Theological Milton

Medieval & Renaissance Literary Studies

Theological Milton

Milton

Deity,
Discourse
and
Heresy
in the
Miltonic
Canon

MICHAEL LIEB

Duquesne University Press
Pittsburgh, Pennsylvania

Published in the United States of America by
DUQUESNE UNIVERSITY PRESS
600 Forbes Avenue
Pittsburgh, Pennsylvania 15282

Library of Congress Cataloging in Publication Data

Lieb, Michael, 1940–
    Theological Milton : deity, discourse and heresy in the Miltonic canon /
    Michael Lieb.
        p. cm. — (Medieval & Renaissance literary studies)
    Summary: "Literature and theology are inextricably intertwined in this
    study of the figure of God as a literary character in the writings of John
    Milton"—Provided by publisher.
      Includes bibliographical references and index.
      ISBN-13: 978-0-8207-0374-9 (cloth : alk. paper)
      ISBN-10: 0-8207-0374-5 (cloth : alk. paper)
        1. Milton, John, 1608–1674—Religion. 2. Christianity and literature—
    England—History—17th century. 3. Christian literature, English—History
    and criticism. 4. Heresies, Christian—History—Modern period, 1500–.
    5. Heresies, Christian, in literature. 6. Theology in literature. 7. Heresy in
    literature. 8. God in literature. I. Title. II. Medieval and Renaissance
    literary studies.
      PR3592.R4L54 2006
      821'.4—dc22

                                                                2005030737

∞ Printed on acid-free paper.

To my wife, Roslyn

Contents

ACKNOWLEDGMENTS

I am genuinely indebted to both the individuals and the institutions that helped to make this work possible. These include Albert C. Labriola and David Loewenstein, to whom I am deeply grateful for their astute and sensitive readings of my manuscript. To the guiding hands of Susan Wadsworth-Booth and the staff of Duquesne University Press, I extend my heartfelt thanks. I thank as well those several institutions that proved so supportive. Under the superb leadership of Mary Beth Rose, the Institute for the Humanities at the University of Illinois at Chicago offered me a year of uninterrupted research and writing, as well as the opportunity to share my work with the other fellows. A summer fellowship from the National Endowment for the Humanities allowed me to focus on particular aspects of the study, and a month at that island of serenity and scenic wonder, the Rockefeller Center at Bellagio, Italy, proved to be among the most fruitful of my career. A travel grant from my own institution helped to support my trip to the Public Record Office in the United Kingdom to examine the manuscript of *De Doctrina Christiana*. Finally, a year as a senior fellow at the Martin Marty Center, University of Chicago Divinity School, allowed me to carry on my research in a wonderfully rich environment. I offer thanks to W. Clark Gilpen, director of the Center, Richard Rosengarten, dean of the Divinity School, and my dear friend and colleague Anthony C. Yu for all their encouragement and support. I am especially indebted to Stanley Fish and Walter Benn Michaels, both of whom have been wonderfully supportive. John T. Shawcross is one to whom this book (and in fact all my work) owes an incalculable debt of gratitude. I also take this opportunity to acknowledge the memory of Michael Masi, colleague, teacher, scholar, and friend. My most profound expression of gratitude and affection I reserve for the one to whom this volume is dedicated, my wife and partner in everything, Roslyn.

Portions of this book represent revisions of previously published studies: chapter 4, "The Theopathetic Deity," previously published as "Reading God: Milton and the Anthropopathetic Tradition," in *Milton Studies* 25, edited by James D. Simmonds (Pittsburgh: University of Pittsburgh Press, 1990), 213–43; chapter 5, "The *Odium Dei*," was previously published as " 'Hate in Heav'n': Milton and the *Odium Dei*," *ELH* 53 (1986): 519–39; chapter 6, "Our Living Dread," was previously published as " 'Our Living Dread': The God of *Samson Agonistes*," *Milton Studies* 33, *The Miltonic Samson*, edited by Albert C. Labriola and Michael Lieb (Pittsburgh: University of Pittsburgh Press, 1990), 3–25; chapter 7, "The Socinian Imperative," was previously published in *Milton and the Grounds of Contention*, edited by Mark R. Kelley, Michael Lieb, and John T. Shawcross, 234–83, 318–33 (Pittsburgh: Duquesne University Press, 2003); chapter 8, "Arianism and Godhead," was previously published as "Milton and 'Arianism,' " *Religion and Literature* 32 (2000): 197–220. Permission to use the foregoing material as part of the present study is gratefully acknowledged.

Notes on Citations

Throughout this book, references to Milton's poetry are to *The Complete Poetry of John Milton*, 2nd rev. ed., ed. John T. Shawcross (Garden City, N.Y.: Doubleday, 1971). References to Milton's prose are to *The Complete Prose Works of John Milton*, 8 vols. in 10, gen. ed. Don M. Wolfe et al. (New Haven: Yale University Press, 1953–82), cited as YP in the text followed by volume and page number. Corresponding references to the original Latin (and on occasion to the English translations) are to *The Works of John Milton*, 18 vols. in 21, ed. Frank Allen Patterson et al. (New York: Columbia University Press, 1931–38), cited as CM.

INTRODUCTION

It has been almost 40 years since the venerable dean of Milton Studies, C. A. Patrides, declared that the treatise known as Milton's *De Doctrina Christiana* is little more than a "theological labyrinth," whereas his epic *Paradise Lost* is "a window to the sun." In his castigation of the theological treatise, Patrides even went so far as to label *De Doctrina Christiana* "an abortive venture into theology." All this took place in an essay that sought to sensitize us to "the language of theology," that is, how theological discourse functions and the way in which it finds expression in poetic discourse.[1] I suppose the moral here is that one can have a deep knowledge of both theological discourse and poetic discourse and still fail to see how the one may overlap with the other. I wish to explore both forms of discourse, to understand how one shades into the next, and, in the process, reestablish the relationship between each. Such an enterprise is of necessity made more complex by the challenges to authorship and canonicity that the theological treatise has endured during the past decade and a half. Having expressed my views on the subject at length elsewhere,[2] I consider the uncertainties of canonicity and authorship an opportunity to reestablish the relationships between *De Doctrina* and Milton's poetry. With these uncertainties in mind, I have adopted as my initial focus the conceptions of God that underlie *De Doctrina Christiana*, on the one hand, and Milton's major poetry, on the other. I do so not to suggest that the theological treatise can in any sense be construed as a "gloss" on the poetry but to demonstrate the extent to which the treatise generates its own conception of deity that offers a fitting context for interrogating the notion of deity that arises in the poetry. Having established the correspondences between the one and the other, I then move into the hotly contested and still unresolved area of the Miltonic conception of godhead, that is, the mystery through which deity assumes the form of a divine relationship in the so-called "persons" of Father and Son, primarily in the celestial realm.[3] Here, one encounters the emergence of those affronts to institutional belief anathematized by the church as "heresy." The place Milton occupies in such matters is the subject of the final portion of my study, which focuses upon godhead, as well as upon God, within the framework of theological and poetic discourse.

To undertake the kind of project I describe here is challenging in the extreme, particularly given the complexities involved in arguing the relationships between the so-called "poetic" and "theological" modes of expression. The question is how one is to approach the language of theology and the language of poetry. At what point do these languages intersect, at what point diverge? Is the language of theology in any sense "poetic," and vice versa? In his reflections on the subject of how theologians reason, G. C. Stead addresses just this conundrum. Citing the Gospel accounts as instances in which the "language of religion" assumes the form at once of poetic enactment and of theological doctrine, Stead explores the cross-fertilization between the two modes of discourse in order to suggest their correspondences. Both, he says, make use of *semeia* (signs) in a way that causes the Gospels to interweave poetry and theology. As a result of that interweaving, the author of each gospel is able to capture the "elusive quality of poetry" at the very point that he is advancing the *kerygma*, or message, that underlies his narrative. According to Stead, occasions of this sort provide the opportunity to observe that, at its most sublime, "theology as a form of human culture resembles art." Despite his energetic and fascinating foray into relationships between poetic and theological discourse, Stead acknowledges that there are certain individuals for whom theology fails at all junctures, with the result that the magic and mystery is lost in the theologian's "dusty prose."[4] For such individuals, theology has no place in poetry and poetry no place in theology. Nonetheless, those sensitive to the multiplicity of meanings generated by the intersection of the two forms of discourse are able to discern crucial dimensions of meaning that help to define precisely what is implied by theological and poetic modes of expression.

The cross-fertilization that occurs when these modes intersect is especially meaningful to an understanding of the works of John Milton. Those willing to entertain the full implications of such discursive modes will be impressed by the extent to which the designation "theological Milton" applies as much to the poet of *Paradise Lost* as it does to the author of *De Doctrina Christiana*. Despite his denigration of *De Doctrina*, C. A. Patrides offers views concerning the relationship between the poetic and theological modes that are very much to the point. As a theological poem par excellence, *Paradise Lost* articulates its insights "not simply in poetic terms," Patrides observes, but "in poetic terms that are bound up inextricably with the whole vocabulary that goes to make up the language of theology." Although this language has been viewed as "odd," its alterity, according to Patrides, is right on target because it is "logically anomalous," that is, ultimately "paradoxical," and such language "is the *staple* of accounts of God's nature."[5] Applied to theological treatises such as *De Doctrina Christiana*, this outlook is very much in keeping with John Milbank's contention in *The Word Made Strange* that the theologian (like the artist or poet) performs the task of "redeeming estrangement." Thus, Milbank elaborates elsewhere, "Explication of Christian practice, the task of theology, tries to pinpoint the peculiarity, the difference, of this practice by 'making it strange,' finding a new language for this difference."[6] The deployment of this "new language" becomes the means by which estrangement is redeemed. Within a Miltonic context, this redemption (which is tantamount to the creation of a work of art or a musical composition) assumes its own unique form in the poetry, on the one hand, and in the theological treatise, on the other. Like poetic documents that are by their nature "theological" in outlook, theological documents can in some sense be called "poetic." Like the language of poetic documents, the language of theological treatises can be the product of alterity. By designating *De Doctrina Christiana* "an abortive venture into theology," Patrides slights the inherent ability of this particular prose treatise to transcend its limits and move toward the production of the "poetic." As I shall attempt to demonstrate in the chapters that follow, the theological language that the treatise adopts, coupled with a methodology that fosters the interchange between doctrinal assertion and biblical proof-text, embodies a poetics of its own.[7] That poetics represents a distinguishing feature of the methodology employed by the author of *Paradise Lost* and *De Doctrina Christiana*.

A caveat: Any study that proposes to address matters of doctrine and expression in *De Doctrina Christiana* must confront the debate about authorship of the theological treatise. Let me declare at the outset that I am a firm believer in Miltonic authorship. I also believe, however, that before venturing such a declaration one must address the question of authorship itself and what it signifies in a work such as *De Doctrina Christiana*. With that vexed issue in mind, one must then attempt to come to grips with the realization that Milton's exact presence in the manuscript of the theological treatise is obscured by a host of factors. Having already explored the question of the authorship of *De Doctrina Christiana* in some depth, I shall not rehearse the arguments of that study here.[8] In keeping with the spirit of that study, I wish only to assert that my approach to Milton as a theologian is one of underscoring a sensibility that is the product not of the serenity that comes from a "calm of mind" but rather of a wisdom that comes from ongoing conflict. It is this very atmosphere of contention that governs my own "take" on the God of Milton's oeuvre. This approach not only acknowledges but embraces the uncertainties that surround the provenance of *De Doctrina Christiana*. Such a stance invites one to appreciate how profoundly rooted Milton's God is in the contentions that distinguish all those debates about who authored the treatise. It is the spirit of these contentions, I shall argue, that energizes the delineation of God in Milton's poetry and prose. Here, I profess a second credo: my Milton is born of conflict, raised of uncertainty, and forever fulfilling all that is meant by the term *agonistes*. For me, the theological Milton exhibits each of these disturbing qualities most admirably. If this Milton is the agonistic Milton, Milton's God is the agonistic God, the *deus agonistes*, the suffering God, the God who not only loves but also hates, the God who fears, the God who repents. Ultimately, he is the hidden God, the *deus absconditus*, the God who defies reason and logic. Milton might not have gone as far as Luther to brand reason the devil's whore, but the dark dimension of Milton's theology most certainly shares the aura of Lutheran angst.[9]

Despite Milton's reputation as the consummate poet of reason and logic, we must acknowledge his intimate ties to the world of the hidden and the perilous. Milton is as "dark" as any other poet (or theologian) that the early modern period produced. His God is the consummate embodiment not only of the light with which he is so often associated but of a darkness in which he is said to reside. To speak of Milton's God through a discourse of light and dark is already present in the angelic celebration of the Father in the third book of *Paradise Lost*. "Thron'd inaccessible," he is conceived as a "Fountain of Light," the "blaze" of which is so intense that his skirts appear "Dark with excessive bright" (372–82). In that description lies the mystery of a deity who encompasses the apophatic extremes of light beyond all seeing and darkness that at once hides and reveals. In this disjunction between the opposites of light and darkness, Milton might well have been responsive to the sensibility reflected in such treatises as Jacob Bauthumely's *The Light and Dark Sides of God* (London, 1650). There, the light side and the dark side represent contrary aspects of deity that are ultimately reconciled, in which, as Bauthumely declares, "light and darkness are all one."[10] Belief in the possibility of such a reconciliation, however, would no doubt have been questioned by Milton as too easy, too automatic, rather too much like yin and yang. But the almost Blakean embrace of opposites engaged him no less, or at least prompted him to conceive a God whose disposition is (for lack of a better term) gnostic. Milton's God is also the God of the Other. To know him is to see him in his contraries. Rather than using the trope of "sides" to gain a sense of how Milton's God is conceived, I adopt the notion of "faces," which better suggests the idea that Milton's God appears in many guises, many masks, many selves. This idea underlies such books as Jack Miles's *God: A Biography*, which explores the roles of God as creator, liberator, lawgiver, and conqueror, but also God as destroyer, executioner and fiend. Essentially literary, Miles's approach sensitizes us to the way in which deity is a multivalent entity in Hebrew Scriptures.[11] It is this multivalency that I find so attractive in Milton's God. Such a conception of deity is crucial not only to the poetry but to the prose, in particular to *De Doctrina Christiana*.

In keeping with this outlook, I begin with an analysis of the God of *De Doctrina Christiana*. Despite all that has been written about the God of *Paradise Lost*, precious little attention has been devoted to the construction of God in the theological treatise. In response to this oversight, I devote almost a third of my study to the way in which God is conceived at the very outset of the treatise. It hardly need be said that *De Doctrina*

Christiana represents the ideal starting point for an encounter with a God, the delineation of whom appears to be Miltonic but because of the questions regarding provenance challenges the reader at every point to question the identity of the true author. In the delineation of the God we encounter in the theological treatise, we are made to ask, "Whose God is this, anyway?" On the one hand, *De Doctrina Christiana* is a work that purports to explain God, indeed, to systematize God, to theologize God. On the other, it is a work that refuses at all points the luxury of knowing, of penetrating to the heart of the mystery. As much as one might hope to gain a foothold on the act of delineating God in Milton's prose treatises, especially *De Doctrina*, problems of text and transmission keep getting in the way. No matter: I begin with the determination to understand the theological systems Milton drew upon to construct his own treatise. In the assessment of the theology that emerges from this construction, we have the opportunity to explore the dialogic interchange between text and proof-text, an interchange that causes the proof-texts to assume a life of their own. God lives in the rich contexts of the proof-texts, and *De Doctrina* is unique in allowing them to enact such a crucial role. The proof-texts represent, in effect, a metatext that releases (one might almost say, "unleashes") new interpretive energies that the text at issue can only begin to imagine. In the dialogic and metatextual dimensions of the treatise a radical hermeneutic emerges.

This is a hermeneutic that explores the dark side of Milton's God. It is the side or "face" that you have always wanted to know about but were afraid to ask. At issue is a dimension of Milton's understanding of deity that prompts both poet and theologian to render God as a "being" wholly passible, indeed, fraught at times with emotional conflict, moved to act in a manner that might otherwise appear to be wholly contrary to our customary notions of how God is to behave. Such notions underlie Harold Bloom's observation that assuming the role of one who is the "author of the author, or writing God, would be an impossible burden for even the strongest of our writers," and "sheer tact has kept them away from it." Like his God, Milton is not known for his tact. Perhaps it is for this reason that Bloom, like so many others, chastises the poet of *Paradise Lost*, "where God's failure as a literary character is the only blemish on an otherwise sublime work."[12] However we might look upon Milton's authoring of the author in his epic, what results is surely not the good God of traditional theodicy.[13] Nor is it the God who emerges in the theologies of those determined to conceive God as an aloof, benign, and fully impassible being. Rather, it is the God that Milton found in the Hebraic notion of deity as manifested in the books of the Old Testament. At the core of Milton's poetic rendering of God in *Paradise Lost* and elsewhere, this is a being who experiences not only anger but hatred. It is, in fact, a being who hates, and through whose example we are encouraged to hate as well. In order to be like God, I argue, one must hate like God.

Hate is only one of a number of emotions that God experiences in Milton's poetry. The whole issue of divine passibility is one that Milton undertakes to examine in what amounts to a theology of the passible in *De Doctrina Christiana*. There, he constructs a world of divinized emotion that reinforces the more frightening aspects of the *deus absconditus* so important to his idea of deity. But Milton goes even further than this to underscore the radical notion of divine passibility in his poetry. Paradoxically, Milton's view of deity is at its most radical when all sense of the passible or the impassible is obliterated. In *Samson Agonistes* God appears in the most disturbing of forms. He appears by not appearing, or, at least, by not appearing in anything like the way he appears in *Paradise Lost* or in *Paradise Regained*. In keeping with the idea of God as an overwhelming force, Milton fashions the God of *Samson Agonistes* in such a manner that he reveals himself as the embodiment of dread, as one, in fact, whose very name is "Dread." In the

dramatic poem, one encounters all the forces and all the energies that underscore the disturbing and off-putting portrayal
of God that emerges in Milton's epics. The difference is that
the sudden manifestation of deity in the dramatic poem is much
more terrifying at the visceral level than that which one discovers in the epics. That is because what I have termed the
personality of God is totally subsumed within the remarkable
force that he becomes in his transformation into a terrifying
phenomenon.[14] No longer are concerns such as the passible or
impassible at issue. In the "wholly other" revelation of deity
that the dramatic poem encodes, all that remains is power or
the sudden breaking out of power that overwhelms everything and everyone that stands in its path.[15] This is the true
deus absconditus come out of hiding. How to interpret this
deity becomes a key to the action of *Samson Agonistes*. By
means of this *clavis* one is able to unlock the theological
implications of the dramatic poem with a sense of renewed
empowerment.

With all the focus on a passible God who hates as well as a
God who is the very embodiment of dread, one might conclude
that we have returned to the era of what might be called
Milton's "bad God," who was the subject of the criticism pro-
mulgated by William Empson, among others.[16] I am not about
to argue with critics of this sort here. My argument as a whole
may be construed as a response (either explicit or implicit) to
those who have taken Milton to task for his conception of deity
in *Paradise Lost* and elsewhere. To rehearse their indictments
is hardly necessary; besides, defenses of Milton's God on several fronts have already undertaken the difficult task of cor-
rection and reclamation. As parties to these defenses, those
responsive to Milton's conception of deity need no longer
resort to the kind of logic implicit in C. S. Lewis's retort that
those who don't like Milton's God, simply don't like God.[17]
By emphasizing the dark side of deity, I am, however, tacitly
acknowledging critics who have not hesitated to grapple with

Milton's God in order to understand his ways. These critics have unleashed certain energies that prompt us to consider the whole question of Milton's God anew. My study is an attempt to understand just how those energies work to render Milton's outlook as poet and as theologian so vital.

As already suggested in these remarks, my study encompasses three areas essential to an understanding of the theological Milton. The first area concerns *De Doctrina Christiana* as a text that not only provides insight into Milton as a theologian but addresses his concept of deity as at once *sui generis* to the doctrinal concerns of the treatise and at the same time crucial to an understanding of the precise theological maneuvers that distinguish his poetry. The second area, in turn, addresses the dimensions of Milton's poetry through which the poet defines himself in theological terms. Here, the primary emphasis is on the figure of God in *Paradise Lost* and *Samson Agonistes*. Each of these poems embodies two radically different modes of discourse, the first represented by the diffuse epic poem, the second by the dramatic poem. Each becomes a conduit for the portrayal of deity. Needless to say, each portrayal is *sui generis*, a fact that suggests the extent to which Milton was prepared to reconceive God from one poem to the next. Moving from "God" as entity to the "godhead" as entity, the third part of the study explores the relationship between Fathers and Sons. In keeping with this focus, we shall consider two movements that are frequently associated with Milton: Socinianism and Arianism. These "heresies" underscore much recent scholarship on what might be termed the heterodox Milton. That heterodoxy derives its impetus from the complex treatment of hypostasis in *De Doctrina Christiana*. In its broadest terms, the subject bears at once upon the preincarnate and the postincarnate Messiah as he assumes a presence in both the diffuse epic and the brief epic, as well as in his other works. Those determined to categorize Milton as an adherent of X heresy, as opposed to Y heresy, have a large stake in maintaining the canonicity of the theological treatise. Because of the way in which the question of authorship is addressed in the present study, I am convinced that our treatment of Milton's understanding of godhead is finally more nearly balanced and judicious than the treatment accorded this crucial issue in the prevailing scholarship. At the very least, the final section on the heresies of godhead invites further study of how godhead is conceived in the theological treatise and in the poems.

This study is as much a foray into the nature of theological discourse in Milton's works as it is an attempt to illuminate specific Miltonic texts. Discourse is the very soul of how those texts perform. In order to come to terms with *De Doctrina Christiana*, on the one hand, and the epic, on the other, one must be aware of the discursive practices they employ and the discursive traditions they draw upon. Accordingly, this book makes a point of providing a context for each of the works discussed, whether that context finds its source in the systematic theologies of the day or in the poetic milieu that proved a source of inspiration for the epics under consideration. The approach I have adopted here is as much historical as it is hermeneutical. If I have succeeded in generating further discussion of the thorny issues addressed here, then I shall consider my undertaking a success. I leave it to others to determine the extent to which my study is finally successful in having brought these issues to light.

Part I

The Discourse of Theology

ONE

Doctrinal and
Discursive Contexts

✦

I

In the first three chapters of this study I shall focus on the figure of God in *De Doctrina Christiana*. Such an undertaking should help to illuminate what might be called the "artistry" of the treatise and at the same time help to provide a context for the nature of God as delineated in Milton's other writings. I am not talking about using *De Doctrina* simply as a "gloss" on those writings (in particular, *Paradise Lost*). As we know from past experience, that method has been weighed in the balance and found wanting.[1] Rather than approaching the treatise simply (and I might add, reductively) as a gloss, I wish to address the treatise on its own terms to see how its portrayal of God functions and to determine how that portrayal is to be understood. To my knowledge, an analysis of this sort has never been undertaken, at least to the extent that I have in mind. The lack of such a study is curious considering the extent to

which Milton as "author" does not hesitate to refer to his treatise as his "dearest and best possession" (YP 6:121). Perhaps
such an estimate has not won as many converts as Milton might
have hoped. As noted, one of Milton's most learned scholars,
C. A. Patrides, did not hesitate to charge the treatise with
being nothing more than "an abortive venture into theology."[2]
If one is dismissive of the treatise in this manner, then the task
of calling its canonicity into question as a genuine Miltonic
work becomes that much more feasible. Nonetheless, most
scholars would no doubt agree that the treatise far exceeds
such "abortive" expectations. Abortive or not, *De Doctrina
Christiana* remains a site of contention among scholars who
have sought to take a stand on the question of authorship.[3]

I would have it no other way: this very atmosphere of uncertainty and contention governs my own "take" on the God of
Milton's oeuvre. In the case of the theological treatise, that
"take" is one *not* of attempting to resolve the matter of authorship. Rather, it is a matter of acknowledging and even embracing the uncertainties that surround the provenance of *De
Doctrina Christiana* in order to appreciate how profoundly
rooted Milton's God is in the contentions that distinguish
current debates about who authored the treatise. The spirit of
these contentions, I shall argue, energizes the delineation of
God in Milton's poetry and prose. There, one encounters a God
born of struggle, of uncertainty, and of controversy. Whether
one considers the God of the poetry or the God of Milton's prose,
one is left with a turbulence of mind that refuses to rest content in the knowledge that now at last one is able to understand fully Milton's God, to know what constitutes this figure
of ultimacy, and to explain the nature of God's ways.

If *De Doctrina Christiana* purports to "explain" God, to "systematize" God, to "theologize" God, it also refuses at all
points the luxury of "knowing," of penetrating to the heart of
the mystery that underlies the *deus absconditus* at the center of its discourse. What results is a *deus absconditus* that

arises as much because of the uncertainties that surround the text qua text as it does because of the nature of the discourse in which the God of its theology is framed. At issue is the notion of deity conceived and executed in a text that is by its very nature problematical, if not at times inexplicable. Here, the state of the text as we know it becomes all important. As those who have worked with the manuscript of *De Doctrina Christiana* will attest, this is a treatise that quite justifiably should be called a "palimpsest," a medium upon which many layers of writing have been effaced and reinscribed by other layers.[4] Inscription/effacement/reinscription: such is the text that lies before us. Emerging from that text are all the uncertainties that underscore the delineation of God. As much as one might hope to gain a foothold on that delineation, the problems associated with its provenance, and by extension its production, keep getting in the way.

A brief review of the circumstances surrounding the provenance and production of the manuscript will remind us just how complex the issues are. I rehearse them here in order to establish the ground rules upon which a discussion of the God of *De Doctrina Christiana* is to be based. To confront the issue of text, one must attend to the paleographical dimensions of the manuscript itself, in particular, the amanuenses responsible for its transcription. Here, several questions immediately arise: Who first constructed the "layers" of transmission? How did the treatise come about? How trustworthy were its scribes? How are they to be identified? These are questions that crop up in any encounter with the manuscript in its present form. However these and corresponding questions are answered, the issues of effacement and defacement become the orders of the day. Implicit in both, of course, is the question of authorship. Whereas what I would call the "Miltonic faithful" are more than inclined to adopt the notion of the One True Author, those who remain attentive to the uncertainties (if not the mysteries) that the text encodes are open to the possibility of other ways of approaching the subject of authorship. We might like to believe in Milton as the One True Author, but we are forever reminded that such a belief is grounded in a need to downplay (if not to ignore) the uncertainties that have beset the treatise from the point of its discovery in the early nineteenth century and continue unabated to the present day. At some level (or levels) Milton might well have had a hand in the composition of the treatise. But one must be sensitive to the fact that the signatures of Milton's presence, his "voice," are often occluded by the signatures of those who played a role in the actual transcription of the work.

With these facts in mind, I think the most effective way of approaching *De Doctrina Christiana* is to reiterate briefly what is known about the text itself, that is, how the text as we know it came about. For only in doing so are we able to place the work in its proper context and thereby to understand how intimately bound up the doctrinal dimensions of the treatise are with the textual dimensions. It is commonly acknowledged that the manuscript of the treatise is essentially the product of two "hands": those of Daniel Skinner and Jeremie Picard. Whereas it is assumed that Picard largely copied out the manuscript in its entirety (possibly from earlier copies), Skinner is said to have begun the process of recopying the Picard draft for the purpose of typesetting. (Although Skinner came well short of completing the process, a sizable portion of the manuscript is in his hand.[5]) In addition to the markings of Skinner and Picard, a group of unidentified hands (not always distinguishable) have also undertaken changes in the manuscript. The problems attendant upon the compositional aspects of the treatise are legion. Issues of chronology, precise methods of composition, and the actual identities of the scribes (beyond those of Picard and Skinner) are only part of the climate of uncertainty that serves to destabilize the text. Attempting to bestow any sort of identity on the individuals to whom the additional hands belong, for example, is rather like trying to find one's way in a dark theater. We know these individuals are *there,* but it is too dark in the theater to make out identities with any certainty. Even knowing the names of Skinner and Picard does not necessarily lead to a full awareness of who they are. What we know (or think we know) of Skinner is that he was an opportunist, perhaps even something of a scoundrel, a prodigal son in pursuit of a father (or at least in a quest to have a new one replace the old). Skinner's dealings with Milton, it appears, were on occasion self-serving. Gaining the confidence of the blind old man, Skinner at first embraced but then disowned the very person whose memory he was to have served.[6] The boy's ambitions finally got the better of him. What we can say with some certainty about Picard is that he faithfully served Milton on several occasions as an amanuensis; some even think that Picard was one of Milton's former students.[7] In his scribal role, Picard may have either transcribed from dictation or recopied from earlier versions documents that Milton held to be important.[8] Among these is what became the theological treatise now extant. As one of Milton's amanuenses in good standing, Picard no doubt came to enjoy a certain prominence and respect in Milton's eyes. But all this is conjectural as well. Even granting the possibility of a close association, Picard's tale quickly palls. A shadowy figure from the outset, Picard might well have been quite mad, for it appears that he suffered consignment to Bedlam toward the end of his life.[9] What does that leave us with? — a mountebank, a madman, and several unidentified scribes to depend upon for the establishment of text.

It is precisely the essential instability of this text that one must be aware of in any attempt to assess the theological principles advanced in *De Doctrina Christiana.* As anyone who has actually examined the manuscript will confirm, this document is almost schizophrenic in appearance. Whereas the first part (in the elegant hand of Skinner) gives the impression of being finished and even polished, the second part is replete with corrections, deletions, interlineations, and marginal notations transcribed not just by Picard but by those other unidentified scribes to whom we have alluded. One is led to assume that Skinner copied over Picard and the others in order to tidy up the text for the compositor, a task he completed for part but not all of the manuscript. In its present form, then, the manuscript is at once finished and unfinished, part fair copy and part foul copy confronting each other with entirely different appearances. Had Skinner completed his task, the instability arising from the juxtaposition of essentially two texts (fair and foul) might not have been at issue. But that issue looms large now. What, after all, lies beneath the Skinner text? Is it, as assumed, the Picard version with all its uncertainties? Dangers threaten to undermine attempts at making a final determination. Although the Skinner transcription is eminently legible, the absence of the ur-text (Picard's text? The text behind Picard's text? The text behind the text behind Picard's text?) is an ever-present reality. Fair copy is a pasteboard mask that hides all and that prevents one from striking through to the world it occludes. Despite the alluring legibility of fair copy, questions about what has been effaced, or defaced, in the act of transcription must remain unanswered. There is simply too much we do not know about the nature of the textual transmission that marks the Skinner text, as clear and finished as it might appear. As much as we would like to rely on Skinner's efforts, then, we are constantly haunted by the trace of a document (or documents) that we assume must have been present at some point. Nonetheless, we must conclude that even were the so-called ur-text within our grasp, we would still be at a loss to know whether it is really, truly the "real thing," for that real thing may itself go back to earlier versions copied and recopied by amanuenses of one sort or another. To speak of the Skinner transcript as the definitive text is, then, to disregard that palimpsest with all its erasures, to disregard the instability of the text that has come down to us. Any attempt to penetrate to the core of the mystery is finally futile. Against the profound uncertainties of this text, one must attempt to understand the way in which God is conceived and formulated in *De Doctrina Christiana*.

As a distinct subject of exegesis, God is addressed in the second chapter of the first book of the treatise under the heading "De Deo." That, of course, is not the only place in the theological treatise in which God as a subject of discourse receives his due. Various aspects of God, his works, his providence, and his nature occupy the treatise well beyond the second chapter. Such is only to be expected. After all, a "theological" treatise is by definition a work about God. Even in a systematic theology that purports to establish the doctrinal basis of religious belief, one cannot (indeed, dare not) presume to confine God within the boundaries of a single chapter. Despite these constraints, the deployment of a chapter devoted to God is fully consistent with the systematic theologies of Milton's day. Like those theologies, *De Doctrina Christiana* seeks to fulfill its mission of providing a context for the theological and doctrinal discussions that follow hard upon what might be called the "God chapter."

In the theological treatise attributed to Milton, a chapter titled "De Deo" is sufficient in itself to indicate its importance in establishing the thrust of the work as a whole. At first glance, the treatment of God in a single chapter suggests what we all know is an impossibility: that the subject of the chapter is "manageable" in so limited a space. If you want to know God, read book 1, chapter 2, of *De Doctrina Christiana*. The issue here is one of containment, or at least the appearance of containment. The impression that one receives in his first encounter with "De Deo" is that of setting boundaries, which seem to foster the notion that it is entirely possible to construct a ballast through which the idea of God might be made manageable. This structure assures the reader that if he wishes to understand God, he need look no further than the chapter of which God is the subject. The irony of such an assumption is further reinforced by the nature of the transcription that has come down to us: clear, polished, and even elegant. Nothing to worry about here, nothing to disrupt us in coming to terms with the truth about God. On the surface, at least, we are left with a sense not only of closure and containment but of the stability and self-assurance that arise as a result of the over-lay of polish, clarity, and elegance reflected in the transcription itself. These characteristics foster the appearance of knowing, containing, and rendering manageable. God is in his heaven (or at least within the boundaries of the chapter that confines him), and all is well with the world.

Assumptions of this kind are all-pervasive in the systematic theologies to which Milton was heir.[10] These assumptions veritably define the milieu from which *De Doctrina Christiana* emerged. Such treatises as William Ames's *Medulla Theologica* (Amsterdam, 1623) and John Wolleb's *Compendium Theologiae Christianae* (Basel, 1626) come immediately to mind.[11] I single out these two works not only because of their importance to Reformed dogmatics but because of the strong ties that critics say exist between the respective treatises of Ames and Wolleb, on the one hand, and *De Doctrina Christiana*, on the other. The influence of Ames and Wolleb on Milton has long been acknowledged.[12] In the biography of his uncle, Edward Phillips readily asserts such an influence. Referring specifically to the theologians "Amesius" and "Wollebius," Phillips maintains that much of Milton's "Perfect System of Divinity" was collected from these "ablest of Divines," among others.[13] The precise relationship between Milton's "Perfect System" and *De Doctrina* remains to be seen. Unlike any of the other systematic theologies that Milton might have cited, Ames's *Medulla* is actually invoked as an authority in *De Doctrina*, and Milton makes reference to Ames elsewhere in his writings.[14] Although Wolleb is not cited directly in *De Doctrina*, the language and the concerns of the *Compendium* are said to resonate at important points in the theological treatise, particularly in book 2.[15]

The prefatory epistle to *De Doctrina* becomes especially important not only in framing the author's recourse to sources but also in providing a sense of how the treatise evolved. It is here in particular that one senses Milton's presence as he plots the course both of his interest in theology and of his composition of the treatise itself. This course, as indicated, extends from his youth to the period of his maturation. In a telling moment of self-disclosure, Milton relates the stages through which his act of producing the treatise took shape. Having in his younger years studied the "shorter systems of theologians," he progressed to "more diffuse volumes of divinity" in which he became attentive to "the conflicting arguments in controversies over certain heads of faith." In response to the systems of theology he digested, Milton presumably devised a set of *loci communes*, or commonplaces, upon which he could rely. He had these "ready at hand when necessary" (a bit like a stockpile of ammunition) to bolster his arguments. As he moved from the shorter systems to the diffuse systems, Milton often found his views at odds with those of the authorities. But he was not to be intimidated. Rather, he struggled on his own to solve the mysteries that defied the authorities. Just where the writings of Ames and Wolleb figured remains to be seen. The important point for Milton was his decision ultimately to rely not on secondary sources of authority (however worthy) but on a direct confrontation with the Bible itself, for this, after all, is clearly the foundational source of "the word of God" (YP 6:118–20). What is so interesting about this narrative of self-disclosure is its attestation to the sequential adoption of two methodologies, the first reflected in the "systems" at hand, the second in the Bible as the ultimate authority. Even in making use of the prevailing theological systems of divinity, Milton suggests a "progress" from the self-evident qualities of a systematizer to a deeper understanding of deity and the attributes that define it. Milton avers that during the course of self-study, he abandoned the first methodology in favor of the second.[16] *De Doctrina Christiana* nonetheless owes aspects of its methodological tactics to the very systems of theology it would otherwise disavow. For this reason, the act of contextualizing the theological treatise according to the practices of those considered to be stalwarts in the field should illuminate the discursive dimensions of *De Doctrina Christiana* and, for our purposes, shed important light on the treatment of God in the work attributed to Milton. To this end, I shall explore the discourse of Reformed dogmatics, centered primarily (but not exclusively) in the treatises of Ames and Wolleb. In addition to other treatises to which I shall refer, the works of these two theologians will help to establish what might be called a "discursive milieu" for approaching the treatment of God in *De Doctrina Christiana*.

II

At the risk of venturing an arbitrary distinction, I refer to a "discursive milieu" as a way of differentiating between specific matters of doctrinal belief and the modes of expression through which such belief is channeled. It hardly needs to be stated that Reformed dogmatics is firmly grounded in the world of Luther, Calvin, and a host of other theologians who carried on the work of the masters. Ames and Wolleb are surely to be counted among those theologians. So much is a given, and even as this observation is advanced as a given, one must always be aware of the differences in doctrine and belief among those who are said to have espoused Reformed dogmatics, a factor in itself that obliges one to qualify just what is implied by the phrase "Reformed dogmatics" at every point. Such issues are not of immediate concern. What is of concern is the manner in which Reformed dogmatics assumed the form of a theological program in the hands of Ames and Wolleb, each of whom systematized theology according to a specific set of dialectical assumptions implemented through an established methodology. The precise assumptions out of which the works of Ames and Wolleb emerged were those of Ramistic dialectic. The product of the sixteenth century French philosopher Pierre de la Ramée (Latinized as Petrus Ramus), Ramistic dialectic is, as we know, the basis of Milton's *Art of Logic*.[17] On the theological front, Ramus authored his own *Commentarium de religione Christiana libri quatuor* (Frankfort, 1577).[18] What is remarkable about this work is its overt disavowal of complex scholastic reasoning and its embrace of an essentially pragmatic view of belief. Theology for Ramus is not so much a system of doctrines concerned with the nature of God as it is a doctrine or art of "living well" (*doctrina bene vivendi*) and of behaving oneself in a manner that reflects a life of rectitude (*recta vitae*). In keeping with the outlook of his other works, Ramus's *Commentarium* reflects his departure from the scholastic presuppositions that had been a staple of dialectic throughout the Middle Ages and the Renaissance. Divided into two parts (the first dealing with faith in God and the second dealing with the works of humankind as the manifestation of that faith), the *Commentarium* seeks "to reduce religion to an art similar to the arts of expression, grammar, rhetoric, and logic" (Ong, *Ramus, Method*, 5). A further characteristic of the *Commentarium* worthy of notice is the way in which its arguments are implemented. Despite all the emphasis upon the Scriptures in Reformed dogmatics, Ramus adopts a methodology that reduces biblical proof-texts to a minimum and invokes instead the philosophical world of Aristotle and the poetry of Virgil.[19]

In keeping with what might be called its pragmatic turn, the whole work reads like a handbook for the education of children. It is the kind of text that invites adoption for classroom use, as well as for individual study.[20] From this pedagogical perspective, the function of the *Commentarium* is to foster a "method" (*methodus*) through which the act of living well might finally be realized. So conceived, method becomes "a series of ordered steps gone through to produce with certain efficacy a desired effect." It is what Walter J. Ong, S.J., calls a "a routine of *efficiency*." Etymologically, the term *methodus* signifies "a following after or pursuit," in particular, "the pursuit of knowledge" by means of a logical procedure. Although such meanings were already present in both classical rhetoric and philosophy, "method could certainly never have got anything like the hearing it got in the wake of the scholastic experience." Challenging the assumptions of scholasticism, Ramus featured method as a phenomenon of crucial importance to his world view. Indeed, "method" (as the means by which to unlock the secrets of the universe) "was to become the most famous item in the Ramist repertory." Indebted not so much to the traditions of logic as to the schemes of rhetoric, method in Ramistic thought found its way into theology. Such an emphasis upon method anticipates "the later sixteenth-and-seventeenth-century spate of method books" that "flooded Europe." In those "method books," the course of reasoning appears to be humanist, rhetorical, and devotional rather than scholastic, dialectical, and speculative. The underlying objective of *methodus* is to effect closure and containment as opposed to indeterminacy and unknowableness. The assumptions upon which method is founded are centered in that which is knowable, graspable, conceivable. Method renders all that can be known as explainable through the "orderly pedagogical presentation" of the argument (Ong, *Ramus, Method*, 225–32).

With the implementation of method, Ramus engaged in a discourse structured schematically through the use of dichotomies. In fact, a preoccupation with dichotomies led to his being known as a "flat dichotomist" (Ong, *Ramus, Method*, 199). Conceiving knowledge through a logic of dichotomy became a hallmark of his thinking. As Ong points out, the use of dichotomies was not a trait uniquely Ramist. In fact, "the Ramist dichotomies have little, if any, real theoretical foundation. There is a bipolarity in being, which echoes everywhere through philosophical history: form and matter, act and potency, Yang and Yin, thesis and antithesis, the one and the many, and so on through an indefinite number of epiphanies." If the Ramist dichotomies reflect this tendency toward bipolarity, such a phenomenon "does not arise from any penetrating insight on Ramus' part." Rather, what amounts to a preoccupation with dichotomization for Ramus has its origin primarily in "the pedagogical appeal of the tidy bracketed tables of dichotomies which he studied in the printed commentaries and epitomies" of the time (ibid., 199). To be sure, this was the very stuff of both earlier scholasticism and emergent humanism. In his struggle with what he considered outworn traditions, Ramus, however, resorted to the strategies of dichotomization and schematization with renewed gusto.

Underlying the Ramistic point of view is the conviction that all that is knowable can be dichotomized and diagrammed in space. Theological commentaries indebted to Ramistic thinking are accordingly replete with tables of various sorts that presume to codify knowledge as both rational and accessible to those equipped to search out and to understand the nature of God and his ways. On a larger scale, the result of this mode of thinking, moreover, was a "quantified, diagrammatic approach to reality and to the mind itself." All knowledge was seen to have a spatial component that could be mapped and diagrammed (ibid., 199–202, 306). In that enactment, the relationship between space and discourse was germane to the practice of theology. As Ong observes, "the origins of Ramism are tied up with the increased use of spatial models in dealing with the processes of thought and communication" (ibid., 30). These models could be used as aids to memory on the part of those involved in a program of theological training. One need only have access to the Ramistic method to understand not just the realm of humans but also the world of God. Thus, knowledge itself is seen to be self-confined within boxes that might be opened through the right application of method. Theological commentaries amounted to keys through which one might gain access to these boxes. Once secured, knowledge was expressed through commonplaces that one transcribed and learned in order to reveal insight into the deepest mysteries. In the Ramistic tradition, the systemization of theology resulted in the compilation of *topoi* that were the discursive formulation of the content released from those boxes. This approach resulted in an epistemology grounded in the idea of truth as "content." Looking beyond Ramus to those who followed in his wake, Ong concludes that "out of the twin notions of content and analysis is bred the vast idea-, system-, and method-literature of the seventeenth century" (ibid., 30, 314–15).

Both in England and on the Continent, theologians of various stripes incorporated the Ramistic approach into their commentaries.[21] Whether one considers Johannes Piscator, Amandus Polanus von Polansdorf, Bartholomäus Keckermann or Johann Heinrich Alsted, each embodies in the Reformed dogmatics of his teachings the kind of outlook fostered by Pierre de la Ramée. As the noted author of *Medulla Theologica*, William Ames is no exception. Among the most frequently printed theological treatises in the seventeenth century, *Medulla* fully reflects the principles of Ramus as applied to theology. At the forefront of Ames's teachings is the Ramistic emphasis upon method. This fact is already reflected in the full title of *Medulla*, translated as *The Marrow of Sacred Divinity, Drawne Out Of The holy Scriptures, and the Interpreters thereof, and brought into Method.*[22] For "*brought into Method,*" the original Latin has "*methodice disposita,*" a phrase that has the force of that which is orderly and methodically placed, arranged, or set in order. What results is a textbook of sorts, "a systematized body of knowledge suitable for teaching, learning, and memorizing."[23] As a handbook or primer, *Medulla* seeks to instruct those who wish not only to learn about God and his ways but to emulate him as well. In this capacity, *Medulla* fulfills its role admirably.

A veritable primer of Reformed dogmatics, Ames's treatise is written to appeal to readers at the most elementary of levels. For that reason, it is aptly called a *medulla* or "marrow," a word that suggests a determination to get to the "innermost part" of the theological ideas that express themselves, finally, in one's behavior.[24] Eschewing the theological intricacies of the scholastics (in fact, eschewing theological intricacies of almost any sort), Ames thus emphasizes practical or experiential knowledge over theoretical reflection. Ames is self-conscious in his awareness of the pragmatic dimension of his treatise. "Some people," he says, "dislike this whole manner of writing, that is, of placing the main body of theology in a short compendium." Such readers, according to Ames, seek after great volumes and weighty tomes. This, however, is not how *Medulla* is to be conceived. Its purpose, Ames contends, is to satisfy all those who have "neither the ample leisure nor the great skill to hunt the partridge in mountain and forest."[25] In keeping with what might be called the pragmatic dimensions of the treatise, Ames views himself as a teacher surrounded by students eager to learn at the feet of the master, and in particular to become infused with the art and spirit to lead better lives. It is the pragmatic Ames who thus steps forward in his treatise to aid in the redemption of souls. With this emphasis in mind, Ames correspondingly does not hesitate to incorporate into *Medulla Theologica* the Ramistic idea of the "doctrina bene vivendi." Other arts may instruct us how to reason, to speak, to number, and to appreciate the natural world, but for Ames theology teaches us how to live. In fact, the very purpose of theology is to enable the true votaries of God's ways to engage in the act of "living to God" (*vivendi deo*). Put into practice under the auspices of Ramistic theology, the idea of "livingness" advocated by Ames carries with it a kind of devotional fervor.[26] This devotional and pragmatic quality distinguishes *Medulla Theologica* throughout. The modus operandi of the treatise is ballasted by the multiple divisions and subdivisions that are so commonplace in Ramistic thought. In keeping with the spirit of this modus operandi, various editions of *Medulla* are appropriately accompanied by elaborate tables that provide a diagrammatic and spatial structure for the neat dispositions that distinguish the treatise. As might well be expected, the underlying structure of the work is grounded in dichotomies, the most pronounced of which is the division of the treatise into two parts that deal with faith and observance. This bipartite division represents what Ames calls "the two parts of theology."[27]

Within the first part of this division Ames addresses the issue of how God is to be understood. A set of preliminary chapters on matters such as the definition and parts of theology, as well as the nature of faith in God, anticipates a corresponding set of chapters on God and the nature of godhead. These latter chapters concern themselves sequentially with God and his essence (1.4), the subsistence of God (1.5), the efficiency of God (1.6), and the decree and counsel of God (1.7). All these chapters are structured as a *catena*, or chain, of commonplaces that move logically from one point to the next in the development of a thesis, resulting in a compilation of commonplace notions about God and his ways.[28] The chapter on God and his Essence (1.4) is a case in point. Here, Ames offers a compilation of 67 *topoi* that define just what is accessible to the faithful in their quest for the one true God. The chapter begins with the idea of the inscrutability of God (what might be called Ames's version of the *deus absconditus*) and then proceeds through a series of pronouncements concerning the issue of epistemology (how to know a God that is otherwise unknowable), the nature of God's "sufficiency," the issue of God's essence, and the various attributes that may logically be applied to God. These *topoi* culminate, in turn, in statements about God's absolute virtues and perfections. The rhetorical form in which the *topoi* are cast has a formulaic quality about it. The result is as if the terse pronouncements were carved in stone so that they might be memorized and recited as a form of education and of worship. We learn, for example, that "God, as he is in himself, cannot be understood by any save himself" (no. 2) and that "The sufficiency of God is his quality of being sufficient in himself for himself and for us" (no. 10).[29] Fully in possession of the "truth," Ames leaves no room for the act of questioning, for challenging, for *interpreting*. His is a hermetically sealed universe that delights in closure and control: nothing left to chance here, no sense of indeterminacy, no sense of play.

The Bible penetrates this hermetically sealed universe only rarely, and this lack of biblical intrusion is an important feature in itself. Ames may declare his allegiance to "the holy Scriptures" in the title of his treatise, but, upon careful examination, one begins to notice the curious lack of proof-texts that might be otherwise invoked to aid Ames's cause. In the chapter on God and his essence, for example, the proof-texts are almost elusive, their presence shadowy. Although Ames does cite several scriptural texts to support his observations, the mere act of invoking these texts runs contrary to the conduct of his argument. As important as the "word of God" purports to be to the radical ideology of those inspired by the tenets of the Reformation, one does not wish to be carried away by this sort of thing, especially if the Bible might in any sense run the risk of implicitly undermining the theological assumptions through which that ideology finds expression. In Ames's *Medulla*, the text of God may be said to give way to the text of Ames, at least as far as the putting forth of an argument is concerned. This is not to say that Ames abandons the Bible entirely: far from it. It is just that his spare use of it at crucial junctures suggests the extent to which he is determined not to be undone by proof-texts that might be read in one way as opposed to the other, or at least as opposed to the sense that Ames wishes to impart. In the creation of the hermetically sealed universe that Ames enacts in his discourse, the most important consideration is consistency and clarity of purpose. In that way, the lesson can easily be learned, the precepts memorized, the text rendered suitable for recitation. The issue of control becomes very important. With its emphasis upon the practical benefits to be gained through the mastery of the precepts that constitute the treatise, *Medulla* does all in its power to arrange its *topoi* in a manner entirely suitable for what Ong calls "storage and retrieval."[30]

For the purpose of enacting storage and retrieval successfully, no technique of aiding memory is as effective as the construction of charts and tables, a staple of treatises inspired by Ramistic logic and discourse. *Medulla Theologica* is no exception. All one need do is examine the multiple tables that accompany the treatise to discover how gridlike the very appearance of the argument becomes.[31] Thus, Ames's treatment of God is entirely consistent with the construction of grids to comprehend the divine. God's essence is thereby embodied in "flow-charts" that render him accessible to all who would take the trouble of making sense of the grids. In effect, these empower one to behold God in the anatomized form of his various attributes.[32] God's attributes are visually and logically "tabulated" in such a manner that (at least as far as Ames and his following are concerned) the full nature of deity is revealed to the informed eye. By means of the tables that accompany the argument, one may presume to know what God is and who God is. At the very least, one will know how to divide God up, how to structure him in space, how to diagram him. One is assured that if a thesis can be discerned (for example, God as "quantity"), an antithesis is not far behind (for example, God as "quality"). Although the table makes clear that ultimately such an anatomization will disclose only the "back parts" of God, the visual construction of a chart or table provides a sense of confidence that God is manageable, graspable, containable, knowable.

If William Ames's *Medulla Theologica* represents one impor-
tant text in the theological milieu out of which *De Doctrina
Christiana* arose, the *Compendium Theologiae Christianae* of
John Wolleb is no less important, despite the fact that *De
Doctrina Christiana* makes no mention of either Wolleb or his
Compendium.[33] A widely read and widely consulted work, the
Compendium is clearly a treatise that must be taken into
consideration in any attempt to assess the theological climate
to which Milton was heir. The currency of the *Compendium*
is widely attested. Reissued in at least eight editions in the seventeenth century, Wolleb's treatise was translated into Dutch,
Hungarian, and English. "At the Reformed universities, it
became the basis of lectures on dogmatics and ethics." In
some circles, it is considered the "best systematic theology of
the day."[34] Its importance is thought to be on a par with that
of Ames's *Medulla*. In the context of Milton's own readings,
this estimate, we recall, is confirmed by Edward Phillips, who
in the biography of his uncle does not hesitate to couple those
"ablest of Divines," "*Amesius*" and "*Wollebius*," as crucial
authorities in the field of systematic theology and as models
for the kind of theological endeavor that had engaged Milton
at that point in his career.

As already observed, the treatises of Ames and Wolleb are
monuments to the Reformation agenda because both seek to
get at the "essence" of Reformed belief through a rhetoric of
concision and condensation. Such is true as much for the
Compendium as for the *Medulla*. Indeed, the quest for essence
is already reflected in the very titles of the respective works.
If *Medulla* is the "marrow" of its subject, the *Compendium*
is the "abridgment" or synopsis of it. In his translation of the
Compendium, the seventeenth century divine Alexander Ross
adopts a title befitting the spirit of condensation implicit in
the work as a whole. Ross translates the title as *The abridgment of Christian divinitie* (London, 1656).[35] As might be
expected, the notion of method is as crucial to the *Compendium*
as it is to *Medulla*; both treatises may be looked upon as the

embodiments of Ramistic discourse. Despite these similarities, the *Medulla* and *Compendium* appear to differ both in outlook and in execution. As much as Ames's treatise reflects a profound interest in the pragmatic dimensions of the religious life, Wolleb's treatise purports to be more concerned with the metaphysical and theoretical dimensions of its subject. The defining perspective of *Medulla* is the devotional idea through which Ames classifies "theology," a discipline, we recall, in which the act of *vivendi deo* is crucial. Although the notion of *vivendi deo* is certainly present in the *Compendium*, the pragmatic element is subsumed within a metaphysical framework, one in which an ever-present awareness of scholastic methodology emerges as a phenomenon deeply indebted to the values inherited from the late Middle Ages. Responding to this scholastic point of view, Wolleb sought to foster what John W. Beardslee calls a "new scholasticism" through which Protestantism laid the foundations for its methodology, one firmly grounded in a metaphysics that provided a distinctly reformist view of doctrinal matters. In its handling of those matters, Wolleb's *Compendium* serves its purpose well. Its brevity, clarity, and its faithful expression of Reformation dogma distinguish it as "an avenue to an over-all picture of the accepted 'orthodox' understanding of the Reformed faith."[36]

One need only glance at Wolleb's "Prolegomena to Christian Theology" to sense the nature and import of his methodology. The prolegomena is divided into two major headings (the first providing a definition of "Christian theology," the second addressing the divisions of theology). These, in turn, are subdivided into propositions. Twenty-two propositions support the first heading; the second heading appears to lack any support by way of proposition. It might be argued, however, that the remainder of the *Compendium* elaborates on the second heading. The first heading is stated baldly as no more than an etymological key to the term "theology": "the doctrine concerning God." But already the first heading anticipates the second by asserting that theology is not only the doctrine or teaching (logos) through which God is known; it is also the means by which God is worshiped. Such is precisely the tenor of the second proposition, which provides closure to the prolegomena by observing that theology has two divisions: the knowledge of God and the service of God. The first consists of faith, the second, of works (*ta pista* versus *ta prakta*), the two essential categories that distinguish dispensational theology. Accordingly, Wolleb divides his work into two books, "The Knowledge of God" and "The Service of God."

Within the 12 propositions underscoring *ta pista*, Wolleb provides crucial insight into his methodology and his exegetical frame of mind, which attests to the primacy of Scriptures above every other consideration in the desire to gain a true knowledge of God. The prolegomena is remarkable in its uncompromising faith in the biblical text as the foundation of all that is necessary to be known about theology, and therefore about God. Wolleb is careful to distinguish between the divine truth embodied in Scriptures and what might be called pure fabrication embodied in all that stands apart from Scriptures. Even though some may incorrectly associate the term "theology" with the teachings of the "ancient sages," true theology emerges from the correct reading of the biblical text. Whatever else it is, theology is not that which emerges from the "poetic or mythical, the philosophical, and the priestly or political" worlds of human endeavor (*Compendium*, 29). No matter how much one attempts either to poeticize or mythologize Scriptures, one is not to compromise the integrity of the word of God. Behind this emphasis upon the biblical text as the one true source of God's word is a polemic against the so-called "papists," that is, the Catholic Church itself. Accordingly, "no tradition outside of Scriptures may be admitted as if it were necessary for salvation." "Divine in origin and authority," Scriptures alone will suffice. Adopting such a stance, Wolleb is doing nothing more than espousing good Reformation doctrine, which decries those who demand the intermediation of the church as the only way to understand theology, that is, to know God (ibid., 33–35). The papists represent the very institution from which one must break away in the pursuit of true theological understanding, and it is this understanding that occupies Wolleb in the prolegomena.

There, Wolleb performs his own anatomy of theology, which is divisible into what he calls "original theology" and "derived theology." Original theology is "the knowledge by which God knows himself," that is, the knowledge by which he knows his own "essence" or personality. Derived theology is a "copy of the original, first in Christ the God-man, and secondarily in Christ's members" (*Compendium*, 29–32).[37] Taken together, original theology and derived theology represent doctrine in its fullest form. My own concern will be primarily with the implications of original theology, for the nature of essence is addressed here, in keeping with the epistemological idea of God's knowing himself. Encountering the concept of divine self-knowledge, one might initially be inclined to assume that Wolleb adopts a view of godhead grounded in a rhetoric of reflexivity, a turning in upon oneself to discover one's true identity. If such a heuristic view were actually present, one could argue that in the act of turning inward upon the self, God becomes "*self*-conscious," made aware of his own consciousness, his own beingness. God would then be both the *end* toward which theologians strive and the *means* through which God assumes the role of the theologian. In keeping with this notion of self-consciousness, one might understandably expect at some point in the treatise a detailed discussion of divine reflexivity and its epistemological implications. Such a discussion would "flesh out" the treatment of God, suggesting a literary rendering through which God becomes a dramatic character very much aware of his own being and motives. As the result of such an encounter with the "self" of God, we would then find ourselves participating in what Wolleb calls the poetic or mythical dimensions of representation.

But this, of course, is precisely the kind of representation Wolleb disavows. In the discourse that constitutes Wolleb's confession of faith, nothing of the literary or dramatic is allowed to compromise the dogmatic pronouncements that are the foundations of the system. What results is a determination *not* to flesh out that which might, under other circumstances, prompt one to conceive of God as an inward-turning or introspective being given to *self*-conscious reflection. Quite the contrary is true: the God of Wolleb's *Compendium* is never allowed the luxury of pondering the inscrutability of his own nature. The experience of discovery (divine or human) is alien to the outlook embodied in Wolleb's systematic theology. Wolleb makes this point in his prolegomena: theology is regarded not "as a faculty of the intellect but as a system of teachings" (*Compendium*, 29–30). This disavowal of the heuristic is a governing principle of Wolleb's outlook. The intellect is that which arises from within; it is the world of self, a world in which one is challenged to speculate, ruminate, ask questions, draw one's own conclusions, and discover new ways of dealing with old conundrums. The exercise of intellect as a vehicle for addressing the problems implicit in accepted modes of belief gives way to a kind of monologic iteration of the known. From the perspective of establishing the nature of deity, a concern with the complexities of selfhood (divine or otherwise) is clearly not the province of Wollebian theology. What constitutes the true province of theology for Wolleb is that indisputable "system of teachings" that cannot be denied. The import of such an outlook is clear. Imposed from without, the system that Wolleb has in mind is precisely what he has produced: a "compendium" or "abridgment" of received dogma. It might be observed, then, that Wolleb's so-called "original theology" is quite unoriginal indeed. Despite all of Wolleb's attestation to the primacy and inviolability of Scriptures, his text (like that of Ames) relies almost entirely on his own doctrinal assertions. Biblical proof-texts are cited sparingly, if at all, suggesting that in confronting dogma in the *Compendium* one is obliged to rely primarily on the voice of John Wolleb himself. If proof-texts are present at all, they are cited to support Wolleb's assertion of dogma. Clarity and concision are the order of the day.

Where, then, does all this leave the God of Wolleb's *Compendium?* At least part of the answer lies in the first chapter concerning God's essence. The very idea that an examination of such a subject can be encompassed within the scope of a few pages is sufficient to suggest the nature of what Wolleb has in mind. The chapter begins with five postulates that provide insight into his habits of thought. Wolleb adopts an outlook that permits him to engage in terse, indeed, formulaic assertions of what otherwise might be considered inscrutable matters of divinity. Implicit in the discourse is the assumption that God's essence is "knowable." Thus, "God is a spirit, self-existent from eternity; one in essence, three in person, Father, Son, and Holy Spirit." Wolleb may seek to distinguish original theology from derived theology, but the very first postulate of his treatise suggests the extent to which these theologies are conflated in Wolleb's thinking. One does not get very far beyond the categories of spirit and eternal self-existence before one encounters the Trinitarian implications of Wolleb's doctrinal position. Thus, if God is known in himself "absolutely in his essence," Wolleb maintains, he is also known "relatively in the persons" that constitute the godhead (*Compendium*, 27). This conflation of original theology with derived theology says a great deal about Wolleb's epistemological assertions regarding the "knowability" of God. Any possible notion of self-referentiality or reflexivity is obviated here.

The posture of assured self-confidence adopted at the outset of the treatise resonates in every sentence. Upon reaching the point of discoursing on the life and makeup of God, Wolleb issues a series of statements that make it entirely clear just how intimately he is empowered to share God's features and characteristics. Thus, we find that not only the life of God but also the intellect and will of God are "absolutely simple and infinite," attributes that would unequivocally dispel any doubts concerning God's essence. These observations are followed by statements of elaboration; for example, "there is no external cause" of God's life, but he is "the cause of the lives of all other living creatures." The intellect of God, in turn, is such that "He knows himself primarily as an infinite object." God "knows everything through himself. He knows in one absolutely simple act; he needs neither revelation nor reason, whether intuitive or deductive." We recall Wolleb's earlier statement in the prolegomena to the *Compendium* that original theology is "the knowledge by which God knows himself," that is, the knowledge by which he is aware of his own "essence" or personality. As much as one might be inclined to read the earlier statement as evidence of Wolleb's belief in the "process" by which the Omniscient seeks to know himself, the discourse on God makes clear that "process" as such is simply not to the point: the Omniscient knows himself quite simply by virtue of his omniscience. Wolleb's assertion that God knows himself "as an infinite object" not only distances God from the mutability implicit in the growth of knowledge (a coming to a greater awareness of self); it also militates against any impulse to conceive God as a participant in the so-called poetic or mythical dimensions of representation. As one whose nature is that of "simplicity," "infinity," "immutability," and "perfection," God is a being "truly and simply one." Wolleb concludes that "there is nothing in God that is not God himself" (*Compendium*, 37–39). Accordingly, any notion of reflexivity in God is effectively countermanded by the set of postulates one encounters in the very first chapter ("The Essence of God") of the first book of the *Compendium*.

The foregoing has only touched on the prevailing traditions of systematic exegesis that underlay Reformation treatises on Christian theology. Especially in the theologies of Ames and Wolleb, one discerns several features that distinguish at least

two of the works that are purported to have been of paramount importance to Milton's own theological endeavors.
The first is the influence of Ramistic dialectic in the conception and execution of the treatises. Here, the application of the
all-pervasive practice of *methodus* provides a sense of closure
and containment to the arguments. One feels that Milton is
in a doctrinal world in which all questions are answered and
the possibility of conflict or at least "difference" is resolved.
In one form or the other, the use of dichotomy appears to be
the distinguishing characteristic. Each treatise assumes the form
of a grid in which the dichotomies are predictable, if not
inevitable. For this reason, the arguments of both treatises are
easily structured in space, diagrammatically anatomized in
tabular form. With the presence of tables, one can much more
easily grasp the system as a whole. As suggested earlier, the
system can be taught, memorized, recited as a set of pedagogical principles, the implications of which are essentially pragmatic. This pragmatism may be more in evidence with Ames
than with Wolleb, but its presence is discernible in the discourse
of both theologians. What is true for Ames is finally true for
Wolleb: in both, the practice of theology is undertaken as a
means of "living to God," a state that fosters the "art of living well." With the system well in hand, one possesses the key
to unlock the mysteries of God. It is within this context that
one might most productively approach the rendering of God
in *De Doctrina Christiana*.

III

In the prefatory epistle to his theological treatise, Milton
underscores what is unique about his method of argumentation. At the heart of this method is the crucial reliance upon
biblical proof-texts. Whereas in Ramist dialectic and its heirs
(such as Ames and Wolleb), proof-texts are invoked sparingly,
Milton features them prominently in *De Doctrina Christiana*.

Most of the authors of systematic theologies, he alleges, make a practice of "filling their pages almost entirely with expositions of their own ideas." If these theologians invoke any proof-texts at all, they customarily "thrust" the biblical references into the margins (*in marginem extrudere*), where the proof-texts appear primarily in the form of brief chapter and verse citation. The Bible is thereby relegated to a subsidiary role in the construction of the argument; it is almost as if the sacred text has a habit of getting in the way. The result is a tradition of systematic exposition more nearly concerned with its own declaration of received dogma than with the authority of the biblical text.

A glance at the language is instructive in coming to terms with Milton's desire to distinguish his practices from those of his compeers. The colorful use of *extrudere* ("to thrust out" or "drive out") suggests not only a displacement of what is otherwise crucial to the enterprise but a kind of violence to the primacy of the biblical text. Milton counters this violence with a violence all his own. Eschewing the idea of marginalizing the Bible through the act of thrusting or driving out, Milton opts instead to "stuff" or "cram" his proof-texts into the space of his own text. That which is decentered, marginalized to the periphery of the page is accorded a place of honor at the very center of the discourse, framed by the margins but not part of them. Thus, Milton declares that he has striven to "cram" his pages, "even to the point of overflowing" with "quotations drawn from all parts of the Bible." In that way, he will have left "as little space as possible for [his] own words, even when they arise from the putting together of actual scriptural texts" (satius duxi mearum quidem paginarum spatia confertis undique auctoritatibus divinis etiam eadem ingerentibus redundare, meis verbis, ex ipso licet contextu scripturarum natis) (YP 6:122; CM 14:10–11). This is a fascinating revelation of compositional practice or method, for it willingly obliterates the self in exchange for the texts that offer themselves in abundance to the reader, who in turn ventures his or her own interpretation (which may or may not be at odds with the views of the expositor). Put another way, Milton privileges the proof-text over that which is to be proven, and the act of marshaling evidence takes on a life of its own. In turn, the Ramistic act of bestowing authority upon doctrinal assertion in a manner that marginalizes the force of the proof-text is effectively undermined by a renewed emphasis upon the primacy of the sacred text.

The phrase *ingerentibus redundare* is crucial to an understanding of how Milton views his office. As Regina M. Schwartz suggests, the idea of cramming one's pages full of biblical quotations to the point of overflowing is engaging because of the "essential violence" it enacts on the text. In its various forms, *ingerentibus* (from *ingero*) implies the act of "inflicting" or "thrusting into" as aspects of battle. So Schwartz observes that Milton has "ransacked the whole Bible and then crammed" his text with scriptural passages, "hardly a deferential approach to his sacred authority."[38] Intensifying the notion of violence, *redundare*, in turn, implies the idea not just of "overflowing" but of "flowing forth in excess." One detects a deliberate flourish here, a rhetorical gesture that produces what might be called an "aggressive abundance." If so, this is an abundance in which "cramming to the point of overflowing" culminates in an "engagement" between reader and text designed not to circumscribe or limit meaning but rather to release it. If the image of the relationship between reader and text sounds a bit like King Canute encountering the sea, such an image is not entirely out of keeping with the conception suggested by *ingerentibus redundare*. In an encounter with *De Doctrina Christiana*, one faces the danger of being overwhelmed by the powers of the sacred text let loose upon those willing to address the multiple meanings implicit in the biblical citations. As for Milton, he is there and not there. Cramming his pages with proof-texts, he is, in the words of Schwartz, "squeezed out of his text": he is obliterated, no longer there. At the same time,

Milton *is* there to the extent that he appropriates the text as a foregrounded series of proof-texts, each with its own contexts and its own assumptions that may or may not agree in full with the other proof-texts that have been invoked to support a particular doctrinal assertion. However the proof-texts are to be conceived, they are cited in such abundance that one is inclined to observe that Milton makes the language of the proof-texts his own. Whereas Milton claims that his commentary is so replete with the Bible that the pages have no room left for his own words, Schwartz is astute in her observation that "in the end, the exiled author returns, stuffing his own pages — cramming them even to overflowing — with himself."[39] Thus, at the very point that Milton claims the liberty to "sift and winnow" each doctrine before advancing it, he makes certain that his conclusions are empowered by what he calls "the authority of the Bible." If others view these conclusions in any sense "heretical" (as well they have been from the discovery of the treatise in the nineteenth century up to the present time), that is an outlook in which Milton takes full delight, because he knows that the truth of what he says is already present in Scripture. "For my own part," Milton reiterates, "I devote my attention to the Holy Scriptures alone. I follow no other heresy or sect" (YP 6:123; CM 14:10–13). Such, in brief, is the nature of the compositional methodology — as well as what might be called the credo — that Milton adopts in *De Doctrina Christiana*.

At the very point that Milton pledges to draw upon "the Holy Scriptures alone" as the medium through which he seeks to validate his doctrinal positions, we are obliged to raise a question of crucial import. What is the precise version (or versions) of the Holy Scriptures that Milton adopts?[40] One need hardly assert that a multiplicity of versions was available to exegetes throughout the early modern period. These versions could be had, for example, in such seminal editions as the *Biblia sacra polyglotta* (1657), compiled by Brian Walton.[41] Providing

Hebrew, Greek, Latin (of the Vulgate), Arabic, Aramaic, Ethiopic, Persian, and Syriac versions in separate columns (along with an interlinear Latin translation of the Hebrew), this multi-volume work has been offered as one of the possible sources for the proof-texts cited in *De Doctrina*.[42] Vying for equal, if not greater, prominence is the Junius-Tremellius-Beza translation of the Old and New Testaments (Junius-Tremellius for the Old Testament and Beza for the New). The "favorite Latin version of seventeenth-century Reformed Divines," this version assumed the position of a veritable *textus receptus* during the period (or periods) that *De Doctrina* was produced.[43] These are only two of the likely sources behind the proof-texts Milton cites. There are other possibilities as well. The point is not to discover the exact source or sources but to realize that the "foundational text" (called the Holy Scriptures) is represented by a variety (if not a multiplicity) of versions, and hence a variety or multiplicity of renderings. This fact not only underscores the sense of complexity with which the proof-texts are imbued; it also suggests the need to go beyond the proof-texts in order to explore the larger contexts from which they emerge.

What is required dealing with the proof-texts is a kind of archaeology of interpretation, one that is sensitive both to the multiplicity of versions that might come into play and to the problems of taking for granted the accuracy of individual translations, whether that of Charles R. Sumner or that of John Carey.[44] At least, one can no longer rely on the translation of a particular proof-text to determine one's interpretive posture. Nor can one feel comfortable relying on the idea that, confronted by the Latin text, one has access to the "original" form in which the proof-text was either cited by Milton or transcribed by the amanuensis during various stages of composition. As Fletcher conjectures, "Vast numbers of the quotations in the *De Doctrina* manuscript have been transcribed, perhaps by different amanuenses, from Milton's own copy of some of them." Meanwhile, other quotations "must have found their way into the surviving manuscript from copies made by other and earlier amanuenses."[45] Once again, we are prompted to ask, "Will the One True Author please step forward?" Failing that, we are content to ask, "Will the actual amanuenses please identify themselves as responsible for transcribing specific passages at specific times?" The issues raised in the treatment of the biblical text in *De Doctrina* serve as analogues to the theological treatise as it has come down to us. Thus, in his discussion of "the Holy Scriptures," Milton makes a point of alerting us to the instability, indeed, the "corruption," of the codices (especially of the New Testament) through which the biblical text has been transmitted over the centuries. The fact of this corruption is reinforced by the "untrustworthy authorities" (cum sub custodibus variis male fidendis) responsible for transcribing the text at various points in its history. These putative authorities or transcribers are responsible for both "an assortment of divergent manuscripts" and "a medley of transcripts and editions" (YP 6:587–88; CM 16:274). As I have discussed, these are the very problems that beset the manuscript of *De Doctrina* itself. By extension, the uncertainties associated with transmission find their way into the fashioning (or transcribing) of the proof-texts. Nothing can be taken for granted. In keeping with the manuscript itself, the proof-texts with which the pages are "crammed" must not be simply analyzed but interrogated. And from this field of discourse, and, with it, this concatenation of proof-texts, the God of *De Doctrina Christiana* emerges.

Having introduced the essential principles upon which his theological discourse is based, Milton begins his treatise with a chapter on the meaning of "Christian Doctrine" and the nature of its "parts." The assumption is that once these matters are resolved then issues such as the nature of God and of godhead may be profitably addressed. "Christian Doctrine," Milton observes, is the lesson that Christ taught by "divine communication" about the "nature and worship of Deity." To that end,

God is glorified (*ad gloriam Dei*) and the salvation of humans (*salutemque hominum*) extolled (YP 6:126; CM 14:17–18). At the outset, we learn that essential to the concept of Christian doctrine is the not only overwhelming need to come to terms with God's nature but the ever-abiding desire to celebrate his glory because of his redemptive plan. Underlying Christian doctrine are the elements of an epistemology, a soteriology, and an ontology. It is important to realize, however, that despite the philosophical overtones that distinguish such considerations, Milton is at pains to divorce himself from all who would presume to "know" God by embarking on any sort of philosophical speculation or by adhering to any set of dictates. We must, Milton accordingly observes, search for God "not among the philosophizing academics, and not among the laws of men" (non ex philosophantium scholis, neque ex humanis legibus), but "in the Holy Scriptures alone and with the Holy Spirit as guide" (YP 6:127; CM 14:18–19). The turn here is important, for, at the very point of embarking upon a systematic disquisition concerning categories such as epistemology and ontology, Milton distances himself from the "schools," where such matters were customarily debated from the Middle Ages to early modern times.[46] Milton maintains that he will have none of it. He is ever ready to assert with the Psalmist that "the secret of Jehovah [*arcanum Iehovae*] is with those who reverence him" (Ps. 24:14). It is this sense of the *arcanum* that drives Milton's arguments regarding deity (YP 6:128; CM 14:24–25).

While disavowing the kind of outlook that would reduce deity to a "logical construct," Milton nonetheless does not hesitate to conceive his arguments concerning issues of theology in general and God in particular through the sort of methodological suppositions that define the Ramistic perspective and that underlie the treatises of Reformation thinkers indebted to Ramus. (So much for disavowing the "philosophizing academics.") Once again, "method" makes itself known, in this case,

as the result of Milton's determination to conceive his work
as part of the larger tradition represented by the works of
Ames and Wolleb. Thus, commenting upon the methodology
he has adopted in his theological treatise, Milton observes
with a modest flourish. "I do not teach anything new in this
work. I am only to assist the reader's memory by collecting
together, as it were, into a single book texts which are scat-
tered here and there throughout the Bible, and by systematizing them under definite headings in order to make reference
easy" (ut quae sparsim sacris in libris leguntur; commode
velut in unum corpus redacta, perque certos digesta locos, ad
manam sint) (YP 6:127; CM 14:20–21). This "modesty topos"
suggests that Milton is doing no more than "gathering" and
"collecting" biblical proof-texts to support what is already
commonly known. Nothing original here: in its own way, De
Doctrina Christiana represents itself as both a marrow and an
abridgement of theological topoi. As such, it is a systematic
"digest" (digesta) or a "redaction" (redacta), a tool through
which the reader is at liberty to resort as he might to any work
of reference. Arranged under certain heads or topics, De
Doctrina is fashioned in a manner to provide easy access to
its arguments. The language of the first chapter thereby resonates with the discourse of the prefatory epistle, which maintains that the treatise itself is no more than "a systematic
exposition of Christian teaching" (doctrinae Christianae
methodicam institutionem) (YP 6:120, 127; CM 14:6–7, 20–21),
one in which Milton seeks to teach the "heads" of Christian
doctrine "methodically" (certo ordine) and systematically. For
Milton, such a plan is entirely in keeping with the biblical
injunction to "hold fast the form" (2 Tim. 1:13). In order to
impart an even greater sense of authority and conclusiveness
to his assertion, Milton makes certain to cite his text in the
original Greek: hypotyposis (from typos). At issue is the importance of "form" or "pattern." In connection with the emphasis upon form, Milton offers corresponding terms such as the

use of *morphosis* ("form," "semblance") in Romans 2:20. This striving after form is putatively the foundation of *De Doctrina*, which views itself as "a complete corpus of doctrine, conceived in terms of a definite course of instruction" (totius doctrinae evangelicae methodicam quandam institutionem) (YP 6:120, 128; CM 14:6–7, 22–23).

For Milton, this sense of completion, of confinement, of circumscription underscores his desire to provide a reasoned, logically grounded, and logically accessible manual or digest of the fundamental doctrines of the Christian faith. It all goes back to method, the underlying objective of which is to effect closure and containment, as opposed to indeterminacy and unknowableness. The assumptions upon which method is founded are centered in that which lies squarely in the realm of the knowable, the graspable, and the conceivable. As a defining feature of Ramistic thought, method renders all that can be known as explainable through the "orderly pedagogical presentation" of the argument. This presentation, we recall, is universally given to the inclination to dichotomize. Ames and Wolleb once again come to mind immediately. Whereas Ames divides his treatise into "faith" and "observance," Wolleb divides his treatise into "the knowledge of God" and "the service of God." So Milton divides his treatise into the same sort of categories: "Faith, or the Knowledge of God; and Love, or the Worship of God" (YP 6:128). All is stable, all is predictable, all is as it should be. The bugaboos of those things that are open ended, indeterminate, and even self-contradictory have no place here, at least on the surface.

If one assumes a Miltonic authorship of *De Doctrina Christiana* the way one takes for granted the authorship of the *Artis Logicae Plenior Institutio ad Petri Rami Methodum Concinnata* (1672), one might well view the theological treatise as a work that reflects the principles given expression in the treatise on logic. As Gordon Campbell has ably demonstrated, the principles upon which the *Artis Logicae* are based inform the methodology of *De Doctrina Christiana*.[47] In fact, both the Ramist outlook and the overarching sense of structure are so pronounced in *De Doctrina* that Campbell is able to provide a detailed table of dichotomies reminiscent of the flow charts that accompany the works of Ames and Wolleb, among others. The idea of *De Doctrina* as a "systematic exposition" is very much in keeping with the statement in the prefatory epistle that what was sought in constructing the treatise was an exposition that "could assist [one's] faith or [one's] memory or both" (YP 6:120). As Campbell observes, the announced purpose of the treatise is the quite practical one of self-reclamation, an event brought about through recourse to the treatise as a "mnemonic aid."[48] It is with this view in mind that Ong does not hesitate to draw parallels between the *Artis Logicae* and *De Doctrina*. Invoking such terms as *institutio* and *methodica*, Ong points out that the language of the prefatory epistle to *De Doctrina* echoes that of *Artis Logicae*. Nonetheless, Ong observes how the theological treatise not only "reduces Christian teaching to 'method' " but also subjects the Bible to the strict logical analysis characteristic of Ramist thought. Implementing a "methodized" logic, Ramist thinking expresses itself through a mode of discourse in which knowledge becomes "a closed field." Whether in the form of *Artis Logicae* or *De Doctrina Christiana*, Ramist discourse is, according to Ong, "complete in itself and separated, like a plot of real estate, from other knowledge."[49] To the extent that *De Doctrina Christiana* is the product of the kind of thinking that produced *Artis Logicae*, both works occupy the same real estate. However, if one were to explore the houses built on both pieces of land, he would find some radical differences.

Despite the apparent similarities between the two structures, the closed world of *Artis Logicae* is not that of *De Doctrina Christiana*. As I have been suggesting all along, the theological treatise is, in effect, *sui generis*. Given the uncertainties of text, amanuenses, and transmission, one would do well not to draw hasty conclusions about how it is to be interpreted. It is here that the criteria of open-endedness and indeterminacy enter the picture. At the very point that the theological treatise appears to be a logically organized, systematic working out of doctrinal premises, the argument assumes what William Shullenberger contends is a "poetic" bearing in which the structured discourse gives way to the allusive and, indeed, elusive language of poetic enactment.[50] Although some might argue that Shullenberger goes too far in his attempt to "poeticize" *De Doctrina,* he is correct in his inclination to read the treatise as more than (indeed, *other* than) the kinds of systematic theologies current during Milton's time.

Two

The Ontological Imperative

✝

I

The discourse on God that occupies the chapter titled "De Deo" in *De Doctrina Christiana* raises major issues that to a greater or lesser degree inform most of the systematic theologies produced in the early modern period. The chapter is essentially divisible into three sections: (1) concerning the existence of God; (2) concerning the knowledge of God; and (3) concerning the names and attributes of God. One might suggest that the chapter moves from the ontological to the epistemological to the phenomenological modes by means of which God is manifested or made known.[1] Categories overlap. If the ontological mode encompasses issues concerning not just the existence of God but the knowledge of God as well, then the epistemological mode encompasses issues concerning not just the knowledge of God but the existence of God. The same may be said of issues concerning the names and attributes of God, which in turn share characteristics with the first two categories. Each mode becomes an aspect of how God is conceived in *De*

Doctrina Christiana. Each represents a means of coming to terms with the faces of God in the construction of that which lies ultimately beyond our ability to construe the absolute in any truly discernible way. The very act of construction, in fact, belies the fact that all such systematic endeavors, including those advanced by the theological treatise under consideration, are incapable of naming the unnamable, construing the inscrutable, setting bounds on that which by its very nature defies all attempts to address matters classified as ontological, epistemological, or phenomenological. Given the nature of *De Doctrina Christiana* as a "systematic theology," these modes are in keeping with the rage for order that underlies the fundamental assumptions upon which the methodology of the treatise is grounded. Responsive to those assumptions, I shall accord that methodology its due in my discussion of "De Deo."

Here, we are immediately caught off guard. The first category, ontology, gives rise to issues that strike us as almost a given in any attempt to systematize God. So important is the question of ontology that we are inclined to observe that it is an issue that must have been a matter of urgency for early modern dogmatics. A glance at the theologies most often cited in connection with *De Doctrina* (namely those of Ames and Wolleb), however, suggests that this is not the case; in fact, quite the opposite is true. As much as *De Doctrina* may be said to implement a methodology consistent with that found in Ames's *Medulla* and Wolleb's *Compendium*, neither treatise focuses on the issue of ontological proof.[2] Although Ames does address the nature of faith in God in the chapter that precedes his chapter on God and his essence, the actual possibility of not believing in God at all does not appear to fall within the agenda that Ames sets for himself. A corresponding lack of interest is likewise discernible in Wolleb, who never once in his chapter on the essence of God considers the possibility that there are those who would actually disavow belief in God in the first place. For neither Ames nor Wolleb, then, does the question of disbelief emerge as a subject worthy of investigation. Various explanations might be undertaken to explain this omission, but at the very least the existence of God is apparently something Ames and Wolleb took for granted. This is somewhat surprising considering the fact that the subject did resonate throughout the early history of the church and beyond, and the question of ontology was not without its adherents in the early modern period. A brief overview should suggest how and in what form the question arises.

In order to address the question of ontology, we must first attend to its place in the discourse of the early church. That place is decidedly philosophical in origin. Grounded in both Platonic and Aristotelian modes of thought, theologians extending back to the early church and forward into the early modern period did not hesitate to consider the fundamental question of ontology. As early as the second century, we find philosophy as a discipline "constantly being pressed into the service of Christian theology." The idea of wedding philosophy with theology gave rise to what Robert M. Grant calls "philosophical theology."[3] Attesting to this kind of theology, Richard Messer observes that "since Plato, and the Neoplatonic influence on early Christian belief, the dominant strand of Western philosophical thought has considered it entirely appropriate to try to prove that God exists."[4] In the Hellenistic period, for example, such ontological concerns are already reflected in the writings of Clement of Alexandria and Origen, among others. The very idea of raising the question of God's existence, however, did not escape resistance. In fact, there were those among the church fathers opposed to what they considered unnecessary and ill-conceived attempts among the theologians of the church to engage in ontological arguments that were better left to the philosophers. Thus, in this vein, Tertullian described the influence of Greek philosophy upon Christianity as an expression of "the foolishness of this world." True theology lay elsewhere.[5] Despite opposition of this sort, theologians whose views of God were the product of distinctly philosophical habits of mind did not hesitate to engage in "the foolishness of this world." Whether in the form of scholastic discourse or other modes of expression, such exegetes demonstrate the extent to which philosophy was put to the service of theology during the medieval and early modern periods. In the Middle Ages, Anselm, Archbishop of Canterbury in the eleventh century, and Thomas Aquinas in the thirteenth, were instrumental in establishing the question of ontology as an essential constituent of philosophical theology.

By means of such works as the *Monologion* and the *Proslogion*, Anselm set the pace for all those interested in pursuing the ontological dimension of philosophical theology. So committed was Anselm to the category of ontology that he is credited by many as the father of ontological reasoning to support the idea of God's existence. To speak of Anselm is to speak of ontology, a dimension of philosophy that came to be known as the "argument of Anselm" (argumentum anselmi).[6] Subscribing to the idea of "faith seeking understanding" (fides quaerens intellectum), Anselm set about in both the *Monologion* and the *Proslogion* to provide a logical structure by which faith might ground itself in the faculty of reason. The *Monologion* engages in an elaborate process of demonstrating that "there must be some one thing that is supremely good, through which all good things have their goodness." That one supremely good thing is the source of all goodness who is God. Undertaking a demonstration of this contention throughout the *Monologion*, Anselm concludes that he is led to the undeniable fact that "there is a certain nature or substance or essence who through himself is good and great and through himself is what he is." As such, God is the "supreme good, the supreme great thing, the supreme being" by means of whom everything is generated.[7] God thereby becomes "something than which nothing greater can be conceived." Anselm asserts that it is "incoherent and self-contradictory" to think of such a Being as not existing. "For," he says, "a nonexistent entity, or a nonentity, would not be the most adequate object of worship, or that than which no more perfect can be conceived."[8]

Arguments of this sort find their way into both the *Monologion* and the *Proslogion*. As Thomas Williams points out, however, the *Proslogion* reflects Anselm's desire to find a simpler way than that reflected in the *Monologion* to advance his views concerning ontology. In the preface to the *Proslogion*, Anselm maintains that he wanted to discover "a single argument that needed nothing but itself alone for proof, that would by itself be enough to show that God really exists." In the second chapter, Anselm's evidence for God's existence manifests itself.[9] Here, his object is to counter any who would presume to doubt the existence of God. The chapter heading says it all: "Truly there *is* a God, although the fool hath said in his heart, 'There is no God [*Quod vere sit Deus, etsi insipiens dixit in corde suo: Non est Deus*]." Anselm invokes the psalmic denunciations of atheists (Ps. 14:1, 53:1) in order to counter the world of doubt they represent. The fool who proclaims that there is no God need only look to his understanding in order to know what that faculty tells him, that God does indeed exist if only the fool would understand his understanding. For, acknowledge it or not, we must be aware that God exists inherently in the understanding. All one need do is find him there. Anselm concludes, "Hence, there is no doubt that there exists a being, than which nothing greater can be conceived, and it exists both in the understanding and in reality."[10] Both in the realm of understanding and in the realm of reality, the ontology of God assumes renewed impetus and urgency in Anselm. His emphasis upon these realms suggests the extent to which he conceives the existence of God to be manifested both in the internal (that is, in the world of thought and of mind: *in intellectu*) and the external (that is, in the world represented by "things": *in re*). The balance between the two supports the contention that the existence of God is indisputable and that only the fool would proclaim: "Non est Deus."[11]

Some two centuries after Anselm produced his ontological arguments on behalf of God's existence, Thomas Aquinas reconceptualized the whole issue of ontology in terms of his own predilections. The result was the great work of medieval scholasticism, *Summa Theologica*.[12] This work is germane because it reflects the belief that through the act of systematizing theology one can arrive with complete confidence at the source of all knowledge, of all method, of all belief about the doctrinal basis of the one true religion. Crucial to this outlook, proof in the existence of God represents the groundwork of all that Aquinas's elaborate arguments in *Summa Theologica* entail. The logic of Aquinas's master plan is discernible in the deployment of the arguments. Thus, the discourse on God opens with the crucial question of "whether there is a God." Under that question, three subquestions delineate the issue even further: "1. is it self-evident that there is a God? [utrum Deum esse sit per se notum]; 2. can it be made evident? [utrum sit demonstrabile]; 3. is there a God? [an Deus sit]" (2.1).[13] From there, the treatise methodically adduces proofs for each of these three questions. The process is one of first raising objections, then introducing supporting evidence with reference to the appropriate authorities, and finally providing requisite arguments to support the main contention. Schematizing God through headings, subheadings, and the constructs of questions, objections, and replies, both the arguments and their deployment are indebted to metaphysical speculation and grounded in disputational modes of discourse. That authority of authorities, namely Aristotle (referred to in the *Summa* as "the Philosopher"), is ever at Aquinas's side to legitimate both the arguments and the methodology enlisted to implement them. Moreover, the structure of the arguments as a whole is firmly ballasted by a determination to consider every possibility and to provide all the answers. In this regard, Aquinas anticipates later methodologies that gave rise to their own metaphysical modes of argumentation and disputation.

During the Reformation, the issue of ontology as a prime category of theological discourse loomed large in several sources. A case in point is John Calvin, who addresses the whole question of ontology most eloquently in *Institutes of the Christian Religion*.[14] Unlike Aquinas, Calvin adopts a mode of discourse that is, in a sense, much more open-ended and less systematic. Above all, it is experiential. Throughout Calvin's treatment of God, one senses the profound experience of his own conversion as related in the preface to his *Commentary on the Psalms* (1557). "As a consequence of that lasting inward change, he lived and wrote as a man constantly aware of God." As a result of that awareness, the *Institutes* is a work "suffused with an awed sense of God's ineffable majesty, sovereign power, and immediate presence." For Calvin, the experience of God is "neither the product of speculative thinking nor an incentive to it." His outlook is never that of "impersonal inquirer." It is not the "nature" of God that concerns him but "what God is in relation to His world and to us." One finds in Calvin's *Institutes* not the "neatly jointed structure of dogmatic logic" but a highly personal revelation of the relationship between the individual and his God.[15] The mode of discourse implicit in this outlook amounts to something like a spiritual autobiography, one in which Calvin's personal knowledge of God is of utmost concern. The work as a whole is one that emphasizes piety and devotion, as opposed to the kind of scholastic speculation one finds in Aquinas. Although the existence of God is a given, the specific knowledge (a kind of existential knowledge) that God exists is not. When it occurs in those privileged to know it, the experience is such that it combines the phenomena of ontology and epistemology to produce a view of God in which being and the knowledge of being complement one another.

In "The Knowledge of God the Creator," the first book of the *Institutes*, "knowledge" subsumes "being" or "existence," two terms that systematic theology customarily takes as a given. Unlike systematic theologies, Calvin's theology emphasizes inward-turning and self-revelatory knowledge. Thus, the title of the first chapter, "The Knowledge of God and That of Ourselves Are Connected," invokes precisely the "truth" that it seeks to demonstrate, followed by an explanation on "How They Are Interrelated." What is so fascinating about this assertion is the extent to which it ties divine knowledge with the knowledge of self. That turning inward as an act that complements the knowledge (and therefore proof) of the other is a development of major import in the confluence of ontological/epistemological speculation. The same act of turning inward is followed by that of looking upward. In a sense, the act of turning inward to know oneself leads to that of turning outward to know God and in the process to acknowledge his presence throughout the universe. The experience of knowing God leads to the corresponding experience of affirming his existence, indeed, his very being is as much within one's self as it is throughout the universe. At this juncture, Calvin is at his most profound and at his most intimate. In a paean that sets the epistemological and the ontological in order, Calvin celebrates not just God but the experience that draws one to God. So he contends that "no one can look upon himself without immediately turning his thoughts to the contemplation of God," for it is in God that one "lives and moves" (Acts 17:28). With this citation of a partial verse from the biblical text, one is left to complete the phrase "lives and moves" by "and have our being." Because the experience of knowing God is innate, we also know that in him we have our being, which is at the same time his being. To know one's self is to know God, to know that he exists, to participate in his "beingness." Epistemology resolves itself in ontology. "Led as by rivulets to the spring itself," we are compelled in that spiritual awakening to "look upward," to acknowledge and worship our creator (1.1).[16]

Moving from the initial comments on epistemology and ontology, Calvin goes on to pursue the experience of God's self-revelation or self-manifestation in all things. Thus, in the fifth chapter of the first book, Calvin maintains that "the clarity of God's self-disclosure strips us of every excuse" not to have faith in God's existence. Such an assertion reflects an awareness of what has been called "doubt's boundless sea," the currents of which made themselves felt throughout the early modern period.[17] In keeping with his work as a whole, Calvin's response to these currents amounts to a hymn of praise to commemorate God's act of "self-disclosure," a process that takes place daily. We cannot, Calvin declares, open our eyes without being compelled to behold God (1.5 and 2.5).[18] With Calvin's *Institutes*, then, the emphasis falls upon the experiential relationship between humans (and their ability to perceive) and God (and his willingness to disclose himself to those capable of living and moving and having their being within the being of God). In keeping with works such as *Summa Theologica*, the discourse of being in the *Institutes* takes center stage. At the same time, the focus of the *Institutes* is one that eschews the systematic, if not paradigmatic, constructions of what is normally associated with scholastic methodology. In Calvin the experiential (one might almost say "existential") mode comes dramatically to the fore. In fact, it not only comes to the fore, but also it is the very stuff of the treatise as a whole. As such, it is a treatise in which ontology assumes a primacy consistent with the concerns of philosophical discourse.

In the traditions of early modern philosophy, the issue of being assumes its most compelling form in René Descartes, whose *Discours de la méthode* (1637) and *Meditationes de prima philosophia* (1641) are pivotal statements in the debate about ontology.[19] For our purposes, *Discours de la méthode* is important because of its emphasis upon method and its concern with ontology. We have already encountered the issue of method in Ramus and his heirs. According to the Ramistic formulation, method reflects a belief in a world of closure and containment as opposed to a concern with indeterminacy and unknowableness. As such, method is centered in the knowable, the graspable, and the conceivable. Method renders all that can be known as determinate by means of the orderly and logical deployment of the argument. For Descartes, the concept of method assumes a decidedly different bearing. Above all else, it is the product of the "self," particularly as that entity embodies or finds expression in "the great book of the world" (*Discours*, 10). This emphasis upon the self is, of course, the crucial signifier of the Cartesian *cogito*, which for Descartes is the foundation for determining the fact of his own existence, not to mention the existence of the external world. All proceeds from the self, the phenomenon through which Descartes is empowered to arrive at his conclusions concerning the nature of things human and divine (ibid., 24–25). Such a view represents not only a turning inward to the self but also a movement from inward to outward in the implementation of method. This method, in turn, involves a revaluation of conventional methodologies governed by a logic based on a knowledge of syllogism and other rules (ibid., 15).

Rather than depending upon "the multiplicity of rules that comprise logic," Descartes posited four principles to ballast his idea of method. These include such basic principles as testing all suppositions before accepting them, subdividing each problem or issue into smaller units in order to engage it more efficiently, undertaking an orderly mode of research and speculation, and finally, making certain to be careful and comprehensive in the implementation of one's plan. The third principle is especially revealing because it involves the movement from those things that are "the simplest and easiest to know" in order to "rise gradually, as if by steps, to knowledge of the most complex," that is, knowledge of the divine (*Discours*,

17).[20] Accordingly, Descartes is confident that his awareness of that which is at once most complex and yet most perfect is the means by which he is able to perceive the fact of God's existence. We can only proceed to implement this methodology, Descartes observes, if we acknowledge that "God is, or exists, that he is a perfect being, and that everything in us derives from him" (ibid., 24–28). It is the phrase "in us" that is key: the inward turn to self underlies all that the *Discours* argues about in matters of deity and the method undertaken to address issues of being.

If *Discours de la méthode* represents one mode of addressing the issue of ontology, *Meditationes de prima philosophia* develops the philosophy of being (human and divine) even further. Assuming the form of six meditations on "first" or originary philosophy, *Meditationes de prima philosophia* seeks to prove at once the validity of the idea of the mind/body dichotomy and the evidence of God's existence.[21] Although these two notions are inextricably linked, the ontological issue is what engages us here. Once again, the emphasis upon mind is highlighted. That humans have the capacity to think, to reflect, to meditate is crucial for Descartes in dealing with matters of ultimacy, that is, with the fact that God exists. The crucial notion of self takes center stage. In the third meditation, Descartes makes clear his belief that as a result of having been created in the likeness and image of God (compare Gen. 1:27), humans perceive deity with the same faculty that they use to perceive themselves. Addressing the concept of humans as the embodiment of the *imago Dei*, Descartes observes in his third meditation that "'tis not to be admired that *God* in creating me should *Imprint* this *Idea* in me, that it may there remain as a *stamp impressed* by the *Workman God* on *me* his *Work.*" This "idea" is one that asserts that there is indeed a God through whose powers the *imago Dei* is given shape. Declaring his belief in the correspondence between divine ontology and human ontology, Descartes likewise ventures the following observation: as one made in the "likeness and Image of God," he as human bears "the same *likeness* and *Image*" in which "the *Idea* of God is contain'd." This *imago,* Descartes avers, "is *perceived* by Me with the *same faculty,* with which I *perceive my Self;* That is to say, whilst I *reflect* upon my self." At this very point, the entire argument about ontology devolves into a series of reflections on the self as the source of what we know about this world and the next. The whole emphasis of Descartes's argument rests upon his conclusion that "I know it Impossible for me to Be of the same Nature I am, *viz.* Having the *Idea* of a *God* in me, unless there really were a *God,* a *God* (I say) that very *same God,* whose *Idea* I have in my *Mind*" (*Meditationes,* 53–54). With the idea of God firmly in mind, the philosopher becomes aware of the extent to which humankind as the *imago Dei* is in a position to see and know the nature of the divine, its presence and its bearing. The meditation is as much about the faculties of mind in the act of perception as it is about that power through which mind came into being in the first place. At the center of the meditation is the *imago Dei,* a concept that embraces two complementary notions: that of God as *imago* and that of humankind as bearer of the divine *imago.* For Descartes, both notions must be taken into account in any consideration of the nature of ontology.

From the perspectives provided by representative texts in the medieval period and beyond, we may now proceed to discuss the place of ontology in *De Doctrina Christiana.* A systematic theology that shares a certain amount of its impetus with that reflected in the treatises of an Ames or a Wolleb, *De Doctrina* is nonetheless *sui generis* in its focus upon such issues as ontology. Here, the treatise adopts a methodology consistent with an entire range of discourses at once strictly "theological" and at the same time "philosophical" in orientation. Reflecting a determination to address ontological matters, *De Doctrina Christiana* most certainly is classifiable as a philosophical theology, a form that the treatise may be said to assume from the very outset. Thus, in his overall attempt to determine who or what God is in the chapter "De Deo," Milton does not hesitate to begin his discussion by raising the crucial issue of God's existence. Milton's assertion is charged with a decidedly argumentative tone that dares the faithless to refute that which is finally irrefutable but that at the same time acknowledges that there are those determined not to believe: "That there is a God, many deny: *for the fool says in his heart, There is no God, Psal.* xiv. 1" (Esse Deum, quanquam haud pauci sunt qui negent esse, *dicit enim stultus in corde suo, non est Deus*) (YP 6:130; CM 14:24). Reminiscent of the position adopted in Anselm's *Proslogion*, the statement is in effect a challenge to all who seek to undermine true faith.

With these *stulti* in mind, Milton follows the first assertion with a second that turns inward to focus on what might be called the crucial concept of mind: "But he has left so many signs of himself in the human mind, so many traces of his presence through the whole of nature, that no sane person can fail to realize that he exists" (tot tamen clara indicia sui Deus in mente humana, tot per omnem penitus naturam sui vestigia impressit, ut ignorare Deum esse, nemo non insanus possit) (YP 6:130; CM 14:24). Neither the translation in the Yale edition nor the translation in the Columbia edition of *De Doctrina* is entirely effective in suggesting the full implications of the original.[22] One is struck immediately by the syntactical balance, as well as patterns of phrasal repetition and variation. Thus, the opening pronouncement *"Esse Deum"* underscores the need to bear up against the assertion of a contrary idea (*negent esse*), offered as a challenge to those determined to undermine all that *esse* represents. But the *Esse Deum* prevails over the denial of God's existence, as *negent esse* gives way to the *Deum Esse* in what becomes a playful pattern of repetition and reversal.[23] What results is a theme and variations on the notion of the existence, the beingness, that is, the *esse* of God. One is struck not only by the artistry reflected in the passage but also by the way in which that artistry reinforces a focus upon "mind" (or "heart") as an entity that is as compelling as that of the external world of "nature." Milton does not hesitate to view the world of mind as all-encompassing, as the means by which the existence of God is doubly confirmed. Milton's belief in this principle is reinforced by his insistence that not to accept the fact of God's existence is to prove oneself as nothing more than *insanus*. The stakes are high, but they demonstrate the extent to which Milton is willing to back his views about God. At the same time, the rhetorical patterning of the language encourages the text to open up, to entertain the possibility of contrary views for the sake of combating them. With such terms as *stultus* and *insanus*, the tone begins to assume the force of polemic, of combat with those who would advocate what is contrary to the true path. The emphasis upon the *indicia*, or "traces," moreover, demonstrates an awareness of the signatures of being through which the mind gains knowledge of God's existence, as well as the efficacy of his presence. One recalls a corresponding outlook in the *Meditationes* of Descartes. The Cartesian phrase "in mente humana" says it all. For Milton, the human mind represents the medium through which deity fully manifests itself. However one conceives the argument at this point, Milton is at pains to accord the human mind a privileged status in his treatment of God. As a result of that treatment, the self and the other become coordinates in a play of dialectic grounded in a belief in the powers of mind. This is a dialectic that underscores the experiential revelations of Calvin as well.

For Milton as for those who embraced a similar point of view, the urgency of establishing the legitimacy of the ontological perspective rendered any suggestion that God does not exist both foolish and insane. Considering the amount of space Milton devotes to the question of ontology in the treatise, it should come as no surprise that the subject of being assumes a good deal of importance indeed. First heralded with a declaration that God most certainly does exist, the argument then moves into corresponding areas, among them the fallacy of believing in nature, chance, fate, and other such phenomena as substitutes for the one true supreme being. It is at this point that the theologian becomes philosopher as he considers the provenance of the terms *natura* and *fatum* and associates them with various pagan schools of thought. "In place of one God," these schools invoke as universal rulers "two goddesses" (duas Deas) who are constantly in a state of antagonism toward one another and are conceived as the opposition of good and evil. This reductionist view of divine "beingness" as nothing more than an impersonal conflict of powers that rules the affairs of its votaries is for Milton "intolerable and incredible." Paradoxically, the absurdity of such views is yet further evidence that "Deus igitur est" (YP 8:130–32; CM 14:24–26). Clearly at play here is the desire to confute such errors as those held by the Stoics and the Manicheans as philosophical schools.[24] In short, the argument from ontology does not hesitate to address what it feels are the essential dangers that beset any attempt to conceive the one true God through notions that fail to comprehend the profound mystery of his existence.

But Milton does not stop there. As part of the argument from ontology, he extends his discussion to matters of behavior and intellection. Specifically, he considers the roles of *conscientia* and *recta ratio* in coming to terms with the issue of God's existence. For Milton, conscience and right reason become interchangeable phenomena through which the existence of God can be proven.[25] "No one," Milton observes, "would refrain from sin because he felt ashamed of it or feared the law, if the voice of Conscience or right reason did not speak from time to time in the heart of every man, reminding him" at all points that "a God does exist" (YP 8:132). Implicit in such assertions is the idea that the ability to reason properly and the capacity to make the correct moral choices are intimately intertwined. For

Milton, the very presence of both the rational imperative and the moral imperative in humankind is in–and of itself sufficient evidence that God exists. An inclination to conceive theology in philosophical terms is essential to the outlook represented here. To demonstrate this end, the references to *conscientia* and *recta ratio* in the treatise reflect an awareness of conceptions of philosophical thought extending from the Stoics to the scholastics. In turn, both categories (conscience and right reason) later became staples of philosophical thought throughout the Renaissance.[26] From the perspective of those concerned with right reason, "the difference between the 'dry light' of 'unaided reason'" (that is, "the nonmoral activity of logical disquisition") and "the dictates of 'right reason'" is that *recta ratio* is a distinctly superior faculty, the kind of reason that has been "morally purified." As a moral and indeed spiritual phenomenon, the faculty of reason is deemed "right" insofar as it seeks "the knowledge of absolute Truth, that is, the Truth of Christianity." Essential to the formulation of right reason, then, is the intimate association of *recta ratio* with the categories of good and bad behavior, that is, with the awareness of the difference between right and wrong. "Reason thus simultaneously disposed, so that it presides with equal validity over the realms of intellect and morality, is what is meant by 'right reason.'"[27]

Such a distinction accounts for the association of right reason and conscience in *De Doctrina Christiana*. Given the high regard in which conscience is held in the treatise, the association is understandable, if not inevitable. In the second book of *De Doctrina*, Milton makes it clear that conscience is an "intellectual judgment of one's own deeds, and an approval of them, which is directed by the light either of nature or of grace" (YP 6:652).[28] Conscience, then, is an innate faculty bestowed upon humankind as a sign of the ability not simply to reason but to make right choices. At the same time, Milton views both conscience and right reason as the product of grace.

This characteristic aligns them with the experience of revelation as the result of what it means to be receptive to the presence of God. Here, secular and sacred, human and divine, the
work of nature and the work of grace, find expression.[29] In order
to perfect the one, the other must be acknowledged. Thus,
Milton argues that as noble and as powerful as conscience and
right reason might prove themselves to be, their true significance must be understood in the context of the revealed word
of God. This experience provides ample evidence that God
exists, that he is the "Lord and ruler of all things," and that
one day everyone must give him "account of his own actions,
whether good or bad." This is already inscribed in the Bible,
which is why "the disciples of the doctrine of Christ may
fairly be required to give assent to this truth before all others,
according to Heb. xi. 6. 'he that cometh to God, must believe
that he is'" (qui accedit ad Deum, credat oportet esse Deum)
(CM 14:28).[30]

Convinced of the primacy of the biblical text in executing
his methodology in De Doctrina Christiana, Milton draws lib-
erally on the Bible to support his contentions. We recall that
the act of amassing proof-texts (in fact, "cramming" them
"even to the point of overflowing") constitutes the establishment of a metatext that potentially gives rise to a whole new
world of resonances. Accordingly, the practice of cramming the
page with proof-texts (all of which are given the same status
or weight as the text they are meant to support) runs the risk
of problematizing matters rather than clarifying them because
a new constellation of signifiers threatens to unleash meanings that extend well beyond the immediate context.[31]
Returning to the opening paragraph of the chapter "De Deo,"
we can see precisely how complex the interchange between
text and proof-text comes to be. The paragraph is essentially
made up of three sentences plus a plethora of proof-texts. The
first sentence, "That there is a God, many deny," is followed
by a brief but memorable proof-text: *"for the fool says in his*

heart, There is no God, Psal. xiv.1." This proof-text is followed
by a second sentence: "But he [God] has left so many signs of
himself in the human mind, so many traces of his presence
through the whole of nature, that no sane person can fail to
realize that he exists." That declaration is followed by a long
series of proof-texts drawn from both the Old and New
Testaments. The concluding sentence rounds out the paragraph
as a whole: "It is indisputable that all the things which exist
in the world, created in perfection of beauty and order for
some definite purpose, and that a good one, provide proof that
a supreme creative being existed before the world, and had a
definite purpose of his own in all created things" (YP 6:130).

The first proof-text provides an excellent sense of the ten-
sions that arise in the use of proof-texts to substantiate a doctrinal pronouncement. As we have seen, the reference to Psalm
14:1 ("for the fool says in his heart, There is no God") immediately brings into focus the polemical castigations that per-
meate the psalm as a whole. For this is clearly a psalm of
denunciation against those who "have become corrupt" and
"have done hateful things" (14:1). Suddenly, the opening observation of the theological treatise ("That there is a God, many
deny") is placed in the context not only of those who are foolish but also of those whose corruption and hateful behavior
are a source of dismay and revulsion: "The Lord looked down
from heaven upon the children of men, to see if there were any
that did understand, and seek God. They are all gone aside, they
are all together become filthy: *there* is none that doeth good,
no, not one" (Ps. 14:2–3). The proof-text broadens out and
shapes our understanding of just what is at stake in denying
the existence of God and in seeking to undermine all faith in
that existence. What begins as a discourse on God, then, immediately moves from an assertion of one of the basic principles
of theology (God exists) to a world of righteous indignation
against any who would say otherwise. This movement leads
to a Jobean insistence on the existence of God, despite all the

pain and suffering Job himself has been made to undergo. Accordingly, the proof-text "Who does not know from all these things" (Job 12:9) is part of a larger network of complaints by Job that he is as one "mocked of his neighbour, who calleth upon God, and he answereth him: the just upright *man is* laughed to scorn" (12:4). In fitting response to the sufferings the just man endures, God "poureth contempt upon princes, and weakeneth the strength of the mighty" (12:21). Job's enemies will "grope in the dark without light" and "stagger like a drunken man" (12:25). From this perspective, the conception of God in *De Doctrina Christiana* begins to be charged with energies unleashed by the cumulative force of the proof-texts. Assuming a central role in the discourse, these proof-texts threaten at every moment to overwhelm their boundaries. Far from being little more than tools to substantiate claims advanced in the main body of the text, the proof-texts take on a life of their own.[32]

II

Milton creates a world in which one may never rest content with the simple assertion of doctrinal principles. Rather, one must contend with the proof-texts, interpret them, and understand what they disclose on their own terms. Milton's God is buried in the proof-texts, just as the author of *De Doctrina Christiana* is buried in the text of his treatise. Of both it might be said, "he is there and not there; now you see him, now you don't." In his analysis of *De Doctrina*, Arthur Sewell reveals a fine sensitivity to the implications of the buried life in which the mind of the author reveals a profound "restlessness" that cannot "wholly satisfy itself by a re-formulation of doctrine on the intellectual plane." Milton reveals a sensibility "troubled" by "its darker intuitions of the nature of God, by its active affections towards God, by its perplexities in what it conceived to be the presence of the mystery of God's purposes."[33]

This is a mystery that transcends reason and intellect, a realm of knowing that is essentially one of not-knowing. This mode complements and deepens the ontological dimensions of deity addressed in the first section of the chapter on God in *De Doctrina*. With that complementarity in mind, we may now consider the second section, which embodies what I have termed the epistemological mode.[34] This is a mode that Milton associates with the so-called "hiddenness" of God. Officially known as the *deus absconditus*, this phenomenon has enjoyed a long and fruitful history in biblical exegesis extending back to the early church and up through the early modern period and beyond.[35] With an understanding of the traditions through which the hiddenness of God emerges, we shall then return to *De Doctrina Christiana* as a work fully responsive to all that the *deus absconditus* represents.

In his study of the phenomenon, Brian Gerrish locates one of the originary biblical sites for the *deus absconditus* in the Acts of the Apostles (17:16–34).[36] According to the narrative, Paul is found disputing with the Athenians in the marketplace, after which he is led by the philosophers to the Areopagus, the Hill of Mars. There, the apostle relates that along his way he discovered an altar with the strange inscription, "To the Unknown God." Whereas the true meaning of the inscription may have been a mystery to the citizens of Athens, Paul "deciphers" it by distinguishing between the "true God" of his message and the idolatrous gods of the Athenians. The distinction is one that not only highlights pagan versus Christian modes of thought but also provides the impetus for later exegetes to formulate their own notion of the *deus absconditus*, one through which the "total otherness of deity" is manifested. That otherness underscores what Gerrish calls "the experience of God," a category at once epistemological and phenomenological.[37] According to Gerrish, that experience appears to manifest itself in two forms, each of which involves its own act of occultation and disclosure.[38] The first form is manifested in the experience of God hidden "*in* his revelation," the second form in the experience of God hidden "*outside* his revelation" (my italics).[39] David Tracy nicely nuances the distinction by suggesting that the first form of hiddenness manifests itself in the *deus crucifixus*, that is, God's paradoxical disclosure of himself to humans *sub contrariis:* "life through death, wisdom through folly, strength through weakness." If the first form is fully embodied in the figure of the Son as Savior, the second form is that of God as "outside" or "behind" or even "beyond" the embodied Word. In this form, hiddenness is conceived as an overwhelming force, an "impersonal reality — 'it' — of sheer power and energy" and is signified by such metaphors as "abyss, chasm, chaos, horror." This is, as it were, "God beyond God."[40] Such is the answer of the *deus absconditus* to the unknown God of the ancient world, God beyond the reach of the ability to know and understand.[41] One senses in all this a kind of metaphysics of hiddenness that arises in the attempt to explain precisely how the roles of God as both hidden and revealed complement each other. However these roles are conceived, one thing is certain: we appear to be dealing with the attempt to understand the experience of God in its most archaic form.

Among those who have defined that experience most fully, Rudolf Otto is especially notable.[42] More than any other scholar, he has forged a terminology through which one might be able to articulate that which eludes expression, a terminology that has assumed an idiomatic presence in accounts of religious phenomena. For Otto the true experience of God is one that recognizes deity as *ganz andere*, or "wholly other," a concept that lies at the heart of all that Otto writes about the encounter with the hidden God, which is the basis of his book *The Idea of the Holy*.[43] In its concern with the phenomenon of "the holy," the book is germane to a full understanding of God's hiddenness. Approaching the subject from an "evolutionary" perspective, Otto speaks of the presence of God in its earliest stages as a "feeling-reflex." Nonrational in nature, this feeling-reflex is a visceral phenomenon that has to do not with the ability to reason but with the capacity to experience. As such, the archaic notion of God as "wholly other" assumes the form of the *mysterium tremendum* as well as that of the *mysterium fascinans,* terms conceived to suggest not just the ineffable nature of deity but also the "power" of a phenomenon at once inviting contact and at the same time too dreadful and awesome to be encountered face to face. Imbued with *numen,* that power beyond all powers is known by its "awe-fulness," as well as by the "dread" and "terror" it engenders.[44] To this end, Otto alludes to "the *emat* of Yahweh ('fear of God'), which Yahweh can pour forth, dispatching almost like a daemon, and which seizes upon a man with paralysing effect." This *emat* is closely related to the *deima panikon* of the Greek, and in the Old Testament it is found everywhere, such as Exodus 23:27: "I will send my fear before thee and will destroy all the people to whom thou shalt come." What results is "a terror fraught with an inward shuddering such as not even the most menacing and overpowering created thing can instil." This power has something spectral in it, Otto observes.[45] The psychological or (more to the point) phenomenological complex that Otto brings to bear upon *das Heilige* is useful in coming to terms with the *deus absconditus* as defined by Gerrish, whose agenda is to construct a historical context for the concept ranging from the period of the early church up to the time of the Reformation.

From the perspective of the early church, the idea of the *deus absconditus* appears in a number of the church fathers. Otto points, for example, to Saint John Chrysostom, "whose sermons break forth with the inconceivable and unapproachable in God." These sermons, Otto avers, are "not the result of any school of theology or philosophy"; rather, they "indicate a profound feeling that God cannot be approached in his majesty."[46] In his own study of divine hiddenness, John Dillenberger explores the nature of the *deus absconditus* in the works of such fathers as Clement of Alexandria, whose *Stromata* specifically speaks of the hiddenness of God, as does Origen's *De Principiis*. So, too, do the works of Saint Augustine "abound with references to the term [*deus absconditus*] and its meanings."[47] The one medieval figure whose works are foundational in any assessment of the inconceivable and unapproachable in God is Dionysius the Areopagite.[48] Indeed, Pseudo-Dionysius's distinctions between kataphatic and apophatic views of deity speak directly to the notion of the *deus absconditus*.[49] Needless to say, his mystical or apophatic view of deity gained a wide audience through the centuries. Although his ideas were hardly accepted without question during the Reformation, the reformers at least took them into account.[50] Gerrish is at once careful to point out the differences between the patristic endorsement of "hiddenness" and the Reformation agenda but also is clearly insistent upon the role that figures such as Pseudo-Dionysius played in the early modern period.[51]

However one conceives of the relationship between apophatic theology and the notion of divine hiddenness in the formative years of the Reformation and beyond, Martin Luther and John Calvin assume primary importance in an encounter with the *deus absconditus*. In the works of Luther and Calvin, the hiddenness of God assumes its own form and impetus. Although critical of the Dionysian mystical theology on many fronts, both Luther and Calvin not only found the teachings of Pseudo-Dionysius appealing but they also incorporated the very language of those teachings in the conduct of their exegesis. In his *Lectures on the Psalms,* Luther accordingly provides his own taxonomy of God's hiddenness as manifested in Psalm 18:11 ("And he made the darkness his hiding-place"). Here, Luther sees a fivefold hiddenness at work. Thus, God hides in the darkness of faith, in light inaccessible, in the mystery of the Incarnation, in the church, and in the Eucharist. Throughout his discourse, Luther speaks of God not simply as "unknown" (*incognitus*), but more precisely as "hidden" (*absconditus*).

The full force of that hiddenness emerges in one of Luther's most profoundly disturbing works, *On the Bondage of the Will*. Written in response to Erasmus's treatise *On the Freedom of the Will*, Luther's treatise took the sage of Rotterdam to task for calling into question the premises upon which the great reformer grounded his own teaching.[52] At the very center of Luther's conception of God's hiddenness is his argument that if a person is saved at all, his salvation is the result of God's having "irresistibly directed the impotent human will, which is utterly incapable of turning itself toward salvation."[53] Why, then, does God not choose to move every person's will from bad to good, since only God has that power? The answer is that there is no answer available to human reason. For Luther, "the source of grace is the predestinating purpose of God." Given these circumstances, Gerrish observes that it is impossible to read Luther and not to recognize that there was "a terror in his encounter with the hidden, predestinating God and that the emotional, religious, or spiritual content of the experience burst the limits of the merely rational and conceptual." From Luther's own testimony, one can see that the encounter with the hidden God was a "shattering" one that "brought him right up to the rim of the abyss."[54] So Luther speaks of the "hidden and awful will of God," which is "not to be inquired into, but reverently adored, as by far the most awe-inspiring secret of the Divine Majesty, reserved for Himself alone and forbidden to us" to probe. As one "hidden in His majesty" and dwelling in "light inaccessible" (1 Tim. 6:16), God must therefore "be left to Himself in His own majesty, for in this regard we have nothing to do with Him, nor has He willed that we should have anything to do with Him." We have "no right whatever," Luther asserts, to "inquire into, hanker after, care about, or meddle with" God's hiddenness. He is a God that we must "fear and adore."[55]

If Luther represents one notion of divine hiddenness in the early modern period, Calvin represents a corresponding notion.

Falling under the heading of epistemology, that notion is of a kind with Calvin's speculations on the all-important issue of ontology, addressed earlier. To the extent that epistemology and phenomenology overlap both with each other and with ontology, Calvin's delineation of the *deus absconditus* is in keeping with what we have already discussed as the "experiential" basis of his theological outlook, one that emphasizes the significance of the "wholly other." For Calvin, the experience of God is fundamentally daunting because his God is essentially unknowable, essentially hidden. Thus, Gerrish observes that the term "secret" (*arcanum*) is Calvin's "most characteristic description" of God's "design" (*consilium*). Calvin speaks repeatedly of God's ways as both "concealed" (*occulta*) and "secret" (*secreta*). God's "wonderful way of governing the world is justly called an 'abyss' because while hidden from us, it ought reverently to be adored." Here, Calvin, no less than Luther, finds himself on the brink of what Gerrish calls an "abyss of sightless darkness."[56] As we have seen, Calvin's most detailed account of what it means to "know" God is at the core of his *Institutes of the Christian Religion*. Under the heading "The Knowledge of God the Creator," Calvin accordingly makes a point to address the full implications of the *deus absconditus*.

Those implications are delineated in the chapter titled "It Is Unlawful to Attribute a Visible Form to God" (1.11), where Calvin shifts the emphasis from the Lutheran issue of "will" (bound or otherwise) to the equally important issue of "representation." Uncompromising in his scathing attack on images of any sort, Calvin invokes the ark of the covenant with its mercy seat and covering angelic guards to argue against any idea of actually presencing God in the world of matter. Here, Calvin sees occlusion, a keeping of the holy inviolate: "The mercy seat [of the ark] from which God manifested the presence of his power . . . was so constructed as to suggest that the best way to contemplate the divine is where minds are lifted above themselves with admiration. Indeed, the cherubim with wings outspread covered it; the veil shrouded it; the place itself deeply enough hidden concealed it" (Exod. 25:17–21). Moving from the Exodus narrative to the prophetic accounts, Calvin next observes that "the prophets depict the seraphim as appearing in their visions with face veiled toward us" (Isa. 6:2). This image signifies "that the splendor of divine glory is so great that the very angels also are restrained from direct gaze."[57] Throughout the theology of Luther and Calvin, God becomes the embodiment of the most profoundly archaic of forces that one can possibly conceive. As the true *deus absconditus*, the God of Luther and Calvin fulfills all that has come to be associated with deity as the most "awe-ful" representation of the "wholly other." This is a representation that underscored the formative stages of the Reformation and that found expression at various points in the early modern period and beyond.[58]

For our purposes, the idea of the *deus absconditus* may certainly be said fully to resonate in Milton's *De Doctrina Christiana*. To be sure, the doctrinal premises of this work run counter in many respects to those put forth by either Luther or Calvin, particularly in the area of predestination. Although predestination does have a place in the theology advanced by *De Doctrina*, the very notion of "bondage of the will" would be deemed anathema by Milton, who takes up issues of this sort at a later stage of his argument.[59] These are matters that lie well beyond the purview of the present discussion. Nonetheless, the emphasis upon the hiddenness of God is still very much an essential part of the outlook embodied in *De Doctrina Christiana*. The God of *De Doctrina Christiana* is as profoundly "hidden" in his own way as any that the *Bondage of the Will* or *Institutes* might imagine.[60] One need only consider the discourse that falls under the heading of "knowing God" to become aware of how important the concept of hiddenness is to the delineation of deity in the theological treatise.

For Milton, the whole project of attempting to know God is already called into question by the fact of God's hiddenness. This phenomenon far transcends the faculty of "knowing" as the product of "nature or reason alone." Thus, "when we talk about knowing God" (de cognoscendo Deo quod loquimur), Milton observes, such an act "must be understood in terms of man's limited powers of comprehension." Indeed, the reliance upon reason to know God "as he really is, is far beyond man's imagination, let alone his understanding" (nedum sensus longe superat) (YP 6:133; CM 14:30). Such an outlook is one that calls into question the rational faculties in matters of divine apprehension, rather than relying upon them as determinants of ultimacy. Milton thereby reveals his determination to conceive the act of knowing God by arguing that God is beyond all power to know. The phrase "nedum sensus longe superat" is particularly telling, for it suggests not so much the "imagination" as that higher faculty that "far overcomes" or "outdoes" the faculty bound by the senses or the understanding. (The Columbia Milton is closer to the sense: to know God "far transcends the powers of man's thoughts, much more of his perception" [CM 14:31]. But even that does not fully capture the spirit of the statement, which alludes to some power through which it is possible to comprehend that which far transcends any other faculty.) The point is that to "know" God in any true sense of that phrase is tantamount to that which is impossible for any of the faculties, whatever they are called. This is finally a God of "not knowing," of transcendent grandeur, a figure who finally cannot be grasped. In the very act of venturing the observation about what he calls the category of cognoscendo Deo, Milton implies that to know is not to know, that is, to undo knowing in the attempt to come to terms with the divine. It is here in particular that the treatise may be said to follow in the path of the hiddenness of God. Essentially at issue is that apophatic theology through which the experience of God amounts to "an obliteration of knowing, understanding, naming, speech, and language" and by means of which one moves into "the realm of unknowing, divine ignorance, the nameless, the speechless, and the silent."[61]

To support his claim that "God, as he really is, is far beyond man's imagination, let alone his understanding," Milton cites 1 Timothy 6:16: "dwelling in unapproachable light" (lucem habitans inaccessam) (YP 6:133; CM 14:30). The citation represents a kind of shorthand for the full biblical text: "Who only hath immortality, dwelling in the light which no man can approach unto; whom no man hath seen, nor can see: to whom *be* honour and power everlasting. Amen." As is clear from the salutation that concludes the verse, the text itself has a liturgical ring to it. One has the impression that the text represents something of a coda to a hymnic celebration of the *deus absconditus*. At the very least, the verse celebrates that paradox through which God's occlusive nature is revealed by the unbearable light with which it is imbued. God's very revelation is one in which he is most hidden. As the ontological passes to the epistemological, we come to realize that this is an epistemology of that which cannot be beheld, known, or understood. This is true of the past, the present, and implicitly the future. Any attempt to ameliorate the harshness of that truth will find itself subverted by the occlusiveness of God's self-revelation as one who dwells in light that is absolutely blinding in its intensity.[62] For this reason, the statement that follows the citation ("lucem habitans inaccessam") appears almost ironic in its belief in the willingness of God to let himself be known: "God has revealed as much of himself as our minds can conceive and the weakness of our nature can bear" (YP 6:133). As an expression of the well-known doctrine of accommodation, this statement must be placed in the context of 1 Timothy 6:16. Based upon the proof-text, we are obliged to conclude that even the most limited or accommodative knowledge of God is totally beyond the reach of human capacity.

Accommodation or not, what emerges from the discussion is the unknowableness of God on any level.[63] This unknowableness is further underscored by the proof-texts that are marshaled to provide biblical evidence for the *deus absconditus*. Milton invokes these texts from both the Old Testament and the New Testament:

> Exod. xxxiii. 20, 23: *no man can see me and live; but you will see my back parts;* Isa. vi. 1: *I saw the Lord sitting on a throne which was raised high in the air, and the fringe of his garment spread over the whole of the temple;* John i. 18: *no man has ever seen God,* and vi. 46: *not that anyone has seen the Father, except him who is from God; he has seen the Father,* and v. 37: *nor have you heard his voice;* I Cor. xiii. 12: *in a mirror, in a riddle, partially.* (YP 6:133)

Although we might view these as standard proof-texts to express the unknowability of God, the fact that Milton elects to cite precisely these texts in this configuration is significant. These aspects of the marshaling of proof-texts should not be taken for granted.[64] First, it is worthwhile to note that, purely from a statistical point of view, the number of proof-texts drawn from the New Testament is greater than the number drawn from the Old Testament, a fact that places special emphasis upon the issue of the Father/Son relationship discussed later in the treatise. Second, the yoking of these texts together is significant in suggesting Milton's determination to endorse an epistemology that embraces both worlds, that of the Old Testament and that of the New. Milton's "method" is already made clear in instances such as these, for the combining of both Testaments is inevitable and generally consistent throughout the treatise. But, as we have already seen, proof-texts represent surface clues to matters that lie far beneath. They are at once signifiers for realms of the hidden and icebergs that offer only a glimpse of what their surface calm might otherwise mask. What is so evident in the foregoing proof-texts in support of epistemology is the extent to which they elaborate even further that which we have already witnessed: the ultimate inability of human beings (no matter how exalted their office) to know God. Once again, to speak of the "God" of *De Doctrina Christiana* is to acknowledge the force of the *deus absconditus* as a guiding principle of the treatise as a whole.

In keeping with this outlook, we begin with the proof-texts from the Old Testament. Because of their emphasis upon a God of awe and indeed of terror, the texts from Exodus and Isaiah are germane. "Exod. xxxiii. 20, 23: *no man can see me and live: but you will see my back parts*; Isa. vi. 1: *I saw the Lord sitting on a throne which was raised high in the air, and the fringe of his garment spread over the whole of the temple.*" Each of the proof-texts enacts the drama of theophany through which God reveals himself in varying degrees to his prophets, first to Moses; second to Isaiah. Eliding two verses (20 and 23) in the Exodus account, Milton encapsulates a crucial moment in the process of divine revelation. That moment is a small but telling part of the cycle of narratives that constitute the sojourn in the wilderness and with the establishment of the covenant at Sinai. In the particular moment to which the elided verses allude, Moses has entered the newly constructed tabernacle wherein the divine presence of God resides. Encountering that presence, Moses speaks to God and God responds to Moses, as it were, "face to face, as a man speaketh unto his friend " (Exod. 33:11). One encounters here the primal scene of approaching deity in the most intimate of terms.

It is as a result of such circumstances that Moses negotiates the terms through which God's divine presence will continue to reside with and protect the Israelites as they continue their journey through wilderness. But even under these circumstances, the drama of negotiation is developed further, as Moses petitions God to reveal himself wholly: "I beseech thee, show me thy glory" (Exod. 33:18). On one level, the drama is reminiscent of that which transpires when Moses receives his calling before the burning bush (Exod. 3–4). Here, too, the prophet-to-be petitions the divine presence within the bush to reveal his identity in the form of its name, in response to which the voice responds cryptically through a locution that occludes as much as it reveals: "I Am That I Am" (Exod. 3:14). In the drama under consideration, God responds just as mysteriously. More than that, however, the interchange is charged with something of a sexual, perhaps voyeuristic, quality that intensifies the drama even further.[65] "Show me thy glory" or "let me see thy glory" is the kind of petition that one finds throughout the tradition of carpe diem.[66] At the risk of comparing "great things with small," I am not urging that the dialogue between God and his servant be viewed overtly in sexual terms, but at some level the interchange appears to suggest this idea. At the very least, the dialogue gives evidence that the petition to see what should not be seen is conceived as a kind of erotics of self-disclosure, an erotics that draws upon what one might term the sexual presence of God to delineate the nature of his transcendence. We arrive once again at the proof-texts that Milton invokes and elides in order to dramatize the ultimate unknowability of God, Exodus 33:20 and 23: "no man can see me and live; but you will see my back parts." The elision acts as a kind of frame that sets off the drama, which includes God's placement of Moses in the "cleft of the rock" as his "glory passeth by" (Exod. 33:22). Protecting his prophet from the mortal dangers attendant upon viewing deity through an unmediated vision, God says that he will "cover" Moses with his "hand" while his glory passes by, and only after that will he remove his hand. Although Moses will not be able to see the actual "face" of God, his servant will be in a position to see and marvel at God's "back parts." The reference to the back parts brings to closure the voyeuristic element with which this particular theophany is imbued. The elision that encompasses what is appropriate for the prophet to see (back parts) and what is appropriate for him not to see (the transcendent self embodied in the face) establishes the terms by which the prophet is empowered to behold God as a manifestation of otherness within the holy realm of the tabernacle. The epistemological dimension that complements the ontological gives rise to a kind of "mysticism," one in which the divine face remains occluded, the *deus absconditus* embodied in the features that transcend all seeing.

Such a view is no less true of the second proof-text cited to delineate the nature of God's presence. That proof-text, we recall, is Isaiah 6:1: "I saw the Lord sitting on a throne which was raised high in the air, and the fringe of his garment spread over the whole of the temple." What begins as an encounter with God's presence in the tabernacle is here reenacted as an encounter with God's presence in the temple. Both acts focus upon the cultic dimensions of the *visio Dei*, first by Moses, and second by Isaiah. In both, the prophet receives his vocation. For Moses, that vocation has to do with the inscription and dissemination of the commandments (Exod. 34); for Isaiah, with admonishing the reprobate to reform (Isa. 6:9). In both cases, the theophany results in a renewal of the covenantal relationship between God and his prophet. The vision that impresses itself upon Isaiah's being is one in which God is beheld seated upon his throne, "high and lifted up, and his train filled the temple" (Isa. 6:1). Here, God is surrounded by his "entourage," that is, the seraphim, each with six wings: "with twain he covered his face, and with twain he covered his face, and with twain he did fly." So situated, each of the seraphim cries to the others: "Holy, holy, holy *is* the Lord of hosts; the whole earth *is* full of his glory" (Isa. 6:3).[67] Once again, the theophany celebrates the "glory" of God. This time, however, the event is mediated through the intercession of the seraphim. They make certain that even the visionary is at least several steps removed from the "actual" source of the theophany, that is, the enthroned deity. This, too, is a *deus absconditus*, one whose hiddenness is further reinforced by the protective seraphim that surround the enthroned figure and by the role that is assigned to this deity as lord of hosts.[68] Such a title suggests the distinctly military bearing of this theophany.

As we move from the Old Testament to the New Testament, the idea of knowing God (*cognoscendo Dei*) assumes renewed significance as a reflection of the proof-texts that Milton draws upon to support his contentions. Exploring the proof-texts and comparing them with those drawn from the Old Testament, we are in a position to understand the extent to which Milton's habits of mind incline one to view the God of the theological treatise as a multifaceted, indeed, a kaleidoscopic figure, one whose bearing gives rise to a host of interpretations. As we have already seen, the New Testament proof-texts are grouped as follows: "John i. 18: *no man has ever seen God*, and vi. 46: *not that anyone has seen the Father, except him who is from God; he has seen the Father*, and v. 37: *nor have you heard his voice*; I Cor. xiii. 12: *in a mirror, in a riddle, partially*." The proof-texts fall into two sets, the first drawn from the fourth gospel, the second from the epistles. Each of the proof-texts speaks to the subject of epistemology. Those from John make it clear that the act of knowing God involves two forms of "perception" — seeing and hearing. The proof-text from 1 Corinthians makes it clear that God is, almost by definition, a mystery; in fact, one might observe an enigma within a mystery. The theme of the combined proof-texts raises the issue of epistemology, only to deny the possibility of its efficacy in this life without the intercession of the Son. The focus is essentially Son-centered, that is, implicitly Christocentric. What emerges is a God who is defined by (because he is known only to) his Son. In effect, this is a reconfiguration of the proof-texts cited from the Old Testament, in which the *visio Dei* is bestowed only upon God's prophets (directly, in the person of Moses and, indirectly, in the person of Isaiah). But even when it comes to God's prophets (in particular, Isaiah), the issue of the intermediary arises. Only through the intercession of the seraphim does the prophet receive his vocation. Of course, the New Testament has its own intermediary, in this case reconfigured as the Son of God. He assumed the form of a servant into order to provide a means for humankind to experience God in all his glory. The proof-texts cited leave no doubt that it is only through the Son that a true knowledge of the Father is possible. For only the Son has seen God. In this context, the *cognoscendo Dei* makes a point of reformulating the whole issue of epistemology.

As a capstone to the argument, the culminating reference to 1 Corinthians 13:12 is germane: "per speculum, per aenigma, aliquatenus" (CM 14:31). The translations of Charles Sumner and of John Carey, respectively, are revealing. Whereas the first has "we see through a glass, darkly . . . in part" (CM 14:30), the second offers "in a mirror, in a riddle, partially" (YP 6:133). It hardly need be stated that the Sumner translation replicates the well-known rendering found in the Authorized Version: "For now we see through a glass, darkly; but then face to face." This rendering has assumed the status of a *topos* in biblical hermeneutics. Not only does the formulation "through a glass, darkly" enjoy something of a poetic legitimacy: it is also consistent with the renderings of the *textus receptus* as reflected in such works as Brian Walton's *Biblia sacra polyglotta* (1657), mentioned in the previous chapter.[69] Both the Greek and Latin "originals" are consistent in this regard. Thus, we find *en ainigmati* in the Greek, and *in aenigmate* in the Latin.[70] But this is precisely the formulation that *De Doctrina Christiana* eschews. In place of the *textus receptus,* the treatise offers the phrase *per aenigma,* the form attested in the Junius-Tremellius version. It is this version that adopts the phrase *per speculum, per aenigma,* as opposed to the rendering *per speculum in aenigmate,* the form adopted in the Latin of the Vulgate, among other versions. Because of the subtle shades of meanings to which each formulation gives rise, the difference in locution is important. At the center of the difference is the use of the term "enigma." In the standard sources, the term is conceived adverbially to designate the act of looking through a *speculum*, or mirror.[71] In the *textus receptus*, such an act is performed *in aenigmate*, in a manner that occludes, rather than discloses, the object of sight. Accordingly, the action through which the object is beheld must be rendered as "darkly," devoid of the illumination that comes only with the vision of ultimate "truth."

The sense of the Junius-Tremellius version, on the other hand, is quite different, especially in its formulation *per speculum, per aenigma*. Here, the Carey translation ("in a mirror, in a riddle") is more nearly reliable than that of the Sumner translation ("through a glass, darkly").[72] Nonetheless, in a rendering of "per," I would retain the sense of "through," rather than "in," as the preposition of choice. Retaining "through" yields: "through a mirror, through a riddle." The phrase allows for the integrity of the configuration through which both *speculum* and *aenigma* are conceived as nouns ("mirror," "riddle") that stand in apposition or at least in a parallel relationship, rather than in what amounts to an adverbial relationship ("glass darkly"). As a result, one might suggest that the *visio Dei* implicit in the pairing up of *speculum* and *aenigma* is one in which the object of vision (that is, God himself) and the experience of vision (that is, the means by which the seer sees God) play off against each other in a metaphorical reciprocity. By means of that reciprocity the idea of *cognoscendo Deo* is not only very much enhanced but rendered that much more complex as well. For now it becomes a matter in which the experience of seeing through a "glass, darkly," gives way to an experience in which the vehicles of mediation (mirror, riddle) at once comment on one another and suggest (at least in this life) the deep mystery that God represents at the very point one risks the blasphemy of presuming to see him at all. As parallel nouns that are apposite but contrastive, *speculum* and *aenigma* perform a figurative function. From that perspective, each object threatens to undo the other. If the *speculum* is a mirror through which one might presume to gain access to God, that very phenomenon places the seer in the untenable position of being seen in return. We presume to see God, to know him, but what we really see is the reflection of our own features in the glass. As a result of a failure to see correctly (in this life with all its darknesses) by means of the *speculum,* we are then challenged to solve the *aenigma* through which God finally discloses himself. Through this ironic and paradoxical condition God proclaims that there will be no recognition of him until he is beheld face to face.

We have only begun to explore the way in which Milton shapes his conception of God as a complex figure rooted in the Old Testament and its counterpart in the New Testament. As we recall, this conception is delineated most fully in the chapter "De Deo," which is a self-contained account of Milton's emphasis upon the "one God" and all that that notion implies. What might be viewed as the conundrums associated with the nature of the godhead (Father-Son relations, the place of the Holy Spirit, Trinitarian versus Antitrinitarian views, and the like) engage Milton in the chapters that follow "De Deo," but the treatment of God in the chapter at hand remains true throughout to its task of drawing upon the Bible as the essential *vade mecum* into the unknowable.[73]

THREE

The Signatures of Deity

I

As this study has attempted to make clear, the discourse on God that underscores the second chapter of *De Doctrina Christiana* provides a framework through which one is invited to come to terms with the ineffable, to categorize that which defies categorization, to systematize that which by its very nature calls into question the logic of systemization. With an awareness of the shortcomings to which any systematic theology is liable, the chapter titled "De Deo" structures its argument according to what I have called the ontological, epistemological, and phenomenological modes of discourse. These involve the existence of God, the knowledge of God, and the names and attributes of God. Having addressed the ontological mode in some depth, I shall now turn to the phenomenological mode, that which concerns the names and attributes of God.[1]

Made evident in the section of "De Deo" that deals with the phenomenological dimensions of deity, Milton's discourse

reveals a sensibility attuned not only to theological and doctrinal notions of God's nature but also to the profoundly occlusive character of God's presencing of himself by means of his
various names and attributes.[2] In his consideration of the
names of God, Milton accordingly focuses upon the perfor-
mative nature implicit in the act of uttering that which cannot (or at least, should not) be uttered. Such utterances become
a sign of the "divine power and virtue" (vim eius atque virtutem divinam) with which the names are imbued. Names like
"Jehovah," "Jah," and "Ehie" bespeak the inscrutable nature
of God, as well as the dangers of compromising the protocols
necessary in any attempt to gain access to the *deus absconditus*.

These and other considerations reveal Milton's familiarity
not just with the Old Testament but with the early rabbinical
pronouncements on the *Tanakh*. Following the discourse on
the names of God, Milton's commentary on the attributes is
consistent with the systematic theologies of the period.[3]
Nonetheless, the commentary on the attributes in *De Doctrina*
departs from early modern systematic theologies to the extent
that the treatise devotes detailed attention to these attributes,
dividing its list into two major headings or groups. Under the
first group, one finds nine attributes that distinguish the
"nature" (*naturam*]) of God; under the second group, one finds
an account of attributes that involve God's "divine power
[*vim*] and virtue [*virtutem*]."[4] The first group includes the following attributes: that he is the true God; that he is a spirit;
that he is characterized by immensity and infinity; that he is
eternal; that he is immutable; that he is incorruptible; that he
is omnipotent; and finally that he is one. The second group,
in turn, includes the attributes of life, intellect, and will. The
nature and extent of the discourse reveals the in-depth manner in which God is conceived in *De Doctrina Christiana*.

A case in point is the assertion that "God in his most simple nature is a SPIRIT" (Deus sit natura simplicissima SPIRI-
TUS) (YP 6:140; CM 14:40).[5] To support this assertion, Milton

offers the following citations: "Exod. iii. 14, 15: *I am who I am;* Rom. xi, 35, 36: *from him and through him are all things;* John iv.24: *God is a Spirit.*" The allusion to John 4:24 might have been deemed sufficient, but it is clear that Milton is intent on moving toward a climax in his use of proof-texts. Interestingly, the allusions to Exodus and Romans do not in-and-of themselves demonstrate the contention that God in *natura simplicissima* is a spirit. Rather, each represents a commentary (or better still, a precommentary) on the text of John. The effect is to recall the contexts of Exodus and the Epistle to the Romans with the idea of querying the rationale behind their presence as proof-texts here, only to be thrust back (in a kind of "sense return") to the first and the second citations, an experience that invites a renewed interpretation. The process as a whole is heuristic: on the one hand, to know what spirit is, one must be familiar with the theophany at God's holy mount, and, on the other hand, one must understand the apostolic pronouncements of one for whom such a theophany assumes a decidedly kerygmatic cast. In the first instance, the act of seeking after the divine name of names as a means of disclosure is met with the realization that such a quest is far beyond the abilities of even God's most valued prophets. This is an event that might be described as a step in the process of coming to awareness of that which defies all knowing. Drawing upon such an awareness, the second instance transforms narrative into exhortation as the apostle declares, "O the depth of the riches both of the wisdom and knowledge of God! How unsearchable *are* his judgments, and his ways past finding out! For who hath known the mind of the Lord? or who hath been his counsellor?" (Rom. 11:33–34). This, of course, is the wisdom that comes of not knowing, of being aware that the true knowledge of God is tantamount to the "divine ignorance" that comes only to those wise enough to understand that this is a God who surmounts all understanding. Like the burning bush aflame with a fire that proved to be a source of generation rather than annihilation, the God of the new dispensation is one of whom, through whom, and to whom "*are all things*" (Rom. 11:36). The heuristic process, then, involves the movement from old to new dispensation as it culminates in the wisdom of not knowing. With this knowledge (a *via negativa* all its own), those who seek to understand the *natura simplicissima* of God come to know the impossibility of knowing.

This fact assumes almost an ironic twist if one examines the context in which the bold statement that "God is a Spirit" (John 4:24) is voiced.[6] That context is the account of Jesus' encounter with the Samaritan woman at the well. As Jesus imparts to this woman wisdom tantamount to the waters of life, it is clear that he speaks not of temporal waters but of eternal waters through which one is reborn. The prototypical Wife of Bath with her five husbands, the nameless woman of Samaria in the biblical account is imbued with a remarkable comic presence as she leaves her water pot and runs to gossip with the citizens of the city: "Come see a man, which told me all things that I ever did: is not this the Christ?" (John 4:29). Our response is one of both amusement and wonder. This is theology in its truest, most engaging form. It is theology reconfigured as play, indeed, as poetry, the ludic dimension that renders the proof-texts with their intertextual resonances so compelling. Enhanced by the artistry of arrangement, the proof-texts assume a life of their own as they implicitly interpret and comment upon one another. In the sequence of text and countertext that Milton cites to ballast his contentions, we move from Mosaic narrative of the most overwhelming sort through Pauline exposition to Gospel narrative distinguished by its lively domestic comedy.

Does all this yield a true knowledge of God as one distinguished by what Milton calls a "natura simplicissima SPIRITUS"? The answer is both yes and no: yes, in the sense that we become aware of the extent to which that *natura* cannot ultimately be known, and no, in the sense that we are content

to remain "lowly wise" in our knowledge that we can in any
way understand what the term *spiritus* means in the first
place. To confirm that observation, one need only glance at the
detailed discussion in the chapter titled "De Spiritu Sancto"
in *De Doctrina* (1.6). In his commentary on the Holy Spirit,
Milton shows his cards at the very outset of the chapter:
Granted, "this is called the spirit both of the Father and of the
Son," but what do we have when we have that? Not a great
deal, for the Bible, Milton continues, "says nothing about
what the Holy Spirit is like, how it exists, or where it comes
from." These rather unsettling observations should serve as a
warning "not to be too hasty in our conclusions" (YP 6:281).
To be sure, one might insist that there is a distinction between
the *spiritus* addressed in the earlier chapter on God and the
spiritus addressed in the later chapter on the Holy Spirit.
Nonetheless, these two entities (if indeed they are two) are close
enough to conclude that one essentially corresponds to the
other. It is this correspondence that is ultimately so disquiet-
ing. For if Milton is willing to acknowledge that the Bible
gives no clue to what precisely the Holy Spirit *is*, what constitutes it, he would be no less forthright in acknowledging that
the nature of the spirit invoked in "De Deo" is likewise perplexing in the extreme.

Reinforcing the sense of perplexity is the determination on
the part of Milton to pursue the issue to its "logical" conclusion. Thus, in his account of God as a "natura simplicissima
SPIRITUS," Milton quickly moves from the realm of not
knowing, that is, of "divine ignorance," into the murky realm
of metaphysics. Resorting to biblical proof-texts that distinguish between flesh and spirit (Isa. 31:3; Luke 34:39), Milton
concludes that from these proof-texts

> it may be understood [*intelligitur*] that the essence of God [*essen-
> tiam Dei*], since it is utterly simple [*simplicissima*], allows
> nothing to be compounded with it, and that the word *hypostasis*,
> Heb. i. 3, which is variously translated *substance, subsistence,*

> or *person,* is nothing but that most perfect essence by which
> God exists from himself, in himself, and through himself [*qua
> Deus a se, in se, et per se est*]. (YP 6:140–41; CM 14:40–42)[7]

At this juncture, it would appear that the commentary on the
"person" of God has undergone something of a transformation.
It has moved almost imperceptibly from God to the Son, the
subject of later chapters. It has also undergone a transformation from an implicit endorsement of the experience of "not
knowing" or of "unknowing," a category of mysticism, to a
concern with the idea of explaining the inexplicable, a category of metaphysics. If the two categories overlap in the treatise as a whole, we nonetheless find ourselves very quickly
immersed in doctrinal disputes concerning matters such as
hypostasis, essentia, substantia, and *subsistentia.* This is the
discourse of knowing in the abstract, of untangling matters of
metaphysics, logic, and doctrine. It is also the discourse of "matter," or at least of the kinds of distinctions that underscore arguments concerning matter as opposed to spirit, or of matter and
spirit as manifestations of deity. The pleasure that arises from
the use of proof-texts to demonstrate that God is beyond knowing is rendered problematical by a determination to explain it
all as rationally and as logically as possible. No stone is left
unturned: it is all right there in the Bible.

If the dynamics that underscore the second attribute (God
as Spirit) provide insight into Milton's habits of mind and his
theological principles, the relationship between exposition
and the use of proof-texts extends to the treatment of corresponding attributes by which God's essential nature is "known."
As indicated, the precise attributes in question (aside from
"Spirit") include God as "true," God as "immense" and as
"infinite" (considered as one), as well as God as "eternal,"
"immutable," "incorruptible," "omnipresent," "omnipotent,"
and "one."[8] This is quite an inventory, but, as we have seen,
an analysis of the proof-texts invoked to support this inventory can yield some fascinating insights concerning the dia-

logue between proof-text and proof-text and text and proof-text. The doctrinal pronouncements that occupy the text encourage such a dialogue.[9] Moving from God as Spirit, we now focus on the category that conceives of God as Omnipotent (*Omnipotens*). I choose omnipotence as a category to explore, first, because Milton places a good deal of emphasis upon it and, second, because the force of this attribute is such that it warrants special attention here. It is clear that Milton fully embraces the concept of an omnipotent God, in part because that concept is important to a full understanding of how an essentially Hebraic God is to be appreciated, indeed worshiped, with a mixture of love and fear, if not dread. As such, Milton's approach to this attribute is both to invoke proof-texts that support a theology of power and to distinguish between this view of omnipotence and other views that might compromise what Milton believes is absolute power, indeed, power divinized. If the proof-texts to support these views are drawn from both the Old Testament and the New Testament, the Hebraic concept of divine power prevails. Texts from the Old Testament outnumber those from the New Testament more than two to one.

Thus, the texts from the Old Testament include 2 Chronicles 20:6, Job 42:2, as well as Psalms 31:9, 115:3, and 135:6, whereas the texts from the New Testament are limited to Matthew 19:26 and Luke 1:37. A glance at these proof-texts should indicate in more detail Milton's view of omnipotence. The first allusion sets the tone: "might and power are in your hand" (2 Chron. 20:6). The occasion is that of an impending battle between the faithful of Jehoshaphat and the children of Ammon and other tribes such as the Moabites. A prayer to God is met with a positive response by the Levite Jahaziel, who was inspired by God to proclaim: "Be not afraid nor dismayed by reason of this great multitude; for the battle *is* not yours, but God's." The oracle is correct: the enemy is totally discomfited by God. The milieu is that of the so-called "Wars of the Lord" or *milkhamot 'adonai*, a phenomenon of ancient lineage.[10] The attribute of omnipotence, as Milton conceives it, assumes a decidedly militaristic bearing from the very outset. The allusion to Job 42:2 ("I know that you can do everything") provides another dimension — reconceiving power in the context of wisdom. Accordingly, the verse culminates in a celebration of the fact that God is capable not just of doing everything, but of knowing everything: "no thought can be withholden from thee [God]." This praise is uttered as a consummate sign of Job's ability, even in the teeth of adversity, to reassert his faith in God yet once more.

The verses from Psalms 33:9 ("He speaks, and whatever is, is"), 115:3 and 135:6, both of which are folded into one citation ("He does whatever pleases him"), reinforce the quality of awesomeness, as well as of power, that the Old Testament associates with God. These characteristics are reconfigured in the New Testament references: Matthew 19:26 ("All things are possible with God") and Luke 1:37 ("There will be nothing impossible with God"). In the first instance, Jesus reassures his disciples that, no matter what the circumstances, God, according to his will, is able to bestow salvation on anyone. In the second instance, Gabriel (that messenger of "strength") arrives to alert Mary that she will be the mother of the Son of God, for whom all things are possible. The transition from the Old Testament to the New Testament is fascinating in its conception of what omnipotence implies. Rather than an emphasis upon physical might to smite one's enemies in battle or the association of power with wisdom in the faith that comes of suffering, the conception is now one of coming to know and understand the renewed significance of grace, sacrifice, and redemption. This is a conception of omnipotence that is essentially salvific and regenerative. Although parallels might be drawn between ideas of omnipotence in the Old Testament and New Testament, the proof-texts cited here are more nearly contrastive than they are comparative. This, of course, does not stop Milton from implying otherwise. Indeed, as quickly as he invokes the New Testament proof-texts, he abruptly returns to Hebraic renderings of power. Having cited the two New Testament proof-texts to support his contention, he then asserts: "Unde et nomen illud Dei El Shaddai" (CM 14:46). That *unde* has to do an awful lot of work. The translations offered by the Columbia Milton and the Yale *Prose* have a hard time of it: "Hence the name El Shaddai, applied to the Deity" (CM 14:47) vies with "Because of this attribute the name El Shaddai is applied to God" (YP 6:145).[11] Neither captures the tension in the transition. Although the purpose of the assertion is to segue smoothly back to the Old Testament, the sense of dislocation between the two Scriptures is only reinforced. If there is a link between the concept of power in the texts cited from these Scriptures, it is the contrastive one. The sense of difference between the Old Testament, on the one hand, and the New Testament, on the other, finally serves to point up what might be called the "savagery" of the Hebraic renderings.

In the treatment of power that concludes the discussion of this vital attribute, the idea of *omnipotens* as essentially destructive or annihilative underlies Milton's reflections on the Hebrew and Greek names for God.[12] A case in point once again is Milton's invoking of the fearsome name "El Shaddai," or "God Almighty." There is no discernible sense of grace or redemption in that name; rather, it instills awe and even dread. To that end, Milton cites Genesis 17:1: "I am the omnipotent God." The larger narrative context of the citation concerns God's "cutting of a covenant" with the patriarch Abram-become-Abraham. Represented by the rite of circumcision, this is a covenant born of violence. The rite is represented by the excision of the flesh of the foreskin to signify that the children of Abraham and their descendants are uniquely "chosen" as the people of God (Gen. 17). This is an ideal context for Milton to invoke *El Shaddai*, a name Milton elaborates upon by ascribing to it the crucial term *sufficiens*: "Unde et nomen illud Dei El Shaddai. Gen. xvii.1 *Ego sum Deus omnipotens*, ad

verbum, *sufficiens*" (CM 14:46–47; YP 6:145). The Columbia
Milton and the Yale *Prose* translate *sufficiens* as "sufficient"
and as "sufficiently powerful," respectively.[13] But both the
phrase "ad verbum, *sufficiens*" and the term *sufficiens* imply
far more than the translations in the authoritative editions
suggest. The phrase "ad verbum, *sufficiens*" means that God
is *literally* sufficient. The force of *ad verbum* is such that *El
Shaddai* becomes not only "*The* Omnipotent" but also "*The*
Sufficient."[14] The term *sufficiens* signifies not only laying the
foundation for something but likewise of imbuing or even
impregnating that thing to the point that it is irradiated with
the quality of "otherness." As we have seen, this otherness is
what Rudolf Otto calls the *ganz andere,* or "wholly other."
Underlying it is the fundamental notion of "the holy" as a form
of religious experience, one that occasions awe and even dread
at the prospect of coming into contact with the *mysterium
tremendum.*[15] However one conceives the name *El Shaddai,*
one must be aware of its dangerous and destructive implications. Thus, the term *Shaddai* itself comes from a root that
means, among other things, to ravage or lay waste. As related
to *shadad,* the term *Shaddai* carries the verbal idea of dealing
"violently" with the object of its wrath.[16] Problematizing this
dimension of the power of God still further is the name *El Elion.*
So God is invoked by Abram/Abraham in Genesis 14:22: "I
have lift up mine hand unto the Lord, the most high God, the
possessor of heaven and earth." Citing this passage as crucial
evidence of God's great power, Milton declares: "Deus iste
maximus, potentissimus, et El Elion" (CM 14:46). With its roots
in the concept of ascending to the "high God," the God of mountains and natural terrain, this phrase is among the most archaic
depictions of God.[17] At the same time, Milton is inexorably
drawn toward this conception.

Determined to find correspondences to such archaic ideas
in the New Testament, Milton invokes the two names *Kyrios
pantokrator* and *monos dynastos* (YP 6:138–39). Both carry sim-

ilar senses, one in which God through his Son becomes at once "the omnipotent Lord" and "the only ruler." Consummate power and the prerogatives of rulership appear to be two of the most significant attributes of the deity, who assumes the supreme office as "the King of Kings and Lord of Lords." To support his contention, Milton cites a series of proof-texts, including 2 Corinthians 6:18, Revelation 1:8, and 1 Timothy 6:15. The purpose of these citations is not only to provide evidence of the truth and accuracy of these titles but also to suggest what might be called the cosmic individuation of God in his various capacities. As a result of these ascriptions, God the Father is clearly "personalized." Thus, in 2 Corinthians 6, Paul undertakes his passionate appeal to the citizens of Corinth to establish a community of the faithful, one fully dedicated to God and his teachings. As a separate, holy community, only these faithful will be accepted by God, whom Paul conceives significantly as a "Father" unto his children, both sons and daughters.

This emphasis upon a community of the faithful centered in God the Father is reconceptualized in Revelation 1:8. Here, the emphasis is upon the *parousia*, which assumes the form of God in the Son coming forth to judge humankind in the last days: "Behold, he cometh with clouds; and every eye shall see him, and they *also* which pierced him: and all kindreds of the earth shall wail because of him" (Rev. 1:7). This apocalyptic context sets the stage for the proclamation that follows: "I am the Alpha and Omega, the beginning and the ending, saith the Lord, which is and which was, and which is to come, the Almighty." By his own proclamation, God is conceived as one who both encompasses worlds and who extends his rule and his being through past, present, and future. In God, the temporal is collapsed into the eternal as a signature of his omnipotence. This, then, is the *pantokrator*, the all-powerful in all his glory. Reflected in his names, God as the *mysterium tremendum* assumes a multitude of forms. Whereas his

savagery and truculence are embodied in his name as *El Shaddai*
and his transcendent stature is figured in his name as *El Elion*,
the concept of God as *Kyrios pantokrator* and *monos dynastos* gives rise to yet additional dimensions of his role and (if I
may be allowed the use of this word) "personality." But the
citations do not end there. With the artistry of a poet, Milton
concludes his biblical references with the allusion to 1 Timothy
6:15. This text is part of a larger action in which Paul charges
his followers to keep God's commandments "without spot,
unrebukeable, until the appearing of our Lord Jesus Christ:
Which in his times he shall shew, *who is* the blessed and only
Potentate, the King of kings, and Lord of lords." The Christocentric outlook is the culminating moment in the catena of
proof-texts that Milton marshals in support of his treatment
of omnipotence as an essential attribute of God. Christ becomes
the power of powers, the potentate whose royal power is all-
encompassing. This figure dwells "in the light which no man
can approach unto; whom no man hath seen, nor can see; to
whom *be* honour and power everlasting" (1 Tim. 6:16). The
liturgical quality of this moment is one that suggests the
extent to which Milton's hermeneutic is as much one of worship as it is of analysis. In order to recognize this dimension,
however, one must be attuned to what the biblical references imply.

One might conceive the biblical references as signs or perhaps musical notations that score the treatise. Those attuned
to the occluded meanings of the score will sense what the text
itself is saying. As we have seen, any attempt to understand
the treatise involves the act of probing the subtexts, the signatures of which are inscribed throughout the text. These
notations open up into the allusive (and, at times, elusive) world
embodied in the text beneath the text. The extent to which
one might wish to read the subtext as part of the body of material that surrounds it is finally the prerogative of the reader
attuned to the "method" that Milton adopts. What results is

a hermeneutics of discovery that makes the experience of reading *De Doctrina Christiana* so engaging and so challenging. In order to participate in the hermeneutics of discovery, however, one must be attuned not only to the biblical contexts. Despite its professed allegiance to the Bible (in its various versions) as fundamental authority, the treatise reflects a knowledge of "secondary" texts as well. When these texts are cited (albeit infrequently), they generally appear not to bolster the argument but to suggest counterarguments that Milton considers misleading or false. Such a situation arises in the discussion of the attribute of omnipotence.

Having provided a range of biblical citations to reinforce his views concerning the nature of God's power, Milton uses the occasion to take up other views of God that run counter to those expressed in *De Doctrina*. His main opponents here are Aristotle and the later scholastics, whose views appear to Milton as being both reductionist and misguided. "Hence," Milton avers, "it appears that God cannot rightly be called Actus Purus, or pure actuality, as is customary in Aristotle" (YP 6:145–46). For Aristotle, in fact, "the highest determinations of Being are Actuality (*entelecheia*) and Potentiality (*dynamis*)." Whereas *entelecheia* is perfection, realization, fullness of Being, *dynamis* is imperfection, incompleteness, perfectibility. Actuality and potentiality are crucial to an understanding of Being. They underlie everything except "the Supreme Cause, in Whom there is no imperfection, and, therefore, no potentiality." This Cause is "all actuality, *Actus Purus*."[18] The idea found its way into the philosophy of the scholastics, who adopted the terms *actus* and *potentia* to translate Aristotle's *entelecheia* and *dynamis*. English has no single word to render either *actus* or *potentia*. Implicit in *actus* are such meanings as act, action, actuality, perfection, and determination. In turn, *potentia* implies potency, potentiality, power, and capacity. Actuality and potentiality, then, are by definition mutually exclusive. Throughout the Middle Ages, the distinction between *actus* and *potentia* was all pervasive in the scholastic system of philosophy and theology.[19] It is this system that Milton is writing against. For him, God is certainly *entelecheia*, but God also embodies that *dynamis* that provides for motivation, movement, all those qualities that underscore character and drama. To adopt the counterargument, Milton maintains, would be to place God in a position in which "he could do nothing except what he does do, and he would do that of necessity, although in fact he is omnipotent and utterly free in his actions" (YP 6:146).[20] In short, Milton would have it both ways. Or, better still, Milton refuses to confine his God to the rules that constitute the metaphysical traditions and their heirs. At the very point of appearing to acknowledge those traditions, he adheres to the representations of deity that underlie both the Old Testament and their counterparts in the New Testament. What results is a composite God, one in whom the metaphysical notions of *entelecheia* and *dynamis* are present but in whom the culture of the Old Testament and the New Testament reign supreme.

II

Nowhere is this fact more compelling than in Milton's discussion of the ninth attribute, that God is "one" (*unus*). Milton's treatment of this attribute is among the longest and fullest in "De Deo." The issue is crucial to an understanding of the figure of God in *De Doctrina*, so crucial, in fact, that if one were to focus only on the proof-texts from the Old Testament that Milton invokes in his discussion of *unus*, he or she might be convinced that this is a sensibility consistent with all those determined to argue on behalf of the essentially Hebraic notion that *adonai 'echad*, God is one (Deut. 6:4). The idea of *unus* is such that it implies that which is not only "one" but that which is *solus*, that is, "alone, only, sole, single." So conceived, *unus* stands in opposition to that which can be anything else, to that which might threaten to conceive it as other

than one. The term *unus* occupies a space of contention, one
in which there exists a threat that deity might be anything more
than one. With the assertion of oneness, we find ourselves in
the world of the Old Testament proclaiming the fundamental
oneness of God in the teeth of any who would counter that
there is not just one God but, in fact, many gods. The notion
of oneness is so important to the principles upon which *De
Doctrina* is founded that Milton proclaims that the attribute
of oneness "proceeds from the eight previous attributes and
is, as it were, the logical conclusion of them all" (YP 6:146).
Unus is not simply essential to the conception of God: it
represents the culminating concept of all that goes before. It
concludes them, completes them, embodies them all. To
demonstrate what should be apparent to all, indeed, beyond
the need for proof, Milton then proceeds to amass a body of
proof-texts that would overcome any intruder who might be
inclined to undermine the conviction of God as *unus*. Proof-
texts are, in effect, "marshaled" as if Milton were a soldier going
to war. Thus, one is presented with the following:

> Deut. iv. 35: *that Jehovah is God and that there is no God except
> him*, iv. 39: *that Jehovah is God in the heavens above and on
> the earth beneath and that there is no God except him*, vi. 4:
> *Hear, Israel, Jehovah our God is one Jehovah*, and xxxii. 39: *that
> I am myself and that there is no God with me*; I Kings viii. 60:
> *that all the peoples of the earth may know that Jehovah is God
> and that there is no one else except him*; II Kings xix. 15: *you
> are the only God of all the kingdoms of the earth*; Isa. xliv. 1:
> *except me there is no God*, and xliv. 8: *Is there any God except
> me? Certainly there is no rock, I know none*; and xlv. 5: *I am
> Jehovah and there is none except me; except me there is no God*;
> and xlv. 21: *there is no other God besides me; there is none except
> me*; xlv. 22: *I am God and there is none besides*. (YP 6:146–47)

Extending from Deuteronomy to Isaiah, the proof-texts reflect
multiple ways of saying the same thing. Phrased primarily in
the negative (*nullus*), the citations assert "No, no, no!" God
must be understood as "one" and not anything else but "one."

Where one or two proof-texts would do, Milton relentlessly marshals a multitude of texts in order to drive home his point. Rather than "analyzing" contexts here, we are encouraged to attend only to the drumroll of iteration that builds to a climax until even the most obdurate is resigned to acknowledge "Yes! yes! already. I give up. God is indeed one." But, no, Milton is still not finished: he feels obliged to clarify: "no spirit, no person, no being besides [*praeterea*] him is God, for 'none' [*nullus*] is a negative of general application [*nullim enim universe negat*]" (also termed a "universal negative"). Both grammatically and semantically, the universal negative that arises from the text is beyond dispute the central unifying theme in the encounter with the *unus Deus* or *adonai 'echad*. There is no compromising here: God is either one or he is not. Repeatedly the Old Testament declares that he is one. Underscored by the presence of that resounding *nullus,* the term viewed as a universal negative brings to mind the rhetorical quip, "What part of 'no' don't you understand?" Just in case the reader still remains in doubt, however, Milton cites another text from Isaiah that drives the point home yet once more: "I am God and . . . there is no God besides me and . . . no one is like me" (46:9). This takes us back to the *praeterea,* a term that carries multiple meanings, including "beyond this or that," "besides" and "henceforth."[21] One might suggest that for the purpose of *De Doctrina,* the term bears all three meanings.

Under the circumstances, it is clear to Milton that his assertions are incontrovertible. It is all so obvious, even to those not on an equal standing with Milton himself. Accordingly, Milton poses the following rhetorical questions: "What could be more plain and straightforward? What could be better adapted to the average intelligence [*vulgi sensum*], what more in keeping with everyday speech [*quotidianumque loquendi*], so that God's people [*Dei populus*] should understand that there is numerically one God and one spirit, just as they understand that there is numerically one of anything else" (YP

6:147; CM 14:50). This represents a curious mix of audiences that extend from those whose *vulgi sensum* renders them insensitive to the very complex arguments that distinguish *De Doctrina*. At the same time, they are the *Dei populus*, a very select group indeed but also possibly characterized by a *vulgi sensum*. At the very least, they are not all comprised of the "fit audience, though few." Nor is there any need that they should be so elite. In fact, they are better off being the common herd, for even those who constitute the common herd cannot miss a distinction between that which is *unus* and that which is more than *unus*. In any case, Milton's stance is rhetorically one of persuading his readers to accede to those things that are so obvious they render long, metaphysical arguments absolutely useless and indeed worse than useless, because such arguments mislead and confound. (In this regard, Milton has in mind the scholastics, customarily one of the major targets in *De Doctrina*.) All one requires is the power of reason and the exercise of common sense to see how self-evident the idea of God's oneness is. It was therefore only fitting, Milton observes, "that God should communicate his first and therefore greatest commandment, which he wanted all people, even the lowest, scrupulously to obey" (referring to Exod. 20:2–3). Nor would there be a modicum of doubt in the true believers concerning what the oneness of God implies. In keeping with the Hebraic sensibility manifested here, Milton concludes with accolades for the Israelites, who, in keeping with the law and the prophets, "always understood that God was without question numerically one and that there was no other besides him, let alone any equal to him."[22]

Adhering to the authority of the Hebraic point of view, Milton then moves to his New Testament proof-texts. There are fewer of these than the proof-texts drawn from the Old Testament, and even within the framework of the New Testament texts, Milton intersperses additional texts from the Old Testament. The discrepancy is understandable, for in the New

Testament one encounters a view of God that in some respects challenges the monotheistic sensibility of the Old Testament. To be sure, those texts in the New Testament that point to the monotheistic perspective are not wanting, and Milton makes a point of citing them. They include passages from the Gospels (Mark 12:28–28, 42; John 17:3) and the Epistles (Rom. 3:30; 1 Cor. 8:4, 6; Gal. 3:20; Eph. 4:6; 1 Tim. 2:5). Nonetheless, Milton's statement that "nothing can be said of the one God that is inconsistent with his unity, and which makes him both one and not one" comes under pressure in light of the Father/Son relationship fundamental to the Christocentric point of view. Milton immediately acknowledges that point of view in a prefatory statement to his citation of New Testament proof-texts: "Now let us look at the evidence of the New Testament. It is no less clear upon the points already dealt with, and in this respect even clearer: it asserts that this one God is the Father [*Patrem*] of our Lord Jesus Christ [*Domini nostri Iesu Christi*]" (YP 6:148; CM 16:52). Now, this is a fascinating assertion indeed, because it implies that as monotheistic as the Old Testament purports to be, the New Testament is even more compelling in its agreement with the essential notion of unity. If this is the case, then any "taint" of divinity one might find in the figure of the Lord Jesus Christ is viewed not as compromising the monotheistic imperative but as fostering it. To this end, Milton cites Mark 12:28–29 as part of his proof. Thus, when Christ was asked, "what was the first commandment of all, he replied, quoting from Deut. vi. 4, a passage already cited, and understood here in no other sense than the customary one: *Hear Israel, the Lord our God is one Lord.*" Accordingly, Milton draws upon Christ's own words to dispel any notion that the God of the New Testament is anything but one, in fact, the very one hailed as *adonai 'echad* in the Hebrew Scriptures. This, despite the fact that Milton himself refers to Jesus as "Domini nostri Iesu Christi." (CM 14). How many *Domini* can there be, one might ask, and not compromise the integrity of the monotheistic imperative? Milton is determined to prove that there is no contradiction here. Maintaining that the God of the Old Testament is exactly the same as the God of the New Testament, Milton accepts as a given that each God is *Dominus* in his own right. The only difference is that, in the New Testament, God as *Dominus* has a son who also happens to bear the title of *Dominus*. One might argue that you can't have it both ways, but surely Milton would disagree.[23] Nonetheless, it is interesting to note that the term *Pater* as a designation for God is used by Milton only once in "De Deo," a very significant point considering how important the term becomes in Milton's discussion of godhead later in the treatise (see *De Doctrina*, bk. 1, chaps. 5 and 6). What is implied by this fact is that for Milton, the term "God" encompasses such roles as "father." There can be but "one God," but this monotheistic imperative accommodates itself to a point of view consistent with the dispensational relationship between father and son fostered by the New Testament.

In the following portion of the "De Deo" chapter, Milton moves from a general account of the attributes of God to a renewed emphasis upon his "divine power and virtue" (vim atque virtutem) (YP 6:149; CM 14:54). It is clear from the phrase "vim atque virtutem" that as much as Milton has already emphasized omnipotence as a crucial attribute, the emphasis upon power is reiterated in striking detail. As an attribute of crucial moment, power once again takes center stage in the treatment of God. This fact is reinforced by the phrase "vim atque virtutem." As far as Milton is concerned, the use of *vim* to denote power is not enough. Divine *vim* requires its synonym divine *virtutem* to complete the picture. *Vim* (from *vis*) means "strength" (physical or mental), "force," "vigor," "power," "energy," "virtue." In some instances, it can imply "hostile strength," "force," and "violence"; in others, the "virile forces or organs." *Virtutem* (from *virtus*), in turn, denotes "manliness," "manhood," "strength," "vigor," "bravery," as

well as "courage" and "excellence." In this regard, the term
can denote "military talents," "courage," "valor," and "bravery." At the same time, it can imply "moral perfection," "vir-
tuousness," and "virtue."[24] There is clearly some overlap here.
The point is that Milton takes pains to adopt precisely the correct term to express his understanding of God. In one form or
another, all these definitions obtain in a delineation of the figure
of God in the theological treatise. Grouping *vim atque virtutem*
under the headings "Life," "Intellect," and "Will," Milton
discusses these as categories or aspects of his treatment of power.

Although Milton devotes little attention to "Life" as an
expression of power, the proof-texts he invokes are meaningful. The texts include Deuteronomy 32:40, Psalm 42:2, and John
5:26.[25] It would be all too easy to neglect these texts, because
Milton's treatment of "Life" is so brief, but that would be a
most unfortunate mistake. Deuteronomy 32:40 ("For I lift up
my hand to heaven, and say, I live for ever") is a case in point.
This verse is part of the song of Moses that concludes the
Deuteronomic narrative. Milton cites the passage in order to
demonstrate that the phrase "the living God" has its source
in Deuteronomy 32:40, but more is at stake in this passage than
at first meets the eye. For the expression "living God" implies
not simply that God is alive or even that he lives eternally.
The expression means a great deal more than that. In his treatment of *das Heilige*, Otto speaks of God's "livingness" as an
attribute of divinity. Here, the idea of livingness underscores
not only the power of God but also his ability to instill profound fear and indeed a sense of utmost dread. To be in the
presence of this livingness is to risk death. So Otto cites
Deuteronomy 5:26: "For who *is there of* all flesh, that hath heard
the voice of the living God speaking out of the midst of the
fire, as we *have,* and lived?"[26] The idea is repeated in Hebrews
10:31: "*It is* a fearful thing to fall into the hands of the living
God." This sense of livingness permeates Deuteronomy 32:40,
the larger context of which is an account of God's power and

his ability to wreak devastation, as well as to generate new life: "See now that I, *even* I, *am* he, and *there is* no God with me: I kill, and I make alive; I wound, and I heal: neither *is there any* that can deliver out of my hand. For I lift up my hand to heaven, and say, I live for ever." Accordingly, eternal life is consonant with immeasurable power, an attribute, as we have seen, that is crucial to *De Doctrina Christiana.* The proof-text from Psalms 42:2 speaks to the anguished desire of the Psalmist to come fully into the presence of the "living God," who will give solace to the downcast and offer hope to those who worship him. A kinder, gentler version of God's livingness than the first proof-text (Deut. 32:40), the passage from Psalms demonstrates even further the multifaceted nature of the notion of livingness. The passage from John 5:26, however, returns us to the face of God as not only threatening but apocalyptic in nature. At the same time, it reconfigures the notion of the *parousia* as an event through which the faithful gain new life. Drawn from the New Testament, the passage in question distinguishes between "Father" and "Son" and in fact emphasizes the role of the Son configured through his apocalyptic designation "Son of man": "Verily, verily, I say unto you, The hour is coming, and now is, when the dead shall hear the voice of the Son of God: and they that hear shall live. For as the Father hath life in himself; so hath he given to the Son to have life in himself; And hath given him authority to execute judgment also, because he is the Son of man" (John 5:25–27). Accordingly, the reference to "Life" is one in which a few proof-texts do the work of what would otherwise be a multitude of references. With only a brush stroke or two, Milton establishes contexts that are both far-reaching and marvelously penetrating.

In contrast with the category of "Life," those of "Intellect" and "Will" receive much more detailed treatment. What is true for so many of the attributes that Milton brings to the fore, these final two categories are supported by proof-texts grounded in the Old Testament. That is not to suggest that the New

Testament is given short shrift. It is just that when Milton speaks of God, the sensibility that emerges is essentially Hebraic in nature. The Old Testament is simply more compatible with the outlook that Milton embraces. With "Intellect," Milton speaks most immediately to God's omniscience but also once again to his omnipotence. The two go hand in hand. An entire constellation of proof-texts from the Old Testament provides insight into a deity who has the power not only to discern human thoughts but also to see into the deepest and darkest recesses of the human psyche. Nothing is hidden from him. Passages from Genesis, 1 and 2 Chronicles, Psalms, Job, Proverbs, Isaiah, and Jeremiah, among others, are brought to the fore to underscore the idea of God's ability to scrutinize the mind, heart, and affections of all humankind. This is a God who sees into our deepest and most hidden thoughts ("secret places") and desires. Nothing escapes him. A corresponding view prevails in Milton's choice of New Testament passages that include Acts, Hebrews, Romans, and Revelation, among others. Passages from these New Testament texts are precisely what Milton has in mind about God's uncanny ability to behold and disclose all that we are desperate to conceal. For example, Milton cites Hebrew 4:13 as a case in point: "To His eyes all things are laid bare, and are opened to their most secret parts" [omnia sunt nuda et ab intimo patentia oculis eius]. Such powers of penetration into the human psyche results in a new name for God: "*kardiognōstes pantōn*, he who knows the hearts of all men" (Acts 1:24). Thus, Milton asserts, God is named "*the only wise* [*solus sapiens*], Dan. ii. 10; Rom. xvi. 27; I Tim. i. 17." God is also distinguished by prescience (*prescientia*) or "foreknowledge absolute." He knows what humans "will think and do even before they are born and even though these thoughts and deeds will not take place until many centuries have passed" (YP 6:150; CM 14:56–57). What is the result of all this? The power to look into the human heart with a penetrating gaze is disconcerting in its directness and force, and the knowledge and power that come with *prescientia* are daunting in their implications. If all this comes under the heading of "Intellect," then the God of *De Doctrina* is distinguished by a presence that is as potentially threatening as it is awe-inspiring, as much the product of a sensibility capable of provoking dread as it is a source of reverence and worship. This is a deity one would think twice about crossing. With those eyes that see all, God does not hesitate to "spy out" any deemed reprobate. The phrase *kardiognōstes pantōn* is not a comforting epithet, nor is it meant to be. In the God of *De Doctrina Christiana* there resides the figure of all-powerful perception, all-powerful discernment, and all-powerful penetration. Seeing and knowing all, God's omniscience is matched only by his omnipotence: the two go hand-in-hand.

Both aspects are instrumental in reinforcing the emphasis *De Doctrina* places on the attributes of purity and holiness as manifestations of God's will. "Supremely pure and holy" (*summe purus et sanctus*), the figure of God is delineated here by proof-texts drawn exclusively from the Old Testament (YP 6:150; CM 14:56).[27] To get to the heart of *purus et sanctus*, the New Testament apparently will not do, at least, not at this juncture. Only passages drawn from such Old Testament texts as Exodus, Joshua, Job, and Isaiah suggest precisely how purity and holiness are to be understood. These texts embody a conception of deity as one removed, aloof, and ultimately terrifying. The text of Isaiah 6:2–3 is a case in point. Invoked earlier to support the idea of God's divine presence, Isaiah's temple vision is crucial to notions of purity and holiness as fundamental attributes of deity. We are reminded of the prophet's receipt of his vocation as he beholds God enthroned "high and lifted up," with his train filling the temple. Enhancing the vision are those six-winged seraphim that celebrate the enthroned figure with the cry of "Holy, holy, holy, *is* the Lord God of hosts: the whole earth *is* full of his glory" (Isa. 6:1–3). The vision is one in which the enthroned figure is at once absolutely transcendent and aloof and at the same time immediately present in the form of the train of holiness that fills not just the temple but the world itself. By means of this encounter with the supremely pure and holy, Isaiah receives his calling as a prophet (Isa. 6:4–9).

The proof-texts from Isaiah are reinforced by those Milton deems worthy of supporting his contention that God is "supremely pure and holy." One or two texts should suffice. The first is Exodus 15:11 ("magnificent in holiness"); the second, Job 15:15 ("the heavens are not clean in his eyes"). The first is drawn from the so-called Song at the Sea, or Song of Moses, in commemoration of the parting of the waters to allow the Israelites to pass through but to destroy the Egyptian hosts. The song of celebration is in keeping with the liturgical dimensions that distinguish Isaiah 6, with its "Holy, holy, holy." The context of the first is that of a triumphant battle hymn. With its emphasis on the distinction between clean and unclean and the wonders of purity, the second returns us to the milieu of the temple and the complex cultic practices associated with the priestly profession: "What is man, that he should be clean? and *he which* is born of a woman that he should be righteous? Behold, he putteth no trust in his saints; yea and the heavens are not clean in his sight. How much more abominable and filthy *is* man, which drinketh iniquity like water" (Job 15:14–16). The remarkable feature of the citation from Job has as much to do with the speaker of the statement as with the significance of the statement he makes. The speaker is Eliphaz the Temanite, one of Job's dubious comforters. (In fact, the etymology of "Eliphaz" — "My God is gold" or "God of gold" — suggests one whose very name might prompt us to view him with suspicion.) Eliphaz's counsel is the product of a perverse desire to cast aspersions on the sufferer ("Is there any secret thing with thee?"), rather than a genuine desire to help alleviate Job's (and thus by implication, mankind's) sufferings. "Miserable comforters *are* ye all," Job declares; "Shall

vain words have an end?" (16:1–2). In the context of the assertion by Milton that God is "summe purus et sancte," the use
of the Jobean reference is one that threatens to complicate matters immeasurably. It is not that we are prompted to question
God as "supremely pure and holy." (Job himself most certainly would not call such an ascription into question.) It is
simply that one must be very careful of taking the proof-texts
at face value. Underlying the passages invoked to support a theological contention is a world of potential conflict and uncertainty. A God who looks upon the heavens as "unclean in his
sight" and his own creations as "abominable and filthy" is a
deity whose ways would be hard to justify indeed. The sense
of uncertainty fostered by such a view is one that should not
be dismissed out of hand in any consideration of the methodology undertaken in the citation of proof-texts in *De Doctrina
Christiana*. This outlook is not ameliorated by the proof-texts
invoked to support the contentions about God's attributes
that follow upon that concerning his purity and holiness.

We might take, for example, Milton's contention that God
is to be seen as a deity who is "summe benignus" (CM 14:56).
In the Carey translation, this phrase is rendered "supremely
kind" (YP 6:150), whereas in the Sumner translation, the
phrase is rendered "most gracious" (CM 14:57). Neither translation is fully to the point. *Benignus* is multivalent. A form
that suggests the combination of *bonus* and *genus*, the adjective *benignus* implies at once "kind," "good," "friendly,"
"pleasing," and "favorable." Reflected in the term are the
qualities of that which can only be described as "abundant,"
"fruitful," "fertile," and "benevolent."[28] The several proof-texts
from the Old Testament Milton draws upon to support this
notion include passages from Exodus, Psalms, and Lamenta-
tions. Attempting perhaps to achieve something of a balance
in the citation of authority, Milton draws upon a comparable
number of proof-texts from the New Testament, including
passages from Matthew, 2 Corinthians, Ephesians, and 1 John.

The proof-texts from the Old Testament are especially interesting. There, *benignus* finds its Hebraic counterpart in the term *chesed*, which, as applied to God, suggests not just "kindness," but God's "lovingkindness" (see *BDB*, s.v.). All the passages speak eloquently to the idea of God's kindness. The passage from Exodus (34:6), however, is particularly engaging, for its use of epithets at once fosters the notion of *benignus* and in the context of the larger narrative implicitly subverts that notion at the very point of asserting it. On the one hand, it outdoes *benignus* through a series of epithets that describe God as "merciful, gracious, patient, of great kindness, and fidelity" (Exod. 34:6). The copiousness of the epithets here is stunning. The irony is that at the very point of venturing such epithets, the biblical text makes certain to assert that as much as God bestows mercy on thousands, he will not "clear *the guilty;* visiting the iniquity of the fathers upon the children, and upon the children's children, unto the third and to the fourth *generation*" (Exod. 34:7). This supremely kind and merciful God, then, is quite capable of wreaking havoc not only on those he deems guilty of transgression but on those future generations who will have been innocent of those transgressions (YP 6:150–51). Viewed in a larger context, the passages offered to support the argument of the theological treatise ironically disclose a kind of secret identity in God. Buried beneath the surface world that comforts and assures us, this subterranean realm is known to emerge at any moment to subvert the very notions that Milton seeks to foster. In other words, the proof-texts take on a life of their own, one as unsettling in its own way as any attempt to harness the various significations that a proof-text or group of proof-texts might embody.

This might account for the fact that in other theological treatises of the period proof-texts in general were relegated to the margins of the text. When Milton elected to bestow upon the proof-texts a place of privilege in the main body of the work, he was undoubtedly aware that such a decision might provide the opportunity for the proof-texts to assert their own identity and their own primacy. It was a risk he was willing to take. This risk becomes especially pronounced in the context of the various narratives that distinguish the Old Testament. In the New Testament, Milton had at his disposal a counterbalancing force. As one might expect, the New Testament passages cited as proof-texts are more nearly in keeping with the idea of God as *summe benignus*. Indeed, underlying the proof-texts drawn from the New Testament is a sense of God as a father whose function is essentially redemptive. So 2 Corinthians 1:3–4: "Blessed *be* God, even the Father of our Lord Jesus Christ, the Father of mercies, and the God of all comfort; Who comforteth us in all our tribulation, that we may be able to comfort them which are in trouble, by the comfort wherewith we ourselves art comforted of God"; and 1 John 4:8–9: "He that loveth not knoweth not God; for God is love. . . . because God sent his only begotten Son into the world, that we might live through him." Here, *benignus* is represented by distinctly theological significations that underscore the kerygmatic dimensions of the text. These dimensions suggest the way in which God's beneficence is distinguished by such virtues as mercy and love. Nothing is called into question here, nothing compromised: we take comfort in the assurance that a God who is love will never betray us.[29] Such is the dispensational perspective adopted by the New Testament. Nonetheless, the multifaceted and unpredictable deity who appears in the Old Testament continues to render problematic the kerygmatic underpinnings of New Testament doctrine.[30] Milton's final statement on the subject nonetheless does not hesitate to confront the harsher elements of even the New Dispensational assumptions. Thus, we are informed that, as aspects of the divine will, even the God of the New Testament is not only "just" but "severe" in his dealings with those who oppose him. For his proof-text, Milton alludes to Romans 11:22: "Behold therefore the goodness and severity of God: on them which fell, severity; but toward thee, goodness, if thou continue in *his* goodness: otherwise thou also shalt be cut off." Milton renders this even more harshly: "abrupt severity to those who fell away." Uncompromising in its severity, this is a sentiment that one is more nearly inclined to associate with the God of the Old Testament than with the God of the New Testament. I fully believe that such an association is the rule rather than the exception throughout *De Doctrina Christiana*.

III

The final section of the second chapter of the treatise brings to the fore all that has been articulated concerning the figure of God as a subject of discourse. For Milton, this section is the flourish that rounds out his attempt to draw exclusively upon the biblical text in order to provide a coherent statement about God, his existence, his nature, and his mode of operation. The summation that the final section represents is accordingly crucial in any endeavor to assess the way in which Milton views deity as well as the language through which deity is conceived in human terms. To be sure, Milton would be the first to acknowledge that it is impossible to represent God discursively. God will not be confined to language, either in the form of systematic representation or in the more nearly capacious form of poetic rendering. Nonetheless, the very impossibility of providing a coherent statement about God is what the chapter "De Deo" is all about. The truth about God may be had only when the theologian acknowledges how ungraspable God is. With that recognition, one may finally arrive at the conclusion that the chapter on God makes clear: God is beyond our knowing in any form, discursive or otherwise. Acknowledging that, we may be said to have arrived at a point at which a heightened awareness of not knowing is inevitable. This is the point that the conclusion to the chapter on God makes in its final flourish. "From all these attributes springs [*efflorescit*] that infinite excellence [*illa summa . . . excellentia*] which constitutes the true perfection [*perfectus*] of God, and causes him to abound in glory [*summa gloria*], and to be most deservedly and justly the supreme Lord of all things [*dominus omnium supremus*]" (CM 14:60–61).[31]

In its use of such terms as *efflorescit*, the discourse here is deliberately — one might almost say, extravagantly — poetic, for only through the use of poetic devices (such as the trope of blossoming or springing embedded in *efflorescit*) is it possible to capture what would otherwise be a conundrum impervious to the "logic" of theological discourse. All that remains is poetry, but in a sense that is all one requires to address the kinds of issues that Milton has taken upon himself to engage. If the "tropological" is not the ultimate source of understanding the range of transcendent issues encompassed in the treatise, the act of "poeticizing" is at least a start. That, too, has its limits, but at least these are limits one can understand and appreciate when dealing with multiple and complex entities that constitute the discourse on God. So by conceiving the discourse ultimately in poetic terms (as in some sense "trope"), Milton views his task as that of having paved the way for the discussion of attributes to spring, blossom, and flower. What emerges is a kind of poetic theology, one through which the presencing of God in language achieves its own sense of the impossible, its own sense of "knowing" the unknowable, in this case through a kind of accommodated form of representation. Responding to that form, we shall become aware of the impossible notion of the other, the transcendent, one whose attributes are ultimately summed up in the idea of "glory" as a reflection of God's excellence and perfection.[32]

God as *summa gloria:* nothing could be more profound than that. The proof-texts that Milton draws upon speak eloquently on "glory" as the embodiment of God's attributes. Except for one or two references to the New Testament, all the proof-texts are drawn yet again from the Old Testament. These proof-texts are germane to the idea of tracing the development of the concept of glory from one biblical moment to the next. To demonstrate that what has gone before is summed up (or better still, "made to flower") in the true perfection of God, Milton cites passages from Psalms, Daniel, Matthew, and 1 Timothy. Whereas the passages from Psalms include an impassioned plea for divine protection (16:11) and a celebration of God's act of manifesting himself in glory and majesty (104:1),[33] the passages from Daniel conceive God in apocalyptic and visionary terms that emphasize the daunting dimensions of God's awesomeness (7:10, 18). In these contexts, God becomes once again what Rudolph Otto terms the *mysterium tremendum*, that *ganz andere* presence at its most profoundly holy.[34] The passages from the oracles delineated in the apocalyptic Book of Daniel speak most eloquently to this consummate dimension of deity, for it is here that we encounter the Ancient of Days, whom the prophet sees in a "night vision." Distinguished by four great beasts (a lion, a bear, a leopard, and a dreadful horned beast), the vision is one in which the Ancient of Days appears enthroned. His "garment *was* white as snow, and the hair of his head [was] like the pure wool." The throne on which he sat "*was like* the fiery flame, *and* his wheels *as* burning fire." From this fearsome enthroned figured issued "a fiery stream," and befitting his exalted office, "thousand thousands ministered unto him, and ten thousand times ten thousand stood before him" (Dan. 7:1–10). What we are to make of this vision remains to be seen. Certainly, in the context of the apocalyptic Book of Daniel, the vision resonates with topical as well as anagogical significance. As far as Milton is concerned, however, the vision serves to dramatize the way in which we are to conceive God's "infinite excellence." For Milton, the apocalyptic and visionary experience portrayed in the Ancient of Days is one that best exemplifies "the true perfection of God," as he "abound[s] in glory." As a result of Daniel's vision, we are given to understand how God is said to be "most deservedly and justly the supreme Lord of all things." Considering the fearsome and indeed bizarre quality of Daniel's vision of the Ancient of Days, it is interesting to find such a proof-text called upon to demonstrate God's perfection, glory, and supremacy. Nonetheless, at the heart of the conception of God in *De Doctrina* is a sensibility that is entirely receptive to what might be called awesome, fearsome, and even bizarre aspects of deity. Calling attention to those aspects (beyond all others), Milton makes bold to declare that his God is not necessarily a deity that all will accept. With its roots very much in the milieu fostered by the Old Testament, this is nonetheless a deity with which one must contend in order to appreciate fully how the God of *De Doctrina Christiana* functions, how he is to be understood, and how he is to be "approached" (in all senses of that term).

The concept of *summa gloria* becomes especially meaningful here. What Milton calls *summa gloria* or *divinae gloriae* is a phenomenon of which there is available or "on record" (*extat*) only a certain amount, and the knowledge of even that amount is limited by one's capacity to know or to "grasp" (*capere*) that which is revealed (CM 14:60; translation mine). The tenor of the argument is that of one fully aware of his limitations to comprehend a phenomenon that defies all knowledge. We are thrust back into the world of divine ignorance, of not knowing, a world that makes itself available on occasion by means of biblical theophanies. To this end, Milton cites representative moments in which the divine glory reveals itself. These moments, Milton implies, are accessible most immediately and almost exclusively through an encounter with the Old Testament. Such an encounter encompasses what might be called the essential theophanic basis of God's self-manifestation. At issue are revelations of the glory of God ranging from the Sinai theophany and visions of God in the minor and major prophets to the apocalyptic renderings both in the Old Testament and the New Testament. As one might expect, passages from Exodus (19:18; 24:10; 33:9, 10, 18) predominate, but the historical books are also taken into account, including 1 Kings 8:10, 11; 19:11; and 22:19, as well as the Book of Psalms, including 18:8 and (once again) 104. In addition to citations from Micah (1:3), Nahum (1:3), and Habakkuk (3:3), the major visionary events, represented by Isaiah (chapter 6) and Ezekiel (chapter 1; 8:1–3; 10:1; 43:2, 3), assume immediate importance. These texts, in turn, are complemented by the so-called apocalyptic material from Daniel (7:9) and Revelation (chapter 4). For Milton, the crucial texts required to understand the meaning of the concept of *summa gloria* or *divinae gloriae* are reminders both of God's grandeur and of his ultimate removal from the realm of human comprehension. At the center of the proof-texts is the vision of the enthroned figure, a vision already touched upon in the account of the Ancient of Days. Any one of the proof-texts that follow upon Daniel 7 cited above emphasizes the regal presencing of God as the ultimate source of power and knowledge. So Exodus 24:10 (as cited in the treatise itself) says: "they saw the God of Israel, and beneath his feet something resembling a pavement of sapphire stone, and like the very body of heaven in brightness" (CM 14:61). This vision anticipates that experience of the prophet Isaiah, discussed above and mentioned here in connection with the *divinae gloriae*. These visions, in turn, anticipate that of Revelation 4, the only text from the New Testament mentioned to provide a sense of the glory of God.

Of all the texts invoked to suggest the true nature of the *divinae gloriae*, one of the most important is the vision that the exiled prophet Ezekiel (chapter 1) beholds on the shores of the Chebar River in Babylon. There, the prophet experiences a whirlwind out of the north, "a great cloud, and a fire infolding itself, and a brightness was about it, and out of the midst thereof as the colour of amber, out of the midst of the fire." With four living creatures (man, eagle, ox, and lion), the vision is further enhanced, if not propelled, by living wheels, each with wheels in the middle of the wheels and each inwrought with a multitude of eyes that gaze at the prophet as much as he gazes at them. Above the heads of the living creatures appears the likeness of a firmament, and upon that resides a figure surrounded by a rainbow as a sign of the covenant, as well as an electrumlike fiery brilliance that encompasses both the seated figure and the vision as a whole. This is the most stunning of the visions encountered in the various proof-texts cited by Milton to delineate the nature of the *divinae gloriae*. Like the visionary enactments already cited, Ezekiel's vision is a fearsome event, but its advent in the prophecy (chapter 1; 8:1–3; 10:1) as the inaugural experience against which all others are to be placed anticipates the return of the *divinae gloriae* to the temple envisioned in the final eight chapters of the prophecy. This final event is summed up in the verses to which Milton alludes: "And, behold, the glory of the God of Israel came from the way of the east: and his voice *was* like a noise of many waters: and the earth shined with his glory. And *it was* according to the appearance of the vision that I saw . . . by the river Chebar; and I fell upon my face" (Ezck. 43:2–3). Abjection is the true posture for those who have come into contact with "the holy" in the fullness of its splendor.[35]

Having glanced at the vision of Ezekiel as a primal source of understanding the nature of the fearsome and awesome deity, we might focus briefly on the place that glory occupies in the overall conception of God. We are thereby prompted to ask the following questions: What precisely is the phenomenon known as *summa gloria* or *divinae gloriae?* How is this phenomenon to be understood, and what connotations accrue to it? Once again, the most direct answer comes from the vision that inaugurates the first chapter of Ezekiel. As the consummate expression of what his vision has disclosed, the prophet declares that he has beheld nothing less than "the appearance of the likeness of the glory of the Lord" (Ezek. 1:28). If this is to suggest that God is to be held at nothing less than three removes (appearance of, likeness of, glory of), then the actual manifestation of God in all his glory represents the subtext of the visionary encounter itself. What then is that glory? In the Old Testament, the term "glory" is known as *kabod*, a phenomenon that has a distinctly materialistic sense associated with it. For this reason, *kabod* can also be a designation for that which is heavy. God may be aloof as he is encircled by the fires and the living creatures that protect him, but his nature is such that his own glory finds its roots in a latent materialism that underlies his manifestations to his prophets. As such, *kabod* embodies both the external accoutrements of royalty and kingship and the internal resonances having to do with honor and virtue (*BDB*, s.v. *kabod*). The term "glory" also underlies the revelation of God to Saint John the Divine in the throne vision to which Milton alludes (Rev. 4). Here, however, "glory" or *doxa* is especially associated with the act of bestowing praise upon the object of worship (see esp. Rev. 4:9), although the Hebraic sense of inherent splendor and majesty is very much present as well.[36]

What all this implies, finally, is that for Milton, the culminating moment of the portrayal of God throughout "De Deo" is one in which deity is beheld at its most fearsome, awesome, and essentially threatening as a mode of representation. It is God at his most "glorious," but it is also God at his most secret, mysterious, and "inconceivable." With such ideas in mind, Milton concludes his chapter by observing that our understanding of God is such that we must recognize him as "Wonderful and Incomprehensible" (mirabilis et incomprehensibilis) (YP 6:152; CM 14:60). The epithets are to the point. Whereas *mirabilis* implies that which is most glorious, extraordinary, and miraculous, the term *incomprehensibilis* implies not only that which cannot be seized or grasped but also that which ultimately defies conceptualization. It is almost as if Milton concludes his discourse by saying that all that has gone before by way of "explanation" is finally nothing more than an attempt to do the impossible, that is, to comprehend that which undermines all attempts at such a task. What we know of God is that we do not know, cannot understand, and will not ever be able to know fully in this life. What we do know (or should know) is our own limitations. Our knowledge of these limitations prompts us to worship that which by its very nature is *mirabilis*. Worshiping God in this manner, we acknowledge our awareness both of his infinite mystery and of the path upon which one must embark to be responsive to all that that mystery implies. In keeping with the method he has adopted throughout, Milton lets the Bible speak for itself through the proof-texts that are invoked to demonstrate the validity of Milton's exegesis. The three texts Milton has elected to cite are (once again) drawn exclusively from the Old Testament: "Judges xiii. 18: *why do you make eager enquiries about my name, since it is an object for wonder?*; Psal. cxlv. 3: *there is no finding out his greatness*; Isa. xl. 28: *his powers of foresight are beyond discovery.*" Of particular interest is the first citation from Judges, in which Manoah asks the angel of the Lord, "What is thy name?" (13:17–18). The request is reminiscent of Moses' own professed desire to know the name of the theophany in the burning bush (Exod. 3:13). The response Moses receives is deeply enigmatic: "And God said unto Moses, I AM THAT I AM" (Exod. 13:14), for it encodes the mysteries of the Tetragrammaton. In the Judges narrative, Manoah is correspondingly presumptuous in asking for something beyond his power to know. Like the answer Moses receives, that which Manoah receives is equally enigmatic. In both narratives, the request is in some sense rebuffed or, at the very least, embedded in mystery. In the first case, Moses is presented with the enigma of the Tetragrammaton, whereas in the second case, Manoah and his wife are given to know that the answer is essentially beyond the scope of their comprehension. The term that the angel of God adopts to provide a name is *piliy'*, which connotes that which is "secret," "remarkable," "wonderful," as well as "miraculous." With its roots in the *peh, lamed, aleph* configuration, it is an invitation to acknowledge, if not to celebrate, God's own mysteries, which are finally unknowable, unsearchable, and beyond the reach of human sense (see *BDB*, s.v. *pala'*).

The discourse on God in the second chapter of *De Doctrina Christiana* concludes with the act of bearing witness to an understanding of deity very much in keeping with views that celebrate God's unknowableness, his wonder-working presence, and his manifestations (or theophanies). These render him as dark and inscrutable as any other deity in the traditions of interpretation that one might possibly conceive. In this respect, at least aspects of the figure of God bear a resemblance, as we have already suggested, to the traditions of the "mystical theology" or of the negative way that extend back at least as far as the fifth or sixth century. There is most certainly a dimension in the conception of the God of *De Doctrina Christiana* that one might well call apophatic. There is more than a trace of the mystical in the conception of deity as it emerges in the theological treatise. In tone and outlook, the views of God expressed in the second chapter of *De Doctrina* appear, however, to be even more closely aligned with the kinds of primal experience Rudolph Otto propounds in *The Idea of the Holy,* with its portrayal of God as the most "archaic" of deities (a veritable *mysterium tremendum*, as it were) that one can possibly imagine. The foundations of such an outlook are fundamental to the Old Testament and, to some extent, the New Testament, as well.

However Milton came by such an outlook, it is clear that the final section of "De Deo" reaffirms the idea that the God of the treatise has as many ties with the realm of the inexpressible, and even the threatening, as he does with all that has to do with the rational, the moral, and the spiritual. If the theodicy of *De Doctrina Christiana* fosters a conviction that we are in the presence of a "good God," we must ever keep in mind that the God of the theological treatise is very much a *deus absconditus*.[37] When he does decide to reveal himself, one need be very careful about approaching the enigma too closely and without due care, lest he find himself the victim of a consuming fire. If one is inclined to speak of the "faces" of God, those many aspects are certainly present in "De Deo." In assessing the nature of that presence, one must be receptive to the wide range of readings that the treatise not only encourages but demands. If there are contradictions, then there are contradictions; not all aspects must agree with one another. But we must allow the proof-texts to express themselves. Then we can say that all the rest is commentary.

Part II

The Poetics of Deity

FOUR

The Theopathetic Deity

✠

I

Having examined how the discourse of theology finds expression in Milton's thought, we move now from an extended analysis of the exegetical bearings of the chapter in *De Doctrina Christiana* on God ("De Deo") to a consideration of the portrayal of God in Milton's poetry. The principal points of focus will be *Paradise Lost* and *Samson Agonistes*. Through an exploration of these poems, we shall gain insight into what might be called Milton's "poetics of deity." As I hope to show, this is a mode of discourse that finds its correspondence in the exegetical world of the theological treatise but that is also both *sui generis* and, as a phenomenon grounded in a distinctly poetic milieu, whole and complete in its own right. That is, in an understanding of the delineation of God as a character in his own poem, one appreciates the correspondences that can be drawn between the work of the poet and the work of the exegete. At the same time, the poetic representation of God must be understood on its own terms, which may or may not be in accord with the treatise through which deity emerges as a distinctly "theological" entity. I am not talking about formal or unyielding structures here. My fundamental point is to allow the God of the theological treatise and the God of the poetry to "breathe," that is, to enjoy distinct identities without being hemmed in or manacled by a determination to view them as one and the same. Approaching Milton's God in this manner should help to ensure the integrity of the texts (theological and poetic) through which deity is imbued with life and meaning. In a consideration of the God of the poetry, I elect to focus on *Paradise Lost* and *Samson Agonistes* because each in its own way offers a distinct view of deity. In *Paradise Lost* the character of God has become the site of heated debate throughout the centuries. However, the same can hardly be asserted of *Samson Agonistes,* a poem in which God as a character does not make a visible appearance at all. Nonetheless, he is "presenced" by almost every character and by almost every speech in the poem. (The question is whether or in what way that presence makes itself known in the devastating climax of the action.) The midsection of this study, then, encompasses the delineation of God in both the epic and the dramatic poem as a means of suggesting how the notion of deity assumes renewed impetus in a poetic setting.

I do not, however, intend to focus on all aspects of Milton's delineation of God in the poetry. In fact, I make a point here of limiting my focus drastically. I do so in order to unearth what might be called the subterranean aspects of deity, aspects that suggest the "dark side" of God, the "other" God, one who exhibits emotional fervor in a manner that can be construed as threatening and even unstable in the extreme.[1] Once again the *deus absconditus* is at issue here. What is true of the theological treatise is no less true of the poetry: Milton's God is in many respects the hidden God come to life, come to haunt both the prose and the poetry. I discuss in detail the delineation of God in *De Doctrina Christiana* because I am convinced that the theological treatise, with all its trappings of logical systematic discourse, provides the warrant for approaching Milton's God in a manner that calls into question the notion of what is commonly known as "Milton's Good God."[2] Once again, I am not claiming that Milton's God is not good. He is a very good God indeed (at least in most respects). But there is a side or "face" to him that is decidedly dark, decidedly disturbing. That disturbing quality emerges in the revelation of his hiddenness. With that revelation comes the release of emotional energy, anger, and even hate. The faces of God we behold in the revelation of the dark side may be troublesome and unsettling, but they are as much a part of the God of Milton as any other aspects one can imagine. If the God of the theological treatise and the God of the poetry do not necessarily correspond in all respects, they do nonetheless represent the means by which much of what is disturbing about Milton's deity assumes both a discursive and a poetic bearing. How to read the second (the God of the poetry) in the context of the first (the God of the prose) will engage us here.

To that end, we return to "De Deo" chapter in *De Doctrina Christiana* in order to address a crucial dimension of the discussion of divine attributes, still to be examined. That dimension has to do with the attribution of emotion to a being who transcends the very notion of the passible, divine or otherwise. Of major import not only to Milton's view of deity but to the traditions of theological exegesis dating back to the early church fathers, the concept known as *anthropopatheia* signifies the nature of God both as an anthropomorphic figure and as a passible being. Adopting the perspective of divine anthropomorphism, *anthropopatheia* moves logically to the corresponding issue of whether or not God experiences emotions and the extent to which those emotions represent an important index both to what might be called the "personality" of God and the means by which one might better understand the nature of that personality.[3]

Because of the role that Scripture plays in the attempt to arrive at an understanding of the divine personality, a discussion of *anthropopatheia* in the context of the debates over passibility should suggest the way in which the delineation of God in the scriptural text gave rise to a theory of reading through which the debates themselves found expression. As was made clear from the earliest attempts to argue on behalf of passibility, on the one hand, or impassibility, on the other, one's view of godhead was largely determined by his willingness (or unwillingness) to take Scripture at its word. One's stance regarding this crucial issue proved decisive in Milton's determination of not only how God is to be understood in scriptural terms but how the Bible itself is to be read, how it functions as a text, and how the reader should view himself or herself as an interpreter of that text. In order to gain a greater awareness of these issues, we shall first glance at the traditions from which the debate over passibility arose, after which we shall proceed to an analysis of Milton's own views in the context of those traditions. In the course of considering the traditions, we shall become increasingly aware of how a theory of reading formed an essential part of the emerging attitude concerning the emotional life of God, particularly as manifested in the notion of *anthropopatheia*.

As scholars have long recognized, *anthropopatheia* as a concept finds its source in early commentaries concerning the nature of God's attributes. Even before the church fathers addressed themselves to this idea, Philo considered it in his treatise, *The Unchangeableness of God*.[4] Approaching the subject from the Hellenistic perspective that he embodied, Philo transformed the biblical deity into a philosophical principle founded upon the idea of immutability. In place of any scriptural suggestions of a passible deity, Philo substituted his own philosophical predilections, which were founded upon the concept of divine permanence.[5] As one who is immutable, God, argues Philo, cannot be "moved," cannot experience emotion,

for emotion implies movement, which, in turn, suggests mutability. Accordingly, God "is not susceptible to any passion at
all." Correspondingly, "the parts and members of the body in
general" have "no relation to God," who is a self-existent
principle (11.52). To suggest otherwise, Philo observes, is to
engage in "the mythical fictions of the impious, who, professing
to represent the deity as of human form, in reality represent
Him as having human passions" (12.59). But the act of attribut-
ing passions to God, as Philo was well aware, is precisely what
the Bible does. On the basis of such a recognition, Philo is
accordingly put to the expense of devising a rationale for God's
delineation as a passible being in the biblical text. Philo does
this through a theory of accommodation that amounts to a denigration of those inclined to take the Bible at its word. Granting
that Moses ascribed humanlike characteristics to God, Philo
maintains that these expressions served only for "a kind of elementary lesson, to admonish those who could not otherwise
be brought to their senses" (11.52). These are the foolish rabble whose natural wit is dense and dull and who do not have
the ability to see clearly: "Thus ill-disciplined and foolish
slaves receive profit from a master who frightens them, for they
fear his threats and menaces and thus involuntarily are schooled
by fear" (14.63; *Philo*, 3:36–37, 40–43). Arguing on behalf of a
completely immutable and depersonalized deity, Philo has
nothing but contempt for the anthropopathetic and anthropomorphic conceptions of God. As these notions are found in
the biblical text, they are used negatively and condescendingly
to admonish an unbelieving and foolish multitude. The true
reader for Philo, then, is one who is able to look beyond the
apparent meanings implicit in the Scriptures. Seeing through
the text, the reader arrives at a truly philosophical understanding of deity.

This notion found widespread acceptance in the early church,
particularly among the Alexandrian fathers.[6] Even those who
adopted it, however, did not do so categorically. Especially

pertinent in this regard is Origen, in whom one discovers an evolution from a belief in impassibility to the adoption of an idea of God as entirely passible. Moving from a concept of divine *apatheia* in such early works as *On First Principles* and *Commentary on John*, he begins to show signs of a shift in position in his *Homilies on Numbers*. By the time he reaches *Homilies on Ezekiel*, however, he has changed his mind completely. Addressing himself in the sixth homily on Ezekiel to the Passion of the Son symbolized by the cross, Origen sees this experience as the emotion of love consummated in the Father:

> Moreover, does not the Father and God of the universe some-how experience emotion, since he is long-suffering and of great mercy? Or do you not know that when he distributes human gifts he experiences human emotion? . . . Therefore God endures our ways, just as the Son of God bears our emotions. The Father himself is not impassible. If he is asked, he takes pity and experiences grief, he suffers something of love and . . . for our sake he experiences human emotion.[7]

This passage demonstrates the extent to which the appeal of the emotional life of God exerted an overwhelming influence even on those committed philosophically to the idea of an impassible deity. The concept of a passible God was difficult to resist. In addition to suggesting the influence of passibility on Origen, the passage also raises other points of interest. Origen views the concept of divine passibility in terms of the relationship between Father and Son. Specifically, the suffering of the Son upon the cross is seen to be intimately related to (in fact, a manifestation of) the suffering the Father undergoes on behalf of humankind. In a very real sense, Christ's Passion is the embodiment of God's passion.[8] God experiences emotion, a phenomenon consummated in that of the Son upon the cross. Although Origen does not elaborate on the idea of precisely how God may be said to feel emotion, the concept is one that engaged an entire range of patristic exegetes from the earliest times onward.

Tertullian may serve as an example. Although an enemy of patripassianism (the idea that the Father himself suffered and died on the cross in the guise of the Son), Tertullian endorses the notion of passibility in the godhead.[9] So in *The Five Books Against Marcion*, Tertullian defends divine passibility against those (notably philosophers of the Epicurean school) who argue that emotion implies corruption, even in God.[10] The heretics contend that "if God is angry, and jealous, and roused, and grieved, He must therefore be corrupted, and must therefore die." Such, Tertullian argues, is the folly of those who "prejudge divine things from human" and conclude that, "because in man's corrupt condition there are found passions of this description, therefore there must be deemed to exist in God also sensations of the same kind." In order to clarify the matter, Tertullian distinguishes between the emotional life of human beings and the emotional life of God. Just as the difference between the divine and the human body is great, so, Tertullian observes, it is with the divine and the human soul, even though the sensations of each are designated by the same names. Just as these sensations in the human being are rendered corrupt by the corruptibility of human substance, in God they are rendered incorruptible by the incorruption of the divine essence. It is absurd to place human characteristics in God rather than divine ones in human beings and to clothe God in the likeness of human instead of humans in the image of God. It is to be seen as the likeness of God in human beings, therefore, that the human soul has the same emotions and sensations as God, although they are not of the same kind. Whereas humans possess these emotions in imperfection, God possesses them in perfection. God, Tertullian concludes, is moved by all these affections "in that peculiar manner of His own, in which it is profoundly fit that He should be affected; and it is owing to Him that man is also similarly affected in a way which is equally his own" (2.16).[11] What makes Tertullian's observation so interesting is its insistence that passibility may be seen not only as a characteristic of God but as an attribute that God bestows upon his offspring, notably humans in the role of *imago Dei*. Although different in kind from that which human beings experience, God's emotion is nonetheless as integral to the divine personality as human emotion is to the human. In Tertullian, then, emotion is accorded a divine psychogenesis, one that legitimates the concept of the "mind" or personality of God.

Tertullian is not alone in having approached the notion of passibility in this manner.[12] Among the church fathers, the one individual who, more than any other, devoted his energies to a defense of passibility is Lactantius. His treatise *The Wrath of God* is a detailed exploration of the issue.[13] Arguing against the Epicureans, who maintained that God experiences no emotion, and the Stoics, who believed that God could be kind but not angry, Lactantius asserts that it is the very nature of divinity to be passible: "What beatitude, then, can there be in God," asks Lactantius, "if quiet and immobile He is ever inactive; if He is deaf to those who pray, if blind to those who worship Him? What is so worthy, so befitting to God as providence? But if He cares for nothing, provides for nothing, He has lost all divinity" (chap. 4).[14] What is true for Tertullian is likewise true for Lactantius: emotion becomes an essential constituent of the divine personality. In both of the church fathers, one discovers a divinization of emotion as it originates in God. This divinization, moreover, applies not only to emotions such as love and compassion, which are normally associated with God; it likewise applies to the emotions of anger and hatred, both of which for Lactantius are manifested in the divine personality of God. Addressing himself to that personality, Lactantius observes: "He who loves the good also hates the evil, and he who does not hate the evil does not love the good, because, on the one hand, to love the good comes from hatred of evil, and to hate the evil rises from love of the good. . . . The one who loves, therefore, also hates, and he who hates also loves" (chap. 5). A loving God is also therefore not only potentially an angry God but a God who, under the appropriate circumstances, is capable of hatred as well. Entering the perilous waters of divine possibility, Lactantius does not hesitate to attribute to deity the most extreme of emotions, but even Lactantius has his limits. He will not allow the possibility that God experiences such affections as fear, sexual desire, envy, avarice, or grief. These affections, he feels, are demeaning to God. "What need is there," he asks, "to speak of the human affections to which our frailty yields?" In the case of fear, for example, Lactantius offers the following reason for its absence from the emotional makeup of deity: God, "on whom there falls neither need, nor injury, nor pain, nor death, can fear in no way because there is nothing that can bear force against Him." Corresponding arguments are put forward for sexual desire, envy, avarice, and grief (chap. 15).[15] What determines the criteria of selection that Lactantius adopts finally seems somewhat arbitrary and suggests the potential dangers awaiting those whose view of deity is determined to immerse godhead in the realm of the passible. Although Lactantius realized that it was easier to conceive deity as an entity totally removed from the possible turmoil and uncertainty that such an immersion might entail, his view of godhead was such that the removal of passibility was tantamount to the removal of divinity itself. Granting the questions that his approach was bound to provoke, Lactantius was fully committed to the notion of a passible God.

Needless to say, the views represented by Origen (in his later writings), Tertullian, and Lactantius proved to be the exception rather than the rule. Committed to the kind of outlook manifested in the philosophical schools, the early church adopted the impassibility of God as an established doctrine. In this respect, Saint Augustine is the consummate spokesman for the orthodox point of view.[16] In the expression of that point of view, he begins with the human perspective and moves to the divine. Arguing in *The City of God* that *pathos* implies "a commotion of the mind contrary to reason" (8.17), he concludes that passion, when uncontrolled and misdirected, is incompatible with blessedness.[17] "It is in the freedom from all disturbance, from all the weakness and defects which in human experience are associated with the various phases of the emotional life, that Augustine sees the divine impassibility."[18] Accordingly, he says, "that which the Greeks call *apatheia*, and what the Latins would call, if their language would allow them, '*impassibilitas*,' . . . is obviously a good and most desirable quality, but it is not one which is attainable in this life. When man shall be without sin, then shall he be able to realize full *apatheia*" (14.9; *City of God*, 454–55). It is precisely this *apatheia* that finds true expression in God. In keeping with those philosophical principles that subscribe to the idea of immutability, Saint Augustine argues that God remains impassible, that is, immutable, even when appearing to undergo *pathos*. Although pathos is ascribed to God, his impassibility is such that what we would call emotion in him is of a nature totally beyond our understanding. So Saint Augustine observes in his treatise *On Patience:*

> Patience is spoken of as belonging even to God. So though God can suffer nothing, while patience takes its name from suffering, nevertheless we not only faithfully believe, but also healthfully confess, that God is patient. But of what kind and how great the patience of God is who can explain, when we speak of Him as suffering nothing, yet not as without patience, but rather as most patient? His patience is therefore ineffable, even as His jealousy, His anger, and any other similar characteristics. For if we think of them as though they were ours, none such exists in Him. For none of them do we experience without vexation, but far be it from us to imagine that the impassible nature of God suffers any vexation. For as He is jealous without any envy, is angry without any perturbation, is pitiful

without any grief, repents without having any evil in Him to correct, so He is patient without any suffering.[19]

In effect, Saint Augustine has it both ways: God is essentially impassible, but appears to exhibit passibility in the most exalted and ineffable form. Whatever that passibility is (or at least appears to be) far transcends our power to know. One thing is certain, however: that which appears to us as passibility occurs without any perturbation in the mind of God or compromising of his divine *apatheia*. "God," says Saint Augustine, "does not repent as does a man, but as God; just as He is not angry after the manner of men, nor is pitiful, nor is jealous, but all He is He is as God." By the repentance of God is signified "the change of things which lie within His power, unexpected by man; the anger of God is His vengeance upon sin; the pity of God is the goodness of His help; the jealousy of God is that providence whereby He does not allow those whom He has in subjection to Himself to love with impunity what He forbids." In short, it is we who read pathos into God: we attribute to him those emotions that we experience as a result of the effects that his actions have upon us.[20]

As with Philo, Saint Augustine explains this act of "reading God" through the idea of accommodation. Unlike Philo, however, Saint Augustine does not view the accommodative dimension of Scriptures in a manner that is necessarily demeaning to the reader. The audience for God as accommodated deity encompasses a wide range of abilities but is essentially limited by one's incapacity to go beyond the boundaries of his own nature. Applying such attributes as anger and repentance to God, the Bible "familiarly insinuate[s] itself into the minds of all classes of men, whom it seeks access to for their good, that it may alarm the proud, arouse the careless, exercise the inquisitive, and satisfy the intelligent; and this it could not do, did it not first stoop, and in a manner descend to them where they lie" (*City of God,* 515). If Saint Augustine adopts the theory of accommodation, he does so not to suggest that what appears to be pathos in God really is so but to explain pathos as a literary manifestation of what might be called God's "figurative" presence in Scriptures.[21] In this regard, Saint Augustine's view of scriptural language as applied to notions of passibility is essentially rhetorical in nature. The Bible adopts metaphors for deity in order to allow the reader to understand what would otherwise be beyond human comprehension. The reader, in turn, is not to interpret these metaphors literally. To do so would be to violate the figurative dimension of the biblical text. When applied to the notion of passibility, reading God for Saint Augustine requires us to distinguish between the way God appears in the text and the way God really is. What appears to be true is so only insofar as it insinuates itself familiarly into the mind of the reader in order to promote his betterment, but it does not provide insight into the actual mind of God, which is finally unknowable. For Saint Augustine, that unknowability and the fact of God's impassibility are synonymous.[22]

If the kind of outlook that Saint Augustine embodied became the norm throughout the Middle Ages, an adherence to the essential impassibility of God was the standard of Renaissance thought on the subject as well.[23] Such is particularly true of Reformation theology. Those among the Reformation exegetes who considered the issue of God's personality generally remained committed to the idea of an impassible deity. Calvin represents a case in point. His allegiance to impassibility appears most fully delineated in his *Commentaries upon the Book of Genesis*.[24] Analyzing Genesis 6:6 ("And it repented the Lord that he had made man on the earth, and it grieved him at his heart"), Calvin maintains that "the repentance which is here ascribed to God does not properly belong to him, but has reference to our understanding of him. For since we cannot comprehend him as he is, it is necessary that, for our sake, he should, in a certain sense, transform himself." The same reasoning is applicable, Calvin observes, to the notion that God grieves. "Certainly," says Calvin, "God is not sorrowful or sad; but remains for ever like himself in his celestial and happy repose: yet, because it could not otherwise be known how great is God's hatred and detestation of sin, therefore the Spirit accommodates himself to our capacity." Calvin's observations are interesting for several reasons. They suggest that the ascription of emotion to God derives not from God as he really is but from human beings as they respond to the accommodated presence of deity in the Scriptures. As a being moved by passions of one sort or another, humans are prompted by that presence to read their own passibility into God, to create God, as it were, in their own image. This is entirely understandable, Calvin would argue, because human beings, as limited creatures, indeed, fallen and sinful creatures, cannot conceive of God in any other way. In order to read God, one must, in a sense, misread. As one does so, however, one must also be aware at every juncture that his or her reading is in fact a misreading. Aware of this misreading, one will know that God is not really passible but only appears to be so. Calvin is no doubt aware of this fact, for, just at the point of advancing the notion of divine *apatheia*, his analysis implicates itself in the very passibility it would dismiss. Arguing that God neither repents nor grieves, his analysis portrays God as a being who exhibits emotions such as hatred and detestation. How does one argue on behalf of *apatheia* and yet refer to God's "hatred and detestation of sin"? For Calvin, as for earlier exegetes, the answer lies in the transformative nature of God's act of accommodation. In Calvin's understanding of that act, God "clothes himself with our affections" in order to "pierce our hearts" more compellingly. This piercing of the heart has the effect of "subdu[ing] in us the love of sin." In accommodated form, God assumes a passible presence for the purpose of heightening our awareness of our own passibility. Such are the spiritual effects of accommodation.[25]

As Calvin was well aware, these effects are intimately bound up with literary dimensions that accommodation assumes in his thought. As a means by which a deity makes itself known, accommodation for Calvin is essentially a troping of God, a literary act, one in which the deity attires itself in the clothing of humanity. As such, accommodation is tantamount to figuration. In fact, Calvin refers to God's "clothing" of himself with humanity's affections as a trope, a figure distinguished by a particular name. "This figure," he says, "which represents God as transferring to himself what is peculiar to human nature, is called *anthropopatheia*." With this statement, Calvin places himself squarely in the tradition of those who read the fact of God's passible presence in Scriptures as a rhetorical event. Determined to reconcile scriptural representation with doctrinal imperative, such exegetes consign passibility to the realm of trope. They rhetoricize possibility in order to avoid compromising any notion of *apatheia*. As a result of this rhetoricizing, the impassible is clothed in passible form. Unlike those for whom the act of rhetoricizing represents a perfectly acceptable means of reconciling the fact of God's *apatheia* with his apparent passibility in Scriptures, Calvin approaches the whole notion of such a rhetoricizing with some trepidation.

His ambivalence is made clear in the *Institutes*. There, he argues that "every figurative representation of God contradicts his being." Among the prophets, Isaiah, for example, "teaches that God's majesty is sullied by an unfitting and absurd fiction, when the incorporeal is made to resemble corporeal matter, [and] the invisible a visible likeness" (*Institutes*, 1:100–101). Accordingly, any image that we conceive in our minds concerning God is "an insipid fiction" (*Institutes*, 1:103.). Nonetheless, humankind does not hesitate to imagine God according to their own conception and to express in various forms (notably in works of art) the sort of deity they have inwardly conceived (*Institutes*, 1:108). Calvin is not totally opposed to such representations. Works of art, he says, are "gifts of God." But works of art must have a pure and legitimate purpose, one fully aware of their own limitations, and even granting the potential usefulness of such works, Calvin still concludes that it is "wrong that God should be represented by a visible appearance, because he himself has forbidden it and it cannot be done without some defacing of his glory" (*Institutes*, 1:112.). No matter how God is portrayed, such portrayals are suspect. This, Calvin implies, is true even of scriptural representations. The fault here, however, lies not in God accommodating himself to human beings' limited capacities. Rather, it lies in our foolish inclination to assume that God's accommodated presence may be interpreted literally. Such, observes Calvin, was the fault of the Anthropomorphites, "who imagined a corporeal God from the fact that Scripture often ascribes to him [God] a mouth, ears, eyes, hands, and feet."[26] This, correspondingly, would be the fault of those who might believe in the passibility of God. In both respects, interpreters who literalize trope do not understand that, "as nurses commonly do with infants, God is wont in a measure to 'lisp' in speaking to us." "Such forms of speaking do not so much express clearly what God is like as accommodate the knowledge of him to our slight capacity. To do this, he must descend far beneath his loftiness" (*Institutes*, 1:120–21). We, in turn, must be on guard not to read literally what must be interpreted figuratively. To do otherwise would create false images of God, that is, misread without being aware that our misreading is precisely that, a belying of the true ineffability of godhead.[27] Then, we would interpret *anthropopatheia* as fact rather than as figure. We would rest content with the clothing of God's anthropopathetic presence rather than removing that clothing in order to perceive the truth of the impassibility that his clothing masks. As one fully committed to the concept of *apatheia*, Calvin looked upon himself as an interpreter determined to preserve the notion of God's impassibility at all costs.[28]

If Calvin fulfilled this ideal in his own work, his adherence to the concept of impassibility became a commonplace of

Reformation exegesis. In this respect, William Ames is representative. Addressing himself to the issue of "God and His Essence" in his *Medulla* (1.4), Ames makes clear his position on the subject of impassibility.[29] True to the title of his work as a "marrow" or *medulla*, the mode of expression that Ames adopts provides the quintessence of prevailing thought on the subject. Pithy and declarative, this mode of expression, we recall, assumes the form of *topoi* or theological commonplaces that by their very nature suggest the extent to which impassibility itself became a Reformation *topos* given to bald pronouncement.[30] Ames issues his pronouncements in the context of what he calls "the knowledge of God." "God, as he is in himself," declares Ames, "cannot be understood by any save himself." Those who do attempt to explain "the things which pertain to God" must do so in "a human way." This human way frequently assumes "a manner of speaking called *anthropopatheia*." Because the attribute of passibility implicit in *anthropopatheia* is accessible to "human comprehension," such an idea is applied to God "according to our own conceiving rather than according to his real nature." For the quality that is called "passive" is simply not in God. Indeed, "the affections attributed to God in scripture, such as love, hatred, and the like . . . apply to God only figuratively."[31] Once again, we are made aware of the way in which the idea of reading God represents an act of creating God. The reader as author projects his own image, that is, his own passible nature, onto what is inconceivable and uncreatable. Ames calls this the "human way" of reading God, one that speaks of deity according to its "own conceiving," rather than according to what really is. Here, as elsewhere, *anthropopatheia* becomes a troping of God, an understandable misreading, given human limitations, but a misreading nonetheless. For Ames, the concept of emotion as a divine attribute loses any real meaning: it is simply metaphor. The God of Ames remains distant and aloof in the blissfully untouched and untouchable realm of *apatheia*.

Nothing out of the ordinary here: the views embodied in Ames's *Marrow* simply reflect the acknowledged beliefs of the Church of England, institutionalized in the Thirty-Nine Articles and reiterated in the Westminster Confession: "There is but one only living and true God, who is infinite in being and perfection, a most pure spirit, invisible, without body, parts, or passions, immutable, immense, eternal, [and] incomprehensible."[32] As expressed here in institutional form, such a statement codifies the prevailing Reformation view regarding God's impassibility, a view shared not only by Ames but by a host of other theologians as well.[33]

II

The foregoing should suggest something of the milieu out of which Milton's own treatment of divine passibility emerged in *De Doctrina Christiana*. There, the subject receives full consideration. Because Milton's treatment, like that of Ames, falls under the larger heading of "knowing God" (*cognoscendo Deo*), this aspect requires renewed attention. In his discussion of knowing God, Milton argues that because God far transcends our limited powers of comprehension, it is impossible to speak of knowing him in any absolute sense. Despite these limitations, however, God makes a point of revealing as much of himself as the human mind can conceive and the weakness of one's nature can bear. God's principal mode of self-revelation is through the sacred writings (*in sacris literis*). To know God as he wishes himself to be known is to read him in Scriptures. It is there that God most fittingly "accommodates" himself to our capacities (ipse se ad captum accommodans nostrum). Encountering God as he has authorized his appearance in the sacred text, we, in turn, should "form such a mental image of Him [*mente nostra concipere*], as he, in bringing himself within the limits of our understanding, wishes us to form."[34] Attending in this manner to God's portrayal of himself in the scriptural text, we shall be spared the errors of those tempted to extend their reach beyond the "the written authority of scripture," only to find themselves lost in the "vague subtleties of speculation" (YP 6:133–34; CM 14:31–33).[35]

Immediately at issue is the nature of God's self-revelation. In Milton's thought, this phenomenon assumes a distinctly textual bearing. The sacred writings for Milton are the vehicle through which God authorizes his own presence.[36] To use the language of *Paradise Lost*, one might say that in the Bible, God becomes "author to himself" (see 3.122). Acting in his capacity as author, God appropriates the Bible as the text in which his accommodated presence is to be most fully and effectively understood. At the heart of Milton's hermeneutics is this all-important emphasis upon intentionality. Reading the Scriptures becomes for Milton an exercise in the discovery of God's intentions, of forming a mental image of him corresponding to that which he, in bringing himself within the limits of our understanding, desires us to form. Responsive to God's authorized presence, Milton adopts a hermeneutics of intentionality.[37] A misunderstanding of intentions can become a particularly risky enterprise because, as a sacred text, the Bible deals in matters of belief. To read God is in effect a religious act: one must be careful to avoid the perils of misinterpretation. Although Milton was well aware that these perils were compounded by the questionable state in which the sacred writings were preserved, he nonetheless believed that between the writings as they had been transmitted to his own times and the Holy Spirit as a guide to God's intentions, the reader had sufficient warrant to know that God revealed himself in his own writings, in that text of which he himself was supreme author.[38] For Milton, this fact bestowed upon the text a primacy that refused to allow its message to be compromised by "vague subtleties of speculation." Responding as we should to what Scripture actually says, that is, to what it has been authorized to proclaim, we should behold Scripture "protesting [its] own plainnes, and perspicuity" in all matters essential to be known and especially that concerning God's portrayal of himself in his own text.[39]

This view of Scriptures is fundamental to Milton's treatment of *anthropopatheia* in *De Doctrina Christiana*. There, Milton appears initially to dismiss the notion of divine passibility, only afterward to reintroduce it in another form. He dismisses it as a trope through which theologians presume to come to terms with God's unknowableness, and he reintroduces it as a fact through which God's unknowableness is manifested in accommodated form to one's limited capacities. This paradoxical maneuver is one that does away with the rhetorical dimensions of passibility while preserving its substantive dimensions. Having argued for the self-sufficiency of the biblical text as a means of knowing God, Milton accordingly ventures the following observation:

> In my opinion, then, theologians do not need to employ anthropopathy, or the ascription of human feelings to God. This is a rhetorical device thought up by grammarians [quam figuram Grammatici] to explain the nonsense poets write about Jove. Sufficient care has been taken, without any doubt, to ensure that the holy scriptures contain nothing unfitting to God or unworthy of him. . . . So it is better not to think about God or form an image of him in anthropopathetic terms, for to do so would be to follow the example of men, who are always inventing more and more subtle theories about him. Rather we should form our ideas with scripture as a model, for that is the way in which he has offered himself to our contemplation. We ought not to imagine that God would have said anything or caused anything to be written about himself unless he intended that it should be a part of our conception of him. (YP 6.134; CM 14.32)

The observation is unequivocal in its expression of Milton's argument on behalf of scriptural self-sufficiency. Responding to the biblical text, the reader need not "invent" God through the attribution of characteristics that are nothing more than a rhetoricizing of God's presence. To do so is tantamount to making of him a pagan deity whose actions are comparable to those one finds indecorously portrayed not only in myths of various sorts but implicitly in the traditions of exegesis dating back to the early church and extending into his own times.[40] Countering those traditions, Milton endorses a theory of reading that refuses to secularize the sacred writings. This is what he feels happens in any attempt to explain God through the use of *anthropopatheia* conceived in rhetorical terms, that is, as a trope by which what is otherwise inexplicable is domesticated, brought down to the human level. So conceived, *anthropopatheia* explains away, rather than explains, and the reader as *rhetor* creates God in the image of human beings. God becomes an *imago hominis*, rather than humans an *imago Dei*. Avoiding this trap, Milton advises against following the example of exegetes who are always inventing more and more subtle theories about God; rather, he advocates following the example of God, through whom appropriate care has been taken to ensure that the text of the Bible is a sufficient vehicle for the revelation of God's will. When meaning flows from author (God) to reader (humans) and not the other way around, *anthropopatheia* as a rhetorical device is obviated.

Given this theory of reading, what then does Milton say about the passibility or impassibility of God? The immediate assumption might well be that in his dismissal of *anthropopatheia* Milton calls passibility itself into question. Precisely the opposite is true. Having done away with *anthropopatheia*, he not only intensifies the idea of passibility but bestows upon it renewed significance. For lack of a better term, this new form of passibility might be called *theopatheia*, as opposed to *anthropopatheia*. Milton generates the concept of *theopatheia* through a reassertion of the divine intentionality that underscores his theory of reading. "On the question of what is or what is not suitable for God," Milton observes, "let us ask for no more dependable authority [*auctorem*] than God himself." This appeal to the author to come forth and speak on his own behalf leads Milton to invoke an entire series of instances in which the passibility of God is authorized in the biblical text. "If *Jehovah repented that he had created man, Gen. vi. 6, and repented because of their groanings,* Judges ii. 18, let us," Milton says, "believe [*credamus*] that he did repent." "If *he grieved in his heart* Gen. vi. 6, and if, similarly, *his soul was grieved,* Judges x. 16, let us believe [*credamus*] that he did feel grief."

> If it is said that God, after working for six days, *rested and was refreshed,* Exod. xxxi. 17, and if he *feared his enemy's displeasure,* Deut. xxxii. 27, let us believe [*credamus*] that it is not beneath God to feel what grief he does feel, to be refreshed by what refreshes him, and to fear what he does fear. For however you may try to tone down [*lenire*] these and similar texts about God by an elaborate show of interpretive glosses [*interpretationis ambitus*], it comes to the same thing in the end. (YP 6:134–35; CM 14:33–37)

In this recitation of proof-texts that establish the validity of *theopatheia*, Milton emphasizes time and again both the primacy of the text as the vehicle of intentionality and the function of the Creator in authorizing his presence in that text. Reading is believing: "let us believe [*credamus*]," Milton reiterates throughout. *Credamus:* let us believe, no matter how disturbing we may find the notion that deity by its very nature experiences such emotions as repentance, grief, and fear.[41]

To allay any doubts about the nature of the emotions that God experiences, Milton makes it perfectly clear that they are of a different order from those experienced by human beings. In the case of repentance, for example, Milton says, "let us not imagine that God's repentance arises from lack of foresight, as man's does" (YP 6:134–35). Although Milton does not elaborate further on the issue of precisely in what manner God repents or feels any other emotion he is said to undergo in the biblical text, it is quite evident from what Milton does say that his theology is founded upon a divinization of the passible. Reflecting an outlook made evident in exegetes as early as Tertullian, this divinization accords the passible a legitimacy, indeed, a sanctity, as compelling as any of the other attributes customarily associated with God.[42] So Milton observes that, "those states of mind [*affectus*] which are good in a good man, and count as virtues are holy in God" (YP 6:135; CM 14:34). With this statement, Milton reclaims the passible as a phenomenon that proved disturbing from the very point at which the early church sought to come to terms with the personality of God. Relying on the authority of the biblical text as an index to that personality, Milton dismisses the kind of latitudinarian approach that seeks to tone down (*lenire*) and make palatable the passible dimension of God's character. As a rhetorical fabrication of the exegetes given to such latitudinarianism, *anthropopatheia* will therefore not suffice for Milton. Only *theopatheia,* as that which implies the true emotional life of God, will do.

If such is the case, Milton's advocacy of *theopatheia* raises corresponding issues as well. Despite the fact that the divine nature by definition cannot be known or defined in any absolute sense, Milton does not hesitate to concern himself with the states of God's mind, that is, with the psychogenesis of the passible in the *animus Dei.* Recalling once again those early church fathers who took the Scriptures at their word, Milton combines the psychogenetic approach with one that takes into account not just the mind of God (what Milton would call the "internal form") but the body of God (what Milton would call the "external form") as well.[43] Associating these two, Milton maintains that "if *God is said to have created man in his own image, after his own likeness,* Gen. 1.26, and not only his mind but also his external appearance [*idque non animo solum sed forma etiam externa*]," and "if God attributes to himself again and again a human shape and form, why should we be afraid of assigning to him something he assigns to himself, provided we believe that what is imperfect and weak in us is, when ascribed to God, utterly perfect and utterly beautiful." Both in mind and in body, then, God's accommodated presence as revealed in the biblical text is one in which deity is conceived as a being who not only experiences a full range of emotions but who is portrayed in a manner that corresponds to the shape and form of man as *imago Dei*.[44] Perfecting the image of God in himself, man becomes a fit reader of the biblical text when he is sensitized to the way in which God as creator of that image accommodates himself to man's understanding. "Let there be no question about it," Milton says; "they understand best what God is like who adjust their understanding to the word of God, for he has adjusted his word to our understanding, and has shown what kind of an idea of him he wishes us to have." This is as much a hermeneutics of reciprocity as it is a hermeneutics of intentionality. As God accommodates himself to man, man adjusts himself to God. The author reaches down; the reader reaches up. The author's intentions are validated in and through the text; the reader's understanding is revealed in its ability to grasp those intentions. Reading is sharing as well as believing. If we refuse to share, that is, if we arrogate meaning to ourselves, we break that hermeneutical circle so fundamental to the concept of reciprocity that Milton endorses. We cannot presume to impose our will upon the text, to create the text. In doing so, we not only violate our role as readers, we misconceive God, who, Milton insists, "has disclosed just such an idea of himself to our understanding as he wishes us to possess." "If we form some other idea of him," Milton concludes, "we are not acting according to his will, but are frustrating him of his purpose, as if, indeed, we wished to show that our concept of God was not too debased, but that his concept of us was" (YP 6:135–36; CM 14:37–39). The assumptions are clear enough: as the embodiment of the *imago Dei*, we should not assume that God debases himself in appearing to be like us; rather, we should ennoble ourselves in attempting to be like him. We should understand God the way he understands us. Only by fulfilling the dynamics implicit in this hermeneutical circle will we do justice to the text in which God's self-disclosure occurs.

Because of Milton's refusal to rhetoricize (and thereby secularize) God's presence in the biblical text, then, accommodation for him is an ennobling experience, not a demeaning one, as it was, say, for Philo, who admonished that foolish rabble incapable of moving beyond the world of trope. Dismissing that world as inapplicable to the real nature of God's accommodated delineation, Milton endorses a hermeneutics of passibility (and therefore a theory of reading) that aligns him with such exegetes as Tertullian and Lactantius (as well as the later Origen), through whom the passible was divinized and Scripture taken at its word. Recalling these figures — and, in fact, going beyond them in extending the range of emotions attributable to God — Milton broke not only with the orthodox traditions of the early church but with the reformed dogmatics of his own time. Doing so, he provoked the kind of critical debate to which *De Doctrina Christiana* was customarily subjected after its publication in 1825.

In this respect, a review that appeared in the *Evangelical Magazine* in 1826 is representative.[45] According to the author of the review, Milton's attribution of divine emotions to God in *De Doctrina Christiana* is nothing more than "a striking example of the power of poetical feeling overbalancing the dictates of a cool and rigorous judgment." In other words, by succumbing to the temptation of divine passibility, Milton for this reviewer abandons the rigors of true theology and writes as a poet. Having argued that those who subscribe to the anthropopathetic view of deity are themselves guilty of a kind of poetical excess, Milton would no doubt find the reviewer's charge somewhat perplexing. Milton would argue that the reviewer, not he, has been taken in by the impulse to abandon the rigors of theology and to align himself with those exegetes that rhetoricize and thereby secularize Scriptures. In fact, this is precisely what the reviewer does in his criticism of Milton. From those biblical passages (notably in the earlier books of the Old Testament) in which "the mutable affections of the human mind, and even the form and members of the human body, are *figuratively* applied to the Infinite Being," Milton, the reviewer charges, would have us conceive God "according to the *literal* meaning of those expressions" (my italics). Such a criticism, of course, makes no allowances for the distinctions Milton draws between human passibility and divine passibility. For the reviewer, both are the same. Collapsing the distinction between human and divine, the reviewer then presumes to reveal the shortcomings of the Miltonic point of view:

> If the Deity be in reality susceptible of disappointment, grief, regret, change of purpose, the relinquishing of old plans upon an unwelcome discovery of their failure, and the setting to work of new ones, with the hope of better success; — it is impossible to avoid the inference that he is a being limited in both knowledge and power, ignorant of many things which are of the first importance that he should know, embarrassed in his views, thwarted, perplexed, and defeated by unexpected circumstances, and, in fine, a being unutterably distressed and unhappy.[46]

Although Milton would hardly have acceded to these charges as in any sense applicable to his notion of deity, the reviewer's concern over the potential dangers that lie in wait for those who endorse the concept of passibility is one of which Milton would have been very much aware in his own reading on the subject. Milton knew that in an imperfect form passibility led to all those shortcomings that distinguish human nature from the divine. Despite his awareness of these shortcomings and the concerns that they provoked, Milton was determined not to compromise his view of deity by underestimating the significance of the passible as authorized by God himself in Scriptures. If such is true of Milton's treatment of deity in his theological tract, it is no less true of his handling of deity in his poetry. Both as theologian and as poet, Milton is consistent in his incorporation of the passible into his delineation of godhead. Among his poems, *Paradise Lost* in particular provides dramatic evidence of this fact.

III

The figure of God in *Paradise Lost* is portrayed as a fully passible being in whom is embodied an entire spectrum of emotions. Although these assertions would appear to be self-evident, the God of *Paradise Lost* continues to be viewed more nearly as abstract principle than as fully realized character.[47] In the very essay that Irene Samuel argues on behalf of a dramatic reading of God, she maintains that he is essentially "Total Being," "Primal Energy," the "Voice of Reason." As an embodiment of "the toneless voice of the moral law," Milton's God "speaks simply what is."[48] For Roland M. Frye, Milton's God is "pure intellect, pure reason, unmixed with passion."[49] Such an outlook is the rule rather than the exception. What makes this outlook so interesting is the extent to which it reflects the antipassible point of view that became the theological norm from the period of the early church up until Milton's own time. The critics of *Paradise Lost* have adopted the role of those earlier exegetes who insisted upon reading the portrayal of God in the scriptural text as the embodiment of *apatheia*. When Milton took this view to task in *De Doctrina Christiana*, it is almost as if he were responding to the future critics of his own poem.

In modern criticism, one of the most influential and brilliant spokesmen for the antipassible point of view has been Stanley Fish. Adopting the perspective of those who argue on behalf of *apatheia*, Fish conceives God as a being totally removed and fully aloof, an abstraction void of dimensionality. Whatever tonal qualities one discovers in God's voice are the result not of what is there but of what the reader ascribes to or "reads *into*" that voice. The entity that projects this voice is, in turn, devoid of both ethos, the quality that constitutes personality, and pathos, the quality that constitutes the emotional substratum of personality. These qualities emerge as the result of the meaning that arises from the reader's encounter with deity: they are bestowed by the reader onto deity rather than inhering in deity itself.[50] Responding to Milton's God in this manner, Fish explains the presence of the passible by transferring emotion from God as portrayed in the text to the reader as he interprets the tonalities that appear in the voice of God. Such a transferral of the passible from text to reader corresponds, in effect, to that which occurs among the theologians who invoke the device of *anthropopatheia* to explain God's apparent passibility in the Bible. Reading the passible into God, the reader, for Fish, in effect creates God in his own image. In Fish as in those theologians committed to an anthropopathetic notion of deity, God becomes an *imago hominis* rather than man an *imago Dei*.[51] As a result of this occurrence, all concepts of the passible in Fish are rhetoricized, "toned down," to use Milton's phrase, and made palatable.

As we have seen, such a view is precisely the opposite of that which Milton held as a theologian who sought to reclaim the passible as a category of deity. Legitimating the passible, Milton divinizes the emotional life by viewing it as an essential attribute of God. Doing so, Milton refuses to rhetoricize God as the product of an anthropopathetic world view. He will not consign the passible to the realm of trope. For Milton, the emotional life of God is real and indeed holy. It originates in God, inheres in him, and is bestowed upon his offspring as manifestations of the *imago Dei*. From this theological perspective, Milton might well have responded to the anthropopathetic trend in modern criticism in terms reminiscent of his answer to the anthropopatheticists in *De Doctrina Christiana:* "In my opinion, critics do not need to employ anthropopathy, or the ascription of human feelings to God. This is nothing more than a rhetorical device thought up by grammarians to explain the nonsense poets write about Jove" (YP 6:134).

Invoking (in somewhat altered form) his statement in *De Doctrina Christiana* and applying it to the modern critics, he would then have effectively divorced himself not only from the prevailing anthropopathetic reading of God in Scriptures but from the current anthropopathetic reading of God in *Paradise Lost*. In the process, he would have distinguished his exalted conception of God in his poem from the "nonsense" the pagan poets write about Jove in theirs. Aligning his poem with the sacred writings, he would have suggested the kind of hermeneutics most appropriate for his poem, a hermeneutics consistent with that which was to be applied to the Scriptures. What Milton says in *De Doctrina Christiana* about the act of reading God as rendered in Scriptures might then be accordingly applied to the act of reading God as rendered in *Paradise Lost:* "It is better not to think about God or form an image of him in anthropopathetic terms, for to do so would be to follow the example of men, who are always inventing more and more subtle theories about him." Rather, we should rely on the way in which God is actually depicted in Milton's poem, for (to adapt Milton's statement to our present purposes) "sufficient care has been taken without any doubt, to ensure that *Paradise Lost* contains nothing unfitting to God or unworthy of him." We should thereby read the God of Milton's epic theopathetically rather than anthropopathetically.[52] If Milton's God is said to be angry, we shall grant him that anger; if he is said to hate, we shall grant him that hatred; if he appears to be compassionate, we shall grant him that compassion; if he appears to be jocular, we shall grant him that jocularity.[53] "For however you may try to tone down these and similar texts about God by an elaborate show of interpretive glosses, it comes to the same thing in the end." What is true of Milton's view of Scriptures is true of the view he holds of his own poem: the text protests its self-sufficiency, indeed, its primacy as the vehicle of intentionality. *Credamus:* reading is believing.

Granting the alignment that Milton makes between Scriptures, on the one hand, and *Paradise Lost,* on the other, a major dilemma nonetheless presents itself in any attempt to derhetoricize the Miltonic portrayal of deity in his epic. That dilemma has to do with the accommodative assumptions on which the Miltonic portrayal is based. In keeping with the discussion that falls under the heading of *"cognoscendo Deo"* in *De Doctrina Christiana,* Milton argues that because God far transcends man's limited powers of comprehension, it is impossible to speak of knowing him in any absolute sense. Accordingly, God reveals as much of himself as the mind of man can conceive and the weakness of his nature can bear. God's principal mode of self-revelation is through the Scriptures, where he most fittingly accommodates himself to our capacities. Encountering God as he has authorized his appearance in Scriptures, we, in turn, should "form such a mental image of him, as he, in bringing himself within the limits of our understanding, wishes us to form." Given such an outlook, it is one thing to argue for an authorized representation of deity on the basis of scriptural self-sufficiency; it is quite another to make the same claim on the basis of poetic reenactment. Milton's epic, after all, is not the Bible, nor can it be said that God authorizes his presence in *Paradise Lost* in the same manner that he does in Scriptures. Milton may dismiss as nonsense what the poets write about Jove, but he was well aware that in presuming to accommodate the transcendent and unknowable to the limited capacities of his fellow mortals, he was treading on dangerous ground, risking the possible "ruin" of "sacred Truths to Fable and old Song."[54] The question remains, then, in what manner the accommodative formulation of deity is to be understood in Milton's epic, and by what authority Milton as a poet presumes to undertake such a formulation. The answer to this question should help to clarify the way in

which the God of *Paradise Lost* is to be conceived in general
and how the theopathetic dimensions of that presence are to
be understood in particular.

Milton himself might be said to provide an answer to this
question in the angelic hymn of celebration that culminates
the celestial council scene in book 3 of *Paradise Lost*. There,
the angelic hosts, accompanied by the music of their harps,
sing a "sacred song" in praise of Father and Son (3.372–415).
The song is executed in such a way as to suggest not only
the theopathetic bearing of God's nature but the means by
which his presence is made known in accommodated form.
The first part of the song (3372–82) celebrates the Father
through a recapitulation of attributes that Milton ascribed to
godhead in *De Doctrina Christiana*. As an entity that defies
all attempts at conceptualization, godhead is celebrated in the
following terms:

> Thee Father first they sung Omnipotent,
> Immutable, Immortal, Infinite,
> Eternal King; thee Author of all being,
> Fountain of Light, thy self invisible
> Amidst the glorious brightness where thou sit'st
> Thron'd inaccessible.   (3.372–77)

The attributes of immutability, immortality, and infinity
totally remove deity from any possibility of conceptualization.
By means of these attributes, the "self" of God is made invisible to any that would attempt to discern it. Enveloped in
brightness, deity overwhelms any inclined to comprehend its
meaning. The language underscores this failure of comprehension through a kind of *via negativa* that at once conceives
deity metaphorically in the vein of the Pseudo-Dionysius and
is made to confront the fact of its own incapacity to do so:

> but when thou shad'st
> The full blaze of thy beams, and through a cloud
> Drawn round about thee like a radiant Shrine,

Dark with excessive bright thy skirts appeer,
Yet dazle Heav'n, that brightest Seraphim,
Approach not, but with both wings veil thir eyes.   (3.377–82)

So totally "inaccessible" is deity, the angels proclaim, that even
when it shades the full blaze of its beams, the brightest seraphim
dare not approach, but veil their eyes with both wings (compare Isa. 6:1–6; Rev. 4:1–8). Enshrined in its own unknowability,
deity blinds with its brilliance: it is "Dark with excessive
bright." At the very point that the language denies accessibility,
however, it invites conceptualization. Deity may be "Thron'd
inaccessible," but it is also the "Author of all being" and the
"Fountain of Light." As such, it is the generative source of all
that it bestows upon those who are the beneficiaries of its illumination. Bestowing this illumination upon those it engenders, deity embodies itself in all those who seek to know it and
understand it, in all those, that is, who are the recipients of
the *imago Dei*. In the dissemination of this *imago*, the unknowable is at once the source of all life and the source of all knowledge. Within the accommodative context of Milton's poem, we
might say that that which is the author of all being is also the
author of all meaning: the two are synonymous.

The most fully discernible form they assume in the manifestation of their presence is that of the Son. So the angelic hosts
next celebrate the first "of all Creation":

Begotten Son, Divine Similitude,
In whose conspicuous count'nance, without cloud
Made visible, th'Almighty Father shines,
Whom else no Creature can behold; on thee
Impresst th' effulgence of his Glorie abides,
Transfus'd on thee his ample Spirit rests.   (3.383–89)

As the visible manifestation of God's embodying of himself in
discernible form, the Son represents the way in which deity
as the author of all being is also the author of all meaning.
Implicit in the Son's presence is that categorical imperative by

which the Father authorizes himself in the text. In the self-consciously literary (as well as theological) terms that the language adopts, the Son accordingly becomes a "Divine Similitude." If this is in any sense a troping of God, it is a form of troping that calls upon the *topoi* of rhetoric in order to suggest the inability of the rhetorical to sustain the weight of what the Son truly signifies. The Son is not simply metaphor (similitude). Or if he is metaphor, he represents an entirely different order of troping from that customarily associated with rhetoric as secular enterprise. To use the language of Milton's God, he is "My word, my wisdom, and effectual might" (3.169–70). He is the logos of God, the word of God's text and the text of God's word.[55] In him as in a text is "impresst" or engraven the effulgence of God's glory. In his countenance is made "conspicuous" (from *specere*, "to look at" or "behold") the Almighty Father as visible entity, "Whom else no Creature can behold." On the Son is transfused the spirit of God, that which moves the Son to enact the Father's will. So the Father at another point celebrates his Son as the "Effulgence of my Glorie, Son belov'd, / Son in whose face invisible is beheld / Visibly, what by Deitie I am / And in whose hand what by Decree I doe" (6.680–83). This "whatness," this "being-ness," is that which the Son manifests both in his appearance and in his actions. In him is embodied all that is otherwise unknowable in God. If such is true of God's essential ineffability, it is especially true of his passible nature. In this respect, the Son is a primary vehicle for the expression of *theopatheia*.

Embodied in the figure of the Son, this theopathetic dimension constitutes the primary focus of the remainder of the angelic song (3.390–410). In the expression of *theopatheia*, the Son becomes the means by which the Father's vengeance, on the one hand, and his mercy, on the other, are manifested. As the product of indignation and wrath, the Father's vengeance is that to which the angels first allude. So they recall the way in which the Son "threw down / Th'aspiring Dominations":

"thou that day / Thy Fathers dreadful Thunder didst not spare, / Nor stop thy flaming Chariot wheels" (3.391–94). In the execution of the Father's vengeance, the Son declares to his Father: "whom thou hat'st, I hate, and can put on / Thy terrors, as I put thy mildness on, / Image of thee in all things," after which his countenance changes into terror as he goes forth in his chariot of vengeance to overwhelm the rebel angels (6.734–36, 825–27). Doing so, he is, in the words of the angels, "Son of thy Fathers might, / To execute fierce vengeance on his foes" (3.398–99). All that the Father experiences in the form of indignation and wrath is transfused into the Son as the veritable embodiment of divine passibility, the vehicle of *theopatheia*.

What is true of the Father's indignation and wrath in the celestial battle is correspondingly true of his pity in the celestial council. Here, God becomes "Father of Mercie and Grace," one moved by "pitie." It is in response to this expression of *theopatheia* that the Son adopts his sacrificial role. Thus, the angels sing:

> No sooner did thy dear and onely Son
> Perceive thee purpos'd not to doom frail Man
> So strictly, but much more to pitie enclin'd,
> He to appease thy wrauth, and end the strife
> Of Mercy and Justice in thy face discern'd,
> Regardless of the Bliss wherein hee sat
> Second to thee, offerd himself to die
> For mans offence. O unexampl'd love,
> Love no where to be found less then Divine.   (3.403–11)

The lines are immensely illuminating for what they tell us about Milton's version of the theopathetic process. That process begins with the perception of God's motives (that which "moves" God) as revealed in a genuine conflict, indeed, an actual "strife" that the Son beholds occurring on the face of his Father. Like those who "read" God in Scriptures, the Son reads his Father in the text of his "beingness." Although the Son is the only one who can read his Father in this manner, the angels acknowledge in their song that such a reading has occurred. The fact of its occurrence attests both to the primacy of *theopatheia* as a phenomenon for Milton that actually transpires in godhead and to the incorporation of that phenomenon as an event in Milton's epic. That event ultimately leads the Son to offer himself as a sacrifice for man: "O unexampl'd love, / Love no where to be found less then Divine." This is the ultimate demonstration of pathos, one that eventuates in what Milton himself calls a *Christus patiens*,[56] through which mankind is redeemed and as a result of which the Son, along with those who are saved, will return after long absence to see God's face, "wherein no cloud / Of anger shall remain, but peace assur'd, / And reconcilement." Then, "wrauth shall be no more" but in God's presence only "Joy entire" (3.261–65). In this manner, then, the theopathetic dimensions of the Father are consummated in the Son. As a being who experiences indignation and wrath, on the one hand, and pity, on the other, the Father is one in whom the passible is divinized: he is the source of emotion at its most perfect, indeed, at its most sacred. Both in his theological writings and in his poetry, Milton did not hesitate to urge this belief home in the most compelling manner.

Because of its emphasis upon the Son of God as the embodiment of the passible in its sublimest form, *Paradise Lost* is a testament to the importance that the Son assumes in Milton's epic. The fact of this importance is sounded in the final lines of the angelic hymn:

> Hail Son of God, Saviour of Men, thy Name
> Shall be the copious matter of my Song
> Henceforth, and never shall my Harp thy praise
> Forget, nor from thy Fathers praise disjoin.   (3.412–15)

These lines are significant not only because they attest to the centrality of the Son to Milton's poetic enterprise but because

they suggest the function that the poet himself assumes in the
act of celebrating both Father and Son as the source of poetic
enactment. In both respects, one discovers a renewed emphasis on the nature of identity. To praise the Son, to make him
the copious matter of one's song, is to praise the Father. The
quatrainal coda to the angelic song of praise represents a reunit-
ing of identities "disjoined" momentarily for the purpose of
suggesting how the ineffability of the divine nature finds
expression in — indeed, is embodied in — that word, that
name, through which it makes itself known in the transmission of its unknowableness. Beyond this, the quatrainal coda
represents the establishment of a new identity in the sudden
shift from the third person references to the angelic hosts
("they sung") to the first person reference to the poet himself
("my Song"). The shift is quite remarkable, but also very
significant. What it signifies is not just a joining of one's voice
unto the "angel quire" or a uniting of one's voice with the "celestial consort," although, of course, such a joining or uniting is
certainly implied. In the shift from third person to first person, the poet goes further than this. His solemn music is one
in which the poet in effect appropriates the "sacred song" of
the angelic doxology and makes it distinctly his own ("my
Song"). All that occurs within the song of praise to which this
quatrain is a coda provides the occasion by which the poet is
textualized as a real presence within his own poem. His voice
is literally that of the angels. Their song is his poem; their identity one with his. What they know, he knows; what is communicated to them on this sacred occasion is communicated
to him. This means that the poet no longer stands on the outside as he writes a poem about what transpired in the celestial realms. Having appropriated to himself both the voice and
identity of the angelic hosts that surround the thrones of God
and the Son, the poet places himself in the profoundly unique
position of offering his poem as the vehicle through which
the voice of God is able to speak. By means of the poet, the

accommodative presence of deity as it is transmitted from Father to Son is able to be made known. Replicating in large what the angelic doxology enacts in small, the poet is thereby authorized to delineate "what surmounts the reach / Of human sense" in a manner that permits the unknowable to manifest itself in poetic form.[57]

Paradise Lost is not the Bible, and Milton's God does not possess the same authorized presence as he does in the Bible. As far as Milton is concerned, however, his poem is the most authoritative reenactment of what happens in the Bible as one can possibly imagine. In the process of that reenactment, the passibility of God is accorded a new and distinctly compelling status, one in which a sublimely feeling, indeed, passionate deity becomes the focal point of all the creative energies that Milton's poem is able to marshal.[58] Bestowing upon the theopathetic a renewed legitimacy, *Paradise Lost* thereby represents Milton's poetic response to the theological traditions through which the ongoing debates over the passibility of God assumed paramount importance both in the early church and in his own times. As they are addressed in Milton's theological tract, on the one hand, and in his epic, on the other, these debates provide Milton the occasion to demonstrate the way in which one should go about "reading God" as a fully passible being.

FIVE

The *Odium Dei*

I

In an illuminating analysis of *Paradise Lost*, John T. Shawcross formulates what he feels to be the thematic basis of Milton's epic. The most crucial theme, Shawcross asserts, is love. "We see it in the providence of God which the poem asserts, in the love of the Son for God the Father and thus for man, and in the realization of Adam in Book 12, which thus justifies God's ways. By contrast, we see the hate of Satan and its generation of revolt, revenge, and deceit. Love leads to eternal life; hate, to eternal death."[1] As a succinct and cogent statement of the theme of Milton's epic, the foregoing observation has the support of Milton's God, who declares that "Heav'nly love shall outdo Hellish hate, / Giving to death, and dying to redeem, / So dearly to redeem what Hellish hate / So easily destroy'd" (3.298–301). At the very thematic center of *Paradise Lost*, then, one discovers that all-important triumph of "Heav'nly love" over "Hellish hate." In its assertion of eternal providence, Milton's epic represents a veritable celebration of that triumph.

Despite the paradigmatic sense through which the theme of *Paradise Lost* is articulated in the triumphant assertion of God's love over Satan's hate, one must nevertheless come to grips with a crucial aspect of Milton's epic — the *odium Dei*. This phenomenon finds its fullest expression in the Son's statement to the Father just before the Son ascends "The Chariot of Paternal Deitie" to overwhelm the rebel angels in book 6 of *Paradise Lost*. Responding to his Father's directive to "Pursue these sons of Darkness, drive them out / From all Heav'ns bounds into the utter Deep" (715–16), the Son says, "whom thou hat'st, I hate, and can put on / Thy terrors, as I put thy mildness on, / Image of thee in all things" (734–36). As this response suggests, it is not only through an encounter with Satan that Adam and Eve come to discover "things to thir thought / So unimaginable as hate in Heav'n" (7.53–54). One must likewise acknowledge that this discovery includes an encounter with a Being who is customarily looked upon as the God of love. If hatred is the characteristic hallmark of absolute evil and love the characteristic hallmark of absolute good, this fact must not overlook the very real presence in *Paradise Lost* of a God who hates. As "unimaginable" as this might appear to be, the nature of the *odium Dei* must be taken into account if the theme of Milton's epic is to be fully understood.

Any attempt to assess the nature of the *odium Dei* in *Paradise Lost* is, of course, not without its dangers. C. S. Lewis long ago attempted to controvert a view still current that, in his portrayal of God, Milton has given us "a cold, merciless, [and] tyrannical Deity." Though eloquent and eminently quotable, Lewis's response to this view has never proven satisfactory: "Many of those who say they dislike Milton's God only mean that they dislike God: infinite sovereignty *de jure*, combined with infinite power *de facto*, and love which by its very nature, includes wrath also — it is not only in poetry that these things offend."[2] The idea that love should include wrath is one thing: anyone will acknowledge the possibility that a

God of love might on occasion become a God of wrath in reaction to the behavior (or misbehavior) of his creations. Although perhaps unsettling, the idea of a God of wrath, in short, is at least finally arguable.

As a biblical concept, in fact, the idea is to be found everywhere, especially in connection with the idea of love. In the Old Testament, God is actually seen to engage in a kind of self-struggle between love and wrath as the result of feeling himself betrayed. So Isaiah 54:6–8: "For the Lord hath called thee as a woman forsaken and grieved in spirit, and a wife of youth, when thou wast refused, saith thy God. For a small moment have I forsaken thee; but with great mercies will I gather thee. In a little wrath I hid my face from thee for a moment; but with everlasting kindness will I have mercy on thee, saith the Lord thy Redeemer." In the New Testament, "wrath is an essential and inalienable trait" in the depiction of God. "When it is realised, as everywhere in the New Testament, that it is a fearful thing to fall into the hands of the living God (Heb. 10:31), that He has power to save and to destroy (James 4:12), and when He is feared because, beyond the death of the body, He has power to destroy both body and soul in hell (Luke 12:5; Matt. 10:28), awareness of God's wrath is at the root."[3] As with the Old Testament, so with the New: love and wrath are mutually inclusive in God: "The wrath of God arises from His love and mercy." So Romans 9:22–25: "*What* if God, willing to shew *his* wrath, and to make his power known, endured with much longsuffering the vessels of wrath fitted to destruction: and that he might make known the riches of his glory on the vessels of mercy, even us whom he hath called? . . . As he saith also in O'see, I will call them my people, which were not my people; and her beloved which was not beloved."[4]

C. S. Lewis is correct: love by its very nature includes wrath. Commonplace as a biblical notion, the association of love and wrath is almost inevitable in a poem that celebrates the overcoming of wrath by grace. So Adam rejoices that, as the result of God's love and as an expression of his mercy in the willing sacrifice of his Son, "much more good thereof shall spring, / To God more glory, more good will to Men / From God, and over wrauth grace shall abound" (12.476–78). Given the nature of the theodicy that Milton's epic embraces, the association of a God of love with a God of wrath is quite understandable, if not, in fact, inevitable. But in what respect does that theodicy envision a God of hate? How is one to reconcile the notion of a God who is putatively the very embodiment of love, who is, in fact, very love itself (compare 1 John 4:8), with that of a God who comes to embody those qualities that are by definition not only the opposite of love but characteristically associated with one whose "Hellish hate" "Heave'nly love" shall ultimately overcome? How is one to reconcile a God of love with a God of hate?

Such is the unspoken assumption of all those who are inclined to maintain, despite attempts to the contrary, that Milton's God is "a cold, merciless, . . . [and] tyrannical Deity," to quote C. S. Lewis once again. To add "hate" to this onslaught of epithets appears merely to reaffirm what the detractors of Milton's God have always thought to be the case. Doing so, in fact, plays directly into the hands of critics like William Empson, for whom the whole notion of deity (and, in particular, the Christian Deity) is suspect at best. In his discussion of Christianity in *Milton's God*, Empson maintains that far from being a religion of love, Christianity is really a barbaric religion, a religion of torture, in effect, a religion of hate.[5] For Empson, "the Christian God . . . is the wickedest thing yet invented by the black heart of man." Rather than overtly aligning Milton's God with the Christian God, however, Empson curiously attempts to "defend" the God of *Paradise Lost* by presuming to demonstrate how unlike the Christian God Milton's conception of deity really is: Milton is to be credited, Empson maintains, for allowing his God to rise above the wickedness of the God of Christian tradition. With defenders like this, Milton doesn't need enemies. But Empson does not succeed even in this regard: the perverseness of his argument still causes him to conceive of Milton's God as essentially a manipulative and ruthless tyrant who rules a totalitarian state with an iron fist. "The picture of God" one receives in *Paradise Lost*, Empson maintains, is "astonishingly like Uncle Joe Stalin."[6] The effect of such a statement is obvious: one is made immediately to think of the figure of Big Brother. In the context of Empson's book, the idea becomes particularly apposite because Empson is at such pains to dissociate his view of Milton's God from that which emerges in Orwell's depiction of Big Brother in *1984*.[7] Needless to say, that depiction is one of hate, for Orwell portrays a society enslaved by an ideology of hate. Undermining its own cause, Empson's argument obliges one to conceive of Milton's God as the very embodiment of that ideology. In so doing, it fails utterly in its attempt to dissociate Milton's God from what it conceives as the Christian God. Either as Big Brother or as the Christian God, Milton's deity is made to preside over a religion of hate.[8]

The outlook expressed by William Empson might well serve as an object lesson: any discussion of the *odium Dei* either as theological concept or as Miltonic formulation must be careful not to fall into the Empsonian trap. At the same time, that discussion must be willing to acknowledge the legitimacy, as well as the significance, of an outlook that embraces at one and the same time two apparently contradictory ideas, that of a God who loves and that of a God who hates.[9] What is needed, in short, is a genuinely sympathetic treatment of the *odium Dei* and the impact of this notion upon an epic poet for whom the concept of hatred as theological phenomenon performed a very real function, indeed, an epic poet for whom the face of divine love finds its counterpart in the face of divine hate, that is, hate divinized.

This concept has both well-established biblical and exegetical antecedents.[10] In the Old Testament, the idea is designated by the term *sane'*. Assuming a religious force, *sane'* stands in opposition to the term for love, *'ahab*. From a divine perspective, the opposition is voiced by Malachi at the outset of his prophecy: "I have loved you saith the Lord. Yet ye say, Wherein hast thou loved us? *Was* not Esau Jacob's brother? saith the Lord: yet I loved Jacob. And I hated Esau, and laid his mountains and his heritage waste for the dragons of the wilderness." Against Esau and his heirs, "the Lord hath indignation for ever" (Mal. 1:2–4).[11] God loves those who are faithful to him and hates those who oppose him. He hates them indeed with a consuming hatred, one that associates divine hatred with an anger that is unrelenting and finally eternal. Those who are faithful to God, in turn, adopt his hatred of the enemy with an almost zealous sense of obligation. So in Psalm 139, David cries out to God: "Surely thou wilt slay the wicked, O God: depart from me therefore, ye bloody men. For they speak against thee wickedly, *and* thine enemies take *thy name* in vain. Do I not hate them, O Lord, that hate thee? and am I not grieved with those that rise up against thee? I hate them with a perfect hatred: I count them mine enemies" (19–22; compare Ps. 26:5, 45:7). This sense of "perfecting hatred," causing hatred to assume its consummate form as religious entity, bestows upon this passage so much force and causes it to become so compelling as an expression of the extent to which the sublime hatred that God feels toward his enemies is emulated by his faithful.[12] In order to become like God, one must hate like God.[13] Granted, this is not an easy concept to come to terms with, but it must be grasped if one is to understand the full nature of the *odium Dei* as a theological phenomenon.

In the New Testament, the concept of hatred is signaled by the term *miseo*. Its opposite is *agape*, the term for love. Drawing upon these terms, Jesus issues a statement that appears to reverse the Davidic idea of hating one's enemies with a perfect hatred. So in Matthew, Jesus proclaims: "Ye have heard that it hath been said, Thou shalt love thy neighbour, and hate

thine enemy. But I say unto you, Love your enemies, bless them
that curse you, and pray for them which despitefully use you,
and persecute you; That ye may be the children of your Father
which is in heaven" (Matt. 5:43–45). To be a child of God is to
love those who hate you. This reorientation in values is a hallmark of the Gospels. If hatred does find expression, its presence
is made known as a way of underscoring the unconditional character of discipleship. So Jesus declares: "If any *man* come to me,
and hate not his father, and mother, and wife, and children,
and brethren, and sisters, yea, and his own life also, he cannot be
my disciple" (Luke 14:26). From the perspective of the Gospels,
then, one is to love his enemies but to hate anyone (including
those who love him) and anything (including his own life)
that might impede him from becoming a true disciple of Christ.

As a counterpart to the Gospels, the Epistles offer their own
rendering of the nature of divine hatred. So in Romans, Paul
invokes the passage from Malachi ("Jacob have I loved, but Esau
have I hated") discussed above not to controvert it but to
endorse it: "They which are the children of the flesh, these *are*
not the children of God: but the children of the promise are
counted for the seed." "*Is there* unrighteousness with God"
because of his hatred for those who are the children of the flesh?
asks Paul, and then responds to his own question with "God
forbid." God shows mercy on those who merit his mercy and
reveals the "power" (*dynamis*) of his might on those, like
Pharaoh, who are hardened against him (Rom. 9:2–18). The idea
finds its correspondence in Revelation, where Jesus expresses
his approval of his church at Ephesus for following his example in hating the deeds of the Nicolaitans (2:6). In this context,
however, hatred is directed not so much at God's enemies as
it is at the deeds they have done. Nevertheless, in Revelation,
more than any other book of the New Testament, those who
oppose God suffer under his scourge. The "vials of the wrath
of God" that are poured out upon the earth are as much an
expression of divine hatred (*miseo*) as they are an expression

of divine anger (*orge*) (Rev. 16:1–17). Here, as elsewhere, divine hatred and divine anger become complementary manifestations of the same idea.[14] In either case, God is depicted not as one who says "in a little I hid my face from thee for a moment; but with everlasting kindness will I have mercy on thee." Rather, he is depicted as one who gives vent to an all-consuming vengeance in response to those he finds entirely odious and fully deserving of retribution. In such instances, God's hate is a perfect hate, his wrath a perfect wrath. The perfection of both is as much a part of the New Testament perspective as it is of the Old. In an encounter with this dimension, one must simply be willing to acknowledge its presence as a biblical imperative. A refusal to do so represents a refusal to come to terms with an essential aspect of the theology that underscores not just the Old Testament but the New Testament as well.

An awareness of that refusal on the part of his contemporaries, in fact, is what prompted the early church father Lactantius to argue on behalf not only of a God of wrath but a God of hate. So once again in *The Wrath of God*, Lactantius maintains that anger "has a befitting occasion in God. For it is not right that . . . He should not be moved, and arise to take vengeance upon the wicked, and destroy the pestilent and guilty." Proceeding from anger to hatred, Lactantius observes, "He, therefore, who loves also hates, and he who hates also loves; for there are those who ought to be loved, and there are those who ought to be hated. And as he who loves confers good things on those he loves, so he who hates inflicts evils upon those whom he hates. . . . Therefore," says Lactantius, "the opinion of those is vain and false, who, when they attribute the one to God, take away the other, not less than the opinion of those who take away both."[15]

Coming to grips with the nature of divine hatred was as of much concern to the theologians of the Reformation as it was to the theologians of the early Christian era. In his *Commentaries on the Prophet Malachi*, John Calvin, for example, makes a point of distinguishing between God's love and God's hate. God's love, asserts Calvin, encompasses an anger that is finally tempered by mercy. If God becomes angry for a while with those he loves, he ever "moderates His wrath" in order that his love might prevail. It is in this respect that God loved Jacob and his posterity. God's hate, on the other hand, encompasses an anger, indeed, a "dreadful wrath," that is never tempered by mercy. Against those who are entirely reprobate, God's hate is ever-lasting. It pursues the reprobate eternally, "ever suspended over their heads" and "ever fixed as it were in their bones and mar-row." It is in this respect that God hated Esau and his poster-ity.[16] In *Commentary on the Book of Psalms*, Calvin further underscores this insistence upon the importance of divine hatred as a legitimate theological enterprise. Indeed, such an enterprise is to be not only acknowledged but also emulated. So, in his analysis of Psalm 139:21–22 ("Do not I hate them, O Lord, that hate thee? . . . I hate them with a perfect hatred"), Calvin declares that "it is a proof of our having a fervent zeal for God when we have the magnanimity to declare irreconcilable war with the wicked and them who hate God." This zeal for God must burn constantly in our hearts and cause us to con-tend with those against whom God himself manifests his hatred. Thus, David "stood forward strenuously in defence of the glory of God, regardless of the hatred of the whole world, and waged war with all the workers of iniquity."[17]

Among the theologians of Milton's own time, one finds a comparable insistence upon the significance of God's hatred. Accordingly, William Perkins, in his *Lectures* on Revelation, admonishes us to "hate that he [Christ] hateth, loue that he loueth, and so shew that we be true Christians and members of Christ." In so doing, we shall be "of the same mind, iudge-ment, will, and affection that he [Christ] is of."[18] In his *Commentary* on Romans, Thomas Wilson correspondingly finds that hatred is applied to God in a number of senses, including that which is directly opposed to love and that which justly decrees and inflicts punishment upon the reprobate. In either case, "God's hatred is the soueraigne and chiefe cause of the damnation of the wicked, their owne sinnes either actuall or originall, or both, being the meritorious cause."[19] In *The Marrow of Theology*, William Ames likewise acknowledges the significance of divine hatred as theological enterprise. For Ames, hatred represents the most extreme form that the wrath of God is liable to assume. In this respect, God is said to "hate" the reprobate (Rom. 9:13). Those who follow God manifest a "zeal of the will" that reflects a comparable hatred of evil, just as it reflects a comparable love of good.[20] As these views suggest, the theologians of Milton's own time were hardly loath to acknowledge the significance of divine hatred as a distinct and legitimate category of value.

If such is the case, the insistence upon divine hatred as theological entity found its counterpart in the speculations of those who sought to devise a psychology of hatred founded upon the *odium Dei*. One such expositor was Edward Reynolds, whose *Treatise of the Passions* takes full account of how the *odium Dei* manifests itself as a psychological phenomenon. For Reynolds, two kinds of hatred are inspired by an emulation of the *odium Dei:*

> an *Hatred of Abomination* or loathing; which consists in a *pure aversion* or flight of the Appetite from something apprehended as *Evill*, arising from a dissonancy and repugnancy betweene their natures: and an *Hatred of Enmity*, which is not a flying, but rather a *pursuing Hatred*, and hath ever some *Love* joyned with it, namely a Love of any Evill which we desire may befall the person or thing which wee hate.

In either case, this form of hatred is entirely justified: it is a "just hatred," in fact, a "transcendent Hatred," inspired by the "Will of God." In order to be "conformable" unto God's will, we must allow this hatred to manifest itself fully within us. So Reynolds observes, "Wee owe *submission* to the *will* of *Gods purpose* and Counsell, and wee owe *conformity* to the *will* of his *Precept* and Command; we must submit to the will, whereby God is pleased to worke himselfe, and wee must conforme to the will, whereby hee is pleased to command us to worke." In that submission and conformity, we shall hate our enemies with a perfect hatred. Doing so, we shall become the means by which the *odium Dei* finds expression in those entirely in accord with God's will.[21]

II

The extent to which Milton assimilates and transforms the foregoing perspectives will be seen upon an investigation of the *odium Dei* in his thinking. Once again, an appropriate starting point is Milton's discussion of the nature of God in the second chapter ("De Deo") of the first book of *De Doctrina Christiana*. We recall from our reading of the theopathetic section of that chapter the extent to which God's delineation of himself in the Scriptures should determine our interpretation of what God experiences. Approaching deity in this manner, Milton is at once careful to avoid what he implies is the excess of anthropopathy, that is, the ascription of human emotions to God after the manner of the pagan deities, and at the same time courageous enough to conceive of God as he has accommodated himself to our limited capacities. Thus, we recall that,

> if *Jehovah repented that he had created man,* Gen. vi. 6, *and repented because of their groanings,* Judges ii. 18, let us believe that he did repent. . . . If *he grieved in his heart* Gen. vi. 6, and if, similarly, *his soul was grieved,* Judges x. 16, let us believe that he did feel grief. . . . If it is said that God, after working for six days, *rested and was refreshed,* Exod. xxxi. 17, and if he *feared his enemy's displeasure,* Deut. xxxii. 27, let us believe that it is not beneath God to feel what grief he does feel, to be refreshed by what refreshes him, and to fear what he does fear. For however you may try to tone down these and similar texts about God by an elaborate show of interpretive glosses, it comes to the same thing in the end. (YP 6:134–35)

Such a view goes far to suggest the function of the *odium Dei* in Milton's thought. Although Milton does not specifically mention the concept of hate in conjunction with those of repentance, grief, and fear, the idea is certainly in keeping with the spectrum of "affections" that he attributes to God as a result of his reading of the biblical text. Those affections that Milton does single out are meant to be representative rather than inclusive, and, judging by the Son's declaration to his Father in *Paradise Lost* that "whom thou hat'st, I hate," the affection of hate would no doubt assume a prominent place among the ones that Milton does mention.[22]

What bearing this view has upon the idea of hatred as a categorical imperative in the human sphere is discernible in Milton's discussion of "The Duties of Man Towards His Neighbor" (chapter 11) in book 2 of *De Doctrina Christiana*. There, Milton acknowledges that "hatred . . . is in some cases a religious duty; as when we hate the enemies of God or the church" (odium etiam pium est; ut cum hostes Dei aut ecclesiae odio habemus). Among the proof-texts that Milton invokes to support this observation, one finds Psalm 139:21–22: "Do I not hate them, O Lord, that hate thee? . . . I hate them with a perfect hatred." Having cited such proof-texts, Milton further intensifies this outlook by maintaining that "we are to hate even our dearest connections, if they endeavor to seduce or deter us from the love of God and true religion" (CM 17:258–61; YP 6:743).[23]

Such an outlook is not confined simply to Milton's theological tract, however; it represents an essential component of his other prose works as well. There, the concept of hatred as a "religious duty" enacted in conformity with the will of God finds full expression.[24] The divorce tracts are a case in point. *The Doctrine and Discipline of Divorce*, for example, maintains that those who "mean to inherit the great reward" of salvation must hate and forsake any who would "divide, or hinder, or but delay our duty to religion." In keeping with the spirit of the Gospel, those hated and forsaken include father, mother and wife. They must be hated "zealously."[25] If such is true of those, like father and mother, with whom we do not cohabit, it is especially true of those with whom we do. Milton has in mind, of course, what he calls the "irreligious" wife, in response to whom hatred is not only justified but mandated:

> how the peace and perpetuall cohabitation of marriage can be kept, how that benevolent and intimate communion of body can be held with one that must be hated with a most operative hatred, must be forsak'n and yet continually dwelt with and accompanied, he who can distinguish, hath the gift of an affection very odly divided and contriv'd: while others both just and wise, and *Salomon* among the rest, if they may not hate and forsake as *Moses* enjoyns, and the Gospell imports, will find it impossible not to love otherwise then will sort with the love of God, whose jealousie brooks no corrivall. (YP 2:263–64)

In the context of the divorce tracts, the irreligious wife inspires an unqualified hatred, a hatred that it becomes a sacred duty to execute in accord with the love and worship of God. This is not a hatred that sins, Milton asserts; rather, it is a hatred that demonstrates one's allegiance to the true way (YP 2:262).[26]

The antipathy between love and hatred in Milton is so pronounced that he even conceives of it in cosmic terms. Thus, in *The Doctrine and Discipline of Divorce*, he proclaims: "There is indeed, a twofold Seminary or stock in nature, from whence are deriv'd the issues of love and hatred distinctly flowing through the whole masse of created things, and . . . Gods doing ever is to bring the due likenesses and harmonies of his workes together."[27] When the issues of love and hatred meet "to their own destruction," they must be separated, divorced. Such a divorcement is conceived not as a subversive act but as one through which order is restored. In keeping with his cosmic metaphor, Milton accordingly speaks of God's "divorcing command" as the result of which "the world first rose out of Chaos" (YP 2:272–73).

In *Paradise Lost*, this "divorcing command" is what under-scores the *odium Dei*. The extent to which such is the case is discernible in the context that Milton establishes to portray the expulsion of the rebel angels at the climax of the war in heaven. If the Son's declaration "whom thou hat'st, I hate" represents the fullest expression of "perfecting" God's hatred, the "Chariot of Paternal Deitie" becomes the veritable embodiment of the *odium Dei*. By means of the Chariot, the Son will enact a divorcement: he will "farr separate" the pure from the impure, so that only those who are truly obedient will remain to sing "unfained *Halleluiahs*" before the holy Mount of God (6.742–45). In this respect, the Chariot assumes the form of a weapon through which the Son answers despite with despite. So the faithful angels are instructed to behold "Gods indignation on these Godless pourd" by the Son. "Not you but mee they have despis'd, / Yet envied; against mee is all thir rage" (6.809–13), the Son proclaims before he changes his countenance to terror "too severe to be beheld" and rushes onward to overwhelm all who stand in his path (6.824–66).

As the emissary of the *odium Dei*, the Son manifests that "*Hatred of Enmity*, which is," in the words of Edward Reynolds, "*a pursuing Hatred.*" "Ever suspended" over the "heads" of its "enemies," this hatred, to quote Calvin, is "fixed as it were in their bones and marrow." Embarking upon such hatred, we recall, "is a proof of our having a fervent zeal for God when we have the magnanimity to declare irreconcilable war with the wicked and them who hate God." In this way do we "perfect hatred." As William Ames maintains, such an act is in keeping with a "zeal of the will" that demonstrates one's faith in and allegiance to God. If the Son demonstrates such zeal by overcoming the rebel angels in the Chariot of Paternal Deitie, his epic enactment of the *odium Dei* is anticipated by Milton's polemical rendering of the idea in the antiprelatical tracts. In the *Apology for Smectymnuus*, for example, Milton envisions "Zeale" as a warrior "whose substance is ethereal." "Arming

in compleat diamond," Zeal "ascends his fiery chariot drawn
with two blazing Meteors figur'd like beasts, . . . the one vis-
ag'd like a Lion to expresse power, high autority and indignation, the other of count'nance like a man to cast derision and
scorne upon perverse and fraudulent seducers; with these the
invincible warriour Zeale . . . drives over the heads of Scarlet
Prelats" in an act of "sanctifi'd bitternesse against the enemies
of truth" (YP 1:900–901).[28]

If this spirit of zeal is what underscores the Son's enactment
of the *odium Dei* in *Paradise Lost*,[29] one must nonetheless be
aware that the Chariot of Paternal Deitie performs a twofold
function: that of destruction and that of reclamation. Its purpose is not just to manifest a "sanctifi'd bitternesse against the
enemies of truth"; likewise, it can be a source of regeneration
and renewal. Milton suggests this twofold function by means
of indirection. When the rebel angels behold the Chariot, they
are, Milton says, "hard'n'd more *by what might most reclame*"
(6.790; italics mine). The sense is clear: the effect of the Chariot
upon those who are "the enemies of truth" is to harden them
in their obduracy. But the Chariot can likewise have the opposite effect: it has the capacity to "reclame," just as much as it
does the capacity to destroy. The way in which these two
capacities not only complement one another but also resolve
themselves in a dialectical interchange that is ultimately
beneficial and restorative will be seen upon further investigation. That investigation will attempt to suggest the relationship between the *odium Dei* and the *amor Dei,* one in keeping
with Milton's idea of how "the world first rose out of Chaos."

My point of departure will be Milton's reference to the
Chariot of Paternal Deitie as that through which the enemies
of truth are "hard'n'd more by what might most reclame." From
the perspective of the *odium Dei,* the enemies of truth are overwhelmed by a hatred that reflects back upon them a hun-
dredfold their own hatred. In that process, they become
"hardened" and therefore desperate. In *De Doctrina Christiana,*

Milton devotes a good deal of attention to this process of "hardening" (*indurando*). As he explains the process, God provides the occasion through which the "will being already in a state of perversion" becomes even more obdurate in its sinfulness. "Out of its own wickedness," the evil "either operates good for others, or punishment for itself, though unknowingly, and with the intent of producing a very different result." Providing the occasion through which hardening may occur, God paradoxically "educes a good and just result, thus as it were creating light out of darkness." A concomitant to this process of hardening is that of "blinding" (*excaecando*). Just as the heart is hardened, the understanding is blinded as a result of God's "withdrawing the light of His grace" and "confounding or stupifying the faculties of the mind." In this respect, God is said to produce good out of evil, light out of darkness (CM 15:71–87). One is reminded of God's statement concerning the fate of the reprobate in *Paradise Lost:* "hard be hard'n'd, blind be blinded more, / That they may stumble on, and deeper fall" (3.200–201).

As the sublime expression of the *odium Dei,* the Chariot of Paternal Deitie provides the fitting occasion by which the complementary processes of hardening and blinding may occur:

> They hard'n'd more by what might most reclame,
> Grieving to see his Glories, at the sight
> Took envie, and aspiring to his highth,
> Stood reimbattell'd fierce, by force or fraud
> Weening to prosper, and at length prevail
> Against God and *Messiah,* or to fall
> In universal ruin last.   (6.791–97)

Recalling Saint Paul's discussion of divine hatred in Romans, the description of the rebel angels here is in keeping with the New Testament idea that it is by means of God's overcoming of the reprobate that his "power" is made manifest: "For the scripture saith unto Pharaoh, Even for this same purpose have I raised thee up, that I might show my power in thee, and that

my name might be declared throughout all the earth" (Rom.
9:17). The passage proved to be of central importance to
Milton's discussion of "hardening" and "blinding" in *De
Doctrina Christiana* (CM 15:83–85). Like Pharaoh, Satan must
undergo the devastation of the *odium Dei* so that God's power
might be made manifest. Overwhelmed by the "pernicious fire"
that shoots forth from the eyes of the Chariot, the "accurst"
are driven to the "Chrystal wall of Heav'n, which op'ning
wide, / Rowl'd inward" like the waves of the Red Sea, which
closed with such finality upon "*Busiris* and his *Memphian*
Chivalry." Thus is their own "perfidious hatred" repaid by the
divine hatred of the *odium Dei,* while God's faithful look on
as "Eye witnesses of his Almightie Acts" (6.844–60, 883; compare 1.306–8).

If the Chariot of Paternal Deitie is the fierce embodiment
of the *odium Dei,* that divine vehicle, we recall, is as much
the source of reclamation as it is the means of destruction.
Although the rebel angels might be "hard'n'd" by the obduracy that they experience in response to the theophany of
God's glorious presence, those who are not corrupted by hellish hate become the recipients of heavenly love. It is in this
capacity that the Chariot of Paternal Deitie assumes the function of a restorative vehicle, one of the primary functions of
which is to "reclame," evident in its ability to restore the
landscape of heaven as it approaches the warring angels:

> Before him [the Son] Power Divine his way prepar'd;
> At his command th'uprooted Hills retir'd
> Each to his place, they heard his voice and went
> Obsequious, Heav'n his wonted face renewd,
> And with fresh Flowrets Hill and Valley smil'd.   (6.780–84)

Such an act of reclamation suggests the extent to which the
odium Dei finds its counterpart in the *amor Dei:* that which
overwhelms with hate can likewise restore with love. If God
hates Esau, he loves Jacob. If he lays Esau's "mountain and his
heritage waste for the dragons of the wilderness," he restores

Jacob's mountain and his heritage as a symbol of divine beneficence. These are the effects of God's "divorcing command," his act of separating the "pure" from the "impure," so that only those who are truly obedient will remain to sing "unfained Halleluiahs" before the holy Mount of God.

The *odium Dei* and the *amor Dei* are complementary aspects of the same idea: they cannot be isolated. The dialectic of Milton's epic is such that the *odium Dei* is always ultimately restorative.[30] Whereas hellish hate "recoils" (4.17; compare *Comus*, 593) back on itself, heavenly hate resolves itself in an act of sublime creativity: divorcement becomes reunion, disorder gives rise to a new order, out of chaos a renewed sense of harmony is born. It is in this way that "Heav'nly love shall outdo Hellish hate." Implicit in that heavenly love is a heavenly hate that is finally as restorative and as regenerative as hellish hate is destructive. In fact, it is by means of this heavenly hate that hellish hate brings upon itself its own destruction. Heavenly hate is the vehicle, the Chariot, through which this self-destruction occurs. In that occurrence, the *amor Dei* triumphs: "Heav'n his wonted face renewd, / And with fresh Flowrets Hill and Valley smil'd." God's "divorcing command" causes the world to rise out of Chaos.

The idea is fully conceptualized in God's act of creating the universe in book 7 of *Paradise Lost*. Once again ascending his great Chariot, "the King of Glorie in his powerful Word" sets forth "to create new worlds" (7.208–9). Before him appears "the vast immeasurable Abyss" threatening "to assault / Heav'ns highth" (7.214–15). Silencing the "troubl'd waves," the "Omnific Word" imposes order on the Chaos before him. Doing so, he enacts a divorcement, a separation of pure and impure in a way that confirms even more graphically the extent to which the *odium Dei* of book 6 finds its counterpart in the *amor Dei* of book 7:

> on the watrie calm
> His brooding wings the Spirit of God outspred,

And vital vertue infus'd, and vital warmth
Throughout the fluid Mass, but downward purg'd
The black tartareous cold, infernal dregs
Adverse to life: then founded, then conglob'd
Like things to like.   (7.234–40)

The idea returns us by implication to Milton's discourse on love and hatred in the divorce tracts. There is "a twofold Seminary or stock in nature, from whence are deriv'd the issues of love and hatred distinctly flowing through the whole masse of created things, and . . . Gods doing ever is to bring the due likenesses and harmonies of his workes together." The war in heaven and the creation of the universe represent a kind of precosmogonic conceptualization of this cosmic idea. If the war in heaven represents a realization of the "issue" of hatred, the creation of the universe represents a realization of the "issue" of love. In the first instance, the divine Chariot embodies that *odium Dei* through which hellish hate eventuates in its own destruction. In the second instance, the divine Chariot embodies that *amor Dei* through which heavenly love is made manifest on a cosmic scale. In both instances, God's "divorcing command" becomes the means by which a new world rises out of chaos. It is in this manner, finally, that "Heav'nly love" does indeed "outdo Hellish hate."[31]

The dialectic through which this process is made manifest may now be understood more fully in the context that the Son himself provides for it before he ascends the Chariot of Paternal Deitie in book 6. Having been instructed by God to "Pursue these sons of Darkness, drive them out / From all Heav'ns bounds into the utter Deep," the Son responds:

        this I my Glorie account,
   My exaltation, and my whole delight,
   That thou in me well pleas'd, declarst thy will
   Fulfill'd, which to fulfil is all my bliss.
   Scepter and Power, thy giving, I assume,
   And gladlier shall resign, when in the end

> Thou shalt be All in All, and I in thee
> For ever, and in mee all whom thou lov'st:
> But whom thou hat'st, I hate and can put on
> Thy terrors, as I put thy mildness on,
> Image of thee in all things.   (6.726–36)

The Son's response to the Father suggests a context for the Chariot that transcends its immediate function as a vehicle for the expression of the *odium Dei*. If the Son assumes the role of emissary of God's hatred, that function must be seen in the larger context that the Son's response as a whole provides. This context implies the *amor Dei* through which the Son will ultimately fulfill his role both as *soter* and as *eschaton*. From this perspective, the Son's ascent upon the Chariot is to be viewed as a type of that fulfillment. In the very enactment of his role as emissary of the *odium Dei*, the Son's overcoming of the rebel angels prefigures his redemptive mission within the frame of human history and his eschatological mission when "time stand[s] fixt" (compare 12.555). The first mission is implicit in the Son's reference to his exaltation and his assumption of "Scepter and Power"; the second mission is implicit in the Son's reference to his resignation of the insignias of office at the moment of the "All in All."

What the Son's response encapsulates, in short, is nothing less than an assertion of the *amor Dei* dramatized in the account that climaxes the dialogue in heaven in book 3. Underscoring that account is the formulation of the Son's redemptive and eschatological roles, the first culminating in his exaltation to God's throne, where he "shalt Reign / Both God and Man . . . / Anointed universal King," the second culminating in his "lay[ing] by" his "regal Scepter" in the emergence of a "New Heav'n and Earth" (3.323–41).[32] Embodying both the redemptive and eschatological dimensions of the Chariot as a vehicle of reclamation, then, the Son's response to his Father's directive in book 6 suggests the way in which the Chariot of Paternal Deitie embraces a typology through which the *odium Dei* is consummated in an *amor Dei* at once messianic and apocalyptic.

As the foregoing discussion has attempted to indicate, *Paradise Lost* is an epic in which the theme of divine love must be viewed within the context of its apparent opposite divine hate. Although a discussion of the *odium Dei* runs the risk of playing into the hands of those for whom God is nothing but a cold, merciless, and tyrannical deity, one must confront the concept of hatred as a theological entity in order to appreciate the complexities of Milton's epic. Such an appreciation will sensitize one to the underlying dialectic through which the *odium Dei* and the *amor Dei* are seen to be complementary expressions of the same idea. That idea finds its fullest expression in the Son's act of ascending the Chariot of Paternal Deitie to overwhelm the rebel angels in book 6 of *Paradise Lost*. This central act[33] brings to the fore an entire range of meanings through which "hate in heav'n" is ultimately consummated in the realization of divine love. Such is the dialectic that underscores the theme of Milton's epic. By means of that dialectic, the concept of divine hate assumes a significance of unique import to the traditions that constitute the *odium Dei*.

Six

"Our Living Dread"

✣

I

In her immensely influential and learned study *Toward "Samson Agonistes": The Growth of Milton's Mind*, Mary Ann Radzinowicz argues that Milton's drama contains his most advanced theological outlook. Dramatizing this outlook, *Samson Agonistes* embodies a theology of "progressive revelation" through which one acquires an increasingly more enlightened understanding of how God's treatment of every man reflects his treatment of Samson. As a result of this understanding, one gains a freer and more rational conception of the nature of God. The movement toward God is the movement toward this heightened sense of rationality concerning God's ways.[1] Rather than appearing on stage to foster this process of understanding, God makes his presence known in the human heart. He is revealed in every time and every place through the behavior of tested men who attest to him. By means of his free agent Samson, God manifests the renewal of freedom to all individuals.

As a final demonstration of the importance of mind and will, "the good mind and the good will issue into an exemplary act which teaches how God gives freedom." God's "unsearchable dispose" is the bestowing of "new acquist of true experience" to individuals through the example of purposeful human beings.[2] For Radzinowicz, the notion of God in *Samson Agonistes*, then, reflects Milton's essential stance both as a rationalist and as a moralist, one whose outlook endorses a progressive process of enlightenment for character and reader alike.

As reassuring as this reading appears to be, it has come increasingly under scrutiny in recent scholarship on Milton's drama. In his powerful study *Milton and the Drama of History*, for example, David Locwenstein calls into question the whole notion of a theology of "progressive revelation" based upon categories of rational and moral discernment. "Critics who argue that *Samson Agonistes* charts the linear course of its hero's regeneration or reveals the tempering of his passions," Loewenstein observes, "tend to smooth over the jagged emotional edges of Milton's tragedy, not to mention the disturbing implications of Samson's vehement iconoclasm." In place of the reassurances of Radzinowicz's reading of the drama, Loewenstein offers a reading that underscores the deeply troubled and conflicted dimensions of the drama. The effect of the drama is one characterized by a profound sense of anxiety about God's incomprehensible ways. For Loewenstein, the process of history in *Samson Agonistes* appears "ruptured and discontinuous, and God's purposes inscrutable." As a result of this vexed view of God and his ways, Milton's drama offers little to comfort or reassure us about the mysterious and indeed terrible actions of deity. All attempts to comprehend the mystery of God in history are repeatedly frustrated by the baffling nature of what transpires. It is within this context that the drama itself culminates in the tumultuous events of its iconoclastic ending. In this theomachic encounter, the clash between God and Dagon becomes "a contest of dramatic spectacles, namely, the drama of Dagon versus the drama of God." Loewenstein sees in that terrifying enactment "something of a deep wish fulfillment on Milton's part: the impulse not only to remake and overturn history, but, in the process, to devastate one's enemies by means of a spectacular act." Rather than silencing the "cataclysmic devastation" associated with the account in Judges, Milton intensifies it.[3]

Although the two readings of Mary Ann Radzinowicz and David Loewenstein could not be further apart in their respective assessments of the action and theological basis of *Samson Agonistes,* I think it essential to acknowledge the extremes these readings represent in order to gain an understanding of the current critical climate and of the choices with which one is faced in coming to terms with what transpires in Milton's drama. As I have attempted to demonstrate in my own study *Milton and the Culture of Violence,* I find the outlook reflected in Loewenstein's reading more nearly consistent with the spirit of *Samson Agonistes.*[4] Like Loewenstein, I see the action of the drama as one infused with a heightened sense of personal wrath and frustration. For me, this drama is far from reassuring in its outlook; rather, it is a work of harsh and uncompromising violence, a work that exults in violence while it gives expression to profound and deeply disturbing elements of vehemence and rage.

Focusing in particular upon the theological dimensions implicit in such a point of view, I wish to explore one aspect of it that has not received the attention it warrants. Arising from what Loewenstein sees as the profound sense of anxiety and uncertainty about God's incomprehensible ways in *Samson Agonistes,* this aspect manifests itself in the one name that is so aptly bestowed upon deity as a result of the cataclysmic devastation in which Milton's drama culminates. That name is "Dread" — "our living Dread," to be precise. It is the Semichorus that gives voice to the expression of dread as an appellation of deity.[5] This appellation is bestowed immediately after the Messenger recounts Samson's destruction of the

Philistines in the Temple of Dagon.[6] Celebrating their destruction, the Semichorus declares of the Philistines:

> While thir hearts were jocund and sublime,
> Drunk with Idolatry, drunk with Wine,
> And fat regorg'd of Bulls and Goats,
> Chaunting thir Idol, and preferring
> Before our living Dread who dwells
> In *Silo* his bright Sanctuary:
> Among them he a spirit of phrenzie sent,
> Who hurt thir minds,
> And urg'd them on with mad desire
> To call in hast for thir destroyer;
> They only set on sport and play
> Unweetingly importun'd
> Thir own destruction to come speedy upon them.   (1669–81)

At issue in this celebration of God's destructive power is the designation "our living Dread who dwells / In *Silo* his bright Sanctuary." To gain a sense of the meaning of deity in *Samson Agonistes*, one must come to terms with the full implications of a God who is not only dreadful but who is the embodiment of dread itself, indeed, whose very name is Dread. If, as Radzinowicz argues, *Samson Agonistes* reflects Milton's advanced theological outlook, this outlook certainly embraces some of the most disturbing elements that one is likely to discover in an encounter with his notion of deity. Assuming Milton's drama moves progressively toward a more enlightened understanding of God and his ways, we are obliged to confront the irony that the culminating event of *Samson Agonistes* is one in which a God whose name is Dread manifests this quality in all its cataclysmic power. As a means of understanding the import of this idea, we shall examine in some detail the notion of dread as an appellation of God.[7]

A consideration of Dread as an actual name of God is best viewed from the overarching perspective of the phenomenon designated "the fear of God." According to R. H. Pfeiffer, this phenomenon is so crucial to the religious temperament reflected in the Old Testament that the earliest term for religion in biblical Hebrew, and in Semitic languages in general, is the phrase "the fear of God."[8] In biblical Hebrew, there are many synonyms for the concept of fear, each with its own network of meanings and shades of nuance.[9] One term alone (that of *yare'*) occurs well over 400 times in the depiction of the individual and his relationship to God.[10] When it comes to "the fear of God," biblical Hebrew is terribly inventive. This fact only serves to reinforce the idea that at some archaic level God and fear are synonymous. In the range of meanings associated with fear, the most extreme form of that concept is what English designates as dread. Although biblical Hebrew has several terms that involve this meaning, that which has the most direct bearing upon our undertaking is *pachad,* which carries with it the notion of extreme terror and awe. So Job declares that "In thoughts from the visions of the night, when deep sleep falleth on men, fear [*pachad*] came upon me, and trembling, which made all my bones to shake" (Job 4:13–14). Later, Job asks, "Shall not his [God's] excellency make you afraid? and his dread [*pachad*] fall upon you?" (Job 13:11).[11] The *pachad* of God may fall upon an entire people in his anger (1 Sam. 11:7).

In the Old Testament, the term *pachad* assumes particular cogency because it is used as an actual name of God. So it occurs in Genesis with the remarkable phrase *pachad yitschaq* (dread of Isaac). The phrase appears in Jacob's response to Laban's accusation that his son-in-law is responsible for the loss not only of Laban's daughters but also of Laban's gods. Jacob declares indignantly: "Except the God of my father, the God of Abraham, and the fear of Isaac [*pachad yitschaq*], had been with me, surely thou hadst sent me away now empty" (Gen. 31:42, 53). What one has here is a series of parallel phrases that define God not only by means of patriarchal relationship ("God of my father," "God of Abraham") but also by means of attribute ("fear of Isaac"). In this rhetorical enactment, a patriarchal relationship

culminates in the transformation of attribute into appellation. The God of the patriarchs is thereby redefined most fear-
somely as very dread, indeed, dread deified.[12] No wonder Laban
is reluctant to pursue the matter further! Although the phrase
pachad yitschaq has elicited a good deal of controversy concerning its precise meaning, the general consensus is that it
is among the most archaic names of a God whose purpose is
to sow terror among his enemies (compare Gen. 35:5).[13]

Such is perfectly in keeping with the formative notions of
deity discernible in the Old Testament. These are notions that
serve as the basis of the dread that surrounds Rudolf Otto's
notion of "the holy" (*das Heilige*). Analyzing the nature of the
holy, Otto makes a point of distinguishing between conceptions of God that define deity by the higher attributes of
"Spirit, Reason, Purpose, Good Will, Supreme Power, Unity,
[and] Selfhood," and conceptions of God that designate deity
by the attributes that one might associate with a much more
archaic view of religion. Such attributes are of a decidedly
nonrational sort. The product of a "creature-feeling" in response
to a power totally beyond the realm of knowing, these attributes characterize the notion of God as a phenomenon replete
with the quality of *numen*, imbuing deity with a sanctity,
indeed, a power, that renders it "wholly other" (*ganz andere*).
Otto defines "wholly other" as "that which exists quite beyond
the sphere of the usual, the intelligible, and the familiar, which
therefore falls quite outside the limits of the 'canny,' and is
contrasted with it, filling the mind with blank wonder and
astonishment." This, for Otto, is the experience of God in its
most archaic form, one that we have earlier associated with
the notion of the *deus absconditus*.[14]

In keeping with that notion, God becomes the embodiment
of the "awefulness" that underlies what Otto calls the *mysterium tremendum*. A manifestation of the holy, the *mysterium tremendum* is characterized by "a feeling of peculiar
dread," "peculiar" because it is a feeling quite distinct from

the familiar emotion of fear. At the very least, it is the most extreme form of fear that one can imagine: fear divinized. By its very nature, the *mysterium tremendum* is that which is dreadful, that which causes the experience of being shaken by involuntary tremor. Both embodying dread in itself and causing dread in others, the *mysterium tremendum* manifests itself in an experience of deity that pours forth the dread that constitutes its essence. This dread can break out without warning and consume with paralysis all who encounter it.[15] As a product of deity, it is associated with such qualities as the "Wrath of God," which Otto sees as "a unique emotional moment in religious experience, a moment whose singularly *daunting* and awe-inspiring character must be gravely disturbing to those persons who will recognize nothing in the divine nature but goodness, gentleness, [and] love."[16]

In keeping with his treatment of the "dreadfulness" of God, Otto offers one other attribute that he views as crucial to the holy — what Otto calls God's "livingness," the fact that he is designated "the living God." For this, Otto cites Deuteronomy 5:26: "For who *is there of* all flesh, that hath heard the voice of the living God [*'elohim chayyim*] speaking out of the midst of the fire, as we *have*, and lived?" As Otto is aware, there are many more biblical examples that might be invoked to support the notion of God's "livingness." Suffice it to say that it, too, is a crucial aspect of the *mysterium*. It is by his "life," Otto observes, that this God is differentiated from all concepts of rationality. By virtue of his "livingness," God becomes ultimately a "non-rational essence" that eludes all philosophical speculation. To appreciate the force of such a view of deity is to acknowledge "the non-rational core of the biblical conception of God."[17] For the Rudolf Otto of *das Heilige*, such a conception is what underscores any notion of God as the product of the *mysterium tremendum*. For our purposes, it is certainly what underscores the idea of God as dread, indeed, as "our living Dread."

Both from the Miltonic perspective and the milieu from which that perspective emerged, such an idea was hardly alien to seventeenth century theologians and exegetes. So commonplace was the idea during Milton's time, in fact, that one might even speak of a theology of dread as a dimension of coming to terms with the nature of godhead and as a means of understanding the relationship between the individual and his God. The seventeenth century, in particular, is replete with sermons and treatises that address the specific concept of dread as a divine attribute as well as a psychological response to that attribute.[18] As one might expect, the concept falls under the general heading of the fear of God. In *A Christian Dictionary* (1622), Thomas Wilson, for example, defines dread or fear as both a natural affection in response to an impending danger and the danger itself as that which is dreaded or feared.[19] In this latter sense, Wilson observes, God is called "the Fear of *Isaac*." Although Wilson does not hesitate to conjecture how the phrase came about, he concludes that it is a "Metonimie" for the name of God and cites several biblical texts to support his thesis.[20] From this perspective, Wilson interprets "the Fear of *Isaac*" as "a metonimie of the effect for the cause." As such, it transfers the response to the object of fear onto the object itself. In the process of transference, fear involves "the whole worshippe of God" for those whose dread is an expression of devotion. In that capacity, it becomes a source of renewal, but for those who refuse to acknowledge the true significance of the "Fear of *Isaac*" and the worship it entails, it becomes a source of chastisement and even destruction. Such is Wilson's view of the notion of fear or dread as a religious phenomenon and as a divine attribute.[21]

Later in the century, John Bunyan produced a remarkable work of crucial import to the theology of dread. Examining dread as a fundamental manifestation of the religious experience, Bunyan's *A Treatise of the Fear of God* (London, 1679) suggests the extent to which the notion of the *mysterium tremendum* represents a defining moment in seventeenth century notions of deity.[22] Bunyan is entirely aware that the phrase "fear of God" in the title of his work is as much a name *for* God as a response *to* God. "By this word FEAR," Bunyan observes, "we are to understand even *God himself,* who is the *object* of our FEAR." The divine majesty is known by this very name. Citing Genesis 31:42 as the crucial text to support this contention, Bunyan says, "This name *Jacob* called him by, when he and *Laban* chod [contended] together on Mount *Gilead,* after that *Jacob* had made his escape to his Fathers house; *Except,* said he, *the God of Abraham, and the FEAR of Isaac had been with me, surely now thou hadst sent me away empty.*" Responding to this text, Bunyan declares that "*God* may well be called the FEAR of his people, not only because they have by his grace made him the object of their FEAR, but because of the dread and terrible Majesty that is in him." Imbued with this dread, the people of God worship him with godly awe and reverence of his majesty. "Let him [God] be your FEAR, and let him be your dread," Bunyan counsels; "let his excellency make you afraid with godly fear." As a prime example of this quality of dreadfulness, Bunyan cites the Samson account in Judges, specifically the visitation of the angel of God to Manoah and his wife at the outset of the narrative (Judg. 13:22). "If *Angels,* which are but creatures, are, through the glory that God has put upon them, so fearful and terrible in their appearance to men," Bunyan observes, "how much more dreadful and terrible must God himself be to us, who are but dust and ashes?" For Bunyan, as for Milton, the key to the Samson narrative is the experience of a God whose very name is Dread (*A Treatise,* 9:5–8).

Exploring that name from a multiplicity of perspectives, Bunyan exhorts the faithful to engage in a proper worship of deity. Just as the presence and name of God are dreadful and fearful in the church, so is God's worship and service. Depending upon the nature of the individual (whether prince, lord, or parent) being worshiped, all manner of service involves dread and fear to a greater or lesser extent. So the divine worship due to God, who is so great and dreadful in himself and in name, is such that "his Worship must therefore be a fearful thing." Those who fail to worship God with the proper fear and dread that are due him are themselves destroyed by God's dreadful judgments. Bunyan cites several figures who, as a result of failing to accord Dread himself the rightful fear that is due him, are overwhelmed by the very fear they fail to acknowledge (*A Treatise*, 9:9–14).[23] Although Bunyan does not single out the Philistines of the Samson narrative on this occasion, he would no doubt concur that they too qualify as prime examples of those who bring down their destruction upon themselves as a result of their disregard of the true significance of the God of the Israelites as the very embodiment of dread.[24]

Within this context Milton generates his own theology of dread throughout his works. *De Doctrina Christiana* is a case in point. For Milton, as for a host of exegetes, any consideration of the nature of dread falls under the heading of the worship of God. So it is considered in the second book of *De Doctrina Christiana*, which in general is concerned with what it calls the *cultus Dei* (worship of God). From the perspective of the *cultus Dei*, Milton examines those virtues belonging to "our duty towards God." Endorsing the need for a "devout affection" (religiosus erga eum affectus) toward God in all matters of worship, Milton singles out the following virtues: "love, trust, hope, gratitude, fear, humility, patience, and obedience." These eight virtues constitute the foundation of the true worship of God (compare Deut. 10:12–13). Addressing the category of *timor Dei* (fear of God), Milton observes that this virtue involves "reverencing God as the supreme Father and judge of all men, and fearing above all to offend him." To support this observation, Milton cites a host of proof-texts, among them, Deuteronomy 28:58 ("fearing this most glorious and supremely reverend name, Jehovah your God") and Psalm 2:11 ("worship Jehovah with reverence and rejoice with trembling"). Clearly, for Milton, fear and reverence are synonymous affections: to violate one is to violate the other (CM 17:50, 60–65; YP 6:656–57, 660–61).

Based upon a reading of *De Doctrina Christiana*, one is inclined to see in Milton the emergence of fear as an important constituent in any consideration of *cultus*. Under this heading, fear assumes a positive, indeed, pious role in providing evidence of one's devotion to God. In its association with the virtues of love, trust, hope, gratitude, humility, patience, and obedience, the category of fear is charged with a kind of moral and spiritual valence that mutes any possibility of its association with the archaic dimensions of dread that distinguish the *mysterium tremendum*, as Rudolf Otto defines it. There is certainly no sense of it as a manifestation of the frightening qualities that we have come to associate with the notion of God himself as the very embodiment of dread. This does not mean that the concept fails to materialize in *De Doctrina Christiana*. It does, in fact, emerge later in the second book of Milton's theological discourse, specifically in the chapter dealing with oath-taking and the casting of lots. In his discussion of oath-taking, Milton begins with the following observation: "When we take an oath we call God to witness that we are speaking the truth, and curse ourselves, either by implication or expressly, if we should be lying." Moving from that observation, Milton maintains that "Both God's command and his example show that the taking of oaths is lawful." To that end, he cites, among other texts, Deuteronomy 6:13: "Thou shalt fear the Lord thy God, and serve him, and shalt swear by his name." This passage is cited in the context of the admonition to fear God lest his anger "be kindled against thee, and destroy thee from off the face of the earth" (Deut. 6:15). Already implicit in the act of swearing oaths in God's name is the fear that is associated with incurring his anger (YP 6:684–85; CM 17:118–21). For Milton, the act of swearing oaths in God's name carries with it a sense of fear and anger implicit in the most archaic notions of deity.

It is here that the concept of God as fear or dread emerges in Milton's treatment. At issue is the unique phrase "Dread of Isaac" (*pachad yitschaq*), which Milton does not hesitate to invoke in his discussion of oath-taking. After citing examples in which not only humans but God swears oaths in his anger (Ps. 95:11), Milton avers that the taking of oaths is made particularly evident by the angels and saints of God. Among the proof-texts that Milton cites to support this statement is Genesis 31:53: "Jacob sware by the fear of his father Isaac" (iuravit Iacob per pavorem patris sui)."[25] In his citation of this text, Milton renders "fear" not by its customary form *timor* but by the more nearly expressive form *pavor*.[26] Whereas *timor* does carry with it the notions of fear, dread, apprehension, alarm, and anxiety, it is more nearly associated in a positive sense with the idea of reverence and veneration earlier delineated under the heading of *cultus*. *Pavor*, on the other hand, carries with it the notions of trembling, quaking, and panting with fear. It is associated in particular with religious fear, awe, and dread, and it has even been known to be personified as a god of fear.[27] This is the sense in which Milton no doubt understands it. For this reason, he explains the passage "Jacob sware by the fear of his father Isaac," by declaring quite unequivocally, "id est, Deum." The explanation is an acknowledgment of the remarkable force of the passage, the fact that it in effect *identifies* God with fear or dread. God not only inspires dread in others: he *is* himself dread. As Milton argues in this chapter of *De Doctrina Christiana*, the swearing of an oath is not something that one undertakes lightly. If one is to swear an oath in God's name, it had better be for a very serious purpose. Especially if one is to swear by the name known as *pachad*, or, to use Milton's term, *pavor*, one must exercise extreme caution (YP 6:684–85; CM 17:118–21). Whether as *pachad* or as *pavor*, then, dread assumes an undeniable importance to the Milton of *De Doctrina Christiana*. What is true of his theological tract is no less true of his other writings.

His psalm translations are a case in point. If, as William Riley Parker argues, these translations reflect the spirit of *Samson Agonistes*, they likewise articulate a theology in which God is conceived in the most archaic terms as the source not just of wrath but also of absolute dread.[28] Here, one beholds dread deified. This is certainly true of the translations of Psalms 80–88. At the very outset of the sequence, Milton imports the motif of divine dread into his portrayal of the Psalmist's calling upon God to save the Israelites in their time of need. Whereas the first verse of Psalm 80 in the Hebrew has simply "[you who] sit [between] the cherubim, shine forth" (yoshev hacrubim hophiyah), Milton transforms this rendering into an elaborate quatrain.[29] Within this quatrain, the Psalmist apostrophizes God as follows: Thou "that sitt'st between the Cherubs *bright/ Between their wings out-spread, | Shine forth, and from thy cloud give light, | And on our foes thy dread*" (5–8). As Milton makes clear in the head-note to his psalm translations, his own additions are indicated "*in a different Character,*" that is, in italics.[30] The additions to the original in the present quatrain are not only considerable but also significant. Implicit in the original is the concept of God as a dwelling presence within the ark of the covenant. So conceived, God shines forth in his glory. Intensifying and elaborating upon this idea, Milton portrays the dwelling presence of God between the outspread wings of the cherubim as not only disseminating light but as overwhelming God's foes with dread.[31] The divine theophany manifests its presence through the light that distinguishes its glory and through the dread that constitutes its divinity. In the juxtaposition that the quatrain structures, light and dread become corresponding entities in the portrayal of deity. As attributes of deity, both are imbued with a kind of materiality, a "thingness," that manifests the brilliance and power of

God's dwelling presence. Disseminating its brilliance through the medium of light, that presence overwhelms all those who would violate its sanctity. This overwhelmingness assumes the form of dread.[32]

II

It is precisely this dread that overwhelms the Philistines in *Samson Agonistes*. Just when the Philistines are most elated by their conquest and blinded by their idolatry, we recall that God as "our living Dread" sends among them "a spirit of phrenzie" that urges them on with mad desire "to call in hast for thir destroyer." The Philistines thereby unwittingly importune "thir own destruction to come speedy upon them." Such is the fate of those who, "jocund and sublime, / Drunk with Idolatry, drunk with Wine, / And fat regorg'd of Bulls and Goats" are filled with a kind of Dionysiac madness as they "chaunt" their idol (1669–81). The Semichorus's celebration of their destruction embodies a paradox that strikes at the heart of the concept of dread. Those who prefer the false god before the true God must experience the full import of dread as that which impels one unwittingly to effect his own demise. For such idolaters, the experience of dread is at once attractive and repulsive. The "spirit of phrenzie" that imbues the Philistines causes them to become increasingly consumed with a delight in the very thing that destroys them. Milton refers to this phenomenon in *De Doctrina Christiana* as a hardening of the heart (*indurando*) and a blinding of the understanding (*excaecando*) that consume the sinner and, at God's own prompting, impel him to bring his own destruction upon himself.[33]

Once again, Rudolf Otto is germane here. In *The Idea of the Holy*, Otto classifies the phenomenon under the heading that he calls "the element of fascination" (*fascinans*). If the numinous appears to the mind as an object of horror and dread, it is nonetheless that which allures its victim with a potent charm. Entirely intimidated and cast down, the individual who trembles before it has at the same time the impulse to embrace it, to make it his own. Although he may be bewildered and overcome by it, he experiences something that "captivates and transports him with a strange ravishment," rising to the pitch of a "dizzy intoxication." This is what Otto calls "the Dionysiac element" in the numinous. According to Otto, it is "at once the strangest and most noteworthy phenomenon in the whole history of religion."[34] Otto is not alone in his account of the paradoxical nature of this phenomenon. In his treatise *The Concept of Dread*, Søren Kierkegaard considers what he terms "the dialectical determinants in dread." Constituting those determinants is the paradox by which dread becomes at once "a sympathetic antipathy and an antipathetic sympathy." The individual is simultaneously drawn to it and repelled by it, that is, attracted to that which repels him and repelled by that which attracts him. "He cannot flee from dread, for he loves it," but "he does not love it, for he flees from it." Under this circumstance, dread becomes an "alien power" that lays hold of him and consumes him, as he sinks in the dread that he loves even while he fears it.[35] Such is the quandary inspired by dread.

As the Philistines of *Samson Agonistes* come to learn only too well and, of course, too late, this phenomenon in its divinized form culminates in their own undoing. "Drunk with Idolatry, drunk with Wine," they experience the full force of that which is at once the *mysterium fascinans* and the *mysterium tremendum*. Drawn to the first through a misplaced allegiance to an idol that ultimately fails them, they are destroyed by the second in the form of a power whose impact they never for a moment expected to encounter. Conceived as a "living Dread" that overwhelms them at the height of their frenzy, this phenomenon unleashes its cataclysmic forces in a manner that is all-consuming. Both the vehicle of that unleashing and the victim of that which is unleashed, Samson becomes the means by which God as dread manifests his power in the theater of Dagon's temple. What results in this Dagonalia is the spectacle of dread enacted in its most dramatic and catastrophic form. It is this enactment toward which the action of *Samson Agonistes* builds from its outset to its devastating conclusion.

Early in the drama, Manoa delineates what will be at stake for his son. "This day," he says,

> the *Philistines* a popular Feast
> Here celebrate in *Gaza;* and proclaim
> Great Pomp, and Sacrifice, and Praises loud
> To *Dagon,* as their God who hath deliver'd
> Thee *Samson,* bound and blind into their hands.

As the result of such a celebration,

> *Dagon* shall be magnifi'd, and God
> Besides whom is no God, compar'd with Idols,
> Disglorifi'd, blasphem'd, and had in scorn
> By th' idolatrous rout amidst thir wine.   (433–43)

The entire drama moves toward this moment, one in which the *agon* becomes a theomachic confrontation of momentous proportions. In response to his father's statement, Samson is painfully aware of the theomachic dimensions of the conflict:

> all the contest is now
> 'Twixt God and *Dagon; Dagon* hath presum'd,
> Me overthrown, to enter lists with God,
> His deity comparing and preferring
> Before the God of *Abraham.*   (461–65)

Yet Samson has faith that God will prevail in this *agon.* "Thus provoked," God "will arise and his great name assert." In the assertion of that name, "*Dagon* must stoop," Samson promises,

> and shall e're long receive
> Such a discomfit, as shall quite despoil him
> Of all these boasted Trophies won on me,
> And with confusion blank his Worshippers.   (468–71)

So Dagon will be overthrown in this cataclysmic event. It is what Milton himself in "The Argument" to his drama calls the catastrophe, which implies both a sudden and widespread disaster and in dramaturgical terms the "overturning" (*katastrophe*) that follows the climax.

As Samson is well aware, this will be the time when "the God of *Abraham*" will finally make his "great name" known. Implicit in the defeat of Dagon and his worshipers is the overturning of the bearer of the false name, that of Dagon, within the confines of his own temple.[36] In this act of overturning, the bearer of the true name reveals his identity. As the Semichorus declares triumphantly, that name is Dread. The name is apt, for, as we recall not only from the biblical sources but also from the seventeenth century commentaries on those sources, the one true name of "the God of *Abraham*" is Dread (*pachad*), the Dread of Isaac (*pachad yitschaq*), to be precise. Imported into the dramatic setting of the Samson narrative, this name might well be declared the Dread of Samson (*pachad shimshon*), and so I designate it here. Such a designation is only fitting considering the fact that the appointed bearer of this dread at the catastrophic moment that culminates the drama is none other than Samson. It is apt that he is ultimately the bearer of this dread because he himself at one time bore that very name. So the Chorus avers that in better times the Israelites had once called Samson their own "great dread" (1474). As the bearer and embodiment of God's dread, Samson had assumed this name as a mark of his identity. If it is an identity he was more than willing to assume in a former life, the catastrophic denouement of the drama provides him the opportunity to assume it yet once more, even at the expense of his own life. The manifestation of the *mysterium tremendum* in all its terror, Samson as the heir of dread fulfills his destiny as the one through whom "our living Dread" asserts its awful power and reasserts its name as *pachad Shimshon*.

Imbued with a sense of the destructiveness that such a destiny entails, Samson at the climactic point of his *agon* takes upon himself the task of implementing the full force of God's awesome power. So the Messenger who has escaped the cataclysm relates what transpired. Having satisfied his captors that he who was once "thir dreadful enemy" is now by Dagon made "thir thrall," Samson first performs great feats of strength before the assembled crowds. Thereafter, he is led between the supporting pillars of the theater, where, "with head a while enclin'd, / And eyes fast fixt he stood, as one who pray'd, / Or some great matter in his mind revolv'd" (1636–38). Then, raising his head, he cries aloud:

> Hitherto, Lords, what your commands impos'd
> I have perform'd, as reason was, obeying,
> Not without wonder or delight beheld.
> Now of my own accord such other tryal
> I mean to shew you of my strength, yet greater;
> As with amaze shall strike all who behold.   (1640–45)

This declaration differs markedly from the biblical source. There, Samson's final words are a simple and direct cry for vengeance: "And Samson called unto the Lord, and said, O Lord God, remember me, I pray thee, only this once, O God, that I may be at once avenged of the Philistines for my two eyes" (Judg. 16:28). What Samson seeks in the biblical account is retribution for his loss of sight. The Samson of the Miltonic account, on the other hand, is a much more mysterious figure. He descends into the depths of himself either to pray or to revolve some great matter in his mind.[37] He does so in preparation for an utterance that is as mysterious as the gesture that precedes it. The force of that utterance is such that it strikes with amazement all who behold what it occasions.

To understand the utterance, one must be attuned to the implications of the language in which it is cast. At issue is the phrase "of my own accord." Much has been made of the phrase. In his seminal study of Milton's drama, Joseph Wittreich, for example, has sought in effect to call into question the pivotal moment in which the phrase occurs by associating it with the discourse of false prophets. *"Of his own accord,"* Wittreich observes, "is always used scripturally to mean by one's own initiative." At this moment in the drama, "it is used to imply a contrast between the false prophets who act of their own accord and the true prophets who act by divine commission."[38] For our purposes, however, an examination of the scriptural context of the phrase makes it abundantly clear that it is used in a technical sense as a formula for the swearing of oaths and that its employment is founded upon the discourse not of humans (whether in the form of false prophets or true) but of God.

Throughout the Old Testament, God acts "of His own accord" in the swearing of oaths. The phrase that appears time and again is *"biy nishba'ti":* (by myself [or of my own accord] I have sworn).[39] Milton cites it repeatedly in his discussion of oath-taking in *De Doctrina Christiana*.[40] There, one finds such proof-texts as Genesis 22:16: "by myself have I sworn, saith Jehovah," and Hebrews 6:13: "because he [Jehovah] could swear by no greater, he sware by himself" (YP 6:85; CM 17:120–21). Drawn from the Old Testament, the first proof-text concerns God's oath to Abraham that he will be blessed as the result of his obedience. Drawn from the New Testament, the second proof-text is in a sense a commentary on the first. God's acting of his own accord in swearing by himself to Abraham demonstrates the magnitude of the oath. In the Old Testament, the locution *biy nishba'ti* often appears in the denunciatory setting of prophecy as God swears of his own accord to destroy rebellious nations: "But if ye will not hear these words, I swear by myself, saith the Lord, that this house will become a desolation" (Jer. 22:5); "For I have sworn by myself, saith the Lord, that Boz'rah shall become a desolation, a reproach, a waste, and a curse; and all the cities thereof shall be perpetual wastes" (Jer. 49:13).[41] To invoke the phrase "of my own accord" or "of his own accord," then, is to align oneself with the discourse of God, who, more than anyone else in Scriptures, acts of his own accord ("by Himself") and customarily in the context of swearing an oath.

Thus, when Samson declares, "Now of my own accord such other tryal / I mean to shew you of my strength, yet greater; / As with amaze shall strike all who behold" (1643–45), he is adopting a locution that in its biblical context has all the denunciatory force of the swearing of oaths by an incensed God prepared to unleash his dread upon his desperate enemies. Rather than simply seeking to be avenged for the loss of his eyes in the manner of his biblical prototype, the Miltonic Samson in effect subsumes within himself the divine role implied by the phrase *biy nishba'ti* (by myself I have sworn) and becomes that force, that *tremendum* through which "our living Dread" is made manifest. His assumption of such a role in the appropriation of divine discourse may have the ring of blasphemy to some. Suppose Samson is *not* divinely inspired to talk like God and thereby to assume that most archaic role of God as "our living Dread"? He does, after all, pull down the same destruction on himself that he metes out to his enemies. I think that such questions skirt the issue. The point is that Samson is able to talk like God because he is able to act like God. That is, he is empowered to be triumphantly destructive in God's cause. In this cataclysmic act, all sense of Samson's "beingness" is obliterated. With this obliteration, it is now his "livingness" that matters. He has become a force, a terror, and a dread: he exists totally within the context of this new role. That is his raison d'être. He is "our living Dread" incarnate.

A figure so totally imbued with this dread that he effectively becomes it, Samson, like God, is *pachad*, dread itself. If God is known as *pachad yitschaq*, Samson fulfills his role as *pachad shimshon*. We recall that Thomas Wilson defined the phrase *pachad yitschaq* as a metonymy of the effect for the cause, a phenomenon in which the response to the object of fear becomes the object itself. So in Samson the metonymy is fulfilled: he becomes that very dread he unleashes. Wilson also maintains that in the metonymic process of transference, fear involves "the whole worshippe of God," an idea intensified by Bunyan's discourse on dread later in the century. Those who fail to worship God with the dread that is due him are doomed to experience the devastating effects of the very dread they disavow. Crucial to the concept of dread, then, is the element of *cultus*, placed within a terrifying context indeed.

That context is fully exploited in *Samson Agonistes*. Centered in the figure of Samson as the embodiment of dread, the overwhelming of the Philistines in the temple of Dagon assumes a decidedly cultic (not to mention terrifying) bearing as a manifestation of godhead in its most archaic form. This bearing is operative in the concept of a "living Dread" whose dwelling presence resides in a specific locale, a site of worship. As the Semichorus makes clear in its celebration of the overwhelming of the Philistines, that site is Shilo, the "bright Sanctuary" of Milton's deity. In order to understand the full impact of ascribing to the God of dread a local habitation and a name, we must attend more closely to the act of situating the God of *Samson Agonistes* within the confines of Shilo. The reference to Shilo is significant because it provides a local habitation for "our living Dread." Deity is brought down and localized both chronologically and topographically within a specific cultic residence, one in fact that was ascribed to God during the period of Judges and beyond. As one of the three premonarchic sanctuaries between the time of Joshua and the time of Solomon, Shilo is associated with the early history of the ark of the covenant.[42] As the events underlying such a history make clear, this was a violent and tumultuous period, one in which the ark was seen to be imbued with a power at once awesome and destructive, on occasion, even unpredictable and unstable. It was a time fully in keeping with a view of deity as the manifestation of the most archaic forces. As such, it not only was seen to reside within its cultic center but also was capable of being transported from the one place to the next for the purposes of unleashing its tremendous and devastating energies upon the enemy. If *Samson Agonistes* moves "toward" anything, it certainly moves toward this most primitive conception of godhead.

The import of such a notion of deity becomes significant in the context of 1 Samuel 4–5. Commonly associated in the Renaissance with the Samson narrative in Judges, this passage represents a crucial subtext for understanding both the destruction of the temple of Dagon and the articulation of deity as a source of ultimate dread in *Samson Agonistes*.[43] According to the narrative, the Israelites, in battle with the Philistines, attempt to overcome the enemy through recourse to the ultimate weapon: the ark of the covenant at Shilo. Their stratagem is founded upon the belief that the ark of the covenant is the portable weapon of utmost power through which God overwhelms his enemies (compare Josh. 6:6–21; 2 Sam. 11:11; Ps. 68).[44] "When the ark of the covenant of the Lord came into the camp, all Israel shouted with a great shout, so that the earth rang again." Hearing the noise of the shout, "the Philistines were afraid, for they said, God is come into the camp" (1 Sam. 4:3–7). The Israelites, however, are in for an unpleasant surprise. Because of the corruptions arising from the sons of Eli as priestly stewards of the ark at Shilo, the stratagem unfortunately proves ineffective. Israel is smitten; the sons of Eli slain; and the ark of God taken captive (1 Sam. 4:10–11). The narrative thereby ironically reverses expectations as a prelude to the eventual destruction of the Philistines in the aftermath of the conflict. Far from calling into question the dreadful power of the ark, the narrative only heightens that sense of power, for it establishes the fact that the power to be unleashed from the ark will occur at moments that are least expected and on occasions that are least anticipated. In this case, the circumstances are appropriate when the power of the Philistines is at its height.

Assuming that they have gained complete power over the Israelites and their God, the Philistines take the ark and install it in the temple of Dagon in Ashdod, directly opposite the idol itself as a potent sign that their god has prevailed over the God of Israel. Here the Old Testament recounts a Dagonalia all its own as a counterpart to the Dagonalia in the Book of Judges. What occurs is a series of events through which the god of the Philistines is overthrown by the power that resides in the ark. The Philistines come to learn of this power through a process of realization that culminates in the destruction not only of their idol but also of themselves. Having placed the ark of the covenant next to the idol of Dagon the first night, they learn to their astonishment the following morning that their god has been overthrown. "And when they of Ashdod arose early on the morrow, behold, Dagon *was* fallen upon his face to the earth before the ark of the Lord." Refusing to acknowledge the force of this lesson the first time, they must be taught it a second time. Thus, they repeat the offense by setting the idol of Dagon in his place again and placing the ark of the covenant next to it. The same thing happens a second time, except with more force. For when the Philistines "arose early on the morrow morning, behold, Dagon *was* fallen upon his face to the ground before the ark of the Lord; and the head of Dagon and both the palms of his hands *were* cut off upon the threshold; only *the stump of* Dagon was left to him" (1 Sam. 5:3–4).[45]

So frightful is this event to the Philistines that, according to the narrative, in later years no individual, not even the priests of Dagon, dares to tread upon the threshold of the place where this event has occurred. The destructive force of the ark is not limited simply to the confines of Dagon's temple, however, for the hand of the Lord reaches forth to destroy both the people of Ashdod and those that occupy the surrounding coasts as well (1 Sam. 5:5–6). The only recourse for those who remain is to attempt to return the ark to its rightful place, for the Philistines realize that they have something entirely uncontrollable and terrifying in their midst, something that has the potential to destroy all who would attempt to violate the

forces of deity that reside in the ark of the covenant and subvert those forces by taking the ark captive.[46]

The circumstances surrounding 1 Samuel 4–5 engaged
Milton as early as the poem *On the Morning of Christ's
Nativity*, which alludes to Dagon as "that twise batter'd god
of *Palestine*" (line 199), an idea that is later reintroduced into
the account of Dagon in *Paradise Lost:*

> Next came one
> Who mourn'd in earnest, when the Captive Ark,
> Maim'd his brute Image, head and hands lopt off
> In his own Temple, on the grunsel edge,
> Where he fell flat, and sham'd his Worshipers:
> *Dagon* his Name, Sea Monster, upward Man
> And downward Fish.   (1:457–63)

Along with his temple, this god, the poet observes, was "dreaded
through the Coast / Of *Palestine*, in *Gath* and *Ascalon* / And
Acaron and *Gaza's* frontier bounds" (1.464–66).[47] The epic
account is apposite in its focus upon the overcoming of that
"brute Image," the very idolatrous presence of Dagon, by the
ark of the covenant made captive but not deprived of its power
by the enemy. Confronted by the true God dwelling within the
ark, the false god falls discomfited, its cult undermined and
its worshipers shamed both within its own unhallowed confines
and beyond to the outlying territories. As much as Dagon is
"dreaded" throughout these territories, the true dread, that
Dread of Dreads resident within the ark, deprives the twice-
battered god of its dreadful pretensions. Such is the Dagonalia
that Milton envisions in *Paradise Lost.*

The biblical narrative and its rearticulation in Milton's epic
are particularly important, because they provide a crucial context for understanding the full implications of the theology of
dread delineated in *Samson Agonistes.* In the Semichorus's celebration of "our living Dread who dwells / In *Silo* his bright
Sanctuary," we encounter the terrifying force of a deity whose

residence in the ark of the covenant, momentarily displaced from its sanctified setting and taken captive by the enemy, becomes the occasion for destroying all who would violate and attempt to subvert the sanctity with which it is imbued. Although the events surrounding the Israelite-Philistine wars and the installation of the ark in the temple of Dagon post-date the Judges narrative, the action of Milton's drama looks forward to these events in its reference to the localized site of a deity who dwells as an awesome presence within the confines of Shilo, that most ancient of sanctuaries. Once those confines are violated and the ark removed to an unhallowed site, God's dreadfulness is unleashed in its full fury. Those who stand in its way are destroyed utterly. The god that the unhallowed worship is correspondingly destroyed. All that remains is his "stump."

It is the undoing of Dagon within the confines of his place of worship that renders the narrative in 1 Samuel so germane to an understanding of our own exploration of the cultic dimensions of dread in *Samson Agonistes*. For it is the dread which permeates God's own dwelling presence in the ark of the covenant that underscores this most archaic notion of deity. To view the Judges account of Samson from the perspective of 1 Samuel is to be made aware of the extent to which dread as a cultic phenomenon depersonalizes any concept of God in Milton's drama. What emerges is an emphasis upon "place" as the site of worship and "thing" as the vehicle through which worship is enacted. God is not only depersonalized but also localized as the manifestation of the overwhelming power that resides in singular objects. As the vehicle of such power, the Miltonic Samson within the temple of Dagon is the means by which the *mysterium* unleashes all the forces of destruction upon the idol and its worshipers.

The manner in which this event is conceived invites us to reassess the notion of deity that emerges in *Samson Agonistes*. No longer is it possible to look upon the God of Milton's drama as the culmination of a movement or progressive revelation toward a more rational conception of the nature of deity. Any attempt to suggest that Milton's God may be understood through what Otto calls the enlightened categories of spirit, reason, purpose, and good will is undermined by what actually transpires. The theology of dread that distinguishes the drama is one in which deity is portrayed in its most archaic and terrifying form. Localized in ancient shrines and manifested in the unleashing of devastating powers, the *mysterium* that underlies the archaic sense of godhead in *Samson Agonistes* is one fully befitting a drama that culminates in mass destruction. If Samson is among those destroyed by the very forces he has unleashed, he nonetheless triumphantly fulfills his role as the true avatar of "our living Dread who dwells / In *Silo* his bright Sanctuary."

Part III

The Heresies of Godhead

SEVEN

The Socinian Imperative

✝

In what appears to be an ongoing tendency in modern criticism, scholars are ever more inclined to align Milton with the various heresies that emerged with renewed vigor during the revolutionary decades of the seventeenth century. Most recently, the essays in Stephen B. Dobranski and John Rumrich's collection *Milton and Heresy* (1998) suggest the extent to which the "orthodox Milton" has increasingly given way to the "heretical Milton." In the volume's introduction, appropriately subtitled "Heretical Milton," Dobranski and Rumrich distinguish between two constructions of Milton that have arisen throughout the centuries, one orthodox (grounded in the time-honored traditions of Christian humanism), the other heterodox (grounded in the radical crosscurrents of Milton's own age). "It seems absurd," they contend, that Milton "could be heard as a voice of orthodoxy. Yet twentieth century scholars have often understated, explained away, or otherwise soft-pedaled his heretical beliefs."[1] Conceived in this manner, Milton is one whose works become the repository of either overt or covert heretical views that, sufficiently understood, invite a reassessment of his radical habits of mind. To be sure, such a conception is hardly new. As Christopher Hill's *Milton and the English Revolution* (1977) made clear more than two decades ago, the conception of a heretical Milton is part of a continuing process of resituating him in the context of the heterodox and often conflicting crosscurrents and movements that distinguish his own radical milieu, one in which Milton himself was a major player.[2] I view the tendency to venture the notion of a heretical Milton not with alarm but with excitement at the potential disclosures that such an approach might yield. At the same time, I am deeply aware that one must resist the temptation simply to label Milton as this kind of heretic or that kind of heretic.

Hill purports to be sensitive to the dangers of labeling: a great fuss, he avers, is sometimes made concerning the precise heresy with which to label Milton. "Was he," Hill asks rhetorically, "an Arian? A Nestorian? A Monarchian? A Sabellian? A subordinationist? Or was he a Socinian?" As Hill knows, labels of any sort are dangerous. He accordingly maintains that Milton was "an eclectic, the disciple of no individual thinker," or heresy, for that matter.[3] As Janel Mueller reminds us, "heresy," as a "keyword" with its root in *hairesis*, carries the meaning of "seizing" or "taking hold," which then implies "choice" in the sense of an "inclination." At its root, it is neutral in its implications.[4] This is an etymology of which Milton was certainly aware and did not hesitate to articulate in his works. Thus, in his *Treatise of Civil Power*, he maintains that heresy "is no word of evil note; meaning the choice or following of any opinion good or bad in religion or any other learning" (YP 7:647). As Milton argues in *Areopagitica*, right choice involves the exercise of reason informed by a full awareness of the distinction between "good or bad." One way or the other, this choice must be made, not because we follow the dictates of others but because we attend to the dictates of our own judgment. "A man may be a heretick in the truth; and if he beleeve things only because his Pastor sayes so, or the Assembly so determins, without knowing their reason, though his belief be true, yet the very truth he holds, becomes his heresie" (YP 2:543). As much as Milton sought to distinguish between one form of heresy or another, he became painfully aware of the extent to which he himself had to suffer the indignity of being cast as heretical by his enemies. Thus branded heretic for his views on divorce, he portrays himself as one among others "nam'd and printed Hereticks" ("On the Forcers of Conscience," 11) in the "gangraenas" and "heresiographies" of his day.[5] In these vehicles of slander, labels of one sort or another abounded during Milton's lifetime. As David Masson observes, one always ran the risk of being decried as an atheist, a mortalist, a materialist, an anti-Sabbatarian, an anti-scripturalist, an Antitrinitarian or a Socinian or Arian. Equally appalling, one might (in the same vein) also be branded a "divorcer" or "Miltonist."[6] Some will no doubt derive a certain satisfaction in realizing that (in Milton's time, at least) to claim oneself a "Miltonist" was tantamount to claiming oneself a heretic. Modern Miltonists (at least, those who view Milton in heretical terms, as opposed to those who view him in orthodox terms) might well consider the label a cause of celebration rather than an occasion of dismay. Instead of writing gangraenas and heresiographies, Miltonists of the heretical bent are producing smart books (like *Milton and Heresy*) that provide a balanced and illuminating assessment of where the heretical Milton stands and why.

In keeping with these studies, as well as with Milton's view of heresy as the product of one's ability to choose wisely through the exercise of reason and informed judgment, I shall focus on one heresy in particular, that of Socinianism (later to be known as Unitarianism), a movement of immense importance to Milton's milieu.[7] As Christopher Hill observes, "there are general histories of Unitarianism and of Socinianism in which Milton's name occurs, but no study [of Milton] in light of this tradition."[8] This is not to say that scholars have been remiss in attending to the Socinian elements in Milton's thought. More than three decades before Hill's book on Milton and the revolution, H. John McLachlan, the great scholar of Socinianism, produced a study of the religious opinions of Milton, Locke, and Newton. Perhaps because of McLachlan's predilections, the "opinions" in question are seen as decidedly "Unitarian," but, despite his inclination to overstate his case at times, McLachlan's work is important in its determination to approach Milton from a decidedly radical perspective. As we shall see, moreover, the notion of pairing Milton's religious views with those of such figures as Locke and Newton is hardly unique to the Unitarian outlook embraced by McLachlan. More recently, Hugh MacCallum has advanced an argument about the Socinian (as well as other radical) elements in Milton's thought that is as illuminating as it is judicious. It lays the groundwork superbly for its own conclusion that Milton's theology "was shaped to a significant extent" by its response to Socinianism.[9]

In keeping with Hill's call for a study of Milton in light of the Socinian tradition and responsive to the important work of scholars such as McLachlan and MacCallum, I shall examine two issues of major import. The first concerns the emergence of Socinianism as a movement and the relationship between that movement and Milton's own doctrinal outlook. The second concerns the afterlife of the movement and the manner in which critics of Milton in the two centuries following his death saw fit to interpret his theological views in Socinian terms. I wish to contextualize Milton and his works in light of the growth of Socinianism, as well as to survey some significant moments in the critical history of reading Milton as a writer of the "Socinian persuasion." I wish not to demonstrate that Milton overtly subscribed to the beliefs that constitute Socinianism (he most decidedly did not) but to suggest that Hill's astute estimate of Milton as "an eclectic, the disciple of no individual thinker" is as true of his ties to the Socinians as it is of his ties to any one of the sectarian movements that distinguish his radical milieu.

I

The Socinian movement has a long and complex doctrinal history, which can only be summarized briefly here. Especially in the case of Socinianism, a summary of this sort is difficult because so much of what is known about the movement must be derived from its critics and opponents. Like the early Christian heresies (Arianism, for example), Socinianism "often suffered from being known largely at second hand." In some respects, Socinianism might be said to have existed as a construction in the works of its enemies. According to McLachlan, "Socinian" was invoked as a general term to encompass different kinds of heterodoxies. Thus, "in an age when nice discrimination between heresies could hardly be expected, 'Socinians' were all who departed radically from the orthodox Christian scheme of redemption or found difficulty with the metaphysical notions enshrined in Catholic doctrinal formulae."[10] The name "Socinus" is derived from the Sienese family known as Sozzini or Sozini. Those opposed to the Socinians invoked the name as a term of opprobrium no doubt with the idea that "Sozzini" as a word has affinities with Italian terms that denote such meanings as "filthy," "nasty," "foul," "obscene" and "polluted."[11] According to Paul M. Zall, detractors spoke of the Socinians with the awareness that "Sozzini" might well imply "filthy little people."[12] Being branded a "Socinian" was accordingly much more demeaning than being branded a "Miltonist."

The history of Socinianism goes back to Lelio Sozzini (1525–62) and his nephew Fausto Sozzini (1539–1604), who were at the forefront of the Antitrinitarian movement that left its

mark on the emergence of religious radicalism in the Reformation. Having established close contacts with Melanchthon,
Calvin, and Bullinger, Lelio Sozzini was suspected of heresy
and obliged to prepare a Confession of Faith, one of the few
surviving documents from his hand. At his death in Zurich,
he left his library and papers to his nephew Fausto. A student
of logic and law, Fausto Sozzini produced several important
works on biblical hermeneutics, Christology, and soteriology.
In 1579, he took up residence in Poland, where he became a
prominent figure in the Polish congregation (Minor Reformed
Church) at Rakow, northeast of Krakow. There, his own theology was later fused with that of the Polish Brethren, who had
already devised a Latin *Catechesis* (1574) to express their own
Antitrinitarian beliefs. A year after Sozzini's death, a revised
Catechesis (1605), the work of four ministers who were close
disciples of Fausto, was published in Polish, followed by
German (1608) and Latin (1609) editions.[13] The 1605 *Catechesis*
appeared under the editorship of Peter Statorius Stoinski,
assisted by Fausto, as far as his time and strength would permit. It is assumed that Fausto's own *Christianae Religionis bre-
vissimo Institutio* (unfinished before his death) was possibly
the first draft of the revised *Catechesis*, but if so, the draft was
entirely recast. Although representing Fausto's views, the 1605
Catechesis was both in arrangement and expression the product of others.[14] During the seventeenth century, the work was
issued in some 15 editions and translated into several languages
(including Latin, Dutch, and English) as it made its way
throughout Europe.[15] Although customarily ascribed to Fausto
Sozzini, the *Catechesis*, or the *Racovian Catechism*, is a composite (and, to some extent, evolving) work that encompasses
a broad range of ideas, not all of them necessarily in accord with
Fausto's own views.[16]

Departing from the customary lines and conventional categories of the Protestant confession (such as the Augsburg and
the Helvetic Confessions), the *Racovian Catechism* bases its

doctrines not on earlier systems of divinity or prevailing creeds but on direct recourse to Scripture.[17] As the ultimate source of all belief, Scripture assumes the form of a *corpus juris* through which a mind trained in the legal methods of reasoning is able to explore its teachings inductively, methodically, and, above all, rationally. As a result of those explorations, one is able to construct a system of theology entirely consistent with the teachings of Scripture. Those teachings may contain things above reason but not in any sense contrary to reason. Through the exercise of reason in the discovery of the teachings of Scripture, one is able to attain eternal life.[18] The text of Scripture is entirely accessible as a means of arriving at a knowledge of God. The knowledge of God and his will as manifested in Christ provides the way to salvation. What results is very much a text-centered and reason-centered theology. The knowledge of God, in turn, involves the knowledge of both his nature and his will. God in his nature is one and only one, not three.[19] God's nature, moreover, is perfectly just, wise, and powerful.[20] There is no room in the Racovian system for the orthodox concept of the Trinity or for an inscrutable God whose ways run counter to our understanding. The preincarnate Son does not exist as a person or entity in the godhead, nor, for that matter, does the Holy Spirit, which is understood as the virtue and power of God.[21] Jesus Christ, in turn, is in his nature a real man, not the product of a mysterious union of divine and human.[22] Thus, the *Racovian Catechism* challenges not only the orthodox idea of the Trinity but also the notion of the hypostatical union.[23]

If Christ's innate deity is denied, God does bestow upon him an adoptive deity, but only as the result of his successfully and gloriously fulfilling his role as suffering servant in this life. That reward is bestowed after Christ's Resurrection and Ascension. Then, Christ assumes his proper place at the right hand of God, where he shares in God's power over the government of the world.[24] Although Christ possesses a fully human nature in this life, he is nonetheless not an ordinary man. His ability to fulfill God's call in living a life of such sanctity is proof of his holiness. As a sign of his holiness, he is given the power to work miracles. In its soteriology, the *Catechism* as a Socinian document emphasizes, then, not the Crucifixion of Christ as the work of salvation but the Resurrection and Ascension of Christ as a sign of the eventual salvation of his brethren in the fullness of time. The work of salvation, however, is not in any way tied to the doctrine of penal satisfaction. Christ does not die in order to atone for our sins, nor is his willingness to undergo the Crucifixion a sign of that atonement.[25] The purpose of Christ's sufferings is to demonstrate how we might best bear our own sins and work out our salvation through Christ's holy example.[26] The *Catechism*, then, dismisses the traditional, orthodox formulations of Christ's role as savior, a role that presupposes in God the need to maintain justice with the concomitant willingness to accept the death of his innocent Son as a substitute for the punishment of the wicked. There is in Socinian theology no sense of the traditional debate between love and wrath in the godhead as a process culminating in the ultimate expression of grace. Such an idea runs entirely counter to the Socinian view of a mild, reasonable, and temperate God.

In the expression of his will, God bestows upon Christ the offices of prophet, king, and priest, a traditional paradigm. But not so traditional is the implementation of that paradigm. As prophet, Christ performs his role of teaching his followers the ways of God, but in the capacity of prophet, Christ does not extend his vocation in this life beyond his knowledge as one who is fully human. Christ performs his priestly role not so much as a sacrifice but as an intercessor in heaven after his Resurrection and Ascension have been realized. In his kingly office, he exercises the supreme power bestowed upon him, once again, after he rises from the dead and is seated at God's right hand. In matters of worship, the *Catechism* recognizes only one sacrament, that of the Lord's Supper, which is viewed as an event commemorating the death of Christ. As an outward act through which Christian converts openly acknowledge Christ as their master, baptism is neither appropriate to infants nor possessed of any regenerative value. Other doctrines voiced in the *Catechism* include a belief in the freedom of the will, as opposed to predestination. Nor is there in Socinian thought an acceptance of the doctrine of original sin that infects all mankind as a result of Adam's fall. In the process, Socinus calls into question the notion of a prelapsarian Adam endowed with peculiar gifts bestowed upon him at birth and lost in the Fall.[27] These, in brief, are some of the major doctrinal beliefs articulated in the *Racovian Catechism* and in Socinian thought in general.

As the most authoritative statement of what came to be known as the theology of Socinanism, the *Racovian Catechism* (1605), in its various translations, found its way into Germany, Holland, England, and France. In England, it made its first appearance in the Latin edition of 1609. With no doubt the hope of gaining royal sanction, those responsible for the Latin edition published the work with a dedication to James I, who subsequently responded by having it consigned to the fires as a pernicious and heretical document. Its initial presence in England, then, was hardly auspicious. Considering the spirit of intolerance toward any ideas deemed heretical during this period, one need hardly be surprised at the reception that the *Racovian Catechism* was accorded. Intolerance was the order of the day. It was not just works deemed heretical that faced immolation: the very bodies of heretics were in danger of enduring the same fate. Between 1548 and 1612 at least 18 persons were burned at the stake for their heretical (particularly Antitrinitarian) views.[28] The author (or authors) of the *Racovian Catechism* would most certainly have qualified in 1609. About a decade after its first appearance in 1609, the *Racovian Catechism* was reissued in one or two surreptitious editions, but with little effect. "In all England," Zall comments, "there seems not to have been a Socinian congregation — at least one meeting openly — before 1652/53 when John Biddle ('the father of English Unitarianism') is supposed to have preached to a like-minded group in London."[29]

Shortly after mid-century, however, Socinianism and its doctrines gained greater currency, principally because of the impact of the movement in Holland, where more than 60 Socinian books had been published, either as reprints of Polish originals or in Dutch and English translations. No doubt, many of these books found their way to English soil. In fact, even before mid-century, harsh precautionary measures were adopted, in part, to stem the tide of Socinianism, which was well known to be gaining ground. In 1640 a convocation of leading ministers in Parliament sitting as a synod framed a new body of Constitutions and Canons for establishing true religion. The fourth canon was directed against "the damnable and cursed heresy of Socinianism." Forbidden was the importation, printing, and dispersion of Socinian books, as well as the preaching of Socinian doctrines. Books that smacked of Socinianism were ordered destroyed. Although the canons were never enforced, they provide clear evidence that Socinianism was on the rise.[30] Ever vigilant to stem the rising tide of heresy, Parliament passed the so-called Blasphemy Act of 1648.[31] A glance at the act leaves little room to doubt that Socinianism is among the heresies that the act seeks to interdict. Those who subscribe to this heresy were to face the possibility of imprisonment or death.[32] In its indictment of Antitrinitarianism (as that which asserts "the Father is not God, the Son is not God, or that the Holy Ghost is not God, or that they three are not one Eternal God"), the act then interdicts any assertion that "Christ is not God equal with the Father." At the same time, the act labels anathema as any "that shall deny his [Christ's] death is meritorious in the behalf of Believers; or that shall maintain and publish as aforesaid, That Jesus Christ is not the Son of God." The act also holds as erroneous any assertion "that man is bound to believe no more than by his reason he can comprehend." These blasphemies and others (all of which smack of Socinianism) are branded anathema by the Blasphemy Act.[33]

To counter the spread of Socinianism, writers such as Francis Cheynell, Ephraim Pagitt, Thomas Edwards, John Owen, Bernard Skelton, Francis Fullwood, Edward Stillingfleet, and John Tillotson rallied to the cause of orthodoxy in their respective works.[34] Reviewing their works reveals the extent to which Socinianism progressively becomes a label for "heresy" in general, a heresy of danger both to the individual and to the state. Thus, in his tract *The Rise, Growth, and Danger of Socinianism* (London, 1643), Francis Cheynell argues passionately against all the corruptions that the heresy of Socinus represents. These corruptions are reflected in the very subtitle of Cheynell's tract: Socinianism, the subtitle declares, is "not the pure Protestant religion, but an hotchpotch of Arminianisme, Socinianisme and popery." According to Cheynell, "the *Socinian* Errour is *Fundamentall*." Those guilty of it "deny Christs satisfaction and so overthrow the foundation of our faith, the foundation of our Justification." Moreover, "they deny the Holy Trinity, and so take away the very object of our Faith; they deny the Resurrection of these Bodies [*sic*], and so take away the foundation of our hope." Still further, "they deny originall sinne, and so take away the ground of our Humiliation; and indeed the necessity of regeneration." Finally, "they advance the power of Nature, and destroy the efficacy of Grace." Socinianism, for Cheynell, is an "*Antichristian* errour, because it takes away the very Essence and Person of *Iesus Christ*." This is the damnable heresy that has infected all of England.[35] Such sentiments are reflected in the writings of other anti-Socinians as well. In sympathy with the kinds of allegations leveled in Cheynell's tract, both Ephraim Pagitt and Thomas Edwards include the Socinians in their respective heresiographies. For Pagitt and Edwards, Socinianism is to be paired with Arianism, both of which are dreaded forms of Antitrinitarianism, a "gangrenous" heresy sweeping the nation in the 1640s.[36]

The anti-Socinian rhetoric that characterizes the 1640s continued throughout the century. The "hammer of the Socinians" John Owen is a prime example of one in whom that rhetoric flourished anew. Commissioned by the Council of State, Owen produced his *Vindiciae evangelicae* (London, 1655), in which he pounded not only John Biddle and the *Racovian Catechism* but Hugo Grotius, whom Owen considered something of a Socinian in his views.[37] Among the issues with which the critics of Socinianism were intolerant is what they argued was the fallacious Socinian overdependence on the supreme efficacy of human reason to determine doctrinal matters. Owen asks rhetorically: "*What Reason* do they [the Socinians] intend? If Reason absolutely, the Reason of things; we grant that nothing *contrary* unto it, is to be admitted. But Reason as it is in this or that Man, particularly in themselves, we know to be weak, maimed, and imperfect; and that they are, and all other Men, extreamly remote from a just and full comprehension of the whole Reason of things."[38] For Owen and a host of other writers during this period, Socinianism becomes not just a danger but *the* archetypal heresy, one that embodies all other heresies, ancient and modern. In keeping with this view, Bernard Skelton thus maintains in *Christus Deus* (London, 1692) that Socinus, like "that grand Impostor *Mahomet*," was not so much a "*Heretick*" as (what is even worse) "the founder of a new Religion," one that is a "composition of the errors of *Arius, Photinus,* and *Pelagius*," among many other heresies that might be mixed in this anti-Christian brew.[39] Worst of all, however, God in Socinian doctrine is transformed from a Christian to a Judaic deity. The Socinian God, Skelton avers, is indeed "purely *Judaical*," a view (for Skelton) tantamount to the very "renunciation of the Christian Religion."[40]

To be sure, the God of the Socinians is *one God*, an outlook in keeping with their "unitarian" theology. More than that, he is in effect a "person." So John Biddle argues in *The Apostolical and True Opinion concerning the Holy Trinity* (1653), "To talk of God taken impersonally, is ridiculous, not only because there is no Example thereof in Scripture, but because God is the Name of a Person, and signifieth him that hath sublime Dominion or Power; and when it is put for the most High God, it denoteth him who with Soveraign and Absolute Authority ruleth over all."[41] Biddle's God, one might suggest, is very much influenced by the delineation of deity in Hebrew Scripture. If not "purely *Judaical*," the conception is certainly indebted to that rendering, upon which the Socinians would look most sympathetically.[42] The anti-Socinians, on the other hand, viewed this, as well as other Socinian doctrines, with suspicion, if not scorn. At the root of this sentiment was a fundamental concern with the Socinian method of interpreting Scripture as a source of doctrinal belief. If one were confident that all doctrine is entirely accessible through the practical application of the principles of logic to the sacred text free of recourse to faith in higher mystery, there is no telling what absurdities might result.

Centered in the rhetoric of anti-Socinianism, this concern was so widespread throughout the century that it even found its way into the "poetical" mainstream. Thus in his *Religio Laici* (1682), John Dryden asks, "Are there not many points, some needful sure / To saving faith, that scripture leaves obscure? / . . . We hold, and say we prove from scripture plain, that Christ is God"; on the other hand, "the bold Socinian / From the same scripture urges he's but man" (307–15). Conflating Arianism and Socinianism in *The Hind and the Panther* (1687), Dryden follows this assault on Socinian methodology by focusing on the central issue of the Son's divinity. Arius and Socinus, Dryden laments, "disavowed" the Son's "eternal god-head" and "condemned" true doctrine through the blatant misreading of "Gospel Texts." Like all such "hereticks," the Arians and Socinians have used the "same pretence" of piety to "plead the scriptures in their own defence" (150–55).[43] The point is that the controversy over Socinian and anti-Socinian (and, with it, Arian and anti-Arian) modes of thought became a staple of the intellectual life of seventeenth century England and beyond. For those determined to root out Socinian thinking, no one was above reproach. This is true even if one protested his innocence in the face of the charge of allegiance (of whatever sort) to the doctrines associated with Socinianism. In response to the question "Are you now, or have you ever been?" one might exclaim "No!" but be judged guilty nonetheless.

John Locke (1632–1704) represents a major instance of this dilemma. Although he disavowed the Socinian label in public, he has been viewed as a Socinian both by friend and enemy alike. Those sympathetic to the Socinian cause have, in fact, deemed Locke (not without justification) "the Socinus of his age."[44] In accord with the Socinian writings, Locke's works are said to reveal "the same lay disengagement from scholasticism, the same purpose of toleration tempered by prudence, the same interest in the minimising of essentials, and the same recurrence to Scripture, interpreted (that is to say, rationalised) by common sense rather than by profound exegesis."[45] The one work that has elicited this claim is Locke's *The Reasonableness of Christianity, as Delivered in the Scriptures* (London, 1695), a tract that seeks to demonstrate that all that is needed for saving faith is present in New Testament teachings (as opposed, implicitly, to the extratestamental teachings of the church). Those determined to enlist Locke to their cause have observed that the very title of the work is consistent with the Socinian emphasis upon Christianity as a religion essentially grounded on the rational precepts of Scripture.[46] In keeping with this thrust is a distinction between what might be called "Scriptural Christianity and the Christianity of the Schools." In the work itself, it is significant that "the word *Trinity* is not so much as mentioned," nor is there "the slightest intimation" that the Trinity is to be regarded "as a fundamental doctrine of the Gospel."[47] Along with the erasure of the Trinity is an emphasis upon the Sonship as a result not of the Incarnation but of the Resurrection, by which means, Locke avers, we may find evidence that Jesus became the "Son of God."[48] It is this sort of evidence, we are told, that leads the careful reader to the realization that Locke supports the Socinian cause. The extent to which Locke was or was not a Socinian is not at issue. What *is* at issue is the way in which those who support the Socinian cause are determined to read him as a Socinian.

During Locke's own time, this kind of reading was the distinguishing characteristic of the anti-Socinians. Although Locke mentions nothing of Socinus or Socinianism in *The Reasonableness of Christianity,* such an omission in no way dissuaded the heresy police (ever attentive to the possibility of heterodoxy) from picking up on what they considered a distinctly Socinian frame of mind. Notable in this regard is John Edwards, the stalwart son of Thomas Edwards of *Gangraena* fame. Responding to Locke's *Reasonableness,* John Edwards produced *Socinianism Unmask'd* (London, 1696), through which he takes Locke to task for exhibiting Socinian tendencies. In his tirade, Edwards goes so far as to transform "Socinianism" into a verb: "Socinianize." Even though one does not claim himself a "Socinian," he may be termed such if he (wittingly or unwittingly) "Socinianizes." As much as one attempts to hide his Socinianizing tendencies, the truth will out. "The plain truth," the ever-vigilant Edwards exclaims, is that Locke "Socinianizes" throughout his work. He does so not directly but obliquely, through a kind of conspiracy of silence. By not mentioning the doctrine of the Trinity, for example, Locke implicitly accepts the Socinian view that such a phenomenon does not really exist. By not mentioning the true doctrine of satisfaction, Locke once again accepts the Socinian view that satisfaction is finally not efficacious. What Edwards lights upon is Locke's "utter silence" concerning sacred matters that are a mainstay of orthodox belief.[49] In short, Edwards reads Locke's silences as evidence of subversive thought, and in the interstices of Locke's exegesis, Edwards sees heresy. It is this criticism by absence that renders Edwards so interesting, for one does not need to be a professed "heretic" before one is in danger of encountering charges of heresy in one's thought and writings.

Locke responded to these charges in two works: *A Vindication of the Reasonableness of Christianity* (London, 1696), followed by *A Second Vindication of the Reasonableness of Christianity* (London, 1697). In both treatises, Locke disavows any ties to Socinianism, its beliefs and its doctrines. Rather, he charges Edwards with trying to frighten people from reading his books by invoking that dreaded bugbear "Socinianism, Socinianism!" Responding to this problem, Locke challenges Edwards to "show one word of Socinianism" in his writings.[50] The point, of course, is that the absence of overt statement does not mean that the heresy is not present. Perhaps Edwards is right, after all: Locke Socinianizes in the most subtle of ways, that is, through a subtext of silence. At least, this is how he has been interpreted by those determined to find in his works elements of Socinian belief. Whether or not those elements are present in Locke's writings, his own outlook embraces a latitudinarianism that infuses all his writings but especially his three letters on Toleration.[51] In the first of these, he declares that, although he has "doubts about the faith of the Socinians," among other forms of heterodoxy, "it is not the diversity of opinions" but "the refusal of toleration to diverse opinions" that has brought about "most of the disputes and wars that have arisen in the Christian world on account of religion."[52] Socinian or not, Locke is a Tolerationist who eschews labels. At the same time, his writings are sufficiently complex to suggest (even in their silences) the possibility of "alien" modes of thought.

Locke is not alone in his embrace of doctrines that might well prompt both his friends and his enemies to read Socinianism in his writings. Of a similar frame of mind is Locke's intimate friend Sir Isaac Newton (1642–1727), who has likewise been thought to subscribe (albeit surreptitiously) to a theology at odds with accepted orthodoxy. Unlike the works that Locke produced on matters of religion, Newton's writings on Christology and soteriology were never made public during his lifetime, perhaps because of fears of reprisal. Accordingly, there was no opportunity for the likes of John Edwards to issue a *Socinianism Unmask'd* in response to Newton's speculations. Although Newton never openly departed from the teachings of the Church of England, his posthumous works and his unpublished papers appear to tell a different story.[53] After Newton's death, his friend John Craig, prebendary of Salisbury, maintained that Newton "was much more solicitous in his inquirys into Religion than into Natural Philosophy," because his thoughts on matters of religion were at times "different from those which are commonly received."[54]

During his lifetime, Newton vacillated about whether to publish any of his theological writings, a notable instance of which is a work in the form of letters exposing as false the customary Trinitarian proof-texts of 1 Timothy 3:16 and 2 John 5:7.[55] In 1690, Newton considered the possibility of publishing these letters anonymously in Holland but then presumably withdrew them "in panic" because of his fears of possible repercussions. Although Newton in old age "committed numerous documents to the flames," he nonetheless "spared these letters and scores of other theological manuscripts," among them, "A Short Scheme of True Religion," detailed commentaries on Daniel and Revelation, and an attack on Athanasius entitled "Paradoxical Questions Concerning the Morals and Actions of Athanasius and His Followers."[56] Newton's manuscripts reveal God as one whose servants live "ever under the Taskmaster's eye."[57] For Newton, God becomes a "dominus deus, pantokrator, Imperator universalis." Although Christ is present, his role is distinctly "recessive."[58] In his account of the God of Newton's manuscripts, Frank E. Manuel ventures a psychological analysis of such an outlook by suggesting that

Newton, as a child born after his father's death, engaged in a search for "the Father" throughout his life. "Overwhelmed by his preoccupation with origins," Newton revealed an "anguished desire" to recover his "lost parent." Questions of theology for Newton were "invested with personal feelings that had their roots in the earlier experiences of childhood." Aware of his special bond to God, Newton looked upon himself as one destined to reveal "the ultimate truth about God's creation." In the words of Alexander Pope, "*God* said: let Newton be! And all was light." Significantly, the phrase "Jeova sanctus unus" became for Newton an anagram for "Isaacus Neuutonus."[59]

However one might respond to such an analysis of Newton's psychological motives, it is clear that his view of God as Father and Lord is consistent not just with his unpublished writings but with views that he expressed in his published works as well. Of seminal importance is the major theological pronouncement that Newton as an old man publicly issued in the second edition of his *Principia* (London, 1713).[60] Responding to the criticisms of the first edition of the *Principia* (London, 1687) by George Berkeley and Gottfried Wilhelm von Leibniz,[61] Newton articulated his conception of God in the form of a general scholium to Proposition 42 in book 3 ("System of the World") of the *Principia*. In the General Scholium, Newton celebrates "the beautiful system of the sun, planets, and comets," in short, the universe at large, as the creation of the "dominion of One." As we have seen, this sense of dominion or lordship, with its implications of power and authority, is crucial to the Newtonian view of God as a Being who is the most supreme *pantokrator* or "universal ruler." In his "beingness," his "livingness," his "oneness," he has a presence and a life over that which he has created. Although God is a Being "eternal, infinite, absolutely perfect," we do not substitute his attributes for his "beingness." "We say, my God, your God, the God of *Israel*, the God of Gods, and Lord of Lords," Newton observes; but we do not say, "my Eternal, your Eternal, the Eternal of

Israel, the Eternal of Gods; we do not say, my Infinite, or my Perfect." To do so would be to call into question our full awareness of God as Lord. "It is," Newton declares, "the dominion of a spiritual being which constitutes a God."[62] One might suggest a concurrence here between Newton's view of God and the view expressed by John Biddle, who likewise emphasizes the significance of "dominion" as a primary function of God's "beingness." Like Biddle's "Judaical" God of Hebrew Scripture, Newton's "God of *Israel*" draws upon conceptions that are decidedly Hebraic in outlook.

In the depiction of God that one discovers in the *Principia*, there is no mention of the Son and certainly no sense of the Christological implications of the Son as redeemer. Although it might well be argued that there is no occasion for such consideration within the context of the issues that Newton addresses in his account of the "System of the World," the absence of any allusion to this dimension is not without significance. It might be argued that one must essentially resort to the unpublished material for a sense of Newton's Christology. But even here, one is at a loss. "There are many theological questions on which Newton never settled into a fixed position. Did Christ exist before all worlds and did he create this one at God's command? Was Christ a higher or a lower being than the angels?" Newton summarizes questions of this sort, but he does not draw definitive conclusions. It is clear that for Newton Christ was not simply a "mere man": "he was the Son of God, not just a human soul who was sent into the world." There is, to be sure, a distinctly Antitrinitarian bias in Newton's unpublished writings. On the other hand, it would be a mistake to invoke Newton's "Antitrinitarianism" in order to "pigeonhole him in one of the recognized categories of heresy," whether Arian, Socinian, or Unitarian. To be sure, Newton's chief villain in the early church is Athanasius rather than Arius. But Newton castigated both for "having introduced metaphysical subtleties into their disputes and corrupted the plain language of Scripture." What is most pronounced in Newton is "a perceptible movement away from the Christological centre of religion." Although Christ himself remains crucial to an understanding of God's providential design, metaphysical distinctions about the nature of the godhead, the hypostatical union, and issues of that sort are relegated to a renewed emphasis upon the "omniscience and omnipotence of God."[63]

However one might be inclined to understand Locke and Newton in the context of the traditions of heterodoxy that flourished throughout early modern England and beyond, it is clear that both reveal an inclination to question the orthodox assumptions upon which the church grounded itself as the century drew to a close. No doubt reflecting his own biases, McLachlan holds that both Locke and Newton "reveal a spirit and temper that closely link them with seventeenth-century Socinianism."[64] As much as this statement is open to question, it provides a framework through which to examine Milton's own works as the product of a thinker responsive to the heterodox crosscurrents of his time.

II

What is true of Locke and Newton is no less true of Milton: within the interstices of his work, within his silences, one may discover patterns of behavior, attitudes, and gestures that on occasion recall aspects of Socinianism. Milton was perhaps one who was "silent yet spake." Are we to interpret from such "utterances" that he might have been "a silent" member of a "small, unorganized," yet "vigorous" movement (interpreted loosely as "Arian" or "Socinian") "that manifested itself openly in the second half of the 1640's and ultimately developed into English Unitarianism"?[65] Our response to this question must be one of extreme caution, for, as we have seen, there are equally strong countertrends in Milton's writings that indicate just how removed he was from embracing an outlook that might

be labeled "Socinian." Hill is right: Milton was indeed "an eclectic, the disciple of no individual thinker" or heresy. Nonetheless,
his writings do at times invite interpretations consistent with
certain aspects of a Socinian point of view.

As indicated, I propose to address these aspects by touching upon both Milton's well-established encounter with
Socinianism and his references (both direct and implied) to the
movement. I shall do that, in turn, as part of a larger project:
that of exploring the history of "Socinianizing" Milton by
those determined to enlist him in their cause. At the very least,
I hope to demonstrate how misguided is Paul M. Zall's observation that "the connection between Socinianism and Milton"
is little more than "a matter of intellectual curiosity."[66]

As is well known, Milton's most immediate contact with
Socinianism arose as a result of the publication and licensing
of the Latin version of the *Racovian Catechism*, or *Catechesis
Ecclesiarum quae in Regno Poloniae, et magno ducatu
Lithuaniae* in March 1651.[67] The book was registered on
November 13, 1651, to William Dugard, the printer to the
Council of State and Milton's friend and publisher.[68] As John
T. Shawcross, among others, makes clear, the heretical nature
of the work occasioned the arrest of Dugard by the council on
January 27, 1652; two days later Dugard had the registry can-
celed. The work was considered sufficiently subversive that
on February 4 the council appointed a committee to examine
Dugard, who, in turn, implicated John Milton as the licenser.
According to Shawcross, Gilbert Millington, the chairman of
the committee, also reported the existence of a note in Milton's
hand licensing the book on August 10, 1650; the note itself,
however, has not been located. In a report of his embassy to
England, the statesman Lieuwe van Aitzema noted on March
5, 1652, the *Catechesis* and Milton's licensing of it. Aitzema
maintains that in his examination by the committee of the
council, Milton admitted licensing the book in keeping with
the spirit expressed in *Areopagitica*.[69]

The extent of Milton's precise involvement in the licensing of the work and the repercussions of that involvement continue to elicit discussion and debate. For example, Stephen B. Dobranski cautions us to be wary of drawing hasty conclusions concerning the relationship between Milton's own views and his role in the licensing of the *Catechesis*.[70] We would do well to take Dobranski's admonitions to heart. Whether Milton's licensing of the *Catechesis* is a reflection of deeply held views concerning the Socinian heresy or simply the product of the circumstances in which Milton as licenser found himself at the time remains to be seen. Dobranski observes that Milton "seems to have suffered no consequences for his involvement in the matter," and, although Dugard was found guilty of publishing "this blasphemous and scandalous Book," Milton continued in his capacity as secretary for foreign tongues. Dobranski warns that we are we not to conclude automatically that the council relieved Milton of his duties as licenser because of the *Catechesis*. That his name does not thereafter appear in this capacity may be the result of his blindness or because he was preoccupied with the composing of his defense tracts.[71] If the circumstances under which Milton licensed *Catechesis* and the repercussions that ensued remain uncertain, nonetheless, it is clear that the publication of *Catechesis* in 1651 is important as a sign not only of the renewed ferment that Socinianism was creating in England at the time but of the bearing that the movement might well have had on Milton's thought and behavior.[72]

To gauge the precise nature of that bearing on Milton's thought is difficult. Milton's own statements about the Socinians are few. In *Tetrachordon*, he refers to the Socinians disparagingly as part of his discussion of Genesis 2:24 ("Therefore shall a man leav his father and his mother, and shall cleav unto his wife; and they shall be one flesh"). Responding to those who argue that this verse demonstrates the inseparability of man and woman in all marriages (whether good or bad), Milton credits Adam with the ability to speak metaphorically, that is, with the power to transcend "corporall meaning" in his discourse. To think otherwise, Milton maintains, is to suggest that "*Adams* insight concerning wedlock reacht no furder" than the literal sense of things. To insist that Adam be limited to the literal meaning of his words is, Milton says, to "make him as very an idiot as the Socinians make him; which would not be reverently don of us" (YP 4:604). The Socinians, of course, maintain no such thing about Adam and his limitations, and they certainly do not conceive him as an "idiot." At most, they question the traditional notion of an Adam endowed with special gifts as a result of his so-called unfallen state. Perhaps the idea of an intellectually obtuse Adam might be attributed to the adversaries of the Socinians.[73] If so, Milton's reference to the Socinian's view of Adam as an "idiot" is about as unflattering an allusion to the body of ideas and beliefs of a particular sect within Protestantism as one can imagine. Whether or not Milton drew upon the rhetoric of the enemies of the Socinians, it is clear that in the mid-1640s, at least, he did not hesitate to use Socinus and his followers in a most undiplomatic way.

By the time Milton published *Of True Religion, Heresy, Schism, Toleration* in 1673, the year before his death, his views had apparently undergone a transformation, at least as far as radical movements such as Socinianism are concerned. It is in *Of True Religion* that we find Milton's most open and direct statements about Socinianism (which Milton, in keeping with the major trends in seventeenth century thought, couples with Arianism). Emerging from a 13-year silence in the publication of tracts on matters of religion and affairs of state, Milton produced a work that, according to an unknown admirer writing two years later, says more on toleration "in two elegant sheets of true religion, heresy, and schism than all the prelates can refute in seven years."[74] The milieu through which *Of True Religion* was produced is one of declarations and counterdeclarations on the part of king and Parliament to determine the limits of religious toleration throughout the commonwealth. In 1672, Charles II issued a Declaration of Indulgence that suspended all penal laws in ecclesiastical matters and allowed Protestant Nonconformists to apply for licenses that permitted public worship. On the surface, the act appeared to be a magnanimous gesture indeed. The problem was that the declaration also implicitly extended its "indulgence" to Roman Catholics. (At least, the declaration did not exclude them.) The response to the possibility of Catholicism's regaining power was swift. Immediately upon publication of the declaration, the cry of "no popery" could be heard in pulpit and pamphlet. Parliament responded by having the declaration canceled and, in its place, passing the Test Act, which (draconianlike) required all civil and military personnel to take the Oaths of Allegiance and Supremacy, to receive the sacraments according to the rites subscribed by the Church of England, and to renounce the doctrine of transubstantiation. That took care of Catholicism, but it also threatened to compromise the "tender consciences" of the Protestant Nonconformists. To help mitigate the harshness of the Test Act, the Commons advanced a bill for the "Ease of Protestant Dissenters," which became a subject of ongoing debate in Parliament. This is the environment in which Milton produced *Of True Religion*, a tract that is clearly Tolerationist in its support both of Protestantism in general (as we might expect) and of Nonconformists in particular. In keeping with the spirit of the Test Act, however, the tract is entirely opposed to popery. The concluding words of the full title of Milton's tract make this opposition clear: "And what best means may be us'd against the growth of POPERY."

In his uncompromising hatred of popery, Milton makes it clear in the tract that "Popery is the only or the greatest Heresie: and he who is so forward to brand all others for Hereticks, the obstinate Papist, the only Heretick" (YP 8:421).

Such an outlook is consistent with his views of Catholicism throughout his career, including his earlier great Tolerationist statement *Areopagitica*. Any attempt to assess the true nature of Milton's attitude toward Socinianism (or any other radical "sect," for that matter) in *Of True Religion* must constantly keep in mind his view of popery. All other sects and schisms that have arisen within Protestantism as the truly "catholic," that is, universal faith, are to be not only tolerated but encouraged as the product of a healthy and energetic church, one in which members seek not to destroy faith but to bolster it. This latitudinarian outlook prevails, as Milton considers Lutherans, Calvinists, Anabaptists, Arminians, Arians, and indeed Socinians. Milton's view of them is consistent — "all these may have some errors but are not Hereticks" — in the sense of knowingly, voluntarily, and maliciously adopting notions that seek to subvert the clear teachings of Scripture. To be sure, there may be elements of error in each of the doctrines advanced by Lutherans, Calvinists, and the like, "but so long as all these profess to set the Word of God only before them as the Rule of faith and obedience, and use all diligence and sincerity of heart, by reading, by learning, by study, by prayer for Illumination of the holy Spirit, to understand the Rule and obey it, they have done what man can do." Even if they are "much mistaken" in "some Points of Doctrine," Milton declares, God "will assuredly pardon them" (YP 8:423–24). Such a statement is a sign not that Milton embraces the precise teachings of the movements he mentions (although he might adopt aspects of them) but that he is willing to view them (as he had in *Areopagitica*) as the embodiment of the efforts of those busy in framing the "spirituall architecture" of the "Temple of the Lord" (YP 2:555). Even in the uncertain period of post-Restoration England, the old, long-silent reformer is determined yet once more to break the silence and have his say.

Having expressed this latitudinarian perspective, Milton then provides an account of the contested beliefs of the movements he has named. He does so not to castigate these movements but rather to highlight particular doctrines that, although perhaps open to question, nonetheless do not compromise the movements as a whole and thereby render their members undeserving of salvation. Indeed, if one "calmly and charitably" inquires into "the hottest disputes among Protestants," Milton observes, one will see that those who engage in such disputes have yet "done what man can do" to justify themselves before God, even when certain of their beliefs may be considered erroneous. He then proceeds to catalog such beliefs and those who hold them. Although the Lutheran subscribes to the doctrine of consubstantiation, for example, this is "an error indeed," Milton observes, "but not mortal." If the Calvinist is "taxt" with a belief in the doctrine of predestination that in effect makes God "the Author of sin," this error is committed "not with any dishonourable thought of God, but it may be over zealously asserting his absolute power." Accused of denying infants "their right to Baptism," the Anabaptist counters that he "denies nothing but what the Scripture denies them." The Arminian, in turn, is condemned for "setting up free will against free grace." But he "disclaims" that "Imputation" by maintaining that he "grounds himself largely upon Scripture only." Milton declares that all these sectarians (including their followers) are not only learned, worthy, virtuous, and zealous men but "perfect and powerful in the Scriptures." Far from deserting these reformers, God would both pardon their errors and accept their "pious endeavours." Following God's example, we too should not persecute them but, as fellow Protestants, "charitably tolerate" them, even if we differ with them on certain matters of doctrine (YP 8:424–26).

It is within this latitudinarian context that Milton addresses Socinianism, which he couples with Arianism. Once again, Milton's purpose is neither to blame nor to praise the specific doctrines these movements profess but to argue on behalf of the idea that those who subscribe to such doctrines (however erroneous we might feel them to be) are sincere in their attempts to ground them in their own reading of Scripture. In his list of movements, Milton places the Arian and the Socinian in the penultimate position between Anabaptist and Arminian. Although the terms of Milton's argument about the various movements within Protestantism are entirely clear, his statement about the Arian and Socinian movements in particular has proven extremely difficult to interpret. For this reason, I quote the pertinent parts of the statement in full:

> The Arians and Socinians are charg'd to dispute against the Trinity; they affirm to believe the Father, Son, and Holy Ghost, according to Scripture, and the Apostolic Creed; as for terms of Trinity, Triniunity, Coessentiality, Tripersonality, and the like, they reject them as Scholastic Notions, not to be found in Scripture, which by a general Protestant Maxim is plain and perspicuous abundantly to explain its own meaning in the properest words, belonging to so high a Matter and so necessary to be known; a mystery indeed in their Sophistic Subtilties, but in Scripture, a plain Doctrin. Their other Opinions are of less Moment. They dispute the satisfaction of Christ, or rather the word *Satisfaction,* as not Scriptural; but they acknowledge him both God and their Saviour. (YP 8:424–25)

This is a complex (if not a convoluted) passage indeed. The passage starts out clearly enough: "The Arians and Socinians," which Milton groups together, "are charg'd to dispute against the Trinity." In grouping the two movements, Milton does not aim to raise complex doctrinal distinctions between Arianism and Socinianism concerning the nature of the Son's preincarnate begetting (for the Arians) and the disbelief in any sort of preincarnate Sonship (for the Socinians), among other issues. Rather, Milton states what (he implies) can be agreed upon by all upstanding Protestants: through recourse to the biblical text (and confirmed by apostolic belief)[75] as the one true source of interpretation, both Arians and Socinians believe in the existence and primacy of the Father, Son, and Holy Ghost. As for vexed terms of theology such as "Trinity, Triniunity, Coessentiality, Tripersonality," both Arians and Socinians reject them as "Scholastic Notions," a phrase that for Milton, as well as for his contemporaries, certainly smacked of "Popery."[76] The point is that the enemy here (as throughout Milton's tract) is popery. The pulpit and pamphlet cry of "no Popery" is lurking within the interstices of the passage.

At issue for Milton is the Protestant emphasis upon the primacy of Scripture in contrast to the "corrupt traditions" that arise out of popery. Whereas the former (Protestant belief) is grounded in the idea of Scripture as "plain and perspicuous abundantly to explain its own meaning," the latter (popish belief) is wedded to "Scholastic Notions, not to be found in Scripture." Reflecting the vain attempt to mystify the nature of godhead, these "Scholastic Notions" are propounded by the papists as an expression of their "Sophistical Subtilties." Such terms as "Trinity, Triniunity, Coessentiality, and Tripersonality" thus assume the aura of a "mystery" in what Milton earlier in *Of True Religion* calls "the traditions of men and additions to the word of God" as the defining force of popery (YP 8:421). As opposed to this fabricated mystery (spuriously generated by the papists), the idea of Father, Son, and Spirit, then, is revealed as "a plain Doctrin" in Scripture. Accordingly, when Milton refers to "a mystery indeed in *their* Sophistic Subtilties" (my emphasis), the antecedent of "their" is that old sophistic-scholastic bugaboo, the Catholic Church (not, as some have suggested, the Arians and Socinians themselves).[77] Almost as an afterthought, Milton then addresses another crucial belief, this one associated with Socinianism: "Their other Opinions are of less Moment. They dispute the satisfaction of Christ, or rather the word *Satisfaction*, as not Scriptural; but they acknowledge him both God and their Saviour." In this case, the antecedent of "their" is obviously not the papists but the Socinians. How is one to interpret the afterthought? Is this belief (like those cited earlier) open to question? I see no reason why not, but this is not the point.

The point once again is that all the beliefs of all the movements Milton cites are such that they do not compromise the essential efficacy of the movements themselves. It would be a mistake, moreover, to invoke the foregoing passage as a basis for claiming that Milton was a Socinian, an Arian, or anything else that constitutes his catalog. To endorse the Arian and Socinian interpretive practice (one that grounds itself in the scriptural text) is not necessarily to endorse the beliefs that emerge from this practice. It is simply to say that this is a practice that all good Protestants (no matter what their stripe) adopt to implement their respective hermeneutics. As such, the passage confirms Milton's allegiance to a particular mode of interpretation (the Protestant mode) as the one true foundation upon which to ground belief. Milton's purpose, then, is interpretive, not doctrinal. He refuses to declare his own doctrinal allegiance beyond maintaining that we should be as accepting of the manifold movements that constitute Protestantism as we are of any group (except the papists) who strive to know God aright. It is ironic, he observes, that "we suffer the Idolatrous books of Papists" to be "sold & read as common as our own. Why not much rather of Anabaptists, Arians, Arminians, & Socinians?" (YP 8:437). Again, the question is not a doctrinal one: it is interpretive. In interpretation the exegete opens himself to an entire range of ideas with which he may or may not agree. He tolerates these ideas, not because he agrees with them, but because he is open to them. He may embrace certain aspects of them and dismiss others, but they all have something to offer, whether or not we are persuaded by them. "There is no Learned man but will confess he hath much profited by reading Controversies, his Senses awakt, his Judgement sharpn'd, and the truth which he holds more firmly establish't." As the result of allowing controversies to flourish, we shall create an environment in which "falsehood will appear more false, and truth the more true." An attitude of this sort will result not only in the realization of truth but in the confounding of falsehood, which is to say, "popery" (YP 8:437). This in brief represents Milton's own Declaration of Indulgence, one that suggests both the virtues and the limits of Miltonic toleration.

Although we cannot depend upon *Of True Religion* to provide detailed insight into the complex particulars of Milton's doctrinal beliefs, either pro-Socinian or anti-Socinian, his tract is instructive in suggesting the extent to which such movements as Socinianism were of uppermost concern to Milton later in his career. His willingness to invoke Socinianism in the context of his belief in the direct and unbiased encounter with the biblical text is likewise instructive not only in illuminating the nature of his hermeneutics but in revealing his allegiance to those who adopt a corresponding approach to the discovery of doctrinal truth.

What then of *De Doctrina Christiana*? This work, too, is important as a means of gaining insight into the extent to which Socinianism is either consistent with or at odds with what might be construed as Milton's theological views. Despite all the uncertainties associated with the theological treatise, *De Doctrina* provides crucial insight into the kinds of thought that engaged its author in response to the doctrines espoused by the Socinian movement. There is yet another, perhaps, more compelling, reason to consider *De Doctrina Christiana* at this juncture. As I shall discuss later in this chapter, the remarkable discovery of the theological treatise almost a century and a half after Milton's death provided the occasion for renewed interest in the issue of his doctrinal affiliations and the relation of those affiliations to such radical movements as Socinianism and Unitarianism. Although I have addressed the events surrounding the discovery and afterlife of *De Doctrina Christiana* at some length elsewhere,[78] the act of engaging them here should serve as a bridge between the present discussion and the earlier discussion of the theology and poetics that constitute Milton's understanding of deity.

We begin with the question of text, specifically, the biblical text as sole and final authority, a crucial determinant of the Socinian agenda. Once again, we recall that in the prefatory epistle to *De Doctrina Christiana*, Milton claims that he will "adhere to the Holy Scripture alone" (libris tantummode sacris adhaeresco). Referring to his treatise as his "dearest and best possession," he implies that his adherence to Scripture will be his guiding principle. Whether or not such an adherence gives rise to what others deem "heretical" as a result of their "conventional beliefs," he declares that he subscribes to "no other heresy or sect" (haeresin aliam, sectam aliam sequor nullam). In fact, he maintains that he "had not even studied any of the so-called heretical writers" when the mistakes of the "orthodox" theologians prompted him to side with their "heretical" opponents in their judicious (if heterodox) reading of the biblical text. If this be heresy, he, like Saint Paul before him (Acts 24:14), willingly accepts that designation as a sign of the true worship of God grounded in the unswerving belief in Scripture (YP 6:121, 123; CM 14:14, 15).

Evident throughout the treatise, that attitude is delineated in detail in the chapter on the Holy Scriptures (1.30). There, Milton emphasizes the outlook reflected in *Of True Religion* and other works that, if studied diligently and carefully, Scriptures are entirely "perspicuous" (*perspicuae*) in everything relating to "salvation" (*salutem*). Accordingly, "the rule and canon of faith" is "scripture alone" (regula itaque fidei et canon, scriptura sola est). (YP 6:574–85; CM 16:249–67).[79] If this sentiment recalls Milton's own statement that the Bible, by "a general Protestant Maxim," is sufficiently "plain and perspicuous" to "explain its own meaning in the properest words, belonging to so high a Matter and so necessary to be known," it also moves us toward the mainstay of Socinian belief in the absolute sufficiency of Scriptures as the exclusive source of all doctrine.[80] On the other hand, Milton is, as indicated, aware of the uncertainties associated with the transmission of the text of Scriptures (particularly the New Testament), an awareness that leads him to conclude that in matters of belief "the Spirit which is given to us is a more certain guide than scripture, and that we ought to follow it" (certiorem nobis propositum ducem spiritum quam scripturam, quem sequi debeamus). This remarkable turn from text to Spirit is reinforced, moreover, by a recognition of what Milton calls a "fallacious" propensity in human reason (humanas rationes plerumque fallaces) at times to misconstrue the truths of "divine doctrine" (divina doctrina) present in the text (YP 6:583, 589; CM 16:264–65, 278–79).[81] As much as Milton emphasizes the ability of reason to arrive at an understanding of Scriptures, he likewise reveals an even greater faith in the power of the Spirit to guide us in matters that appear to transcend the ability of reason to comprehend things beyond its limited sphere. One might say that Milton reflects the Socinian propensity to value reason as the means to derive divine doctrine from Scriptures but at the same time reflects a profound awareness of the limits of reason in the face of inscrutable circumstances with which the text of Scriptures on occasion confronts the reader, at least partially as the result of the problems associated with its transmission from the earliest times.

Affinities with and departures from Socinianism come into play particularly in the context of the conception of godhead as delineated in De Doctrina Christiana. Among the characteristics of God that Milton lists is that all-important attribute of "oneness," the most important aspect of deity in Milton's thinking and the one in which all the others culminate. A mainstay of Socinian thought, this uncompromising emphasis upon oneness underscores what eventually becomes the theology of Unitarianism. The assertion of a monotheistic deity is hardly a characteristic that distinguishes the Socinian point of view from mainstream belief, but the methodology through which such an outlook is implemented compellingly recalls the kind of logic-based methodology characteristic of Socinianism.[82]

Citing a multitude of biblical proof-texts to support this all-important emphasis upon monotheism, Milton, as we have seen earlier, poses the rhetorical question: "What could be more plain and straightforward? What could be better adapted to the average intelligence, what more in keeping with everyday speech, so that God's people should understand that there is numerically one God and one spirit [unum numero Deum, unum spiritum], just as they understand that there is numerically one [numerando unum] of anything else." There is no doubt that this is a "unitarian" pronouncement that grounds its suppositions in the plain and logical assessment of number available to all. It is not metaphysics: it is just plain sense, a sense of deity both "fitting" and "thoroughly in accordance with reason" (aequum . . . et rationi summe consentaneum) (YP 6:146–47; CM 14:50–51). Maurice Kelley is correct in his notation that the conception here is essentially rational and "mathematical" (YP 6:146 n. 51).

The pattern is all pervasive in the view of godhead endorsed by the treatise. Later in the treatise, Milton reasserts his credo concerning the "one true and independent supreme God" that will permit no compromise in this mathematics of oneness, and in the process Milton "personalizes" deity by extolling the "Jews," from whom the concept of "one God" is derived: "God's people, the Jews," he says, "have always interpreted the term 'only one person' [unam duntaxat personam] to mean one in number" (YP 6:213; CM 14:196–97).[83] Coupled with the emphasis upon oneness is a kind of "creatureliness" that finds its ultimate source in what Milton associates with the "Jews," that is, God's chosen, whose most ancient conception of deity is portrayed in Hebrew Scriptures. As we have seen, the move toward the Judaic outlook is one customarily looked upon as a signature of the Socinian sensibility.

As much as De Doctrina Christiana reveals tendencies commonly associated with Socinianism, important aspects of the treatise do suggest a decidedly anti-Socinian point of view. For example, *De Doctrina Christiana* makes clear in its discussion of Christ as redeemer (1.14) that although the preincarnate Son of God was not "supreme" (etsi non summus), he was nonetheless "the firstborn of all creation" (omnis tamen rei creatae primogenetus). It follows, then, "that he must have existed before his incarnation [ante assumptam carnem extiterit necesse est], whatever subtleties may have been invented to provide an escape from this conclusion [ad haec evadenda subtilius excogitarunt], by those who argue that Christ was a mere man [quicquid illi qui Christum merum hominem esse disputant]" (YP 6:419; CM 15:262–63). The not-so-veiled reference, of course, is to the Socinians, with whom Milton strongly disagrees at this crucial juncture.[84] Such a disagreement strikes at the heart of Socinian theology, which, in its conception of "one God" categorically disallows the existence of the preincarnate Son. Arguing on behalf of the concept of a preincarnate Son, Milton makes clear that the Son occupies a decidedly subordinated stature in relation to the Father (1.5).

The differences between the theology of the Socinians and of *De Doctrina Christiana* extend to the view of the Incarnation as well. Whereas the Socinians view the "historical Jesus" as an individual whose nature is entirely human (although of a remarkable nature indeed), Milton views Christ's nature as the product of a hypostatical union, that is, divine and human. "Christ, then, although he was God [Deus cum esset], put on human nature and was made flesh [humanam naturam assumpsit]," yet he "did not cease to be numerically one Christ" (YP 6:418, 420; CM 15:262–63). In his embrace of this concept, Milton, in effect, declares his departure from any who would maintain the full humanity of Christ. On the contrary, the incarnate Christ is to be conceived as *theanthropos* in the hypostatic union of divine and human. This view of the incarnate Christ is one that celebrates the mystery of the event. In fact, it is an outlook that sides with those who look upon the Incarnation as "by far the greatest mystery of our religion" (mysterium religionis nostrae longe maximum esse). We are obliged to "let such mysteries alone and not tamper with them," and, because God has not revealed to us how such a mystery comes about, "it is much better for us to hold our tongues and be wisely ignorant" (sapienter potius nescire) (YP 6:424; CM 15:272–73). Such a view is entirely opposed to the Socinian idea of extolling reason at all costs.

By embracing mystery in his treatment of the Incarnation, Milton would dispel all notions that might otherwise promote heresy. So Milton exclaims: "How many opportunities for heresy we shall remove! How much of the raw material of heresy we shall cut away! How many huge volumes" we shall "fling out of God's temple as filth and rubbish [inquinamenta ac rudera]!" This "cleansing" includes even those who are teachers in the reformed church (YP 6:421; CM 15:264–65). For Milton, these teachers, one suspects, may well be of the Socinian persuasion. If such is the case, then the act of cutting and cleansing in which Milton engages is one that challenges the latitudinarian outlook reflected in *Of True Religion*. Milton is apparently in no mood (at least at this point) to "indulge" the errors, even of the reformers of his own stripe. Much mistaken in points of doctrine with which Milton does not agree, these are heretics whom God will assuredly not pardon. Whatever the extent of Milton's own participation in the production of the theological treatise, this is a work that further confirms both the embrace and at times the categorical rejection of positions associated with the Socinian point of view.[85]

From the perspective of Milton's overt statements in *Tetrachordon* and *Of True Religion*, as well as of the oblique references in *De Doctrina Christiana*, we are given insight not only into his awareness of Socinianism but of his response to it as a movement. This insight is further heightened by Milton's involvement in the licensing of the *Racovian Catechism*, often conceived as the foundational statement of the Socinian doctrinal system. Whatever we might think of Milton's allegiance or nonallegiance to Socinianism, it is clear that, had the likes of John Edwards attacked Milton the way Edwards was to attack Locke, Milton might well have suffered a fate similar to that of the author of *The Reasonableness of Christianity*. John Edwards would surely have "unmask'd" Milton's "Socinianism" by reading both the overt statements and the silences of his works. Doing so, John Edwards would have been eager to follow in the footsteps of his father Thomas by rooting out the gangrenous corruptions that plagued the body of Milton's heretical works. Fortunately, Milton escaped all such attempts to cleanse the world of any putatively Socinian leanings. Had *De Doctrina Christiana* been published in Milton's lifetime, God knows what the repercussions might have been, especially with the issue of authorship not in doubt. This is surely one of the most tantalizing possibilities that offer themselves to those who consider *De Doctrina Christiana* as a Miltonic text. For this reason, the afterlife not only of the theological tract but of Milton's works in general represents a fascinating means of understanding both the nature of his writings and of the reception of his theological ideas in the centuries that followed upon his death. Such an understanding is germane to an appreciation of how Milton's poetry (especially *Paradise Lost*) was interpreted both before and after the advent of *De Doctrina Christiana*.

III

From the perspective of Socinianism (coupled with that of Arianism), Milton's reputation between the time of his death in 1674 and the publication of *De Doctrina Christiana* in 1825 was generally free of the charge of Antitrinitarian heterodoxy. As John T. Shawcross observes, "many people in England seem to have learned their Bible with *Paradise Lost* at hand, for it was considered an exposition of the orthodox creed. This was true for most people during the century." Shawcross makes

clear, however, that despite the association of Milton with orthodoxy, charges of Antitrinitarianism were not entirely absent.[86]
The foundations of such charges lay in part with the imposing figure of John Toland, controversialist, pamphleteer, and
Milton biographer. In his *Life of Milton* (1698), first published
in a collected edition of Milton's prose, Toland makes no direct
reference to the possibility of Socinian leanings, but he does
not hesitate to single out, as well as to quote in full, the
specific passages from *Of True Religion* on Arianism and
Socinianism that we have addressed above. Responding to
these passages, Toland endorses Milton's argument that, as
Toland says, "no true *Protestant* can persecute any persons for
speculative Points of Conscience, much less not tolerat his fellow *Protestant*, tho in som things dissenting from his own
Judgment." What Toland is particularly taken with in his reading of the passages he cites from *Of True Religion* is that
"nothing can be imagin'd more reasonable, honest, or pious"
than the Tolerationist sensibility they reflect. The spirit that
infuses the argument in *Of True Religion* as a whole reminds
Toland of the Tolerationist position adopted by Locke. Citing
works such as Locke's *Letters on Toleration*, as well as his *Essay
Concerning Human Understanding*, Toland views Milton in
the context of a Lockean tradition of latitudinarianism that,
according to Toland, all reformers should emulate.

Taking into account theological issues, it would have been
interesting indeed to know what Toland might have thought
of *De Doctrina Christiana*, had it been available to him; for,
following hard upon his discussion of Milton's Tolerationist
point of view in the context of Locke's endorsement of
Toleration, Toland mentions the existence of Milton's so-
called "*System of Divinity*," the location of which is uncertain
and the purpose of which ("whether intended for public view,
or collected merely for his [Milton's] own use") Toland is
unable to determine.[87] As Shawcross observes, Toland's *Life
of Milton* provoked controversy in large part because of the

heterodox beliefs (among them, Socinianism) that Toland himself was thought to have held.[88] Judging by such works as Toland's *Christianity Not Mysterious* (London, 1696), one can understand the rationale underlying the questioning of his religious views by those who subscribed to an unwavering orthodoxy.[89]

Following upon Toland, the charge of heterodoxy in Milton appeared thereafter in venues such as John Dennis's "The Grounds of Criticism in Poetry" (1704), Jonathan Richardson's *Explanatory Notes and Remarks on Milton's "Paradise Lost"* (London, 1734), and various items in the *Gentleman's Magazine* and the *Daily Gazetteer* (1738–39). The tone adopted by those commenting upon Milton's poetry (specifically, *Paradise Lost*) in such venues is either tentative or dismissive because they are largely founded upon the subtle nuances that arise from the language of the verse, rather than from the systematic process of argumentation that might otherwise distinguish a theological tract. It is interesting, in fact, to see how the critics respond to nuances they discover in the verse, absent the supposedly corroborating evidence that a "System of Divinity" would afford. Citing the angelic hymn to God and the Son in the third book of *Paradise Lost* (3.384–96), John Dennis, for example, observes: "I have the rather mention'd these Verses, to show that *Milton* was a little tainted with Socinianism, for by the first Verse 'tis evident, that he look'd upon the Son of God as a created Being."[90]

The verse to which Dennis refers is "Thee next they sang, of all Creation first, / Begotten Son, Divine Similitude" (3.384–85). Although Dennis does not elaborate precisely why this verse leads him to see in Milton the "taint" of Socinianism, one may assume that the emphasis the verse places upon a "created" being in the form of the Son (as "Begotten") suggests to Dennis the presence of Socinian inclinations on Milton's part. Dennis, of course, fails to take account of the fact that in the Socinian doctrinal system, the notion of a preincarnate deity known as the Son does not even exist. But that does not matter, for, as far as Dennis is concerned, the Son is already the incarnate Messiah, even before he becomes the historical Jesus. That the Son is created or begotten at all is sufficient to convince Dennis of what might be called the creatureliness of the Son as a begotten being. Fine theological distinctions simply do not obtain. Nor is there a system of divinity to confirm, clarify, or (ironically) further unsettle Dennis's conclusions regarding Milton's unfortunate state of being "tainted."

Perhaps it is the various uncertainties surrounding the matter of Milton's alleged Socinianism or Arianism that led Jonathan Richardson some 30 years later to allude to the contentious environment that prevailed during his own time. In his *Explanatory Notes*, Richardson observes that it is just this environment that "will not permit [him] to Pass over in Silence" the conjecture "that *Milton* was an *Arian*." This conjecture, he observes, "is built on Certain Passages in *Par. Lost*." Once again failing the presence of an actual system of divinity to which one can resort, charges of heterodoxy must ground themselves in passages from the poetic document. "Some of those [passages]" or perhaps even "all of them for Ought I know," Richardson maintains, "are very Capable of an Orthodox Construction." In other words, these passages can be read either way, as is so often the distinguishing mark of a poetic text. The honesty and forthrightness that such an assertion reflects are refreshing in suggesting Richardson's determination not to accede to readings he considers doctrinaire. In a gesture reminiscent of the admonition to be "wisely ignorant" in *De Doctrina Christiana*, Richardson refuses to "Meddle" in a "Dispute" that does not appear to be able to produce indisputable results and that is based solely on "Conjecture" ("Overrul'd by So many Pious and Learned Divines").[91] Richardson will take the high road and refrain from insisting on heterodoxy in his reading of poetic statement that is open to an entire range of interpretation. No doubt implicit in Richardson's reluctance to proclaim Milton's heterodoxy is precisely the kind of view that arose shortly afterward in the letter of "Theophilus" in the *Gentleman's Magazine* (1738): Milton "has certainly adopted the *Arian* Principle into his *Paradise Lost*." I wish we all had the luxury of being so certain about the doctrinal foundation of Milton's poetry. But Theophilus is convinced that in his heterodox views, Milton "as little believed the Religion of his Country as *Homer* or *Virgil* did that of theirs." These charges were, in turn, subjected to countercharges by the likes of "Philo-Spec." and others in succeeding issues of *Gentleman's Magazine.*[92] Clearly, in the exchange of charge and countercharge, one might be prompted to observe that "Hills amid the Air encounterd Hills," but with little fear that all "Had gon to wrack, with ruin overspred."

Although the whole debate appears to have become quiescent for the remainder of the century, it did not die out completely. In fact, with the growth of Unitarianism, the desire to enlist Milton in the cause flourished with renewed vigor. Theophilus Lindsey represents a notable instance of this renewal. A fellow of St. John's College, Cambridge, Lindsey took Holy Orders after the award of his bachelor's degree in 1747. Having received various ecclesiastical appointments, he adopted latitudinarian views that prompted him to reassess his position as a cleric. His own allegiance had become decidedly Unitarian, a transition that caused him in 1774 to sever ties with the Church of England. Defending his decision to resign his vicarage, he issued an *Apology* (London, 1774), in which he sought not only to justify his behavior, but, in the process, to offer a history of the doctrine of the Trinity and Unitarianism.[93] As one might expect, the treatise elicited both hostile and supportive criticism. To this criticism, Lindsey responded with *A Sequel to the Apology* (London, 1776), a work considered "the most elaborate, and in many respects the most valuable, of his contributions to dogmatic theology."[94]

What is fascinating about these writings is the extent to

which Lindsey draws upon Milton to bolster an essentially heterodox Christology, one in keeping with a Unitarian outlook grounded in Socinian principles. *A Sequel to the Apology* is apposite in this regard. In the *Sequel*, Lindsey defends the notion of an essentially human Jesus whose youth is distinguished by a remarkable growth in self-awareness and a distinct precociousness. Citing Origen and Grotius as figures whose childhood achievements are deemed remarkable, Lindsey observes that "these and similar instances discover what great things the human mind is capable of, by a careful cultivation, and the divine blessing." But even such exemplary individuals as Origen and Grotius pale beside the young Jesus, whose childhood gives every evidence of "the maturity of wisdom and goodness to which the holy Jesus had arrived in very early youth." At issue is the sense that, like Origen and Grotius, Jesus was essentially a man (albeit, an extraordinary man) whose formative years give every evidence of maturation to a higher plane. His "moral improvements, however gradual and impressive," Lindsey states, "always far surpassed those of any others of mankind." This very growth of self-awareness, coupled with the idea of maturation, led Lindsey to argue that the Jesus of Scriptures was (for all his qualities) a human being, not, at that point at least, the Son of God incarnate.

According to Lindsey, the foremost poetic exponent of this reading of Scriptures is John Milton. His *Paradise Regained* provides the most profound evidence of a distinctly human Jesus whose early youth is distinguished by a recognition of his human condition. In keeping with that view, Lindsey offers Jesus' soliloquy having to do with his childhood experiences. Then, "no childish play" was "pleasing" to Jesus. As one "above [his] years," he not only read and delighted in "the law of God" but also grew in his knowledge "to such perfection" that, at the ripe age of 12, he was able to propose to the "teachers of our law" in the temple "What might improve [his] knowledge, or their own" (1.201–13). Clearly, this for Lindsey is one of many examples that the Jesus of *Paradise Regained* is essentially human, for "our Lord's condition in this world is constantly represented [in Milton, as in Scripture] like that of other men." It is for this reason that Lindsey takes to task other critics of Milton (such as Thomas Newton) who are "strenuous advocate[s] for the *godhead* of Christ." Jesus must be human in this life, Lindsey argues, for "the *Deity* can never be changed or transformed." Indeed, it is axiomatic that "*God can never become a child, or a youth.*" In recognizing this fact in his poems, Milton reveals insight into the true nature of Jesus. "I know scarce any more perfect disciple of *Jesus* than *Milton*," Lindsey declares. In fact, the poet's own life, "from the prime of early youth to old age," is consistent with both the maturation and the nobility of Jesus as a man who grows and matures in knowledge and experience. Lindsey even goes so far as to make a distinction between the godhead of *Paradise Lost* as essentially Arian and the Christology of *Paradise Regained* as essentially Socinian. For Lindsey, Milton is respectively of the Arian and Socinian parties in his great epics.[95]

It should be noted, however, that Lindsey subsequently had a change of heart in his reading of Milton. In his *An Historical View of the State of the Unitarian Doctrine and Worship from the Reformation to our Own Times* (London, 1783), Lindsey retracted the views about Milton's Jesus that he had expressed in his earlier *Sequel*. Referring to his past discussion, he avers that he will now "take the liberty to correct a former inadvertence of [his] own," that is, his all too easy "Socinianizing" of the Jesus of *Paradise Regained*. Of the soliloquy from Milton's brief epic that he had cited in the *Sequel*, Lindsey confesses that this passage "too easily persuaded [him], that Milton was at that time come off his former orthodox sentiments, and was become a believer of the proper humanity of Christ."[96] What prompted Lindsey to retract his former interpretation is not immediately apparent. At the very least, Lindsey's change of heart suggests the extent to which the act of reading heterodoxy into texts that yield an entire constellation of interpretations can be (in fact, *is*) a tricky affair. Lindsey was forthright enough to acknowledge that difficulty and did not hesitate to record his altered views as the occasion demanded. However Lindsey's readings are to be judged, he was a critic who struggled with the complex theological nuances of the Miltonic text without whatever "benefit" *De Doctrina Christiana* might have afforded.

With Robert Lemon's eventful discovery of *De Doctrina Christiana* in the Middle Treasury Gallery, Whitehall, in 1823, and the subsequent publication of the Latin text, along with Charles R. Sumner's English translation in 1825, the issue of Milton's so-called heterodoxies reappeared with renewed vigor. Unlike thc pre-1825 critics obliged to labor without recourse to any Miltonic system of divinity, critics now had at their disposal a theological tract, both in the Latin and in an English translation, to squabble over the beliefs that Milton was thought to have held, if not throughout his entire career, then during a good portion of it. It would be an understatement to suggest that the issue of Milton's alleged Antitrinitarianism (whether in its Arian form, its Socinian form, or something of an amalgamation of both forms) loomed large in the discourse of the day. The issue is already present in Sumner's "Preliminary Observations" to his translation of *De Doctrina Christiana:* "Doubts have always been entertained as to the real sentiments of Milton respecting the second person of the Trinity." Now, Sumner says, our suspicions that the Arian and Socinian leanings are discernible in the poetry have been confirmed by the systematic discussions in the theological tract, which establish without question that "the opinions of Milton were in reality nearly Arian" and possibly Socinian as well. As one who subscribes to the orthodoxy of his own clerical calling, Sumner regrets that the great poet exhibits such heterodox views.[97]

As Francis E. Mineka observes, responses (supportive and critical) concerning such matters represent a distinguishing feature of the various periodical reviews that greeted the publication of *De Doctrina Christiana*. The treatise at once "shocked the orthodox" and "delighted the unorthodox."[98] Accordingly, one reviewer laments in *Evangelical Magazine* (1825) that "it is, indeed, harrowing to the feelings to learn, from Milton's own showing, that he believed the Son of God to be nothing more than an exalted creature."[99] To confute Milton's heresies, the *Evangelical Magazine* published a series of articles in 1826 by one "J. P. S." (John Pye Smith) on the subject. It is clear, according to the confuter, that Milton's "generous sympathy with the oppressed would dispose him to the most favourable feelings for the Socinians of Poland."[100] The reviewer for *Congregational Magazine* (1825) mounted a scathing attack on both the style and the theology of *De Doctrina Christiana:* It "cannot be read; and, if it could, would do nobody any good." More than that, it is dangerous, for it contains heresy enough "to delight all the Socinians, Arians, and other triflers with sacred Scriptures, in both hemispheres."[101] In the same vein, the reviewer for the venerable High Church and Tory *Gentleman's Magazine* (1825) shudders that in its delineation of God, *De Doctrina Christiana* relegates Christianity to Judaism.[102] (This is a criticism that was lodged against the Antitrinitarians from the onset of Arianism in the fourth century through the advent of Socinianism in the early modern period and beyond.)

What was disturbing to the orthodox[103] proved a welcome sign to the dissenters. For the Unitarians, the discovery and publication of *De Doctrina Christiana* proved to be a godsend. Although the Unitarians were uncomfortable with certain aspects of the theology delineated in the treatise, the attack upon the orthodox view of the Trinity prompted them to regard Milton as a valuable ally.[104] Accordingly, *Monthly Repository* (1825), founded in 1806 to give voice to the Unitarian viewpoint, devoted three issues to providing an extended account of *De Doctrina Christiana* as a text that prompted one to align Milton with the mighty names of John Locke and Sir Isaac Newton as foremost Unitarians.[105]

What is true of the English cultural climate is no less true of the American, especially on the Unitarian front. William Ellery Channing is a case in point. Deemed "the single most important figure in the history of American Unitarianism," Channing found himself at the very center of the burgeoning Unitarian movement that flourished in New England.[106] Doing battle in his writings against the prevailing theological views and ecclesiastical policies of his Calvinist contemporaries, Channing produced such writings as the pamphlet *Unitarian Christianity* (1819), a latitudinarian document that has since become "the virtual manifesto of the liberal movement in theology, now explicitly Unitarian." A Christian humanist in his own right, he fostered an atmosphere receptive to "the creation of an authentic American literature that would celebrate the dignity and self-awareness of humanity."[107] It is little wonder, then, that Channing's response to the publication of *De Doctrina Christiana* would be of more than passing interest. Entitled *Remarks on the Character and Writings of John Milton; Occasioned by the Publication of His Lately Discovered Treatise "Of Christian Doctrine"* (1826), Channing's detailed appraisal is important both in its own right and for what it says about the theological implications of the Unitarian outlook at that time.[108]

Channing's response to the treatise as a whole is muted. Although Channing is not particularly enthusiastic about the work as a product of the great poet and reformer, he nonetheless acknowledges that it must be accorded careful attention as a reflection of the mind and sensibility of the author. These aspects especially interest Channing, who delights in those "passages in which Milton's mind is laid open to us" in a manner that obliges the author to defend the radical nature of his positions, which include the act of "render[ing] the Supreme Being more interesting by giving him human shape." Although

Channing objects to the idea of embodying God in this manner, he is astute in his responsiveness to the materialism that underlies the theology of the treatise.[109] What most excites Channing is the treatment of the Son of God and the Holy Spirit. We are all aware, Channing observes, that in his delineation of the godhead Milton has "declared himself an Anti-trinitarian, and strenuously asserted the strict and proper unity of God." For Milton, the Son of God is "a distinct being from God, and inferior to him, that he existed before the world was made, that he is the first of the creation of God, and that afterwards all other things were made by him, as the instrument or minister of his Father." The Holy Spirit, in turn, "is a person, an intelligent agent, but created and inferior to God." It is this emphasis upon *person*, this *personhood*, that Channing finds so remarkable. Whether in the form of God, the Son or the Holy Spirit, the quality of creatureliness is an aspect to which Channing as a Unitarian responds so powerfully. Such creatureliness is for Channing a fundamental aspect of the mind and sensibility of Milton. Even at the risk of imposing an overdetermined reading on the theological tract, Channing is willing to draw conclusions concerning it that reveal as much about his own mind and sensibility as they do about Milton. Thus, Channing brings to the fore elements of the theology that he embraces when he remarks that "we are unable within our limits to give a sketch of Milton's strong reasoning against the supreme divinity of Jesus Christ." Although one might have wished Channing to develop this reading in more detail, it little matters, for, as far as Channing is concerned, Milton has sufficiently proven himself the great spokesman of Unitarianism.

This is a triumph that prompts Channing to wax lyrical in his praise. "We must thank God," Channing declares, "that he has raised up this illustrious advocate of the long obscured doctrine of the Divine Unity." In opposition to the "Trinitarian adversaries [who] are perpetually ringing in our ears the names of Fathers and Reformers" to bolster their cause, Channing

invokes his own trinity, "the three greatest and noblest minds
of modern times," as "witnesses to that Great Truth, of which,
in an humbler and narrower sphere, we desire to be the defenders." The minds to which Channing alludes as witnesses to
the Great Truth are Milton, Locke, and Newton. For Channing,
this is the new trinity indeed. "Before these intellectual suns
the stars of self-named Orthodoxy 'hide their diminished
heads.' To these eminent men God communicated such unusual
measures of light and mental energy, that their names spring
up spontaneously, when we think or would speak of the greatness of our nature." "Shackled by no party connexions" and
"warped by no clerical ambition," they approached the subject of the godhead "in the fulness of their strength, with free
minds open to truth, and with unstained purity of life."
Breaking free of the trammels of their own time and unbowed
by the threat of penal law, they refused to discover in the
Scripture a "triple divinity." Rather, they extolled "the One
Infinite Father" and "ascrib[ed] to Him alone supreme self-
existent divinity" and "proper Unity."[110] One might suggest
that Channing represents the culmination of the desire to enlist
Milton in the Unitarian cause, a movement that traces its roots
to a time well before the discovery of *De Doctrina Christiana*
but is certainly given even greater impetus as a result of the
accessibility of this highly contested work.[111] What is especially
interesting is the inclination to pair Milton with Locke and
Newton, the luminaries of the age of the new philosophy and
the new science. The Unitarian inclination to situate Milton
in this manner suggests once again the extent to which the traditions that find their ultimate source in the figure of Faustus
Socinus reemerged in the later periods with renewed vigor
and intensity.

If this chapter has attempted to clarify the relationship
between Milton and the Socinian heresy both during his own
time and in the later periods, it has also sought to provide a
sense of how the intersection between a writer and his audience

can illuminate our own understanding of what transpires in his works. It little matters whether we can prove that Milton accepted one or the other aspect of Socinianism. What does matter is that the Socinian heresy was a crucial movement in his own time and that he responded to it at various points in his career. What also matters is that those who did express their allegiance to the movement were inclined to draw upon certain elements in Milton's work to proclaim him as one of their own. They must have seen *something* in his delineation of doctrinal matters (either implicit in the poetry or explicit in the prose) to justify their readings. That *something* became for them even more pronounced after the discovery and publication of the theological tract that the heterodox are determined to claim as his and that the orthodox are determined to claim as the work of someone else. The debate over the authorship of *De Doctrina Christiana* is deeply implicated in the theological views that Milton's readers hold. As much as some readers might desire, the debate over the authorship of the tract will not go away; nor will the debate over the heterodox Milton, as opposed to the orthodox Milton. The two debates are inextricably interlinked. I trust that the foregoing exploration provides a means of undertaking future investigations into Milton as a writer whose views gave rise to an entire constellation of interpretive possibilities. At the same time, I trust that we shall have gained a greater sense of Milton's place in the development and afterlife of a movement of the first import to the history of religious thought.

EIGHT

Arianism and Godhead

☦

I

It is a truth universally acknowledged that the debate over Milton's beliefs regarding the nature of the Trinity is as lively now as it has been for well over two centuries. In his essay on Milton's putative Arianism, John P. Rumrich argues that this debate goes back at least as far as Jonathan Richardson's defense of Milton's orthodoxy in 1734, almost a century before the publication of *De Doctrina Christiana* in 1825, an event that heralded the rise of increased speculations about the extent of Milton's heterodox views.[1] With William B. Hunter's pioneering efforts to call the authorship (or at least, the sole Miltonic authorship) of the theological treatise into question, the stakes (if not the uncertainties) are even greater than they were before.[2] Whereas scholars always thought it possible (and indeed advantageous) to draw upon the arguments of *De Doctrina* to gloss the poetic complexities of *Paradise Lost*, that exegetical maneuver is now fraught with peril; and, as I assert

261

in the introduction and elsewhere, as much as one might seek to dismiss Hunter's findings, the more he insists on returning to haunt the world of Milton scholarship.[3]

Particularly in the area of Trinitarianism, the question of Milton's so-called heterodoxies is not merely academic. As we have seen, those who held heterodox beliefs (especially Antitrinitarian beliefs) during Milton's time faced the real possibility of imprisonment and death.[4] The very embodiment of Antitrinitarianism, Arius haunted the early modern mind as much as he haunted the consciousness of the early church. The story of the violent and bizarre manner of Arius's death in 336 A.D. is one that Milton surely knew, and it is one that resonates throughout history. In the words of Socrates Scholasticus, Arius met his end through "a terror arising from the remorse of conscience" that suddenly seized upon him, and, with that terror, "a violent relaxation of the bowels." Overcome by faintness, along with the evacuation of his bowels, he experienced "a copious hemorrhage, and the descent of the small intestines," accompanied by the "excretion of his spleen and liver in an effusion of blood."[5] In the seventeenth century, the death of Arius was recalled by the likes of Ephraim Pagitt, whose often-reprinted work *Heresiography* rails against what it calls the "Antitrinitarians, or *new* Arrians" through an appropriate rhetoric of violence. Associating the Arians with "*Judas* the Traitor" (compare Acts 1:18), Pagitt reminds his readers that Arius died with "his Bowells falling out of his belly." Pagitt, who branded Milton himself a heretic, delighted in recounting how such Arians as Bartholomew Legate and Edward Wightman, two notorious heretics, "have been heretofore burnt among us."[6]

Considering the extent to which Arianism was viewed as anathema by the early church, the highly charged atmosphere surrounding the heresy from the time of the Council of Nicaea in 325 A.D. to the seventeenth century and beyond is perfectly understandable, if not inevitable. Throughout the centuries,

Arianism was regarded as what Rowan Williams calls "the archetypal Christian deviation, something aimed at the very heart of the Christian confession."[7] As such, Arianism was "irrevocably cast as the Other in relation to Catholic (and civilized) religion." Moreover, Arius was viewed as the Antichrist among heretics, a heresiarch whose "superficial austerity and spirituality cloaked a diabolical malice." In the ecclesiastical art of the early Middle Ages, he was accordingly represented alongside Judas as the consummate betrayer of Christ, a notion invoked, as we have seen, by Ephraim Pagitt in the seventeenth century. In fourth and fifth century accounts, Arius's death was already clearly patterned after the death of Judas in the Bible. No other heretic has undergone such a thoroughgoing process of demonization.[8]

Despite this demonization and the polemic that fostered it, we must be aware that Arianism, conceived as a coherent system, one founded by a single authoritative figure and sustained by his disciples, is nothing more than a "fantasy," largely fabricated by the polemic of the Nicene writers (principally Athanasius) to support their Trinitarian views. According to Williams, "the textbook picture of an Arian system, defended by self-conscious doctrinal dissidents, inspired by the teachings of the Alexandrian presbyter is the invention of Athanasius' polemic; most non-Nicenes would have probably been as little likely to call themselves Arians as Nicenes were to call themselves Athanasians."[9] Under these circumstances, the epithet "Arian" itself is scarcely justified as an accurate term. In fact, the sheer uselessness of the Arian label becomes more apparent with every new piece of research on the subject. "The time has probably come," Williams observes, "to relegate the term 'Arianism' at best to inverted commas and preferably to oblivion."[10]

The problematic nature of the Arian label is made evident not only by the polemic that defines it but by the inaccessibility of Arius's own writings. Except for a handful of texts thought to be authored by Arius (and even these are essentially ascriptions), the corpus of his writings must be derived exclusively from the reports of his enemies.[11] This means that whatever doctrines are ascribed to Arius are inescapably tainted by the polemic through which they are articulated. To exacerbate matters even further, that very polemic is inconsistent in its portrayal of these doctrines as they are delineated from one account to the next. If one considers Athanasius's account of Arius's so-called *Thalia* (presumably conceived as a metrical formulation or "songbook" of his theology) in the *contra Arianos* and the *de synodis*, the extent of the difficulties becomes immediately apparent. On the one hand, the *contra Arianos* not only denigrates the *Thalia* as a frivolous work that adopts a metrical form associated with lascivious comedy but also introduces (as part of the extracts) such paraphrastic phrases as "he says" and "he is presumed to say," a rhetorical gesture that raises issues of attribution. On the other hand, the *de synodis* treats the *Thalia* as a work characterized by a style that is elevated and almost incantatory. Neither the *contra Arianos* nor the *de synodis* purports to offer a complete version of the *Thalia*; and, as one moves from one version of this work to the next, one discovers both breaks and changes of direction in the argument, as well as major distinctions in tone.[12] Moreover, if one compares the versions of the *Thalia* (themselves different in tone and outlook) with the letters attributed to Arius, the essential doctrine of the absolute unknowability of the Father (a distinctive feature of the *Thalia*) is noticeably absent from the letters.[13]

What may be asked of the *Thalia* may be asked of all Arius's putative writings: What is the true source of his theology; which document is more nearly authoritative than other documents; and how do we know we have a truly "Arian" document when we see one? Based on the instability of the Arian corpus and the polemical contexts through which it emerges, we are invited to conclude that Arianism is indeed a con-

struction (or, in the words of Rowan Williams, a "fantasy")
devised by the polemicists to counter the threat of heterodoxies
that were notoriously on the rise in the early church.[14] Within
the highly charged atmosphere of ecclesiastical controversy
during this formative period, Arianism as the Other was
construed as the spawn of that heresiarch Arius, who was
demonized as a Judas-like Antichrist who died with his bowels falling out of his body. Poor Arius, to suffer such a fate at
the hands of the adversary!

I bear down so hard on the nature of Arianism as a construction not because I wish to make light of the controversies that surrounded the heresy and resulted in both the Nicene
anathemas and the excommunication of the heresiarch after
whom the heresy is named. Rather, I wish to dispel the tendency, particularly among Miltonists, to regard Arianism as a
monolithic phenomenon with a well-defined set of doctrines
clearly and indisputably traceable to the thought and writings
of a particular individual. Having ventured this caveat, I do
nonetheless think it possible to gain a sense of the doctrines
that underscore what is commonly regarded as the Arian
heresy. According to J. N. D. Kelly, the fundamental premise
upon which these doctrines are based is "the affirmation of the
absolute uniqueness and transcendence of God, the unorigi-
nate source [*agennetos arkhe*] of all reality." This absolute
uniqueness is consistent with the so-called Arian declaration
that "We acknowledge one God, who alone is ingenerate [*agen-
neton*], alone eternal, alone without beginning [*anarkhon*],
alone true, alone possessing immortality, alone wise, alone good,
alone sovereign, alone judge of all." Because the being or
essence (*ousia*) of God is unique, transcendent, and indivisible, it cannot be shared or communicated. To suggest that God
would impart his *ousia* to some other being, however exalted,
is a logical impossibility: it would imply that he is divisible
(*diairetos*) and mutable (*treptos*), which is inconceivable. If any
other being would participate in the divine nature, this would,

moreover, result in a duality of divine beings. Therefore, whatever else exists must have come into being, not as the result of the communication of God's *ousia* but by an act of creation on God's part. Because of the incommunicability of God's being to the beings he creates, his creations must perforce have been called into existence out of nothing.[15]

What then of the Son or Word, whom God used as his organ of creation and cosmic activity? First, the Word must himself be a creature, a *ktisma* or *poiema,* whom the Father by his fiat formed out of nothing. The all-important term "beget" (*gennan*), applied to the generation of the Word, must accordingly assume the sense of "make" (*poiein*). This act of making requires us to conclude that, although he is a perfect creature exalted far above the rest of creation, he is not self-existent or ingenerate (*agennetos*). Second, the Son has a beginning. Although born outside of time, he nonetheless did not exist before he was generated, hence, the familiar, monotonously reiterated Arian slogan: "There was when he was not" (en pote ote ouk en). The orthodox idea that the Son is eternal, that is, coeternal with the Father, ran entirely contrary to such beliefs because it implied the destruction of monotheism. Third, the Son can have no communion with or direct knowledge of the Father, who remains ineffable to the Son. Although the Son is God's Word and Wisdom, he is distinct from the Word and Wisdom that constitute God's *ousia.* Because of the Son's status as a creature, he bears the titles Word and Wisdom as a signature of his exalted station. In himself, however, he (like all other creatures) is "alien from and utterly dissimilar to the Father's essence and individual being." As a finite creature with a different order of existence, the Son is not able to comprehend the infinite God. "The Father," according to the doctrine attributed to Arius, "remains ineffable to the Son, and the Word can neither see nor know the Father perfectly and accurately," but what he does see and know, he comprehends in proportion to his capacity, just as what we lower creatures see and know is comprehended by us in proportion to our capacities. Fourth, the Son is subject to both mutability and sinfulness. Remarkably, this belief implies that the Son might indeed have fallen as the devil fell. Whereas the Son's nature is in principle peccable, God in his providence foresaw that the Son would remain virtuous.[16]

Doctrines of this sort were held to be anathema at the Council of Nicaea. In its creed, the council first declares its orthodox belief in "one God, the Father All Governing [*pantokratora*], maker [*poieten*] of all things, visible and invisible" and in the "Son of God, begotten from the Father, as only begotten, that is, from the essence of the Father [ek tes ousias ton patros], God from God, Light from Light, true God from true God, begotten, not made [gennethenta, ou poiethenta], of the same essence as the Father [homoousion to patri], through whom all things came into being." The Holy Spirit, apparently not at issue in the Council's deliberations, receives short shrift in the form of a phrase: "And [we believe] in the Holy Spirit." Having established the basic principles of its creed, the council (without mentioning Arius or his followers by name) then proceeds to the so-called Arian anathemas: "As for those who say, There was a time when He was not, and, Before being born He was not, and that He came into existence out of nothing, or who assert that the Son of God is from a different *hypostasis* or *ousia*, or that he is a creature or changeable, or mutable, the Catholic Church anathematizes them."[17]

Focusing on such terms as *ousia, homoousios, hypostasis, gennan, poienin,* among others, modern scholars (like their patristic forebears) have waged metaphysical battle in their attempts to decipher the meanings, as well as the changes in meaning from generation to generation, to which these terms give rise. Particularly in the transition from the Eastern to the Western church, the reconfiguration of Greek concepts as Latin terms renders the issues underlying the debates that much more difficult.[18] Is *ousia* the same as *essentia*, or is *ousia* really *substantia*? As Kelly observes, there are few words "susceptible of so many and so confusing shades of meaning as *ousia*," along with its compound adjective *homoousios* (reconceived in the corresponding form *homoiousios*).[19] If *ousia* is so vexed, what about *hypostasis* and the Latin equivalents *persona* or *subsistentia*? As soon as one finishes sorting through the terms and is convinced he or she has them straight, they all become a muddle again. In the face of the uncertainties attached to these terms, one is tempted to utter the anguished cry of Martin Luther: "My Soul loathes this word *homoousios*" (odit anima mea vocem homoousion), a cry befitting all the inkhorn terms that have plagued the minds of the theologians debating the nature of the Trinity over the centuries.[20]

There is a story arising presumably from Eusebius of Caesarea that Constantine inserted the word *homoousion* into the Nicene Creed as a kind of bureaucratic gesture.[21] The story had currency well into the seventeenth century, during which time Isaac Newton lamented that the adoption of *homoousios* by the Nicene fathers was misguided indeed, for they permitted the unbaptized Constantine to impose this term on the council against the wishes of the majority.[22] Whether or not this story is accurate does not matter. What does matter is the extent to which its currency throughout the centuries causes the very terms of the Trinitarian/Antitrinitarian debate to ground themselves not only in the "high truths" of theological/philosophical disputation but in the bureaucratic maneuverings of political compromise.[23]

As Maurice Wiles makes clear, the debates surrounding the nature of godhead that occupied the early church found renewed expression in the seventeenth century, particularly during the age of Milton.[24] These debates, we recall, might well eventuate in the untimely end of heretics determined to adhere to their sinful ways. We have already witnessed the respective fates of Bartholomew Legate and Edward Wightman. Despite the painful fortunes of these poor souls, we should not, however,

get the idea that the sufferings they endured were pointedly
the result of the kinds of complex disputes about godhead
that we have witnessed in the early church. Although on occasion one's theological commitment to the nature of the divine
ousia and *hypostasis* might be at issue, the political ramifica-
tions inherent in what was perceived as one's predisposition
to adopt antinomian or heretical views in general was at least
as important in identifying him as a heretic of the Arian stamp.
So, even though Wightman, for example, was branded an Arian,
the official indictment against him involved a whole list of heresies (including those of the Arian, Ebionite, Valentinian,
Manichean, and Anabaptist variety) that rendered him potentially dangerous to the state. The list does not suggest any serious concern over the precise nature of Wightman's theological
views. Especially in the context of the animus toward Antitrinitarian belief of any sort, Arianism was conceived in a general way as the egregious shortcoming of those who refused
to subscribe to accepted orthodoxy.[25] For the seventeenth century as for the earlier periods, Arianism became the archetypal deviation, the Other, charged with meanings that were
as much political as they were theological. In a sense, the two
are inseparable. So they were for the radical reformers. So they
were for Milton.

II

Given Milton's own radical leanings, one might well expect
the reformer to embrace from the very outset the kinds of heretical views that distinguished the Nonconformists of his age.
In the case of Arianism or the so-called Arian heresy, however,
precisely the opposite occurs. To confirm this fact, one need
only glance at the antiprelatical tracts of the early 1640s. In
the very tracts that champion the cause of Reformation and
the return of doctrine to its original purity, Milton adopts a
stance directly in opposition to Arianism.[26] In *Of Reformation,*

for example, Milton declares that the Arians, like the Pelagians, were "no true friends of *Christ*" (YP 1:533–34), and he praises the Council of Nicaea for warning the churches about Arianism (YP 1:545), an attitude reflected in the *Reason of Church-Government* as well (YP 1:839). Moreover, in *Of Reformation* Milton takes Constantine to task for the emperor's "unsoundnesse in Religion" in ultimately "favoring the *Arrians* that had been condemn'd in a Counsell, of which [Constantine] himselfe sate, as it were President." For Milton, Constantine may well have adjudicated the Nicene Council in a manner to suggest his support of theological orthodoxy, but, in fact, he was guilty of turning his back on those clerics he appeared to endorse. Although hailed as "the Load-starre of *Reformation*," Constantine for Milton is to be faulted for having conversed with those that subscribed to heretical views, as well as for his initial unwillingness to be baptized and his "excessive devotion" to superstition. Milton argues that not only did Constantine, the source of ecclesiastical corruption, embrace Arianism, but his offspring were guilty of the same excess (YP 1:555–60).[27]

Milton's attitude toward Arianism is no less critical in his other antiprelatical tracts. He worries in *Animadversions* that such heretics as the Arians and the Pelagians might infect the people "by their hymns, and formes of Praier" (YP 1:685), a view later reiterated in his antimonarchical tracts, notably, *Eikonoklastes* (YP 3:507–8). Judging by Milton's statements in the very antiprelatical tract in which he takes Arianism to task, we would certainly be able to declare that his theological orthodoxy is intact, a view that Milton elevates to the status of poetic discourse. Railing against Arianism in *Of Reformation*, Milton accordingly concludes his tract with a triumphant hymn to that "one *Tri-personal GODHEAD*" as the consummate source of his inspiration: "Thou therefore that sits't in light & glory unapproachable, *Parent* of *Angels* and *Men!* next thee I implore Omnipotent King, Redeemer of that lost remnant whose nature thou didst assume, ineffable and everlasting *Love!* And thou the third subsistence of Divine Infinitude, *illuminating Spirit,* the joy and solace of created *Things!* One *Tri-personall* GODHEAD! Looke upon this thy poore and almost spent, and expiring *Church"* and shield us from the enemy (YP 1:613–14).[28] Like the poet who extolled the "Trinal Unity" in *On the Morning of Christs Nativity* (line 11), the polemicist of the antiprelatical tracts does not hesitate to hymn the Trinity when he is inclined to don his singing robes in an act of devotion to the Nicene godhead.

I am hardly one to suggest that this perspective did not change during Milton's later years. After all, that very "Monarchy" he likewise hymns in conjunction with the "*Tri-personall* GODHEAD" in *Of Reformation* (YP 1:614) became anathema not long afterward to the Milton of the antimonarchical tracts. Under these circumstances, there is no reason he might not have changed his view of Trinitarianism as well. If he did undergo such a change in outlook, then we are invited to ask about the extent and nature of that alteration and in what form it is to be discerned. As we have seen, the most direct statement of a possible alteration occurs in what may be termed Milton's last and most mature statement on the subject of heterodox views of the godhead (among other such heterodox views) — *Of True Religion, Haeresie, Schism, Toleration* (1673), which was published about a year before his death. This tract is immensely significant because in it Milton considers dispassionately and without rancor the whole issue of heterodoxy. Those Miltonists who have been engaged so long in debates about Arianism that resemble the contentious battles of the early church and that resonate in all the suffering that occurred over such issues in Milton's own time would do well to heed Milton's words, ones that call upon adversaries to adhere to "the main Principles of true Religion" and "avoid and cut off many Debates and Contentions, Schisms and Persecutions" (YP 8:420). We recall from Milton's references to Arians and

Socinians that, although they are accused of undermining the doctrine of the Trinity, they nevertheless claim to believe in the Father, Son, and Spirit as they are revealed in Scripture and delineated in the Apostle's Creed.[29] As such, both Arians and Socinians stand in direct opposition to the "corrupt traditions" that arise out of popery, which is wed to "Scholastic Notions, not to be found in Scripture." Reflecting the vain attempt to mystify the nature of godhead, these "Scholastic Notions" are variously termed "Trinity, Triniunity, Coessentiality, and Tripersonality." Propounded by the papists as an expression of their "Sophistical Subtilties," such terms accordingly assume the aura of a "mystery" in what Milton earlier (in his castigation of all things papistical) calls "the traditions of men and additions to the word of God" (YP 8:421).[30] As opposed to this fabricated mystery, the idea of Father, Son, and Spirit is revealed as "a plain Doctrin" in Scripture.

Does such a reading suggest that Milton is an Arian? I would respond, "No more than he is a Socinian." My response is in keeping with what we already know: that, as a Protestant, Milton is responsive (early and late) to the basic notion that Father, Son, and Spirit find expression in the scriptural text. As self-evident as this might appear, Milton takes the occasion to argue its importance as a way of presenting us with an idea that we can all agree on. The very fact that it is self-evident is what Milton in *Of True Religion* draws upon to argue his case for the universality of Protestant belief and the need to adopt a posture of latitudinarianism toward those whose own beliefs might differ in some respects (none of them fundamental) from our own. Thus, Milton certainly agrees with the Arian impulse to ground belief in Scripture, but just what the Arians (and Socinians) make of Father, Son, and Spirit in Scripture is another matter entirely.

If such is the case, do we gain any further insight into Milton's views of Arianism by attending (as we had with Socinianism) to *De Doctrina Christiana*? Once again, the answer gives rise to more questions than it resolves. It is here once again that the all-important chapter on the Son of God (1.5) comes into play. Assuming that the views expressed in this chapter are precisely those of Milton, they both correspond with and differ from those of Arius in important respects. Clearly, there is an Arian ring to this chapter. One or two points of contact should suffice. Addressing the ongoing subject of the "Divine Decree" of God, the chapter on the Son draws upon an earlier distinction between God's "Internal Efficiency" and His "External Efficiency" (1.3). Whereas "Internal Efficiency" is that which resides with God himself, indeed, within his own mind (YP 6:153), "External Efficiency" is the means by which his decree is executed (YP 6:205). Under this heading, there are three categories: first, the generation (*generatio*) of the Son, second, the creation (*creatio*) of the universe, and third, the government (*gubernatio*) of the universe. Under the first category, God becomes the Father in the sense that he "begets" (*generare*) the Son (YP 6:205; CM 14:178). As the author of this chapter is aware, the primary source of *generare* is the second psalm, which Milton had translated among his other psalm translations. The text at issue is 2:7: "I will declare the decree: the Lord hath said unto me, Thou *art* my Son; this day have I begotten thee" (YP 6:204–8). This text is invoked as evidence that the begetting itself "took place within the bounds of time [*in tempore*], for the decree itself must have preceded its execution (the insertion of the word *today* makes this quite clear)." Because of the literality of the begetting, Milton argues at length that one cannot have a Son unless a Father exists before the Son. This is so because God as the Father quite literally begot the Son within the limits of time (YP 6:209–10; CM 14:188). As the so-called Arians were wont repeatedly to recite of the Son (as a creature begotten "today"): "There was when he was not" (en pote ote ouk en). On this front, at least, the thrust of *De Doctrina* appears to be in agreement with the views ascribed to Arius.

At least as far as the Council of Nicaea is concerned, those views held to be anathema are deemed so because they insist that the begetting of the Son is *exclusively* a literal enactment, an event that occurred on a particular "day" during a particular moment in time. Contrary to such a doctrine, the council declares that the Son is "begotten, not made" (*gennethenta, ou poiethenta*). The distinction is important, for it suggests that the act of begetting (*gennan*) is of a different order from the mere act of making (*poienin*). Begetting is a transcendent, if not a timeless, act of generation that moves beyond the literal, if not the temporal. Its context is that which is always already happening throughout eternity, rather than that which happens once in time. Defying circumscription within the temporal, it finds its place within the world of the timeless. In the parlance of literary discourse, begetting for those who subscribed to the Nicene Creed can be described only through metaphor: it inhabits the divine world of trope, as opposed to the mundane world of letter. For the Nicene fathers, it is precisely this world of metaphor that distinguishes that which is begotten from that which is made, *gennethenta* from *poiethenta*.

Given the professed allegiance in *De Doctrina Christiana* to begetting as that which literally occurs within the limits of time, one might well expect this to be the view that prevails throughout the chapter on the Son of God. Ironically, it is none other than Maurice Kelley who acknowledges that Milton appears to contradict this very idea by viewing the act of begetting in distinctly metaphorical terms.[31] Drawing upon a range of scriptural proof-texts, Milton does in fact argue that the term "begot" is essentially a "figure of speech" (*loquendi tropo*) that embodies an entire range of meanings having to do with the Son's Resurrection, exaltation, anointing, kingship, and the like. Even the saints are said to have been "begotten by God." This does not mean that the Son is *not* literally begotten within the bounds of time: it simply delineates the tropological dimensions of the concept in other contexts. An awareness of these multiple dimensions opens up the possibility of corresponding interpretations, so much so, in fact, that Milton concludes that however the Son was begotten, this event is to be seen in conjunction with the various metaphorical acts of begetting that distinguish the role of the Son according to the scriptural text. By embracing the tropological, along with the literal, Milton goes so far as to construe the act of begetting with the telling phrase *quovis modo:* "whatever that means," or "in whatever sense that expression is to be understood" (YP 6:206–8; CM 14:184–87).[32] This is a view that any self-respecting Arian would eschew at all costs, but it is one that Milton ventures nonetheless to suggest the extent to which the metaphorical is an interpretive category embodied in the act of begetting itself. The result is an outlook that is at once orthodox and heterodox. It is, in short, *sui generis.*

What engages Milton throughout the chapter on the Son is the nature of the godhead itself and how that nature is to be understood, particularly as it is embodied in the relationship between the Father and the Son. At the heart of the discussion is the belief that the Son, although divine, is clearly not coequal or coeternal with the Father, nor is the Son in any sense either omnipotent or omniscient (YP 6:227–28, 263). Just how powerful the Son really is and how much he actually knows of the Father, among other considerations, are not issues that Milton makes clear.[33] What is clear is that Milton takes great pains to distinguish between those properties that may be said to constitute Father and Son. Milton then launches into a long and detailed metaphysical discussion of *essentia* and *substantia,* which makes it entirely clear that, as far as Milton is concerned, Father and Son share the same substance but do not share the same essence (YP 6:213). What precisely is meant by *essentia* and *substantia* is another matter, one that Miltonists continue to squabble over. All that can be said at this point is that Milton engages in a remarkable maneuver in his consideration of such concepts. First, he disavows the power of reason to articulate issues having to do with the nature of *essentia* and *substantia* as sacred categories: "Let us renounce reason in sacred matters" (Nos itaque in sacris rationi renuntiemus). This disavowal is followed by a solemn promise not to embark upon a long metaphysical discussion concerning "the drama of the personalities in the godhead" (personalitum illud totum drama advocem) (YP 6:213; CM 14:196).[34] Both disclaimers, however, are followed by exactly what Milton promises to eschew, a long, detailed, metaphysical argument concerning the nature of *essentia* and *substantia*. Once again, interpretive dilemmas — if not apparent contradictions — in Milton's argument arise, and once again Maurice Kelley draws our attention to them.[35] This is clearly a treatise replete with problems of one sort or another, not the least of which is the detailed discussion concerning the metaphysics of godhead. As I mentioned earlier, the very terms *essentia* and *substantia* (along with all the others that define godhead) have a long, befuddling, and contradictory history.

One thing, however, is perfectly clear. In Milton's attempt to distinguish between Father and Son on the metaphysical grounds of *essentia* and *substantia*, he is performing an act that is about as "contra Arianos" as any act can be, for in the theology attributed to Arius *there is no such distinction*. Had Arius cast his terminology in Latin, rather than in Greek, he would not have distinguished between *essentia* and *substantia*. It thus runs contrary to what we know of Arian thought to suggest that in distinguishing between Father and Son through a terminology of *essentia* and *substantia* that the Milton of *De Doctrina* is Arian. In the Nicene anathemas, as well as in the rhetoric of Arius's enemies, the heresiarch is faulted for alleging that the *ousia* of the Father and the *ousia* of the Son are categorically different, a difference grounded in the inescapable belief that the Son is generated from nothing. This is the crucial determinant, not a putative distinction between *essentia* and *substantia*, a distinction that is quite beside the point in

Arian thought. The major consideration is *nothing*. Nothing means nothing: It does not mean a little bit of this and a little bit of that. It does mean that the Son's *ousia* is not the Father's *ousia*, and the Father's *ousia* is not the Son's *ousia*.[36] With its foundational emphasis upon *creatio ex Deo*, the theology of *De Doctrina Christiana* is entirely out of keeping with the so-called Arian notion of *creatio ex nihilo*. On this decisive issue at least, Milton of the theological treatise and the poor, anathematized heresiarch are products of different realms of discourse.

At the very least, we are not at liberty to conclude, on the basis of what one finds in *De Doctrina Christiana*, that Milton is an Arian. Such a conclusion simply does not make very much sense. As we have seen, the very terms "Arius," "Arian," and "Arianism" are hotly in dispute among historians of the early church. Observing the disagreements among Miltonists about whether Milton is an Arian, these historians might well question whether even Arius is an Arian. Particularly in the context of the early modern period, the tradition that gave rise to Arianism as the great "fantasy" that plagued the church in its infancy emerged as the highly politicized Other that resulted in the sufferings of those besmirched with its taint. Accordingly, even when the terminology is not in dispute, any dispassionate attempt to come to terms with the theology of Arius apart from the polemical milieu that defines it is fraught with peril. So much for Arius. On the Miltonic front, we are no better off. Even if the authorship of *De Doctrina Christiana* were not in contention, daunting problems remain, not the least of which concerns the very meaning of "authorship" itself in light of the present state of the manuscript and the complex and uncertain process of recension out of which the manuscript presumably arose. On the basis of what we know (that is, the theology that the author of the theological treatise is said to articulate), terms of art (*generatio, essentia, substantia,* and the like) are replete with their own problems and uncertainties that must be taken into account in any attempt to establish the doctrinal nature of the treatise.

Anyone who explores the nature of godhead in Milton's poetry (especially *Paradise Lost* and *Paradise Regained*) will confront these issues in the movement from theological text to poetic text. Anyone who attempts to establish the "Arianism" of Milton's poetry through recourse to the theological treatise or even to the so-called Arian doctrines grounded in the discourse of the early church had better be aware of the pitfalls. Nothing can be taken for granted. We may pay lip service to this fact, but in dealing with poetic concepts within a theological context, we would do well to err on the side of caution rather than to venture conclusions that may come back to haunt us. In some respects, this chapter represents a caveat to any who would see in Milton an unqualified allegiance to the systematic theology of one school as opposed to another. Such a caveat is particularly germane in any consideration of Milton's view of godhead. With a certain touch of irony, I shall leave the final words to Maurice Kelley. Addressing Milton's view of godhead, Kelley observes that it "seems singularly Milton's own" (YP 6:71).[37]

NOTES

Notes to Introduction

1. See C. A. Patrides, "*Paradise Lost* and the Language of Theology," *Language and Style in Milton: A Symposium in Honor of the Tercentenary of "Paradise Lost,"* ed. Ronald David Emma and John T. Shawcross (New York: Frederick Unger, 1967), 106, 108.

2. Michael Lieb, "*De Doctrina Christiana* and the Question of Authorship," *Milton Studies* 41, edited by Albert C. Labriola (Pittsburgh: University of Pittsburgh Press, 1990), 172–230.

3. The question of the place of the Spirit in the enactment of this conception is a subject unto itself. For studies that establish the religious contexts that underlie the conception of the Holy Spirit in literature and art, see Albert C. Labriola, "The Holy Spirit in Art: The Theological Bearing of Visual Representation," *Proceedings of the Fifth-First Annual Convention of the Catholic Theological Society of America* (New York: St. John's University Press, 1996), 51:143–62; "Biblical Typology and the Holy Spirit: The Tree of Jesse and the Crucifixion," *Cithara: Essays in the Judaeo-Christian Tradition* 39 (November 1999): 3–12; "The Annunciation and Its Hebraic Analogues," *Cithara: Essays in the Judaeo-Christian Tradition* 40 (May 2001): 27–36; and "The Holy Spirit in Selected Manuscript Illumination," *Cithara: Essays in the Judaeo-Christian Tradition* 42 (November 2002): 13–31. Like the figure of the Incarnate Savior, the figure of the Spirit extends beyond the boundaries of this study.

4. G.C. Stead, "How Theologians Reason," in *Faith and Logic,* edited by Basil Mitchell, 108–31 (London: George Allen & Unwin, 1957).

5. Patrides, "*Paradise Lost* and the Language of Theology," 112. Patrides cites Ronald W. Hepburn, *Christianity and Paradox* (London: Watts, 1958), 16. See I. M. Crombie, "The Possibility of Theological Statements, in *Faith and Logic,* 31–83.

6. John Milbank, *The Word Made Strange: Theology, Language, Culture* (Oxford: Blackwell, 1997), 1; Milbank, "Postmodern Christian

Augustinianism: A Short *Summa* in Forty-Two Responses to Unasked Questions," in *The Postmodern God*, edited by Graham Ward (Oxford: Blackwell Publishers, 1997), 268.

7. On this issue, see William Shullenberger, "Linguistic and Poetic Theory in Milton's *De Doctrina Christiana*," *ELN* 19 (1982): 262–78.

8. See Lieb, "*De Doctrina Christiana* and the Question of Authorship."

9. See Martin Luther, "The Last Sermon in Wittenberg" (1546). I address the subject of the *deus absconditus* later in this study, but I do so without taking account of Milton's views of the will.

10. Jacob Bauthumely, *The Light and Dark Sides of God* (London, 1650), 10. Active in the New Model Army, Bauthumely was a leading Ranter in the '1640s and '1650s.

11. Jack Miles, *God: A Biography* (New York: Alfred A. Knopf, 1995), passim. Unlike Miles, I limit my study more nearly to an examination of the dark side or face of God, rather than to the light side or face. For a discussion of this dimension of deity, see my "Adam's Story: Testimony and Transition in *Paradise Lost*," in *Living Texts: Interpreting Milton*, edited by Charles W. Durham and Kristin Pruitt, 21–48 (Selinsgrove, Pa.: Susquehanna University Press, 2000), followed by a response by J. Martin Evans, "Afterthoughts on Adam's Story," 48–56.

12. Harold Bloom, *The Book of J* (New York: Grove Weidenfeld, 1990), 316–17.

13. See Dennis Danielson, *Milton's Good God: A Study in Literary Theodicy* (Cambridge: Cambridge University Press, 1982), passim.

14. At the opposite end of the spectrum is Mary Ann Radzinowicz, *Toward "Samson Agonistes": The Growth of Milton's Mind* (Princeton: Princeton University Press, 1978), 267, 271, 283–84, 349.

15. See Rudolf Otto, *The Idea of the Holy: An Inquiry into the Non-Rational Factor in the Idea of the Divine and Its Relation to the Rational*, trans. John W. Harvey (Milford: Oxford University Press, 1928). For "the holy" as a category of experience in Milton's works, see my *Poetics of the Holy: A Reading of "Paradise Lost"* (Chapel Hill: University of North Carolina Press, 1981).

16. The critical literature is replete with indictments of the "bad God." Foremost is William Empson, *Milton's God* (1961; reprint, Cambridge: Cambridge University Press, 1981). For an argument correspondingly stimulating and challenging, see Michael Bryson, *The Tyranny of Heaven: Milton's Rejection of God as King* (Newark: University of Delaware Press, 2004).

17. C. S. Lewis, *A Preface to "Paradise Lost"* (1942; reprint, New York: Oxford University Press, 1961), 130.

Notes to Chapter 1

1. I refer, of course, to Maurice Kelley's *This Great Argument: A Study of Milton's "De Doctrina Christiana" as a Gloss upon "Paradise Lost"* (Princeton: Princeton University Press, 1941), an exhaustive study in its own right.

2. C. A. Patrides, "*Paradise Lost* and the Language of Theology," in *Language and Style in Milton: A Symposium in Honor of the Tercentenary of "Paradise Lost,"* edited by Ronald David Emma and John T. Shawcross (New York: Frederick Ungar, 1967), 108.

3. Among those who have questioned the provenance of *De Doctrina Christiana,* none is more important than William B. Hunter, whose *"Visitation Unimplor'd": Milton and the Authorship of "De Doctrina Christiana"* (Pittsburgh: Duquesne University Press, 1998) reignited the debate over the issue of authoring the manuscript now lodged at the Public Record Office in the U.K. For a complete account of the bibliographical details, see my "*De Doctrina Christiana* and the Question of Authorship," *Milton Studies* 41, edited by Albert C. Labriola (Pittsburgh: University of Pittsburgh Press, 1990), 172–230.

4. On the issue of the palimpsest, see Gordon Campbell, et al., "The Provenance of *De Doctrina Christiana,*" *MQ* 31 (1997): 67–12, esp. 95.

5. Skinner recopied large portions of the manuscript (1–196, 308, 571–74, as well as other passages). Pages 197–308a, 309–548, 553–71 and 575–735 are in the hand of Picard.

6. The precise extent of Skinner's relationship with Milton remains a matter of conjecture. According to John T. Shawcross, Skinner may have simply "met Milton in the last months of his [Milton's] life, or simply knew Elizabeth [Milton's third wife] or one of the nephews" (letter to the author, June 12, 2003).

7. See Hunter, *"Visitation Unimplor'd,"* 30–33. Hunter identifies Picard as not only a former student of Milton but also a possible author of the treatise itself. See Hunter, *"De Doctrina Christiana: Nunc Quo Vadis,"* *MQ* 34 (2000): 97–101. Hunter's views are conjectural at best. See the chapters on *De Doctrina* in John Shawcross, *Rethinking Milton Studies: Time Past and Time Present* (Newark: University of Delaware Press, 2005).

8. According to Shawcross, Picard probably did recopy manuscripts that became *De Doctrina,* as well as other documents during 1658–59, but the precise nature of his responsibilities remains uncertain (letter to the author, June 12, 2003).

9. See William Elton, "New Light on Milton's Amanuensis," *HLQ* 26 (1963): 383–84. Even assuming that the Bedlam Picard is our Picard, the possibility of his madness does not imply that he was a candidate for Bedlam while he served Milton. We simply do not know one way or the other.

10. In my discussion, I focus almost exclusively on theologians of the Reformation and, even within that limited context, theologians most immediately or demonstrably related to *De Doctrina*, whether as the result of overt allusion or implicit reference. Underlying the whole concept of systemization, of course, are medieval theologians such as Thomas Aquinas, whose *Summa Theologica* is the grand masterpiece of systematic method. According to that method, Aquinas adopts a "scheme" that is replicated throughout the *Summa:* there is first the question to be considered, followed by the arguments to be countered; this, in turn, finds its view based upon detailed argument, and culminating in a reply to possible objections. Within this paradigm, Aquinas structures an entire self-contained theology. For diagrams of Aquinas's scheme, see the synoptical charts in Saint Thomas Aquinas, *Summa Theologica*, trans. Fathers of the English Dominican Province, 5 vols. rev. (Westminster, Md.: Christian Classics, 1981), passim.

11. Milton was familiar with (and made use of) an entire host of theologians during the course of his studies. The antiprelatical and divorce writings are a case in point. During the period 1641–45, Milton, Maurice Kelley observes, "refers to some forty-two works," many of them "systematic theologies." Although allusions to these works in Milton are quite overt, *De Doctrina Christiana* "mentions none of the systematic theologies or treatises on disputed heads of faith." We must extrapolate from Milton's oblique references in the epistle such diffuse volumes of divinity as "Placaeus on the Trinity, Beza on polygamy, Polanus on Christian liberty, and Zanchius on the hypostatic union and the Mosaic law." But these are conjectures (YP 6:21, 22 n. 25).

12. So Arthur Sewell, *A Study in Milton's Christian Doctrine* (London: Oxford University Press, 1939): "Milton's *De Doctrina Christiana* takes its shape from Ames's *Medulla* and Wollebius's *Compendium*" (38). In *This Great Argument*, Maurice Kelley follows suit (27, 38). Kelley's views on the subject are iterated throughout his edition of *De Doctrina* in the Yale *Prose*.

13. "The Life of Mr. John Milton" (1694), in *The Early Lives of Milton*, ed. Helen Darbishire (New York: Barnes and Noble, 1932), 60–61, compiled at the time "when he first undertook the Education and Instruction of his Sister's two Sons," Edward and John (ca. 1639–40). Although he promises to say more at a later point, Phillips unfortunately dropped the subject of Milton's foray into the production of a systematic theology at the time the poet was tutoring his nephews.

Accordingly, the relationship between the "Perfect System" and *De Doctrina* is largely conjectural. The epistle to *De Doctrina Christiana* alludes to Milton's course of reading in preparation to compile his own theology. Moving from the "shorter systems of theologians" to the "more diffuse volumes of divinity," Milton traces the course of his production of his own theological treatise (YP 6:119–22).

14. See the reference to Ames in *De Doctrina Christiana*, YP 6:705. Milton cites Ames directly and indirectly (but not always with approval) in *The Doctrine and Discipline of Divorce* and in *Tetrachordon* as well (YP 2:232, 275, 610). For a discussion of Milton and Ames, see Maurice Kelley, "The Composition of Milton's *De Doctrina Christiana:* First Phase," in *Th'Upright Heart and Pure*, edited by Amadeus P. Fiore, 35–44 (Pittsburgh: Duquesne University Press, 1967). See also the entries on Ames and Wolleb, in *A Milton Encyclopedia*, 9 vols., gen. ed. William B. Hunter (Lewisburg, Pa.: Bucknell University Press, 1978–83), 1:44–45; 8:173–74.

15. For a careful analysis of Wolleb's putative influence on *De Doctrina Christiana*, see Maurice Kelley, "Milton's Debt to Wolleb's *Compendium Theologiae Christianae*," *PMLA* 50 (1935): 156–65.

16. According to Hunter, the production of *De Doctrina* has resulted in two forms of discourse: the first a "simplistic and elementary collection of quotations from Wolleb supplemented by Ames and filled out by prooftexts"; the second a "complex, much longer response to such earlier naiveté which has been written over many chapters of that original" (*Visitation Unimplor'd*, 52). As tempting as Hunter's observations are, one must recall that the precise method of production is finally based on internal evidence.

17. Published in 1672, Milton's *Artis logicae plenior institutio ad methodum Petri Rami Rami concinnata* consists of Ramus's text, which, according to the summary offered by Walter J. Ong, S.J., is "transcribed virtually intact, amalgamated into a longer explanation of the same material worked up by Milton from George Downame (or Downham) and other commentators on Ramus and from some ideas of his own, the whole supplemented with an exercise in logical analysis adapted from Downame and an abridgement of the *Petri Rami vita* by Johann Thomas Freige (Fregius)" (YP 8:144).

18. Appearing posthumously, the *Commentarium* is the only theological work that Ramus produced. For an account of the treatise, see Walter J. Ong, S.J., *Ramus, Method, and the Decay of Dialogue* (Cambridge: Harvard University Press, 1958), 5, 28, 29, 32–33, 190, 315; hereafter cited in the text.

19. See Ramus, *Commentarium*, 6, 10, 12–15.

20. Reflected in the pedagogical emphasis, there is almost something of a catechetical quality to the method here. The "practical dimensions" are of utmost importance.

21. My brief summary is indebted to Keith Sprunger, "Ames, Ramus, and the Method of Puritan Theology," *HTR* 59 (1966): 133–52. For Milton's debt to Ramus and his followers in Milton's prose works,

see Keith Sprunger, "Ramistic Logic in Milton's Prose Works" (Ph.D. diss., Princeton, 1941).

22. I make use of the 1643 translation based on the third Latin edition of 1629, attributed to John St. Nicholas, in *The Marrow of Sacred Divinity*, ed. John D. Eusden (Durham, N.C.: The Labyrinth Press, 1968). The Ramistic emphasis upon method is discernible throughout Ames's works. Ames's interest in Ramus finds expression in his commentary on Ramus, *P. Rami Veromandui regii professoris, Dialecticae libri duo: quibus loco commentarii perpetuii post certa capita subjicitur, Guilielmi Amesii demonstratio logicae verae* (Cambridge, 1672) and *Demonstratio Logicae Verae* (Cambridge, 1646). Of particular importance to the issue of Ramistic logic is Ames's *Technometria* (London, 1633). See the excellent edition and translation, *Technometry*, ed. and trans. Lee W. Gibbs (Philadelphia: University of Pennsylvania Press, 1979). For my purposes, the importance of the work is reflected in the title of Keith L. Sprunger's "Technometria: A Prologue to Puritan Theology," *JHI* 29 (1968): 115–22. For Milton's Ramistic discussion of method, see his *Art of Logic*, book 2, chapter 17, titled "On Method" (YP 6:390–95; CM 11:470–85).

23. Sprunger, "Technometria," 142–43.

24. The "marrow," or *medulla*, was a well-recognized form in the seventeenth century and beyond. Examples include William Ainsworth, *Medulla Bibliorum, The marrow of the Bible; or, A logico-theological analysis of every several book of the Holy Scripture* (London, 1652).

25. Ames, *Medulla Theologica*, 69.

26. Sprunger, "Technometria," 145–46.

27. Ames, *Medulla Theologica*, 79.

28. One should be aware that what is initially conceived as a *catena* or chain is, in the Latin, also possibly conceived as a fetter, or a form of enslavement.

29. Ames, *Medulla Theologica*, 83–84. This, of course, translates the Latin, which provides even more evidence of the formulaic dimension of the utterance.

30. Ong, "Logic and the Epic Muse: Reflections on Noetic Structures in Milton's Milieu," in *Achievements of the Left Hand: Essays on the Prose of John Milton*, edited by Michael Lieb and John T. Shawcross (Amherst, Mass.: University of Massachusetts Press, 1974), 255, and passim. See also Phillip J. Donnelly, "The *Teloi* of Genres: *Paradise Lost* and *De Doctrina Christiana*," *Milton Studies* 39, edited by Albert C. Labriola (Pittsburgh: University of Pittsburgh Press, 2000), 74–100.

31. Such tables were not necessarily a part of the editions published during Ames's lifetime. In fact, they are more characteristic of the later editions. Nonetheless, their presence in these editions testifies to their importance. See Eusden, *Marrow of Sacred Divinity*, [71] n. 3.

32. The term "flow chart" is taken from Ong, "Logic and the Epic

Muse," in Lieb and Shawcross, *Achievements of the Left Hand*, 248. Referring to the diagrams that customarily accompany later editions of Ames's *Medulla* or *Marrow*, Ong remarks that "these celebrated dichotomized charts or outlines, into which one can purportedly break down or 'analyze' any well-organized discourse to display the 'method' by which it necessarily proceeds. . . . are, in fact, we now recognize, exactly the same in design as flow charts used to program computers today for storage and retrieval" (248).

33. References to the *Compendium Theologiae Christianae* are to the translation of the work in *Reformed Dogmatics*, ed. and trans. John W. Beardslee III (New York: Oxford University Press, 1965); hereafter cited in the text.

34. Kelley, "Milton's Debt," 157. As suggested, Kelley demonstrates that the presence of the *Compendium* is especially discernible in book 2 of *De Doctrina Christiana*.

35. The full title of Ross's translation is *The abridgment of Christian divinitie: so exactly and methodically compiled that it leads us as it were by the hand to the reading of the Holy Scriptures, ordering of commonplaces, understanding of controversies, clearing of some cases of conscience*, 3rd edition (London, 1656).

36. See Beardslee, *Reformed Dogmatics*, 8–11.

37. With derived theology one enters the vexed and uncertain terrain of the relationship between God and Son and between the godhead and the members of the body of believers. Here, we are confronted with such questions as the dynamics of godhead, the nature of sonship, the role of Christ, the hypostatical union, and the place of the church in matters of dogma. Such are the issues that engaged the church councils and are the stuff of systematic theology.

38. Regina M. Schwartz, "Citation, Authority, and *De Doctrina Christiana*," in *Politics, Poetics, and Hermeneutics in Milton's Prose*, edited by David Loewenstein and James Grantham Turner, 227–40 (Cambridge: Cambridge University Press, 1990), 232.

39. Ibid., 232.

40. For a detailed account of this issue, see Harris Francis Fletcher, *The Use of the Bible in Milton's Prose* (Urbana: University of Illinois Press, 1929), especially the third chapter, "The Use of the Bible in *De Doctrina*," 50–89. Although this work has been open to criticism of various sorts (Kelley, "Introduction," YP 6:45 n. 8), it is still extremely useful.

41. *Biblia sacra polyglotta: Complectentia textus orginales*, 6 vols., comp. Brian Walton (London, 1657).

42. See the entry "Bibles" by John T. Shawcross, in *A Milton Encyclopedia*, 1:163. Shawcross is convinced that *De Doctrina* makes use of the *Biblia sacra polyglotta*. Assuming a Miltonic authorship of the theological treatise, one finds the same conclusion in William

Riley Parker, *Milton: A Biography*, 2nd ed., 2 vols., ed. Gordon Campbell (Oxford: Clarendon Press, 1996), 1:499. Parker makes clear, however, that since the copy of the Walton polyglot in question has not survived, Milton's possession of it, though likely, can not be confirmed. In his catalog, *Milton's Library* (New York: Garland, 1975), Jackson Boswell lists the Walton Bible under the heading "A possible or likely candidate for inclusion" (xiii, p. 255, item 1474). See Boswell's list of other Bibles that Milton may have (or in fact certainly) owned (pp. 31–32, items 184–91). The only copy extant is Milton's so-called "family Bible," the Authorized or King James Version of 1611, which contains autograph marginalia (p. 32, item 188).

43. The Junius-Tremellius Bible (the work of Franciscus Junius and Immanuel Tremellius, two Heidelberg scholars) was published in stages between 1575 and 1579. The first London edition appeared in 1580. Later editions contain Theodore Beza's New Testament translation. References in my text to the Junius-Tremellious Bible are to the *Biblia Sacra, sive, Testamentum Vetvs, ab Im. Tremellio et Fr. Ivnio ex Hebraeo Latine reddrium* (London, 1680). Their version was adopted by William Ames as the basis of his own proof-texts in the *Medulla Theologica* (Kelley, "Introduction," YP 6:45). Boswell lists the Junius-Tremellius Bible (along with Beza's New Testament translation) as verified to have been in Milton's library. See Fletcher, *Use of the Bible*, for a thorough analysis of selected proof-texts in *De Doctrina* from the Junius-Tremellius version (52–67).

44. Sumner was the original translator of the treatise as it appears in the Columbia University edition of Milton's complete works. Carey is the translator of the treatise as it appears in the Yale University edition of Milton's prose works.

45. Fletcher, *Use of the Bible*, 54.

46. As made abundantly evident in the Prolusions, Milton was intimately familiar with scholastic debates on a wide range of subjects. During his tenure as a student at Cambridge, he both mastered the discourse of these debates and at times professed to hold them in contempt. See, for example, Prolusion 6. The scholastic dimension of the debates is something that he questions in *Of Education*.

47. Gordon Campbell, "*De Doctrina Christiana:* Its Structural Principles and Its Unfinished State," *Milton Studies 9*, edited by James D. Simmonds (Pittsburgh: University of Pittsburgh Press, 1976), 243–60.

48. Ibid., 243.

49. Introduction to the edition and translation of the *Artis Logicae* in YP 8:178–79, 198–99. For corresponding notions, see Franklin Irwin, "Ramistic Logic in Milton's Prose Works" (Ph.D. diss., Princeton University, 1941), among other works.

50. William Shullenberger, "Linguistic and Poetic Theory in Milton's *De Doctrina Christiana*," *ELN* 19 (1982): 262–78.

Notes to Chapter 2

1. Such terms as "ontological," "epistemological," and "phenomenological" are of relatively recent vintage and must be used with care. According to the *OED*, the first term extends back to the eighteenth century, and the second and third forward from the nineteenth century.

2. See Ames, *Medulla*, 80–87; and Wolleb, *Compendium*, 37–40. In his *Syntagma theologiiae Christianae* (2.4) (1624), Amandus Polanus von Polansdorf, on the other hand, does address the issue of God's existence (see YP 6:130n).

3. Robert M. Grant, *The Early Christian Doctrine of God* (Charlottesville: University Press of Virginia, 1966), 14, 18, 25–26.

4. Richard Messer, *Does God's Existence Need Proof?* (Oxford: Clarendon Press, 1993), 4.

5. Ibid., 4. For a wide-ranging collection of essays that address ontology, as well as related subjects, see *Critiques of God: Making the Case against Belief in God*, edited by Peter A. Angeles (Amherst, N.Y.: Prometheus Books, 1997).

6. See the hypertext essay on Anselm by Thomas Williams, "Saint Anselm"; available at http://plato.stanford.edu/entries/anselm. According to Williams, we owe the phrase "ontological argument" to Kant (3).

7. See the *Monologion*, chap. 4, in *Monologion; and Proslogion*, trans. Thomas Williams (Indianapolis: Hackett, 1996).

8. John Hick, ed., *The Existence of God: A Reader* (New York: Macmillan, 1964), 23, 25.

9. References to the *Proslogion* are to *The Ontological Argument: From St. Anselm to Contemporary Philosophers*, ed. Alvin Plantinga (Garden City, N.Y.: Doubleday, 1965). Latin interpolations are from *Proslogion: English and Latin*, ed. M.J. Charlesworth (Notre Dame: University of Notre Dame Press, 1979).

10. *Proslogion*, chap. 2, in *The Ontological Argument*, 3–4.

11. The argument launched in chapter 2 of the *Proslogion* extends to chapters 3 and 4. In response to Anselm's ontological arguments, Guanilo, a contemporary of Anselm, produced a critique of Anselm's reasoning. Titled "In Behalf of the Fool," this critique takes Anselm to task not for his conclusion ("God exists") but for his methodology. See Plantinga, *The Ontological Argument*, 6–13. Anselm responded to Guanilo in later chapters of the *Proslogion*.

12. References are to Saint Thomas Aquinas, *Summa Theologica*, 5 vols., trans. Fathers of the English Dominican Province (Westminster, Md.: Christian Classics, 1981). Latin interpolations are from *Summa Theologica* (London, 1727).

13. *Summa*, 1:11–14.

14. References are to John Calvin, *Calvin: Institutes of the Christian Religion*, 2 vols., ed. John T. McNeill, trans. Ford Lewis Battles (Philadelphia: Westminster Press, 1960); hereafter cited in the text. The *Institutes* underwent many changes between its first Latin (1536) and French (1537) editions and final Latin (1559) and French (1560) editions. The work is clearly one that grew with Calvin over the years.

15. Introduction, *Institutes*, 1:li.

16. *Institutes*, 1:35–36.

17. I allude not only to John Wilmot, Earl of Rochester's "Satyr" but to Don Cameron Allen, *Doubt's Boundless Sea: Skepticism and Faith in the Renaissance* (Baltimore: Johns Hopkins University Press, 1964). The subject of skepticism in the Renaissance has been widely discussed.

18. *Institutes*, 1:35–36, 51–52.

19. References to the *Discours de la méthode pour bien conduire sa Raison et chercher la Vérité dans les Sciences* (1637) are to *Discourse on Method and Related Writings*, trans. Desmond M. Clarke (London: Penguin Books, 1999). References to *Meditationes de prima philosophia* (1641) are to *Six Metaphysical Meditations*, trans. Thomas Molyneux (London, 1680). Page numbers are hereafter cited in the text.

20. One immediately recalls Milton's own emphasis in *Of Education* upon the process of moving from simple to complex forms of being, "because our understanding cannot in this body found it selfe but on sensible things, nor arrive so cleerly to the knowledge of God and things invisible, as by orderly conning over the visible and inferior creature" (YP, 2:367–69).

21. The notion of a mind/body dichotomy would, of course, be alien to the point of view represented by *De Doctrina Christiana*.

22. The Sumner translation reads as follows: "Though there be not a few who deny the existence of God, 'for the fool hath said in his heart, There is no God,' Psal. xiv. 1. yet the Deity has imprinted upon the human mind so many unquestionable tokens of himself, and so many traces of him are apparent throughout the whole of nature, that no one in his senses can remain ignorant of the truth" (CM 14:25). This rendering misses the force of the assertion about the existence of God.

23. In his *Accedence Commenc't Grammar*, Milton makes a great deal of the significance of *esse* in its various forms: "The Verb which betokeneth *being*," he observes, "is properly this Verb *Sum* only, which is therefore call'd a Verb Substantive." Following this, Milton proceeds to conjugate the verb, according to the paradigms labeled "Indicative," "Imperative," and "Infinitive." He concludes forms of the infinitive with *Esse, Fore,* and *Fuisse* (YP 8:98–99).

24. See Kelley's comment, YP 8:131 n. 3. Although Kelley does not mention the Manicheans, their philosophy seems to be as present as that of the Stoics.

25. "Quin et Conscientia, sive eadem recta ratio" (CM 14:28): conscience and right reason appear to be interchangeable. At a later point in *De Doctrina*, Milton refers to "right reason" again in his discussion of the prelapsarian mentality (CM 15:116). Compare *Paradise Lost:* "But God left free the Will, for what obeys / Reason, is free, and Reason he made right" (9:351–52).

26. See Robert Hoopes, *Right Reason in the English Renaissance* (Cambridge, Mass.: Harvard University Press, 1962).

27. Ibid., 166–67, 4.

28. As even a cursory examination of the concordances to Milton's works will indicate, the subject of "conscience," like that of "reason" (and "right reason"), appears repeatedly and in different contexts. My main concern here is with the treatment of conscience and right reason in the context of the theological arguments advanced in *De Doctrina Christiana.* I have not introduced the references to conscience and right reason in the other works because I wish to have the theological treatise speak for itself.

29. See Lotte Mulligan, "'Reason,' 'Right Reason,' and 'Revelation' in Mid-Seventeenth-Century England," in *Occult and Scientific Mentalities in the Renaissance,* edited by Brian Vickers, 375–401 (Cambridge: Cambridge University Press, 1984). Mulligan argues that "right reason" and "revelation" are correspondingly operative in the pursuit of truth.

30. I use the Columbia Milton translation here because it is closer to the original.

31. To gain a sense of the precise proof-texts Milton adopts to support his arguments, see Michael Bauman, *A Scripture Index to John Milton's "De doctrina christiana"* (Binghamton, N.Y.: Medieval and Renaissance Texts and Studies, 1989).

32. For a discussion of the way in which Milton's allusive practices are such that they produce "anti-texts," see Julia M. Walker, "The Poetics of Anti-Text and the Politics of Milton's Allusions," *SEL: Studies in English Literature* 37 (1997): 151–71. A similar situation results in the use of proof-text in *De Doctrina Christiana.*

33. Arthur Sewell, *A Study in Milton's "Christian Doctrine"* (London: Oxford University Press, 1939), 108–11. Sewell sees the influence of Calvin in this respect. I would add Luther as well. I emphasize the significance of Sewell's study because it has been largely disregarded as the result of Maurice Kelley's criticism in *This Great Argument: A Study of Milton's "De Doctrina Christiana" as a Gloss upon "Paradise Lost"* (Princeton, N.J.: Princeton University Press,

1941), passim. But Sewell is very important and, despite the flaws that Kelley criticizes, illuminating as well.

34. The first section ends with a very curious reference to the Jews, who, for not learning the lesson of true faith in God and the principles of Christian doctrine, must suffer the fate of having been dispersed throughout all parts of the world up to and including the present day (YP 6:132). This strikes me as odd, for it is entirely out of keeping with the discussion that has gone before and the discussion that follows it. To my knowledge, such a digression at this point is unique. Evidence of earlier manuscript revisions (1652–55?) would have proven helpful here.

35. For a discussion of the hidden God in Milton, see especially Victoria Silver, *Imperfect Sense: The Predicament of Milton's Irony* (Princeton: Princeton University Press, 2001), 45–93.

36. Brian Gerrish, " 'To the Unknown God': Luther and Calvin on the Hiddenness of God," *Journal of Religion* 53 (1973): 263–92. The idea of God's hiddenness, of course, is fundamental to the Old Testament as well. See Samuel E. Balentine, *The Hidden God: The Hiding of the Face of God in the Old Testament* (Oxford: Oxford University Press, 1983). Present in a multitude of texts ranging from Genesis through the later prophets, divine occultation is a *topos* that is enacted and reenacted in various Old Testament settings.

37. The experience of God is a category of apperception in keeping with the discipline known as the phenomenology of religion. It is the phenomenological approach through which the *deus absconditus* is most fruitfully addressed. See Gerrish, " 'To the Unknown God,' " 263–64, 269.

38. Gerrish designates these as "hiddenness 1" and "hiddenness 2" (ibid., 268). In his act of designating this double hiddenness, Gerrish acknowledges the work of Theodosius Harnack and Ferdinand Kattenbusch, among others (265–67). Likewise important to Gerrish is the study of John Dillenberger, *God Hidden and Revealed* (Philadelphia: Muhlenberg Press, 1953), esp. 16–17.

39. Gerrish, ibid., 268, and passim. Distinctions of this sort have undergone a good deal of scrutiny both before Gerrish advanced them and in response to his take on how hiddenness works.

40. David Tracy, "Form and Fragment: The Recovery of the Hidden and Incomprehensible God," *Center of Theological Inquiry Reflections* 3 (1999): 62–89. See also David Tracy, "The Hidden God: The Divine Other of Liberation," *Cross Currents* 46 (1996): 1–12.

41. Gerrish, " 'To the Unknown God,' " 268.

42. Rudolf Otto would appear to be working in the field known as the phenomenology of religion. What that field involves gives rise to multiple meanings. Practitioners (aside from Otto) include such figures as William James, Gerardus van der Leeuw, Mircea Eliade and

Joachim Wach. Most convenient as an Internet resource is the entry on the "History and Phenomenology of Religion" in the *Encyclopaedia Britannica Online;* available at www.britannica.com.

43. On deity as *ganz andere,* see Rudolf Otto, "The Sensus Numinus," *Hibbert Journal* 30 (1931–32): 430; cited by Dillenberger, *God Hidden and Revealed,* 88. All other references in my text are to Rudolf Otto, *The Idea of the Holy: An Inquiry into the Non-Rational Factor in the Idea of the Divine and Its Relation to the Rational,* trans. John W. Harvey (London: Oxford University Press, 1928). First published in 1917 as *Das Heilige: über das Irrationale in der Idee des Göttlichen und sein Verhältnis zum Rationalen,* Otto's book has gone through some ten editions. According to Dillenberger, *The Idea of the Holy* has become a "religious classic" (70). As Gerrish attests, his treatment of the *deus absconditus* is in sympathy with Otto's book ("'To the Unknown God,'" 269 n. 20). For the application of Otto's categories to Milton's poetry, see Michael Lieb, *Poetics of the Holy: A Reading of "Paradise Lost"* (Chapel Hill: University of North Carolina Press, 1981).

44. Otto, "The Idea of the Holy," 5–41.

45. Ibid., 14.

46. Ibid., 8–11.

47. Dillenberger, *God Hidden and Revealed,* xvii.

48. Also at issue is the school of the Pseudo-Dionysius, most notably exemplified by John Scotus Eriugena (ninth century A.D.). For an analysis of the visionary outlook fostered by Dionysius the Areopagite and John Scotus Eriugena, see my *The Visionary Mode: Biblical Prophecy, Hermeneutics and Cultural Change* (New York: Cornell University Press, 1991), 234–49, 263–76.

49. Kataphatic theology is the theology of the positive or rational way, the theology of affirmation. Apophatic theology is the theology of the negative or mystical way, the theology of denial. The first deals with delineating deity in perceptible terms, that is, through the images we have of God. The second approaches God's "hid divinity" through what is imperceptible and unknowable. Apophatic theology is an encountering of God through the denial of all those things we assume he embodies. See detailed explanations in Lieb, *Visionary Mode,* 236–37, and passim.

50. Luther and Calvin are a case in point. For Luther's putative "mysticism," see Bengt R. Hoffman, *Luther and the Mystics* (Minneapolis: Augsburg Publishing House, 1976). According to Hoffman, Luther, although occasionally quoting Pseudo-Dionysius, "expunged dionysian theology from his works." Luther is more nearly in keeping with Johann Tauler and the anonymous writer of *Theologica Germanica* (120–21). Gerrish, on the other hand, is much more inclined to see the presence of Pseudo-Dionysius in Luther's

thought. Although critical of the mystical theology on many fronts, Luther not only found the teachings of Pseudo-Dionysius appealing but also adopted the very language of those teachings in the conduct of his own exegesis.

51. Although it would be an overstatement to suggest a direct, unproblematical correlation between the Pseudo-Dionysius and the Reformation theologians, apophatic theology did enjoy something of a presence in the early modern period.

52. Erasmus's *De libero arbitrio* appeared in 1524; Luther's *De servo arbitrio* in 1525. Erasmus thereafter published *Hyperaspistes Diatribae de Libero Arbitrio* in two parts (1526, 1527) to defend his earlier contentions.

53. Cited by Gerrish, " 'To the Unknown God,' " 271. For Luther's full treatment, see *On the Bondage of the Will,* in *Luther's Works,* 56 vols., ed. Jaroslav Pelikan et al. (Philadelphia: Fortress Press, 1972), esp. 33:138–44.

54. Cited by Gerrish, " 'To the Unknown God,' " 272, 274.

55. Luther, *Bondage of the Will,* in *Works,* 33:140–44. In response to such a vision of the *deus absconditus,* Luther finds no place for what he calls "carnal Reason." As he proclaims famously in "The Last Sermon in Wittenberg" (1546), reason, that "mangy, leprous whore," is "nothing but the devil's bride." In the face of God's hiddenness, we must "hold reason in check" and be careful not to be seduced by her "cogitations." Heeding the *mysterium* in all its splendor, we would do well to "trample reason and its wisdom under foot" and to castigate reason by proclaiming, "You cursed whore, shut up!" (*Works,* 51:374–76).

56. Gerrish, " 'To the Unknown God,' " 279–85.

57. John Calvin, *Calvin: Institutes of the Christian Religion,* 2 vols., ed. John T. McNeill, trans. Ford Lewis Battles (Philadelphia: Westminster Press, 1960), 1:95–105.

58. See, for example, Blaise Pascal, whose *Pensées* (1660) is a testament to the *deus absconditus.* Thus, Pascal observes that Scripture attests to the fact that God is a "hidden God," in support of which Pascal invokes Isaiah 45:15: "Vere tu es Deus absconditus" (verily, thou art a God that hidest thyself) (Pascal, *Pensées,* The Classical Library edition, 1999, 4:242; available at http://www.classical-library.org/pascal/pensees/index.htm. In his sermons, Lancelot Andrewes comments on the same passage from Isaiah: "Of God, the prophet Esay saith, *Vere Deus absconditus es tu;* God is of Himself a mystery, and hidden; and that which is strange, hidden with light which will make any eyes past looking on Him" (Project Canterbury Library of Anglo-Catholic Theology; available at http://anglican-history.org/andrewes/index.html).

59. Milton discusses predestination in book 1, chapter 4 of *De Doctrina Christiana.* It is clear from his treatment of this issue that

"bondage of the will" is about as far from his beliefs as a doctrine can get. Nonetheless, predestination does figure prominently in his thought, but he applies it only to "election," as opposed to reprobation. This means that those who are predestined to election as a blessing enjoy salvation as the result of God's beneficence, but it does not mean that predestination is the reason that the reprobate suffer damnation. The reprobate are in no way "appointed" to God's anger. They assume that "bad eminence" as the result of their own free will. On the other hand, there are those fortunate beings appointed to salvation because they have been singled out, "elected," to reap their heavenly rewards as the result of God's mysterious will (YP 6:168–213). Among the many discussions of these issues in Milton studies, see Maurice Kelley's treatment of Milton and Arminianism in the introduction to YP 6:74–86.

60. *De Doctrina Christiana* might be considered closer to Erasmus than to Luther and Calvin concerning the relationship between the operations of the will and the hiddenness of God. For Erasmus, it is perfectly acceptable to maintain the freedom of the will, on the one hand, and the *deus absconditus,* on the other. See Erasmus, "The Obscurity of Scripture," from his *On the Freedom of the Will,* in *Luther and Erasmus: Free Will and Salvation,* ed. E. Gordon Rupp and Philip S. Watson (Philadelphia: Westminster Press, 1969). Erasmus (ever the humanist) likens the hiddenness of God to "that cavern near Corycos of which Pomponius Mela tells, which begins by attracting and drawing the visitor to itself by its pleasing aspect, and then as one goes deeper, a certain horror and majesty of the divine presence that inhabits the place makes one draw back" (38). Erasmus effectively describes what Otto calls the *mysterium fascinans.*

61. Lieb, *The Visionary Mode,* 236–37.

62. For a full discussion of the dwelling presence of God manifested as the phenomenon of divine light, see Lieb, *Poetics of the Holy: A Reading of "Paradise Lost"* (Chapel Hill: University of North Carolina Press, 1981), 185–245. See also Harold Swardson, *Poetry and the Fountain of Light: Observations on the Conflict between Christian and Classical Traditions in Seventeenth-Century Poetry* (Columbia: University of Missouri Press, 1962), passim.

63. Judging by the proof-texts that Milton elects to marshal, one is prompted to remark that the Son alone appears to be in the position of "knowing" the Father, as much as a generated or "begotten" entity of that station has it in his power to "know" the unknowable. This point will be addressed in subsequent chapters.

64. Such texts are cited by Ames, *Medulla,* to support the notion that God is inaccessible. See YP 6:133 n. 11.

65. In the context of Milton's poetry, the voyeuristic dimensions of divine seeing are explored by Regina Schwartz, "Through the

Optic Glass: Voyeurism and *Paradise Lost*," in *Desire in the Renaissance: Psychoanalysis and Literature,* ed. Valerie Finucci and Regina Schwartz (Princeton: Princeton University Press, 1994), 146–68.

66. One thinks of all those poems that call upon the object of desire to "come forth," "suffer herself to be desired," and "not blush so to be admired." The reference, of course, is to Edmund Waller's "Go, lovely Rose" (13–15), a well-known poem in the *carpe diem* tradition. The lines are cited from the *Oxford Book of English Verse: 1250–1900,* ed. Arthur Quiller-Couch (Oxford: Oxford University Press, 1919).

67. Isaiah 6 is crucial to Milton's view of himself as one whose lifetime task is that of celebrating God. See the statement in *The Reason of Church-Government:* His inspiration will be bestowed upon him as a result of his prayers "to that eternall Spirit who can enrich with all utterance and knowledge, and sends out his Seraphim with the hallow'd fire of his Altar to touch and purify the lips of whom he pleases" (YP 1:820–21). The allusion resonates throughout Milton's poetry as well.

68. For a detailed account of the vision in biblical and postbiblical literature, see Lieb, *The Visionary Mode,* 192–98. In *Poetics of the Holy,* I explore the vision in the context of its influence on Milton's poetry and prose.

69. In its rendering of the Latin, Walton's polyglot Bible follows the Vulgate to the letter.

70. For the Greek, see *The Precise Parallel New Testament,* gen. ed. John R. Kohlenberger III (New York: Oxford University Press, 1995), and for the Latin, see *Biblia Sacra Iuxta Vulgatam Versionem* (Stuttgart: Deutsche Bibelgesellschaft, 1969).

71. In the standard Latin version, *aenigma* (conceived as *in aenigmate*) assumes the form of the ablative to indicate the way in which something is performed or undertaken.

72. I am a bit uncomfortable with Carey's locution, because it implies that the action is one of seeing *in* a mirror or *in* a riddle, rather than seeing *through* each of them.

73. Addressing the concept of "godhead" (*theotès*) in "De Deo," Milton comments that because "God by his very nature transcends everything, including definition," to have sense of the divine nature in this life is beyond our limited capacities.

Notes to Chapter 3

1. As it is integrated specifically into the discussion of Milton's poetry, the epistemological mode is incorporated into the second part of this study under the heading "The Poetics of Deity."

2. The deity portrayed in this portion of "De Deo" is one that confirms the sense of God as ineffable, the very embodiment of all that is holy. Such a view is consistent with themes that I have already explored at some length in my book, *Poetics of the Holy: A Reading of "Paradise Lost"* (Chapel Hill: University of North Carolina Press, 1981), 171–84. I do not seek to rehearse the conclusions of that study here; rather, I simply wish to emphasize some of the primary points about the "holy name" (or names) of God raised in the earlier study. To do so is to suggest once again the extent to which Milton was responsive to the most deeply held beliefs about the hidden God.

3. Although the issue of "attributes" is broached in both Ames and Wolleb, for example, it is not handled with the same sense of acuity and comprehensiveness that it is in *De Doctrina Christiana*. In *De Doctrina*, the attributes of God are crucial to the act of disclosing (what ultimately cannot be disclosed): the essence of God. Discussions of the divine attributes have a long history. Among the many analyses of the subject, see Louis Farnell, *The Attributes of God* (Oxford: Clarendon Press, 1925).

4. In keeping with the notion of power, the notion of "virtue," of course, refers not to the category of ethics but to the category of manliness, vigor, and strength.

5. In *De Doctrina*, an entire chapter is devoted to the Holy Spirit (YP 6:281–98), a most complex phenomenon indeed.

6. Despite the emphasis on God as a "spirit" *De Doctrina Christiana*, the fact of God's "materiality" remains crucial to the outlook of the treatise. See Neil D. Graves, "'The whole fulness of the Godhead dwells in him bodily': The Materiality of Milton's God," *Christianity and Literature* 52 (2003): 497–521.

7. Interestingly, the one proof-text cited to support the metaphysical contentions that bear upon the idea of *hypostasis* is Hebrews 1:3. It is no doubt significant that only the source of the proof-text (Heb. 1:3), rather than the text itself, is cited. What the proof-text does put forth is the primacy of the Son "who being the brightness of *his* glory, and the express image of his person, and upholding all things by the word of his power, when he had by himself purged our sins, sat down on the right hand of the Majesty on high." This text serves as the basis of the long and involved interpretation that follows.

8. Actually, the original is *"ubique praesens"* (SP 9/61, p. 14), which differs in connotation from "omnipresent," as translated in CM 14:41. According to John T. Shawcross (letter to the author, June 15, 2003), the phrase *ubique praesens* implies that "God is present in all things and all people," in the sense of God's being a part of all things rather than "simply observing everything and everyone." The precise meaning of *ubique praesens*, however, is something that Milton

acknowledges as impossible finally to understand. In short, it is unfathomable.

9. Of these attributes, some are positive (*affirmativa*), some negative (*negativa*). Milton says almost nothing about this distinction. Nor does he specify which of the attributes is *affirmativa*. He does, however, say a bit more about the so-called negative attributes (*negativa*). "Some are negative, in that they show God is not imperfect as created things are. For example, when God is called immense or infinite, or immortal, these are negative attributes" (YP 6:149; CM 14:52–54). This aspect of the argument appears almost as if it were an afterthought, one that certainly lacks sufficient development. Underlying it, I suspect, is the discourse of the Pseudo-Dionysius.

10. See my treatment of holy war in *Poetics of the Holy*, 246–312.

11. A possible translation might be something like "Whence this name of God *El Shaddai*," with the verb understood.

12. For the significance of the divine names, see Lieb, *Poetics of the Holy*, 171–84.

13. In a note to the phrase "sufficiently powerful," Kelley cites Junius-Tremellius and others to reinforce the reading of *Shaddai* as *sufficiens*, but I believe that the term carries meanings that extend beyond the rather nondescript "sufficient." See *Testamenti veteris Biblia sacra, Libri canonici*, comp. and trans. Immanuel Tremellius (London, 1580), s.v.

14. I am grateful to John T. Shawcross for suggesting these implications.

15. Rudolf Otto, *Das Heilige* (Breslau: Trewendt and Granier, 1922). Translated by John W. Harvey as *The Idea of the Holy* (London: Oxford University Press, 1923), 1–41. See also Lieb, *Poetics of the Holy*, 3–40.

16. See *The New Brown Driver Briggs Gesenius Hebrew and English Lexicon*, comp. Francis Brown, in conjuction with S. R. Driver and Charles A. Briggs (Peabody, Mass.: Hendrickson, 1979), s.v. (hereafter cited as *BDB*), based on the *Lexicon* of William Gesenius (1906).

17. Milton also notes that the term *adonai* ("lord," "master") is frequently used for God (CM 14:48).

18. Aristotle addresses the idea of the *Actus Purus* in the *Metaphysics* (books 9 and 11), as well as in the *Physics* (books 7 and 8). I am indebted here to the entry on Aristotle in the *Catholic Encyclopedia*, available at http://www.newadvent.org/cathen/01713a.htm.

19. See *"Actus et Potentia"* at ibid. Thomas Aquinas is a case in point. In his *Summa Theologica*, he addresses the distinction under the heading of how the intellectual soul (*anima intellectiva*) knows itself. "Therefore," he says, "it is that the Essence of God [*essentia Dei*], the pure and perfect act [*actus purus et perfectus*], is simply and perfectly in itself intelligible; and hence God by his own Essence knows Himself, and all other things also" (1.87).

20. Milton completes this section by observing that, "the power of God is not exerted in those kinds of things which, as the term goes, imply a contradiction." That is, "he cannot deny himself" (2 Tim. 2:3). The notion is a commonplace; see Kelley's comments (YP 6:146 n. 49).

21. *A Latin Dictionary,* comp. Charlton Lewis and Charles Short (Oxford: Clarendon Press, 1879), s.v.

22. As Kelley points out (YP 6:147 n. 54), the language here is very close to that of *Paradise Lost* (8:406–7).

23. As a sign of the recognition of the dilemma to which the God of the Old Testament as opposed to the God of the New Testament gives rise, Milton observes that even in the Old Testament, the very term *'elohim'* is a plural form ("gods") construed in a singular sense: "God" (YP 6:148).

24. See the entries in *A Latin Dictionary,* s.v.

25. For the reference to Psalms, the Yale *Prose* (6:149) has "Psal. xliii. 3," whereas the Columbia Milton (14:54–55) has "Psal. xlii. 3" in the Latin and "Psal. xlii. 2" in the English. The discrepancy occurs, in part, because the manuscript is smudged at that point, and there are unaccountable brackets around certain of the proof-texts. In an e-mail message to me of May 17, 2003, John T. Shawcross observes once again the many textual problems associated with the manuscript, its transcriptions in published form, and, of course, the translations in both the Yale *Prose* and in the Columbia Milton. All this simply confirms my conviction that unless one works with the original, interpretive conclusions rest on potentially dangerous ground. On these and related questions, see Shawcross, *Rethinking Milton Studies: Time Present and Time Past* (Newark: University of Delaware Press, 2005).

26. Otto, *Idea of the Holy,* 78–79.

27. See Lieb, *Poetics of the Holy,* passim.

28. *A Latin Dictionary,* s.v.

29. Quite the opposite is true of texts such as Exodus 34:6, which renders *chesed* a distinctly problematical phenomenon. Indeed, the very term *chesed* can imply the opposite of "kindness." On occasion, *chesed* carries the meaning of "shame" and "reproach." See *BDB,* s.v. *chesed* in its various forms.

30. Even the redemptive outlook of the New Testament assumes a harshness in the advent of the coming judgment. The specter of that event haunts the citations Milton puts forward in the final portion of "De Deo." Thus, the reference to God as *"Verax . . . et Fidelis"* ("true and faithful") recalls Revelation 19:11: "And I saw the heaven opened, and behold a white horse; and he that sat upon him *was* called Faithful and True, and in righteousness he doth judge and make war."

31. The translation in the Columbia Milton is much more to the point than that in the Yale *Prose,* which treats *efflorescit* as a noun

("flower": "the flower of all these attributes"). The term is better left a verb than a noun. I am not particularly happy with the Columbia Milton "springs" either. On the other hand, *efflorescit* can imply "*bloom, spring up, flourish.*" See *A Latin Dictionary,* s.v.

32. For an account of "glory" in the Miltonic context, see John Rumrich, *Matter of Glory: A New Preface to "Paradise Lost"* (Pittsburgh: University of Pittsburgh Press, 1987). In the case of Milton, the materialistic implications of "glory" become all important.

33. For Psalm 104:1, *De Doctrina* employs the phrase "glory and majesty" (gloriam et maiestatem), rather than "honor and majesty," as attested in the AV. Although the translation in the Columbia Milton is "honor and majesty," the Latin uses *gloriam.* In the history of transmission, Psalm 104:1 assumes various forms. See *Testamenti veteris Biblia sacra, Libri canonici,* comp. Immaneul Tremellius, s.v.

34. Otto, *Das Heiligᴜ,* pp. 1–41.

35. See my treatment of the subject in *Poetics of the Holy,* passim. I have addressed the early underpinnings of Ezekiel's vision in *The Visionary Mode.* There, I undertake a detailed analysis of the visionary experience conceived through the notion of the *ma'aseh merkabah* or Work of the Chariot, a phenomenon of crucial importance to biblical exegesis throughout both medieval Judaism and the Christocentric appropriations.

36. See the entry for *doxa* in *A Greek-English Lexicon of the New Testament and Other Early Christian Literature,* trans. and ed. W. F. Arndt and F. W. Gingrich (Chicago: University of Chicago Press, 1957), s.v.

37. For the idea of the "good God," see Dennis Danielson, *Milton's Good God: A Study in Literary Theodicy* (Cambridge: Cambridge University Press, 1982).

Notes to Chapter 4

1. The phrase "dark side" is not exclusive to the *Star Wars* films. It is an appellation current during Milton's own time. See the treatise of the seventeenth century Ranter Jacob Bauthumley, *The Light and Dark Sides of God* (London, 1650).

2. See Dennis Danielson, *Milton's Good God: A Study in Literary Theodicy* (Cambridge: Cambridge University Press, 1982).

3. The concepts of divine passibility versus divine impassibility have received extensive treatment both historically and theoretically. For a brief but informative discussion of the idea in general, see Robert S. Franks, "Passibility and Impassibility," in *Encyclopaedia of Religion and Ethics,* 12 vols., edited by James Hastings (New York:

Charles Scribner's Sons, 1917–22), 9:658–59. The fullest historical study is John K. Mozley, *The Impassibility of God: A Survey of Christian Thought* (Cambridge: Cambridge University Press, 1926). Correspondingly important studies of the historical background include G. L. Prestige, *God in Patristic Thought* (London: SPCK Press, 1952), esp. 1–15; and Robert M. Grant, *The Early Christian Doctrine of God* (Charlottesville: University Press of Virginia, 1966), 14–33, 111–14. Among other treatments of the subject from a theoretical point of view, see Richard E. Creel, *Divine Impassibility: An Essay in Philosophical Theology* (Cambridge: Cambridge University Press, 1986).

4. In *Philo*, 10 vols., trans. F. H. Colson and G. H. Whitaker (London: William Heinemann, 1960), 3: 10–101; hereafter cited in the text by section and page number.

5. The kinds of ideas that Philo as Neoplatonist has in mind are discernible in the discussion of God's immutability in the *Republic* (2.380–81).

6. Represented by church fathers such as Clement of Alexandria and Origen, the Alexandrian school refashioned God in a manner consistent with its attempts to construct a Christian philosophy of religion. In his *Stromata* (5.11), Clement, for example, maintains that God, as that which is totally immutable, is "without passion, without anger, without desire." God's life is quite simply free of such affections. Following the example of God's impassibility, the Christian gnostic, counsels Clement, should rise above all emotions, which bind him to this world. Striving for the world of God, the gnostic should cleanse himself as much as possible from the taint of emotions. See Mozley, *Impassibility of God*, 52–59.

7. Cited by Grant, *Early Christian Doctrine*, 30. See Grant's entire discussion, 28–31. See also Mozley, *Impassibility of God*, 60–63.

8. According to Grant, *Early Christian Doctrine*, Origen here reflects the influence of Ignatius, who often speaks of the suffering of Christ as a manifestation of the "passion of God." Ignatius, in turn, is in keeping with Tatian and Clement of Rome (31). For additional elaboration, see Mozley, *Impassibility of God*, 7–8; and Prestige, *God in Patristic Thought*, 6.

9. For a discussion of patripassianism, see Tertullian, *Treatise against Praxeas*. See also Mozley's treatment of modalistic monarchianism (*Impassibility of God*, 28–37); and the entry on patripassianism in the *New Catholic Encyclopedia*, 15 vols., ed. CUA Staff (New York: McGraw-Hill, 1967), 10:1103.

10. In *The Ante-Nicene Fathers*, 10 vols., ed. Alexander Roberts and James Donaldson (New York: Charles Scribner's Sons, 1908), vol. 3. References to Tertullian in the text are by chapter and section number and are from this edition.

11. *Against Marcion,* in *The Ante-Nicene Fathers,* 3:309–10.

12. See also Novatian's discussion of the anger, indignation, and hatred of God in *Treatise Concerning the Trinity* (chap. 5), in *The Ante-Nicene Fathers,* 5:615. In the next chapter, Novatian addresses the notion of God's body (5:615–16).

13. Lactantius, *The Wrath of God,* in *The Fathers of the Church,* 112 vols. to date, gen. ed. Joseph Deferrari (Washington, D.C.: Catholic University of America Press, 1965), vol. 54: 65–67. References to Lactantius in my text are to this edition. For the influence of Lactantius on Milton, see Kathleen E. Hartwell, *Lactantius and Milton* (Cambridge: Harvard University Press, 1929).

14. In this respect, Lactantius is at odds with his putative teacher Arnobius of Sicca. See Arnobius's *The Case Against the Pagans,* 2 vols., trans. George E. McCracken (Westminster, Md.: The Newman Press, 1949), esp. 197–207.

15. *The Fathers of the Church,* 54:63–69, 96–99.

16. My treatment of Saint Augustine's views follows Mozley, *Impassibility of God,* 104–9.

17. Saint Augustine,*The City of God,* trans. Marcus Dods (New York: Modern Library, 1950), 263; hereafter cited in the text.

18. Mozley, *Impassibility of God,* 104.

19. Cited in ibid., 107.

20. Cited in ibid., 106.

21. Compare Mozley, *Impassibility of God:* "As to the scriptural expressions, he [Saint Augustine] regards them as the best manner of speech possible, in view of the necessary limitations of language when any attempt is made to describe the life of God." For Saint Augustine, "God is said to have a soul only by analogy (*tropice*)" (105).

22. This theory of reading is reinforced by Saint Augustine's discussion of scriptural tropes in the treatise *On Christian Doctrine.* See, in particular, book 1, chapters 2 and 39; book 2, chapters 6 and 10; and book 3, chapters 9, 10, and 11 in *On Christian Doctrine, A Select Library of the Nicene and Post-Nicene Fathers of the Christian Church,* ed. Philip Schaff, 1st ser., 14 vols. (Buffalo: Christian Literature, 1886–89), 2:523, 534, 537, 539, 560, 561.

23. Such is particularly true of the Scholastics. Whether one considers figures like Scotus, Anselm, or Aquinas, the essential impassibility of God is a decisive factor in the theological formulations of the later Middle Ages. See Mozley, *Impassibility of God,* 109–19.

24. John Calvin, *Commentaries upon the Book of Genesis,* 2 vols., trans. John King (Edinburgh: Calvin Translation Society, 1847), vol. 1. References in my text are to sixth chapter of the opening commentary, 1:248–49.

25. Among the Reformation theologians, the attribute of passibility was an issue of major import. One might glance at *The Substance*

of Christian Religion (London, 1600) of the Reformed scholastic theologian Amandus Polanus. Whereas Polanus is a firm believer in the *deus absconditus* (see 15–16), he also emphasizes the anthropopathetic dimension of God, who appears to express a wide array of emotions but in reality is quite impassible (see 26–36).

26. Founded in the fourth century by Audius in Mesopotamia, this sect taught that since man was made in the image of God, God possesses a human form (see the note to *Institutes*, 1:121). Interestingly, Luther was more accepting of the Anthropomorphites. See his *Lectures on Genesis*, in *Luther's Works*, ed. Jaroslav Pelikan (Saint Louis: Concordia Publishing House, 1958), 1:14–15.

27. Proper reading as a religious act meant a great deal to Calvin, who was aware of and cited with approbation Cicero's own association of the word "religion" with the word for "reading" (*Institutes*, 1.12, 1:117). See Cicero's discussion in the *De Natura Deorum* (2.28.72–73), a work likewise concerned in part with the way in which the gods are represented in human terms. In this work, Cicero maintains that the term "religious" is ultimately derived from the idea of reading or rereading (*legere* and *relegere*). Although the accuracy of this etymology is open to question, it does suggest the way in which the ancient commentators emphasized the association between religion and reading. See *De Natura Deorum* in *Cicero*, trans. H. Rackham (Cambridge, Mass.: Harvard University Press, 1951), 192–93.

28. In the language of contemporary hermeneutics, Calvin's approach is one that advocates the idea of "demythologizing" the rhetoric of God's passibility in order to declare with full assurance the fact of his *apatheia*. For a discussion of the principles upon which such an approach is based, see Rudolf Bultmann, *New Testament and Mythology*, ed. and trans. Schubert M. Ogden (Philadelphia: Fortress Press, 1984). For an analysis of the demythologist point of view, see Paul Ricoeur, "Preface to Bultmann," in *Essays on Biblical Interpretation*, ed. Lewis S. Mudge (Philadelphia: Fortress Press, 1980), 49–72. For an analysis of Milton and the contexts of Bultmann's program for demythologization, see Thomas Merrill, *Epic God-Talk: "Paradise Lost" and the Grammar of Religious Language* (Jefferson, N.C.: McFarland, 1986).

29. In addition to Ames, other influences on Milton include Johannes Wolleb, who skirts the issue of passibility entirely. See his discussion of "The Knowledge of God," in *Compendium of Christian Theology*, trans. John W. Beardslee III, in *Reformed Dogmatics* (New York: Oxford University Press, 1965). The whole issue of passibility goes unnoticed in Heinrich Heppe, *Reformed Dogmatics*, trans. G. T. Thomson (London: Allen and Unwin, 1950). References are to *The Marrow of Theology*, trans. John D. Eusden (Durham, N.C.: The Labyrinth Press, 1968).

30. Such an approach is consistent with Renaissance theological treatises of the same type, among them the *Loci Communes* of Melanchthon and Peter Martyr Vermigli. For a discussion of the form, see John M. Steadman's entry on *De Doctrina Christiana* in *A Milton Encyclopedia*, 9 vols., gen. ed. William B. Hunter Jr. (Lewisburg, Pa.: Bucknell University Press, 1978–83), 2:118–19.

31. Ames, *Medulla*, 83–87.

32. The Westminster Confession of Faith (chapter 2), in *Creeds of Christendom*, 3 vols., comp. Philip Schaff (Grand Rapids, Mich.: Baker Book House, 1977), 3:606. Compare the statement in the Thirty-Nine Articles (1): "There is but one lyuyng and true God, euerlastiyng, without body, partes, or passions" (3.487). The Westminster Confession elaborates by maintaining that God, although passionless, "hat[es] all sin."

33. For additional examples, see such works as Roger Hutchinson, *The Image of God or Layman's Book* (1550), in *The Works*, ed. John Bruce, The Parker Society (Cambridge: Cambridge University Press, 1842), and Thomas Jackson, *A Treatise of the Divine Essence and Attributes* (London, 1628), 226–32.

34. Milton's concept of accommodation has been much discussed. See, in particular, Roland M. Frye, *God, Man, and Satan: Patterns of Christian Thought and Life in "Paradise Lost," "Pilgrim's Progress," and the Great Theologians* (Princeton: Princeton University Press, 1960), 9–13; C. A. Patrides, "*Paradise Lost* and the Theory of Accommodation," *TSLL* 5 (1963–64): 58–63; Patrides, *Milton and the Christian Tradition* (Oxford: Clarendon Press, 1966), 9–11, and passim; Patrides, "*Paradise Lost* and the Language of Theology," *Language and Style in Milton*, edited by Ronald David Emma and John T. Shawcross, 102–19 (New York: Frederick Ungar, 1967); and William G. Madsen, *From Shadowy Types to Truth* (New Haven: Yale University Press, 1968), 70–74, and passim.

35. As Milton states in the *De Doctrina Christiana*, "Each passage of scripture has only a single sense," although Milton allows for other senses under particular circumstances. The notion of the written authority of Scripture and the force of the biblical word are treated by Hugh MacCallum, "Milton and the Figurative Interpretation of the Bible," *UTQ* 31 (1962): 397–415, which likewise addresses itself to the various modes of accommodation ("social accommodation" versus "epistemological accommodation") in Milton's thought. Also important in this regard is Theodore Huguelet, "Milton's Hermeneutics: A Study of Scriptural Interpretation in the Divorce Tracts and in *De Doctrina Christiana*," (Ph.D. diss., University of North Carolina, 1960).

36. From the perspective of Milton's sense of the poet as authorizing presence in his own works, see John Guillory, *Poetic Authority:*

Spenser, Milton, and Literary History (New York: Columbia University Press, 1983).

37. For a full statement of this idea with reference to *Paradise Lost,* see John T. Shawcross, *With Mortal Voice: The Creation of "Paradise Lost"* (Lexington: University Press of Kentucky, 1982). Shawcross's study illuminates the significance of the rhetoric of intentionality to Milton as writer and thinker.

38. See Milton's important discussion of the Old and New Testaments in the *De Doctrina Christiana.* There, he discusses the texts of these documents, the nature of their preservation, and how they are to be interpreted (YP 6:574–92).

39. As early as *Of Reformation,* Milton declared:

> The very essence of Truth is plainnesse, and brightnes; the darknes and crookednesse is our own. The *Wisdome* of *God* created *understanding,* fit and proportionable to Truth the object, and end of it, as the eye to the thing visible. If our *understanding* have a film of *ignorance* over it, or be blear with gazing on other false gilsterings, what is that to Truth? If we will but purge with sovrain eyesalve that intellectual ray which *God* hath planted in us, then we would beleeve the Scriptures protesting their own plainnes and perspicuity. (YP 1:566)

A similar idea is put forward in the *De Doctrina Christiana* (1.30).

40. It is not entirely clear what Milton means by the parenthetical statement in the original that *anthropopatheia* is "quam figuram Grammatici ad excusandas poetarum de suo Iove nugas olim excogitarunt" (CM 14:32). The translation in the Yale *Prose* is that indicated in my text: "This is a rhetorical device thought up by grammarians [*quam figuram Grammatici*] to explain the nonsense poets write about Jove." The Columbia Milton has: "a figure invented by the grammarians to excuse the absurdities of the poets on the subject of the heathen divinities." In either case, it is clear that Milton, in keeping with his customary practice, is conceiving Jove as a heathen divinity in contrast to the true divinity of God. (Compare, in another context and by ironic contrast, Milton's statement about Jove in Prolusion 6: "The poets, who are the wisest delineators of truth, represent even Jove himself [*etiam Jovem*] and the other heavenly beings lending themselves to jocularity in the midst of their banquets and potations" (CM 12:220–21). As to the specific "*Grammatici*" to whom Milton refers, that too is an open question. Apparently, he has in mind the paganizing tendencies that Arnobius of Sicca argued against in *The Case Against the Pagans.* In any case, the general thrust of what Milton has in mind is abundantly clear.

41. Milton says in the *De Doctrina Christiana,* "No inferences should be made from the text [of Scriptures], unless they follow

necessarily from what is written. . . . What we are obliged to believe are the things written in the sacred books, not the things debated in academic gatherings." "The rule and canon of faith, therefore, is scripture alone." Despite the importance of the text of Scriptures, "the pre-eminent and supreme authority, however, is the authority of the Spirit, which is internal, and the individual possession of each man" (YP 6:580–88).

42. Included here are attributes that Milton discusses as distinguishing the essential nature of God. These include (among others) the fact that he is infinite, eternal, immutable, incorruptible, omnipresent, omnipotent, omniscient, and incomprehensible (YP 6:139–52). Although applied to God, such attributes (especially that of immutability) in no way compromise for Milton the fact of God's passibility. Unlike other theologians, Milton sees no contradiction in holding that God is at once passible (in other words, subject to being "moved") and immutable (that is, "unmovable").

43. For further treatment of the concept of form as internal and external, see "On Form" (1.7) in Milton's *Art of Logic* (YP 8:231–35).

44. For detailed discussions of this concept, see Hugh MacCallum, *Milton and the Sons of God: The Divine Image in Milton's Epic Poetry* (Toronto: University of Toronto Press, 1986), esp. 113–32, and passim; and Anthony C. Yu, "Life in the Garden: Freedom and the Image of God in *Paradise Lost,*" *Journal of Religion* 60 (1980): 247–71.

45. [John Pye Smith], "On Milton's Treatise on Christian Doctrine," *The Evangelical Magazine,* n.s. 4 (1826): 92–95. Although the editors of the Yale *Prose* (6:136n) attribute this piece to Smith, I could find no reference to a specific author.

46. Ibid., 92–93. The reviewer traces Milton's emphasis upon *anthropopatheia* to the influence of the Polish Socinian writers (43).

47. Although Danielson, *Milton's Good God,* does not deal specifically with God as a fully conceived figure in Milton's epic, his study is implicitly predicated on the assumption of God as principle.

48. Irene Samuel, "The Dialogue in Heaven: A Reconsideration of *Paradise Lost,* III, 1–417," in *Milton: Modern Essays in Criticism,* ed. Arthur E. Barker (New York: Oxford University Press, 1965), 233–45; reprinted from *PMLA* 72 (1957): 601–11. For a detailed exploration of the function of the celestial dialogue in *Paradise Lost,* see Michael Lieb, "The Dialogic Imagination," *The Sinews of Ulysses: Form and Convention in Milton's Works* (Pittsburgh: Duquesne University Press, 1989), 76–97, 157–58.

49. From Frye's entry on "The Father," in *A Milton Encyclopedia,* 3:98.

50. See Stanley Fish, *Surprised by Sin: The Reader in "Paradise Lost"* (London: Macmillan, 1967), 57–91. Fish's approach has been further articulated in *Is There a Text in This Class: The Authority*

of Interpretive Communities (Cambridge, Mass.: Harvard University Press, 1980). In *Surprised by Sin,* Fish maintains that God's adoption of what to us are emotionally laden words (such as "ingrate") are tantamount to "scientific notation[s] with the *emotional* value of an *X* or a *Y*" (65). Although Fish's most recent book on Milton, *How Milton Works* (Cambridge, Mass.: Harvard University Press, 2001), does not address the issue directly, similar assumptions are present.

51. Even for those who hold to some form of passibility, emotion is conceived anthropopathetically. In this respect, Georgia B. Christopher, *Milton and the Science of the Saints* (Princeton: Princeton University Press, 1982), is representative. Although apparently disagreeing with Fish's contention that God's language is "purely scientific and denotative," she maintains that "the angry voice of God in Book III, which has elicited so many critical attempts to justify or ameliorate its tone, belongs not to God as he *is* but to God as the sinner perceives him." As a result of that perception, the reader in effect "creates God" as he moves from the first to the final presentation of deity as a character. Exploring the various changes in tonal register from God's first to his final appearance, Christopher argues that "the 'development' of God's character thus measures the jagged course of the narrator's [and, by extension, the reader's] religious experience." Each stage in the experiential journey of both narrator and reader is marked by a change in God's tone. Essentially, Christopher views God as progressing from a figure of wrath to a figure of tenderness and love. What amounts to an anthropopathetic reading of God is tied by Christopher to the prevailing Reformation views of deity (114–19).

52. Corresponding to this theopathetic conception is the materialistic one. See Neil D. Graves, " 'The whole fulness of the Godhead dwells in him bodily': The Materiality of Milton's God," *Christianity and Literature* 52 (2003): 497–521.

53. These emotional extremes make themselves felt throughout Milton's epic. Based upon Psalm 2, the laughter of God, for example, rings throughout the war in heaven: "Mightie Father," the Son declares, "thou thy foes / Justly hast in derision, and secure / Laugh'st at thir vain designes and tumults vain" (5.735–37; compare 2.731, 12.59). Manifested in the council scene, the anger of God is likewise discernible in the celestial warfare (6.56–59). God's sternness is seen in his warning to Adam not to eat the fruit of the forbidden tree (8.333–34). Despite this evidence of a deity who is "moved," scholars continue to remove Milton's God from the emotional fray. William B. Hunter, *"Paradise Lost:* Passionate Epic," *Milton Studies* 31, edited by Albert C. Labriola (Pittsburgh: University of Pittsburgh Press, 1994), 88, explores the emotional valences of Milton's epic in depth. But there is no mention in the body of the text to a possible deity —

except for an appendix titled "Problems of the Theopathetic Tradition." Because Hunter divorces Milton from *De Doctrina Christiana* entirely, he feels justified in maintaining that emotion in God is attributed to him only by others. In and of himself, Milton's God is absolutely impassible.

54. The reference, of course, is to Andrew Marvell's commendatory poem, "On *Paradise Lost,*" which prefaced the 1674 edition. Addressing the theory of accommodation implied by the association of the *De Doctrina Christiana* and *Paradise Lost,* William G. Madsen, *From Shadowy Types to Truth: Studies in Milton's Symbolism* (New Haven: Yale University Press, 1968), 73–74, and passim, voices similar concerns: "Unless we are willing to grant that John Milton was literally inspired," there seems to be no meaningful way to relate the idea of accommodation as delineated in *Christian Doctrine* to that implied in Milton's epic. As a viable alternative, Madsen opts to read the concept typologically. Although such a reading is possible, I still feel that it is necessary to interpret accommodation in accord with Milton's discussion of the subject in his theological tract.

55. For some of the Reformation contexts of this idea, see Christopher, *Milton and the Science of the Saints;* and Robert L. Entzminger, *Divine Word: Milton and the Redemption of Language* (Pittsburgh: Duquesne University Press, 1985).

56. See Milton's outlines for tragedies in the Trinity College Manuscript (CM 18:240). See also Milton's early but unfinished poem, "The Passion."

57. Compare Raphael's classic statement: "what surmounts the reach / Of human sense, I shall delineate so, / By lik'ning spiritual to corporal forms, / As may express them best" (3.571–74). In effect, this is what the poet does in his own depiction of God throughout.

58. Embodied in deity as a divinized attribute, the passible, of course, finds apt contrast with the debased form it assumes in fallen creatures, both human and satanic. There, it results in the overcoming of the rational faculties by the emotional and the discovery of oneself "in a troubl'd Sea of passion tost" (10.718). Man is plunged into this sea after he succumbs to the temptations of the Adversary. Although a discussion of these matters lies well beyond the purview of the present undertaking, they are germane to it. For a treatment of the psychological dimensions of such matters in the Renaissance, see J. B. Banborough, *The Little World of Man* (London: Longmans, Green, 1952).

Notes to Chapter 5

1. John T. Shawcross, *With Mortal Voice: The Creation of "Paradise Lost"* (Lexington: University Press of Kentucky, 1982), 31.

2. C. S. Lewis, *A Preface to "Paradise Lost"* (1942; reprint, New York: Oxford University Press, 1961), 130. Despite studies such as Denis Danielson, *Milton's Good God: A Study in Literary Theodicy* (Cambridge: Cambridge University Press, 1982), the negative view of Milton's God has not disappeared.

3. *Theological Dictionary of the New Testament,* ed. Gerhard Kittell, trans. Geoffrey W. Bromiley, 10 vols. (Grand Rapids: Eerdmans, 1964–76), 5:395. See the full entry on "wrath" (5:382–445, esp. pp. 392–429) for an enlightening account.

4. Ibid., 5:397.

5. Although Empson does not make this accusation directly, it is implied in the discussion as a whole. See William Empson, *Milton's God* (1961; reprint, Cambridge: Cambridge University Press, 1981), 251.

6. Ibid., 146.

7. Empson actually slights Orwell's book, which he calls "a silly prophecy" (ibid., 236). Nonetheless, one detects a decidedly ambivalent attitude on Empson's part toward the implications of Orwell's portrayal of Big Brother as the ruler of the Totalitarian State (see ibid., 69, 234–36).

8. In the section entitled "Final Reflections," appended to the 1981 edition of his book, Empson says, "I still find people mentioning casually in journals, as a well-known fact, that Empson hates God and uses Milton for propaganda against him, presumably by twisting the text of the epic to suggest that Milton hates him too. Such is the chief thing I need to answer" (ibid., 319–20). Empson fails. But he does succeed in convincing us even further of the association between his view of a Christian God of hate and a Big Brother of hate. Invoking Luther's God, Empson maintains that in order to accept such a figure, "one had to 'gouge out the eyes' of reason, but that in itself was no great sacrifice; one had also to *love* Big Brother, or endure his tortures for all eternity" (320). Here, once again, is the Orwellian figure with whom Empson's argument inclines us to associate Milton's God.

9. To complement this study of the distinction between a God of love and a God of hate, an additional analysis that explores the all-important distinction between a God of good (*bonum Dei*) and a God of evil (*malum Dei*) would be appropriate. In attempting to assess the full nature of Milton's theodicy, scholars have not come to terms with this distinction. Like the notion of a God of love, a God of good is a commonplace; conversely, however, like the notion of a God of hate, a God of evil has not been made the subject of extensive inquiry. The notion is nonetheless present in Milton, as, for example, in the description of hell: "A Universe of death, which God by curse / Created evil, for evil only good" (2.622–23; compare 5.117–18).

10. My analysis of the biblical background is much indebted to the enlightening entry on "hatred" in the *Theological Dictionary of*

the New Testament, 4:683–94. This entry likewise discusses the nature of hatred in the world of ancient Greece, as well as the place of hatred as theological entity in the post-apostolic world. I have also made use of the entry on "hatred" in *The Interpreter's Dictionary of the Bible*, ed. George Arthur Buttrick et al., 4 vols. (New York: Abingdon Press, 1962), 2:536–37; in the *Encyclopedia Judaica*, 16 vols., ed. Cecil Roth and Geoffrey Wigoder (Jerusalem: Keter, 1971), 7:1473–74; and in *A Dictionary of the Bible*, 4 vols., ed. James Hastings (New York: Charles Scribner's Sons, 1903), 2:308–9. In most respects, my conclusions are in agreement with the foregoing studies, but, as far as I am concerned, none of the entries goes far enough in its discussion of the extent to which divine hatred is a factor in either Old Testament or New Testament theology. This may be because the very idea of hatred seems antithetical to those values with which God has been traditionally associated in Western theology. When the attributes of God are discussed in various contexts, hatred is either conveniently overlooked or treated so provisionally and tangentially as to deprive it of any real meaning as a category of value. Theologians, in general, feel uncomfortable with the notion of a God who hates.

11. In *De Doctrina Christiana*, Milton discusses this passage at some length. Taking into account Saint Paul's reference to the passage in Romans 9:13, Milton sets out to establish his reading of the theology of election. The concept of "hatred" per se, however, is not at issue, except as it applies to those whose past actions render them reprobate, on the one hand, and those whose future actions remain to be judged, on the other (CM 14:159–63).

12. Compare 2 Samuel 22:35–41: God "teacheth my hands to war; so that a bow of steel is broken by mine arms. Thou hast also given me the shield of thy salvation: and thy gentleness hath made me great. . . . I have pursued mine enemies, and destroyed them; and turned not again until I had consumed them. . . . Thou hast also given me the necks of mine enemies, that I might destroy them that hate me" (compare Psalms 18:40).

13. Compare Proverbs 6:16–19: "These six *things* doth the Lord hate: yea, seven *are* an abomination unto him: A proud look, a lying tongue, and hands that shed innocent blood, An heart that deviseth wicked imaginations, feet that be swift in running to mischief, A false witness *that* speaketh lies, and he that soweth discord among brethren."

14. According to the entry on "wrath" in the *Theological Dictionary of the New Testament*, there is a sense in which divine wrath assumes "an irrational and in the last resort inexplicable" quality that manifests itself "with enigmatic, mysterious, and primal force." In the Old Testament, in particular, one even finds what might be called a "demonic element" in Yahweh that "is not in the last resort imported

into His nature, but is there from the very first . . . bound up with the innermost being of this God and His religion." It is a zealous wrath that destroys whole nations. "This is particularly clear in the post-exilic period, which experienced the attack of the nations on Israel's existence, the hatred of Edom, and the destructive urge of Babylon and other nations" (5:403–4).

15. Lactantius, *The Wrath of God*, in *The Fathers of the Church*, 112 vols. to date, gen. ed. Roy Joseph Deferrari (Washington, D.C.: Catholic University of America Press, 1965), 54:65–67.

16. John Calvin, *Commentaries on the Twelve Minor Prophets*, 5 vols., trans. John Owen (Edinburgh: Calvin Translation Society, 1849), 5:467–68. See also Calvin's *Commentaries on the Epistle of Paul the Apostle to the Romans*, trans. John Owen (Edinburgh: Calvin Translation Society, 1849), 353–62.

17. John Calvin, *Commentary on the Book of Psalms*, 5 vols., trans. Rev. James Anderson (Edinburgh: T. Constable, 1849), 5:221–23.

18. William Perkins, *Lectures upon the Three First Chapters of the Revelation: Preached in Cambridge Anno Dom. 1596* (London, 1604), 152–53. However, Perkins also counsels us to "moderate our hatred" to the extent that we hate the sins of men, as opposed to the men themselves. Despite this outlook, Perkins does nonetheless acknowledge the fact that David as prophet felt called upon to "hate . . . mens persons" and "prayed for the destruction of his enemies, both soule and body." We who lack David's prophetic "instinct," however, must "keep us within this compasse, that we hate onely their [men's] sinnes, and not their persons."

19. Thomas Wilson, *A Commentary on the Most Divine Epistle of S. Paul to the Romans*, 2nd ed. (London, 1627), 355.

20. William Ames, *The Marrow of Theology* (1628), trans. John D. Eusden (Boston: Pilgrim Press, 1968), 87, 156, 223, 315. There are those, of course, who attempted to downplay God's hatred. One such expositor is Matthew Poole, *Annotations upon the Holy Bible*, 2 vols. (London, 1683), who either avoids the subject altogether (as in his analysis of Psalm 139) or compromises it entirely. Thus, in his analysis of Malachi, Poole says that God's hatred of Esau was tantamount to his not showing the same kindness to Esau as to Jacob (vol. 2, sigs. Ooo2^v, 4D3^v, and 5P3^r). William Cowper, *The Anatomy of a Christian* (1623), *The Workes of Mr. William Cowper* (London, 1623), 311–15, discourses upon the love and hatred of the true Christian without ever acknowledging the legitimacy of hatred as a positive virtue.

21. Edward Reynolds, *A Treatise of the Passions and Faculties of the Soule of Man* (1640), ed. Margaret Lee Wiley (Gainesville, Fla.: Scholars' Facsimiles and Reprints, 1971), 111–30. See also Thomas Wright, *The Passions of the Minde in Generall* (1604), ed. Thomas O. Sloan (Urbana: University of Illinois Press, 1971), 263–78.

22. Compare Milton's translation of Psalm 5: "All workers of iniquity thou [God] hat'st; and them unblest / Thou wilt destroy that speak a lie" (13–15).

23. I prefer the translation in the Columbia Milton over that in the Yale *Prose,* here.

24. In *Of Education,* Milton would have the students of his proposed academy instructed not just in "the knowledge of Vertue" but in "the hatred of Vice" (2:396). Even from the pedagogical point of view, hatred constitutes an important part of Milton's moral outlook. In this context, of course, hatred of vice is much more palatable than in the specifically religious contexts that Milton provides for it in *De Doctrina.* Nonetheless, its presence as a positive entity exists in one form or another throughout Milton's works.

25. See also *Tetrachordon:* "He who hates not father or mother, wife, or children hindring his christian cours, much more, if they despise or assault it, cannot be a Disciple, *Luke* 14." In response to such as would hinder this "christian cours," Milton counsels a "zealous hatred." Milton endorses a "religious cause of separating, executed with . . . an urgent zeal." "What God hates to joyn, certainly he cannot love should continue joyn'd" (YP 2:682–83).

26. Such hatred is essential to the moral outlook that constitutes *Samson Agonistes.* Accordingly, Samson responds to Dalila in the following manner: "Love seeks to have Love; / My love how couldst thou hope, who tookst the way, / To raise in me inexpiable hate, / Knowing, as needs I must, by thee betray'd?" (837–40).

27. Compare Milton's discussion of the conflict between Day and Night in Prolusion 1: "It happens that light and darkness have disagreed among themselves with bitterest hatred [*odio*] from the very beginning of things" (CM 12:133). For an analogue, if not a source, of Milton's concept of the "Seminary" nature, see Spenser's description of the Garden of Adonis (*Faerie Queene* 3.6.36–37).

28. For a full discussion of the polemical underpinnings of this idea, see my "Milton's 'Chariot of Paternal Deitie' as a Reformation Conceit," *Journal of Religion* 65 (1985): 359–77. See Milton's discussion of zeal as a theological virtue in *De Doctrina Christiana,* CM 17:152–66.

29. As a figure who fully embodies the concept of zeal in all its fervency, Abdiel, that fiery servant of God, becomes a type of the zeal manifested in the Son. In fact, Abdiel's encounter with Satan both before and during the war in heaven (5.805–907; 6.111–202) anticipates the Son's own encounter with the rebel angels.

30. For a discussion of the place of dialectic in *Paradise Lost,* see my *The Dialectics of Creation: Patterns of Birth and Regeneration in "Paradise Lost"* (Amherst: University of Massachusetts Press, 1970). Although I do not discuss the concept of the *odium Dei* as such here, I do focus on the generative implications of dialectic.

31. In book 3, the specific context for invoking the idea of "Heav'nly love . . . outdo[ing] Hellish hate" is the Son's sacrificial act of incarnating himself as man, as the result of which Christ will "be judg'd and die, / And dying rise, and rising with him raise / His Brethren, ransomd with his own dear life" (3. 274–303). The overcoming of hate by love, then, speaks to the Son's messianic role. This role is distinctly generative, in fact, regenerative, as Adam comes to learn when he declares, "O goodness infinite, goodness immense! / That all this good of evil shall produce, / And evil turn to good; more wonderful / Then that which by creation first brought forth / Light out of darkness!" (12.469–73).

32. The redemptive dimension of the account includes the Incarnation, the Crucifixion, and the Ascension. The eschatological dimension of the account includes the Last Judgment, when the Son "attended gloriously from Heav'n / Shalt in the Sky appeer." At that "dread Tribunal," the Son "shalt judge / Bad men and Angels, they arraign'd shall sink / Beneath . . . [his] Sentence" and "Hell her numbers full, / Thenceforth shall be for ever shut." This apocalyptic event, in turn, shall be followed by a conflagration and ultimate renewal. As suggested, both the redemptive and the eschatological dimensions are prefigured by the Chariot of Paternal Deitie. In this regard, see Mother M. Christopher Pecheux, "The Conclusion of Book VI of *Paradise Lost*," *SEL* 3 (1963): 109–17; William B. Hunter Jr., "Milton on the Exaltation of the Son: The War in Heaven in *Paradise Lost*," *ELH* 36 (1969): 215–31; and Shawcross, *The Complete Poetry*, 383n.

33. As is well known, the Son's act is numerically, as well as thematically, central. In the 1667 edition of *Paradise Lost*, the word "Ascended" (6.762) occurs, as Shawcross points out in his edition of *The Complete Poetry*, at the precise numerical midpoint of the epic, "since 5275 lines precede it and follow it" (383n).

Notes to Chapter 6

1. Mary Ann Radzinowicz, *Toward "Samson Agonistes": The Growth of Milton's Mind* (Princeton: Princeton University Press, 1978), 267, 271, 283–84, 349.

2. Ibid., 346.

3. David Loewenstein, *Milton and the Drama of History: Historical Vision, Iconoclasm, and the Literary Imagination* (Cambridge: Cambridge University Press, 1990), 133. 30–31, 136, 145.

4. Michael Lieb, *Milton and the Culture of Violence* (Ithaca, N.Y.: Cornell University Press, 1994), 226–63.

5. One must account for the fact, of course, that this is the view of God reflected in the outlook of the Semichorus, which functions

as one character in a drama comprised of several characters, each no doubt with his own "theology." As I attempt to demonstrate, however, the theology implicit in the view expressed by the Semichorus is so fundamental to the outlook that the drama as a whole embraces that the concept of God as Dread is inescapable in any assessment of the nature of deity in *Samson Agonistes*.

6. This is the context of the *kommos*. For a discussion of the nature and function of the *kommos,* see William Riley Parker, *Milton's Debt to Greek Tragedy in "Samson Agonistes"* (Baltimore: The Johns Hopkins Press, 1937), 103–9.

7. The very idea of ascribing a name to God at all runs counter not only to the Samson narrative in the Book of Judges but also to the spirit of the Old Testament. "And Manoah said unto the angel of the Lord, What is thy name, that when thy sayings come to pass we may do thee honour? And the angel of the Lord said unto him, Why askest thou thus after my name, seeing it *is* secret?" (Judg. 13:17–18). What is true of the *malach 'adonai',* that is, the angel or messenger of God, is certainly true of God himself, an idea enunciated on more than one occasion in the Old Testament (compare Gen. 32:29, Exod. 3:15). In the case of the Samson narrative, however, the refusal to disclose the divine name is particularly interesting, for in that very act of refusal there is an implied disclosure. Although the Authorized Version has "Why askest thou thus after my name, seeing it *is* secret," the term used for "secret" (*peliy'*) derives from a root denoting that which is extraordinary or wonderful. It is for this reason that, after refusing to disclose his name, the angel enacts it in the very next verse: "and *the* angel did wondrously; and Mano'ah and his wife looked on" (Judg. 13:19). The angel has fulfilled his name, which is "Wonderful." Isaiah, we recall, articulates the same idea in his celebration of the messianic child: "For unto us a child is born, unto us a son is given: and the government shall be upon his shoulder; and his name shall be called Wonderful, Counsellor, The mighty God, The everlasting Father, The Prince of Peace" (Isa. 9:6).

8. R. H. Pfeiffer, "The Fear of God," *Israel Exploration Journal* 5 (1955): 41–48, explores the cultural contexts of fear in the ancient world. Citing Statius's observation in the *Thebaid* (3.661) that "fear first on earth created gods [*Primus in orbe deos fecit timor*]," he notes that Hammurabi in his Code (1.31) officially designates himself "fearer of the gods."

9. One need only resort to the standard concordances, such as that of *Veteris Testamenti Concordantiae Hebraicae atque Chaldaicae,* 3 vols., comp. Solomon Mandelkern (Tel Aviv: Sumptibus Schocken Hierosolymis, 1971), s.v., and to the standard lexicons, such as *The New Brown-Driver-Briggs-Gesenius Hebrew and English Lexicon, With an Appendix Containing the Biblical Aramaic, Based on the*

Lexicon of William Gesenius (Peabody, Mass.: Hendrickson, 1979), s.v. (hereafter referred to as *BDB*), to discover these terms and to trace the complexity of their significations. I found 18 different terms for fear (each term with its own root) extending throughout the Old Testament. These are confirmed by the list of words under the heading "fear" in William Wilson, *Old Testament Word Studies* (Grand Rapids: Kregel, 1978), 159–60.

10. See the discussion of *yare'* in *Theological Dictionary of the Old Testament*, 13 vols., ed. Johannes Botterweck and Helmer Ringren (Grand Rapids: Eerdmans, 1978–), 6:290–315. The most common term for "fear" in biblical Hebrew is *yare'*, which carries with it such meanings as "be afraid," "stand in awe of," and "reverence." The term appears as a *topos* in such admonitions as "The fear of the Lord is the beginning of knowledge" (Prov. 1:7). So pervasive is the term *yare'* in the Old Testament that it, along with its derivatives, occurs well over 400 times. Along with *yare'*, there are many other synonyms as well.

11. The term *pachad* also assumes a sexual bearing, as in Job's celebration of the behemoth: "sinews of his stones [*pachdo:* thigh, testicle] are wrapped together" (40:17). See *BDB*, s.v. From the Miltonic perspective, this dimension is particularly interesting, given the emphasis upon sexuality in *Samson Agonistes*. Thus, Samson laments the loss of his own virility and his having been shorn by Dalila "like a tame Weather" (537–38), that is, a castrated male sheep. In regaining his own ability to become a figure of dread, Samson is in a sense regaining his *pachad*, the power of his testicles.

12. According to Jason Rosenblatt (letter to the author, January 16, 1995), in their commentaries on *pachad yitschaq*, both Rabbi David Kimchi on Genesis 31:42 and Abraham Ibn Ezra on Genesis 31:53 cite the *akeda*, the so-called binding of Isaac related in Genesis 22:1–19. For these rabbinical commentators, *pachad yitschaq* signifies at once God himself ("the one whom Jacob's father feared," Ibn Ezra) and Isaac ("whose awe of God at the *akeda* caused him to give himself over to slaughter," Kimchi).

13. See, in particular, the discussion of contrary views (along with relevant bibliography) by Emile Puech under the heading "Fear of Isaac," in *The Anchor Bible Dictionary*, 6 vols., ed. David Noel Freedman (New York: Doubleday, 1992), 2:779–80. Also relevant is B. W. Anderson, "Fear of Isaac," *The Interpreter's Dictionary of the Bible*, 4 vols., gen. ed. George Arthur Buttrick (New York: Abingdon Press, 1962), 2:260.

14. Rudolf Otto, *The Idea of the Holy: An Inquiry into the Non-Rational Factor in the Idea of the Divine and Its Relation to the Rational*, trans. John W. Harvey (Milford: Oxford University Press, 1928), 1–11.

15. Drawing upon one of the many terms for dread in the Old Testament, Otto singles out the term *'eymah* ("terror") and cites, as an example of *'eymah*, Exodus 23:27: "I will send my fear before thee, and will destroy all the people to whom thou shalt come, and I will make all thine enemies turn their backs unto thee." Citing other instances as well, Otto comments: "Here we have a terror fraught with an inward shuddering such as not even the most menacing and overpowering created thing can instill. It has something spectral about it." As such, it is a demonic dread that penetrates to the very marrow and makes one's hair bristle and his limbs quake (ibid., 12–14).

16. In his exploration of this daunting dimension of the *mysterium*, Otto cites the *locus classicus* of the idea as it is revealed in one of the most inexplicable texts in the Old Testament, Exodus 4:24: It came to pass that the Lord met Moses by the way and "sought to kill him." The unaccountable behavior of God in this instance is for Otto a prime example of the most frightening dimensions of the *ganz andere*. It is a dimension that undermines all expectations of deity as that which reinforces human ideas of morality, rationality, and beneficence (ibid., 12–14).

17. Ibid., 78–79.

18. For an interesting discussion of the psychological dimensions, see John Flavell, *Two Treatises: The First of Fear, From Isa. 8.v.12, 13, and part of the 14* (London, 1682). In a similar vein, see Edward Young, *A sermon concerning the wisdom of fearing God* (London, 1693). From an apocalyptic perspective, see the sermon of the Quaker Humphrey Smith, *The Sounding voyce of the dread of Gods mighty power* (London, 1658).

19. See the entry for "Fear" in Thomas Wilson, *A Christian Dictionary, Opening the signification of the chiefe Words dispersed generally through Holy Scriptures of the Old and New Testament* (London, 1622), s.v.

20. Among the texts that Wilson cites are Psalm 76:11; Isaiah 8:12, 13; Malachi 1:6; and Genesis 31:42 and 32:9 (*A Christian Dictionary*, s.v.).

21. According to Wilson (*A Christian Dictionary*, s.v.), fear can be "an instrument of diuine vengeance" upon those who are wicked (Isa. 2:1).

22. References are to John Bunyan, *A Treatise of the Fear of God: Shewing What it is, and how distinguished from that which is not so* (London, 1679), in *The Miscellaneous Works of John Bunyan*, 11 vols., ed. Richard L. Greaves (Oxford: Clarendon Press, 1976–86), vol. 9; hereafter cited in the text. On the relationships between Milton and Bunyan, see Roland Mushat Frye, *God, Man, and Satan: Patterns of Christian Thought and Life in "Paradise Lost," "Pilgrim's Progress," and the Great Theologians* (Princeton: Princeton University Press, 1960).

23. Alluding both to the Old Testament and the New Testament, Bunyan cites Nadab and Abihu (Lev. 10:1–3); Eli's sons (1 Sam. 2); Uzza (1 Chron. 13:9–10); and Ananias and Saphira (Acts 5).

24. In his reference to the sons of Eli, Bunyan alludes to the later story of the overcoming of the idol of Dagon by the God of Shilo, a text we shall examine in some detail.

25. I use the Sumner translation in the Columbia Milton here. The Carey translation in the Yale *Prose* misconstrues: "Jacob swore by what his father feared." This places the phenomenon of fear in the person of Jacob, but both in the Hebrew and in the Latin of *De Doctrina Christiana*, the construction is that of the possessive. As I argue, that is precisely the point: fear itself is an entity identified with God.

26. So it is rendered in the *Testamenti Veteris Biblia Sacra siue Libri Canonici Priscae Iudaeorum Ecclesiae a Deo Traditi, Latini Recens ex Hebraeo facti, brevibusque Scholiis illustrati ab Immanuele Tremellio & Francisco Iunio* (London, 1585), a work that Milton frequently used as the basis for the proof-texts in *De Doctrina Christiana*. According to Kelley, introduction to *De Doctrina Christiana*, YP 6:45 n. 8, the Junius-Tremellius Bible was "the favorite Latin version of seventeenth-century Reformed divines," including Ames and Wolleb. (For both Genesis 31:42, 53, the Junius-Tremellius version has *pavor:* "Nisi Deus patris mei Deus Abrahami & pavor Jitzchaki ad fuisset mihi" (Gen. 31:42) and "Deus Abrahami & Dii Nachoris judicent inter nos Dii patris eorum: cui juravit Jahhakob per pavorem patris sui Jitzchaki" (Gen. 31:53). The Vulgate, on the other hand, adopts *timor*. Thus, the *Biblia Sacra Iuxta Vulgatam Versionem*, 2 vols., ed. Bonifatio Fischer et al. (Stuttgart: Wurttembergische Bibelanstalt, 1969) has "nisi Deus patris mei Abraham et Timor Isaac adfuisset mihi" (Gen. 31:42) and "Deus Abraham et Deus Nahor iudicit inter nos Deus patris eorum iuravit Jacob per Timorem patris sui Isaac" (Gen. 31:53). In the Vulgate, *timor* assumes a personified presence as "Fear" or "Dread."

27. See the respective entries on *pavor* and *timor* in *A Latin Dictionary*, ed. Charlton T. Lewis and Charles Short (Oxford: Clarendon Press, 1975), s.v.

28. William Riley Parker, *Milton: A Biography*, 2 vols. (Oxford: Clarendon Press, 1968), 1:322.

29. My translation is from the *Biblia Hebraica Stuttgartensia* (Stuttgart: Deutsche Bibelstiftung, 1967). The Authorized Version has "thou that dwellest *between* the cherubims, shine forth."

30. So Milton points out in his headnote that "*all but what is in a different Character* [that is, italicized], *are the very words of the Text, translated from the Original.*" In *John Milton's Complete Poetical Works, Reproduced in Photographic Facsimile*, 4 vols., ed. Harris Francis Fletcher (Urbana: University of Illinois Press, 1943), 1:86.

31. In *Poetics of the Holy: A Reading of Paradise Lost* (Chapel Hill: University of North Carolina Press, 1981), I discuss this psalm in connection with the function of the ark of the covenant and dwelling presence in Milton's thought (219).

32. The terrifying nature of that quality, moreover, is even further reinforced as a result of the way in which the final line of the quatrain is structured in Milton's rendering. Whereas God in his dwelling presence is called upon to "shine forth" and "give light," there is no corresponding verb to indicate what he is actually to do with his dread. The assumption, of course, is that what he does with his dread is tantamount to what he does with his light: he disseminates it. In Milton's addition to the original, however, the Psalmist calls upon the dwelling presence in a way that obliges us to supply the missing verb: "And on our foes thy dread." The effect is that of intensifying the identification of subject (God in his dwelling presence between the outspread wings of the ark) and object (dread) even further. God *is* the very dread that distinguishes him in his dwellingness. To violate the sanctity of that dwellingness is to be overwhelmed by the dread that is God.

33. See Milton's full discussion of this phenomenon in the first book of *De Doctrina Christiana* (CM 15:70–87; YP 6:331–38). See also *Paradise Lost:* "But hard be hard'n'd, blind be blinded more, / That they may stumble on, and deeper fall" (3:200–201).

34. Otto, *Idea of the Holy,* 31–41.

35. Søren Kierkegaard, *The Concept of Dread: A simple psychological deliberation oriented in the direction of the dogmatic problem of original sin* (1844), in *Kierkegaard's "The Concept of Dread,"* trans. Walter Lowrie (Princeton: Princeton University Press, 1957), 38–40. The relationship between Milton and Kierkegaard has been explored in depth by John S. Tanner, *Anxiety in Eden: A Kierkegaardian Reading of "Paradise Lost"* (New York: Oxford University Press, 1992).

36. As discussed below, Milton accepted the putative derivation of the name Dagon from *dag* (fish). If such is the case, one might note the etymological association between *dag* as "fish" and *da'ag* (a form of *dag*) as both "fish" and "dread" (compare Isa. 57:11). The *BDB* confirms this association. Whether Milton was aware of it remains to be seen. If so, his Samson as the embodiment of divine dread overwhelms Dagon as the embodiment of profane dread in a conflict between divine and profane forms of dread.

37. Stanley Fish, "Spectacle and Evidence in *Samson Agonistes,*" *Critical Inquiry* 15 (1989): 556–86, argues on behalf of the complete indeterminacy of this moment. Although I agree with this outlook, I take issue with the conclusion that Fish ventures: Samson "may be speculating on the shape of Hebrew history or wondering whether

anyone will ever pick up his best robe from the laundry; that is, the matter he revolves in his mind (if he is revolving one at all) may be great or it may be trivial" (567). This, I suggest, is hardly the case. Although it is a profoundly mysterious moment, it is clearly not one that lends itself to trivialization. See Fish, *How Milton Works* (Cambridge: Harvard University Press, 2001), 432–73, for an elaboration of this outlook.

38. Joseph Wittreich, *Interpreting "Samson Agonistes"* (Princeton: Princeton University Press, 1986), 111–12. Wittreich associates Judges 16 with John 11, that is, the temple holocaust with the prophecy of Caiaphas. Despite the liturgical basis of the association that Wittreich offers, I am not convinced that the two texts can be profitably paired. The other Scriptural references that Wittreich cites (2 Cor. 8:17; Acts 12:10) likewise do not appear to illuminate the use of the phrase "Of his own accord" as it appears in *Samson Agonistes*. Fish is generally in agreement with such a reading and cites it with approval. Asserting that he will act "of his own accord," Samson, according to Fish, behaves in a manner "for which he has no final warrant except what he himself at the moment thinks best to do" ("Spectacle and Evidence," 579–80 n. 18). In *Shifting Contexts: Reinterpreting "Samson Agonistes"* (Pittsburgh: Duquesne University Press, 2002), Wittreich addresses the issue yet once more (see esp. 121).

39. In addition to the texts discussed in the body of this essay, see Jer. 51:13, Isa. 45:23, and Amos 6:8. God also swears by his holiness (Ps. 89:35), by his name (Jer. 44:26); and by his right hand (Isa. 62:8).

40. Compare God's declaration in *Paradise Lost:* "your Head I him appoint; / And by my Self have sworn to him shall bow / All knees in Heav'n" (5:606–8). Milton was fond of the phrase; it appears several times in his prose works. Of particular interest is its use in *A Treatise of Civil Power*. There, it is applied to Saint Paul: "None more cautious of giving scandal then St. *Paul*. Yet while he made himself *servant to all,* that he *might gain the more,* he made himself so of his own accord, was not made so by outward force, testifying at the same time that he *was free from all men,* 1 *Cor.* 9.19" (YP 7:267). For Milton, Paul represents a prime example of the inspired prophet-servant who acts of his own volition.

41. Although Jacob does not adopt the *biy nishba'ti* locution, he makes a point not only of invoking God as the Dread of Isaac (*pachad yitschaq*) but of swearing by that Dread as well (Gen. 31:53).

42. The other two premonarchic sanctuaries are Gilgal and Shechem. For a discussion of Shilo, see Baruch Halpern, "Shiloh," in *The Anchor Bible Dictionary,* 5:1213–15; and N. K. Gottwold, "Shiloh," in *The Interpreter's Dictionary of the Bible,* 4:328–30.

43. In the Renaissance, the pairing of the Samson narrative in Judges and the fall of Dagon in 1 Samuel was commonplace. The second

narrative was looked upon as a commentary on the first. See in this respect, Sir Walter Raleigh, *The History of the World, in Five Books* (London, 1617), book 2, chap. 15, sec. 1–2; and Matthew Poole, *Annotations upon the Holy Bible*, 2 vols. (London, 1683), vol. 1, sig. Nnnn2^v–Nnnn2^r.

44. See my chapter on holy war in *Poetics of the Holy*, 246–312.

45. Although this is the translation that appears in the Authorized Version, it should be noted that the phrase "the stump of Dagon" is not in the Hebrew. Rather, the Hebrew has "roc dagon nishar alav" (only dagon was left to him). It is a very vexed phrase that has been variously translated. The Septuagint and the Vulgate have their own variant readings. See *BDB*, 186. Exegetes during Milton's time were aware of the issue. See, for example, Poole, *Annotations upon the Holy Bible*, vol. 1, sigs. Nnnn2^v–Nnnn2^r. According to Poole, "*roc dagon*" refers to "that part of it [the idol] from which it was called *Dagon*, to wit, the Fishy part, for *Dag* in *Hebrew* signifies *a Fish*." Interestingly, Poole also has a marginal gloss for "stump" as "the filthy part," but this may actually be "the fishy part."

46. Even after it is returned to the Israelites, moreover, it wreaks havoc. See 1 Samuel 6.

47. Milton understood "Dagon" as a bipartite figure "upward Man / And downward Fish," in part, because of the prevailing etymology of the term "Dagon" as derived from *dag* (fish). One should be aware, however, that the precise etymology of the term is still very much debated. For discussion, see the entries on "Dagon" in Lowell K. Handy, *The Anchor Bible Dictionary*, 2:1–3; J. Gray, in *The Interpreter's Dictionary of the Bible*, 1:756; and H. Ringrenn, *Theological Dictionary of the the Old Testament*, 3:139–42. Among the many treatments of "Dagon" in the Renaissance, see John Selden, *De Dis Syris Syntagmata* (London, 1629), 262–80; and Poole, *Annotations*. According to Poole, "this Idol of *Dagon* had its upper parts in human shape, and its lower parts in the form of a *Fish*; for such was the Form of divers of the *Heathen* gods, and particularly of a god of the Phoenicians (under which Name the *Philistines* are comprehended)" (vol. 1, sig. Nnnn2^v–Nnnn2^r).

Notes to Chapter 7

1. *Milton and Heresy*, ed. Stephen B. Dobranski and John Rumrich (Cambridge: Cambridge University Press, 1998), 1.

2. Christopher Hill, *Milton and the English Revolution* (New York: Viking Press, 1977).

3. Ibid., 285. Hill does not hesitate, of course, to argue on behalf of what he feels is Milton's implicit relationship to the underground

radical traditions (particularly those centered in the Muggletonians) of the seventeenth century.

4. Janel Mueller, "Milton on Heresy," in Dobranski and Rumrich, *Milton and Heresy*, 22–25.

5. According to Shawcross, ed., *Complete Poetry*, 212 n. 7), Milton in "On the Forcers of Conscience" refers to Thomas Edwards's *Gangraena; or, A Catalogue and Discovery of Many of the Errours, Heresies, Blasphemies and pernicious Practices of the Sectaries of this Time* (London, 1646), which includes Milton's *Doctrine and Discipline of Divorce* under error 154, among the 180 errors or heresies in its arsenal. Also pertinent in this regard is Ephraim Pagitt's *Heresiography; or, A description of the Heretickes and Sectaries of these latter times* (London, 1645). For excerpts on the "heretical Milton" from these and other works, see *Milton's Contemporary Reputation*, compiled by William Riley Parker (1940; reprint, New York: Haskell House, 1971), esp. 75–77. For an exhaustive listing of works by and about Milton during the seventeenth century, see *Milton: A Bibliography for the Years 1624–1700*, comp. John T. Shawcross (Binghamton: Medieval and Renaissance Texts and Studies, 1984).

6. David Masson, *The Life of John Milton: Narrated in Connection with the Political, Ecclesiastical, and Literary History of His Time*, 6 vols. (1896; reprint, Gloucester, Mass.: Peter Smith, 1965), 3:15. According to Shawcross, "the two earliest uses of *Miltonist* on record specifically refer to a follower of Milton in his views on divorce." These two references are in Christopher Wasse's *Electra of Sophocles* (The Hague, 1649), sig. E8r; and in Charles Symmons, ed., *The Prose Works of John Milton* (London, 1806), 250. See Shawcross's entry. "Miltonian, Miltonic, Miltonist," in *A Milton Encyclopedia*, 9 vols., gen. ed. William B. Hunter, Jr. (Lewisburg, Va.: Bucknell University Press, 1978–83), 5: 139–40.

7. Although Socinianism and Unitarianism are often viewed as interchangeable, differences between the two emerged in the evolution from the first movement to the second during the later seventeenth century and beyond. See H. John McLachlan, *Socinianism in Seventeenth-Century England* (London: Oxford University Press, 1951), 316–35. Among other studies of the subject, see Earl Morse Wilbur, *A History of Unitarianism: Socinianism and Its Antecedents* (Cambridge, Mass.: Harvard University Press, 1946), and *A History of Unitarianism: In Transylvania, England, and America* (Cambridge, Mass.: Harvard University Press, 1952). The development of Unitarianism is tied to the passing of the Toleration Act (1689) and the publication of the Unitarian tracts (1691–1703).

8. Hill, *Milton and the English Revolution*, 6.

9. H. John McLachlan, *The Religious Opinions of Milton, Locke, and Newton* (Manchester: Manchester University Press, 1941). Hugh

MacCallum, *Milton and the Sons of God: The Divine Image in Milton's Epic Poetry* (Toronto: University of Toronto Press, 1986), 55, and passim. For an earlier reading in accord with the idea of associating Milton with the Socinians, see George Newton Conklin, *Biblical Criticism and Heresy in Milton* (New York: Columbia University Press, 1949), 37–40. See also John Rogers, "Milton's Circumcision," *Milton and the Grounds of Contention*, ed. Mark Kelley, Michael Lieb, and John T. Shawcross (Pittsburgh: Duquesne University Press, 2003), 188–213. Also of significance is Rogers, "Delivering Redemption in *Samson Agonistes*," presented at the December 1999 MLA convention in Chicago and at the April 2001 meeting of the East Coast Milton Seminar in Princeton. Finally, see William Kolbrener, "*The Charge of Socinianism:* Charles Leslie's High Church Defense of 'True Religion,'" *Journal of the Historical Society* 3 (Winter 2003): 1–23.

10. McLachlan, *Socinianism in Seventeenth-Century England*, 3.

11. See "sozzamente," "sozzare," "sozzezza," "sozzo," "sozzume, sozzura," in *Cassell's Italian Dictionary*, comp. Piero Rebora (New York: Funk and Wagnalls, 1967), and corresponding references in *The Follett/Zanichelli Italian Dictionary*, comp. Giuseppi Ragazzini et al. (Chicago: Follett, 1968), 1716.

12. See the entry on "Socinians" in *A Milton Encyclopedia*, 8:12–13.

13. This summary is indebted to the entry on Socinianism by G. H. Williams in the *New Catholic Encyclopedia*, 15 vols., ed. CUA Staff (New York: McGraw-Hill, 1967), 1:397–98.

14. Wilbur, *History of Unitarianism: Socinianism and its Antecedents*, 39.

15. George Huntstan Williams, ed., *The Polish Brethren: Documentation of the History and Thought of Unitarianism in the Polish-Lithuanian Commonwealth and in the Diaspora, 1601–1685*, 2 vols. (Ann Arbor: Edwards Brothers, 1980), 1:184–85, 188 n. 7. Interestingly, the Polish Brethren (so-called "Socinians") were accused by their enemies of being Arians. The views of the Brethren were similar to those of Michael Servetus. See Piotr Wilczek, "Catholics and Heretics: Some Aspects of Religious Debates in the Old Polish-Lithuanian Commonwealth"; available at http://www.ruf.rice.edu/~sarmatia/499/wilczek.html. For the relationship between Michael Servetus's views and those of Milton, see M. A. Larsen, "Milton and Servetus: A Study in the Sources of Milton's Theology," *PMLA* 41 (1926): 891–934.

16. See in this regard George Huntston Williams, *The Radical Reformation* (Philadelphia: Westminster Press, 1962), 756–63.

17. Supplemented in my notes by references to passages in *The Racovian Catechism*, this doctrinal account is indebted to Wilbur, *History of Unitarianism: Socinianism and Its Antecedents*, 412–14; and Williams, *The Radical Reformation*, 750–55.

18. According to the *Racovian Catechism*, with right reason "we could neither perceive with certainty the authority of the sacred writings, understand their contents, discriminate one thing from another, nor apply them to any practical purpose." Scripture is entirely "sufficient for our salvation" (15). References in my text are to *The Racovian Catechism*, translated by Thomas Rees (London: Longman, Hurst, Rees, Orme, and Brown, 1818), hereafter designated *RC*. This version replicates that of the 1652 translation ascribed to John Biddle. (See McLachlan, *Socinianism in Seventeenth-Century England*, 187–88, 190–93.)

19. "The principal thing is to guard against falling into the common error . . . that there is in God only ONE essence, but that he has three persons." The essence of God "cannot, in any way, contain a plurality of persons." We must always endorse the belief in one God and only one God, and we must ever disavow the belief in the Trinity, for such a belief is simply illogical (*RC*, 33, 44–45).

20. There are four things pertaining to the nature of God, the knowledge of which is necessary for salvation: "first, That God is; secondly, That he is one only; thirdly, That he is eternal; and fourthly, That he is perfectly just, wise, and powerful" (*RC*, 26).

21. For the notion of a preincarnate Son, the *Racovian Catechism* maintains that there is in Scripture no mention of an eternity in which the Son (or the Son of Man) is said to have existed (*RC*, 66, 69). "The Holy Spirit is never expressly called God in the Scriptures. Nor is it to be inferred that it is itself God, or a person of the divinity" (*RC*, 36, 287).

22. "Jesus Christ was truly a man." After his Resurrection, "he was constituted by God both Lord and Christ, made the head of the church, and appointed to be the judge of quick and dead." Christ by nature was "truly a man: a mortal man while he lived on earth, but now immortal." On earth, Christ was not a "mere man." "For being conceived of the Holy Spirit, and born of a virgin, without the intervention of any human being, he had properly no father besides God." At the same time, "he also had a mortal father, of whom Christ was the son" (*RC*, 46, 51–53).

23. On the question of the hypostatical union of divine and human in Christ, the *Racovian Catechism* says: "If by the terms divine nature or substance I am to understand the very essence of God, I do not acknowledge such a divine nature in Christ; for this were repugnant both to right reason and to the Holy Scriptures." As a man, Christ, moreover, possesses only limited knowledge; he is not aware, for example, of the day of judgment (*RC*, 55–56, 59).

24. Through the Resurrection, Christ was begotten "a second time." Once he has undergone Resurrection and Ascension, "he is made to resemble, or, indeed, to equal God" (*RC*, 54, 131).

25. The words "Christ died for us" (1 John 3:16) means not *pro quo* (for whom) but *propter quem* (for [or on account of] whom) (*RC*, 309–10). For the *Racovian Catechism* this distinction is absolutely crucial.

26. The notion of satisfaction is "false, erroneous, and exceedingly pernicious." One cannot conceive that Christ "suffered an equivalent punishment for our sins, and by the price of his obedience exactly compensated our disobedience." It is repugnant to Scripture and to right reason to single out the Crucifixion as the sign of satisfaction (*RC*, 303–6).

27. See the discourse on original sin in Faustus Socinus, *Praelectiones Theologiae Fausti Socini Senensis*, in *Fausti Socini Senensis Opera Omni in Duos Tomos distincta* (Irenopoli, 1656), 540.

28. McLachlan, *Socinianism in Seventeenth-Century England*, 31.

29. From Paul M. Zall's entry "Socinians," in *A Milton Encyclopedia*, 8:12–13.

30. Wilbur, *History of Unitarianism: In Transylvania, England, and America*, 184–87.

31. "An Ordinance for the punishing of Blasphemies and Heresies, with the several penalties therein expressed" [2 May, 1648], in *Acts and Ordinances of the Interregnum, 1642–1660*, 2 vols., ed. C. H. Firth and R. S. Rait (London: Wyman and Sons, 1911), 1:1133–36. See also "An Act against several Atheistical, Blasphemous, and Execrable Opinions, derogatory to the honor of God, and destructive to humane Society" [9 August, 1650], in Firth and Rait, *Acts and Ordinances*, 2:409–12.

32. Although the act stipulates the possibility of death for repeat offenders, such extreme measures were not actually carried out.

33. In keeping with Socinian belief, the act interdicts the mortalist belief "that the soul of man dieth or sleepeth when the body is dead" (1:1135). For a fine discussion of Milton's own ambivalent response to the Blasphemy Act, as well as of the significance of his silences in the face of radical sectarian controversies that raged during his career as polemicist, see David Loewenstein, "Milton among the Religious Radicals and Sects: Polemical Engagements and Silences," *Milton Studies* 40, edited by Albert C. Labriola (Pittsburgh: University of Pittsburgh Press, 2002), 222–47.

34. See Francis Cheynell, *The Rise, Growth, and Danger of Socinianism* (London, 1643), and *The Divine Trinunity of the Father, Son, and Holy Spirit* (London, 1650); Pagitt, *Heresiography*; Edwards, *Gangraena*; John Owen, *A Brief Declaration and Vindication of the Doctrine of the Trinity* (London, 1676); Bernard Skelton, *Christus Deus, The Divinity of Our Saviour* (London, 1692); Francis Fullwood, *The Socinian Controversie* (London, 1693); Edward Stillingfleet, *A Discourse Concerning the Doctrine of Christ's Satisfaction* (London,

1696); and John Tillotson, *A Seasonable Vindication of the B. Trinity* (London, 1693), among many others.

35. Cheynell, *The Rise, Growth, and Danger of Socinianism*, 24.

36. See Pagitt, *Heresiography*, 134–36, 152–54; and Edwards, *Gangraena*, 13.

37. McLachlan, *Socinianism in Seventeenth-Century England*, 128–29. See Owen, *Vindiciae evangelicae; or, The Mystery of the Gospel vindicated and Socinianism examined* (London, 1655).

38. Owen, *A Brief Declaration*, 87.

39. Skelton, *Christus Deus*, 7. Pelagius is invoked because Socinianism disavows original sin. For Photinus (as for Socinus), the Son does not exist until the human birth of Christ. Socinus declared that the Son of Mary was a man.

40. Ibid., 10. By the time Skelton was writing, "Socinian" and "Unitarian" had become interchangeable. See Skelton's comments (8). See also Stillingfleet, *A Discourse Concerning*, iv, xxvii.

41. John Biddle, *The Apostolical and True Opinion concerning the Holy Trinity, Revived and Asserted* (1653; reprint, London, 1691), 1.

42. Stephen Nye, *A Brief History of the Unitarians, Called also Socinians, In Four Letters Written to a Friend* (London, 1687), confirms this view. The whole Scripture "speaks of God as but one Person; and speaks of him and to him by singular Pronouns" (19). Nye ventures this observation in the context of disputing the Trinity. In so doing, he also refines the commonplace conflation of Arianism and Socinianism, both of which were looked upon as nascent forms of the "Judaizing" of godhead. Although both the Arians and the Socinians agree that God is only "one Person," Nye says,

> they differ concerning their views of the Son and Holy Spirit. The Son, according to the *Arians*, was generated or created some time before the World, and in process of time. . . . The Holy Ghost (they say) is the Creature of the Son, and subservient to him in the Work of Creation. But the *Socinians* deny that the Son our Lord Christ had any Existence before he was born of Blessed *Mary*, being conceived in her by the holy Spirit of God. (33)

According to Nye, both Socinians and Arians are nonetheless called Unitarians and look upon each other as true Christians, "because they agree in the principal Article, that there is but one God, or but one who is God" (34). McLachlan observes that that the term "Unitarian" as employed by Nye is used generically for all who believe in the "Unipersonality of the Supreme Being." From that time forth, "Unitarian" was used as a term that embraced Antitrinitarians of various sorts, including Arians, Socinians, and Sabellians. It is of some note that Nye's *Brief History* is the first book in which the term

"Unitarian" appears on the title page (*Socinianism in Seventeenth-Century England,* 320).

43. References are to John Dryden, *The Poems of John Dryden,* ed. Paul Hammond (London: Longman, 1995). Similar attitudes were expressed by Alexander Pope in *An Essay on Criticism* (1711). See especially lines 543–49.

44. McLachlan, *Socinianism in Seventeenth-Century England,* 326. According to McLachlan, the autograph catalog of Locke's library, as well as book lists of works in his possession, reveals how extensive is his collection of Sociniana. McLachlan enumerates the plethora of Socinian titles, both English and continental. These works were Locke's "tools, authorities, and sources for reference, as extracts from his commonplace books reveal" (326–30). See also Dewey D. Wallace, Jr., "Socinianism, Justification by Faith, and the Sources of John Locke's *The Reasonableness of Christianity,*" *JHI* 45 (1984): 49–66.

45. Alexander Gordon, *Heads of English Unitarian History* (London: Philip Green, 1895), 31, cited by McLachlan, *Socinianism in Seventeenth-Century England,* 326.

46. Such an outlook, one might argue, is present in Locke's other works, such as *An Essay Concerning Human Understanding* (London, 1690) and *Reason and Religion* (London, 1694).

47. Robert Wallace, *Antitrinitarian Biography; or, Sketches of the Lives of Distinguished Antitrinitarians,* 3 vols. (London: E. T. Whitfield, 1850), 1:406.

48. John Locke, *The Reasonableness of Christianity, as Delivered in the Scriptures* (1695), in *The Works of John Locke,* 10 vols. (1823; reprint, Aalen: Scientia Verlag, 1963), 7:108. Unless otherwise noted, references to Locke are from this edition.

49. John Edwards, *Socinianism Unmask'd: A Discourse Shewing the Unreasonableness of a Late Writer's Opinion* (London, 1696), 4, 28–29, and passim. For other contemporary views, see John Milner, *An Account of Mr. Locke's Religion, Out of His Own Writings, and in His Own Words* (London, 1700).

50. *A Second Vindication,* in *The Works of Locke,* 8:859.

51. Locke's first published work, the *Epistola de Tolerantia* (1689) was translated into English by William Popple (1689). This, in turn, was followed by *A Second Letter concerning Toleration* (1690) and *A Third Letter concerning Toleration* (1692). For Miltonic influence on Locke's letters on Toleration, see John T. Shawcross, " 'Connivers and the Worst of Superstitions': Milton on Popery and Toleration," *Literature and History* 7, no. 2 (1998): 51–69.

52. John Locke, *Epistola de Tolerantia* (1689), trans. J. W. Gough, ed. Raymond Klibansky (Oxford: Clarendon Press, 1968), 96–97, 143–45.

53. As Frank E. Manuel, *The Religion of Isaac Newton* (Oxford: Clarendon Press, 1974), observes, "during Newton's lifetime nobody cast aspersions on his Anglican orthodoxy," nor did he participate "in any public manifesto on matters of doctrine" (7). See also McLachlan, *Socinianism in Seventeenth-Century England*, 330–31. For McLachlan, those opinions are decidedly Socinian.

54. Manuel, *Religion of Isaac Newton*, 12.

55. The work is entitled "A Historical Account of Two Notable Corruptions of Scripture," a copy of which Newton sent to John Locke. In his response to 1 Tim 3:16 and 2 John 5:7, Locke argues that both texts are interpolations into later editions of the New Testament and calls into question the biblical authenticity of concept of the "three that bear witness in heaven."

56. Manuel, *Religion of Isaac Newton*, 11–13. These manuscripts (and others) have since been published by McLachlan, ed., *Sir Isaac Newton: Theological Manuscripts* (Liverpool: University Press, 1950). These documents (addressing variously the doctrine of the Trinity, the controversy between Arius and Athanasius, the question of the essence that constitutes Father and Son, the nature of Jesus, and the person of the Holy Spirit) are particularly revealing in what they disclose about Newton's theological views. For discussion of much of this material, see Wallace, *Antitrinitarian Biography*, 1:428–68.

57. The phrase is Manuel's (ibid., 16). One assumes that Manuel alludes to Milton's *Sonnet 7:* "As ever in my great task-maisters eye."

58. Ibid., 16.

59. Ibid., 17–18.

60. The first edition of *Philosophiae naturalis principia mathematica* appeared in 1687. In my treatment of *Principia*, I refer to *Sir Isaac Newton's Mathematical Principles of Natural Philosophy and His System of the World*, trans. Andrew Motte (1729), rev. and ed. Florian Cajori (Berkeley and Los Angeles: University of California Press, 1946).

61. For an account of Bishop Berkeley's and Leibniz's respective criticisms, see the appendix to Cajori's edition of the *Principia*, 668–69. In his *Principles of Human Knowledge* (1710), Berkeley finds in Locke's treatise a "dangerous dilemma . . . of thinking either Real Space is God, or else that there is something besides God which is eternal, uncreated, infinite, indivisible, unmutable." Both of these notions "may justly be thought pernicious and absurd." In a letter of May 5, 1712, to one Hartsoeker (a Dutch physician at Dusseldorf), Leibniz, in turn, questions Newton's arguments on similar grounds.

62. Newton, *Principia*, 545–46. For additional statements on the nature of God, see Newton's *Opticks; or, A Treatise of the Reflections, Refractions, Inflections, and Colours of Light*, 4th ed. (London, 1730), passim. The issues raised in the Berkeley and Leibniz responses to

the first edition of the *Principia* continued beyond the second edition. In that context, the issues were further developed in the exchange between Leibniz and Samuel Clarke. See *The Leibniz-Clarke Correspondence, Together with Extracts from Newton's "Principia" and "Opticks,"* ed. H. G. Alexander (New York: Philosophical Library, 1956). Especially interesting is Leibniz's charge that Sir Isaac Newton and his followers have a very "odd opinion concerning the work of God." "According to their doctrine, God Almighty wants to wind up his watch from time to time: otherwise it would cease to move." For Leibniz, the Newtonians conceive God as a clockmaker "obliged to clean" and "mend" his mechanism now and then (11). This approaches Deism. See John Leland, *A View of the Principal Deistic Writers,* 3 vols. (London, 1757).

63. Manuel, *Religion of Isaac Newton,* 57–64.

64. McLachlan, *Socinianism in Seventeenth-Century England,* 330–31.

65. Kelley, introduction to *Christian Doctrine,* YP 6:68.

66. Zall, "Socinians," in *A Milton Encyclopedia,* 8:13.

67. The 1651 version is consistent with the earlier Latin versions. In the 1651 version, the place of publication is "Racovia," but is, in fact, London. An English translation appeared as *The Racovian Catechism* in 1652. The translation has been attributed to John Biddle.

68. References are to John T. Shawcross's entries on William Dugard and *The Racovian Catechism,* in *A Milton Encyclopedia,* 2:183–84 and 7:88–89, respectively. For accounts of the affair, see Masson, *Life of John Milton,* 4:438–39; and William Riley Parker, *Milton: A Biography,* 2 vols., 2nd ed., rev. Gordon Campbell (Oxford: Clarendon Press, 1996), 1:395, 2:994. For pertinent documents, see J. Milton French, *The Life Records of John Milton,* 5 vols. (New Brunswick, N.J.: Rutgers University Press, 1954), 3:157, 206.

69. Shawcross, entry on *The Racovian Catechism,* in *A Milton Encyclopedia,* 7:88. For a discussion of Aitzema, see Paul R. Sellin's entry on Lieuwe van Aitzema in *A Milton Encyclopedia,* 1:34–35. The Aitzema document, along with a translation, appears in French, *Life Records of John Milton,* 3:206.

70. Stephen B. Dobranski, "Licensing Milton's Heresy," in Dobranski and Rumrich, *Milton and Heresy,* 139–58. Dobranski maintains that "with so little evidence corroborating Aitzema's report, we ought to hesitate before using the episode to judge Milton's activities as licenser." See also Dobranski, *Milton, Authorship, and the Book Trade* (Cambridge: Cambridge University Press, 1999), 125–53. J. Milton French, who reproduces the report in *Life Records of John Milton,* notes that he has not seen the original manuscript held in the Dutch archives in The Hague and admits that its authenticity "is not certain" (144).

71. Dobranski, "Licensing Milton's Heresy," 143.

72. It has been conjectured that the Bodleian copy of the marginal notes to Paul Best's *Mysteries Discovered* (1647) are by Milton. The attribution was first made by the Unitarian R. Brook Aspland in *The Christian Reformer*, n.s. 9 (1853): 561–63; and in his *Paul Best, The Unitarian Reformer* (London, 1853), 13–15. Because of Best's Socinian leanings, the attribution (were it true) might go far to help establish even further Milton's ties to the Socinians. The notes to Best are printed in CM 18:341–44 (along with editorial confirmation at 18:572), and the Miltonic authorship is asserted on various occasions, most importantly in McLachlan, *Socinianism in Seventeenth-Century England*, 160–62. Had the Miltonic authorship been established, the substance of the notes would have confirmed a Socinian Milton beyond the shadow of a doubt. But such was not to be. Maurice Kelley, "Milton and the Notes on Paul Best," *Library*, 5th ser., 5 (1950): 49–51, establishes beyond a doubt that Milton is not the author of the notes.

73. The attribution is that of Arnold Williams, in his notes to his edition of *Tetrachordon*, YP 2:604 n.

74. Parker, *Milton: A Biography*, 1:628. The precise occasion of the tract and the circumstances that provoked it have been treated eloquently by Masson, *Life of John Milton*, 6:690–99; Parker, *Milton: A Biography*, 1:622–29; Keith Stavely, preface to *Of True Religion*, YP 8:408–15; and Nathaniel Henry, "Milton's Last Pamphlet: Theocracy and Intolerance," in *A Tribute to George Coffin Taylor*, ed. Arnold Williams (Chapel Hill: University of North Carolina Press, 1952), 197–210; and Henry's entry *"Of True Religion,"* in *A Milton Encyclopedia*, 6:22. See also Sanchez, "'Worst of Superstitions,'" *Prose Studies* 9 (1986): 21–38; and Sanchez, *Persona and Decorum in Milton's Prose* (Madison, N.J.: Fairleigh Dickinson University Press, 1997). My brief overview of the events that prompted the publication of Milton's *Of True Religion* is indebted to the foregoing.

75. The Apostles' Creed (which professes belief in God the Father, Jesus Christ the Son, and the Holy Spirit) is the statement of faith adopted not only by Roman Catholics but also by Anglican and many Protestant churches as well. Although the Creed was traditionally looked upon as a document composed by the 12 apostles, it is the product of the early church. It reached its final form in the late sixth or early seventh century. In his *Apology for Smectymnuus*, Milton counters the argument "that if wee must forsake all that is Rome's, we must bid adieu to our Creed." In response, Milton declares, "I had thought that our Creed had been of the Apostles; for so it beares title." But if it must be abandoned in order to do away with the Catholic Church, "let her take it." For, he says, "we can want no Creed, so long as we want not the Scriptures" (YP 1:943). The Bible itself is the ultimate "creed."

76. The association would have been so automatic as to obviate the need for proof. In Milton's works, see texts ranging from the "Attack on the Scholastic Philosophy" in the third Prolusion (YP 1:240–48) to the references in *Animadversions* to "doltish and monasticall Schoolmen" (YP 1:718) and in the *Doctrine and Discipline of Divorce* to "those *decretals, and sumles sums,* which the *Pontificial Clerks* have doted on" ever since the birth of Catholic divines with their "scholastick Sophistry, whose overspreading *barbarism*" has corrupted the church (YP 2:350–51). Throughout his career, Milton's works reflect this attitude.

77. Among those who interpret the passage differently, the most outspoken is William B. Hunter, *Visitation Unimplor'd: Milton and the Authorship of "De Doctrina Christiana"* (Pittsburgh: Duquesne University Press, 1998), who adopts this passage to argue on behalf of Milton's orthodox Trinitarianism. Approaching the passage from the perspective of statement and response, Hunter argues that the phrase "a mystery indeed in their Sophistic Subtilties, but in Scripture, a plain Doctrin" is Milton's response to the Arian and Socinian position. According to Hunter, "such a division of the sentences shows clearly that Milton recognizes the position of the Arians and Socinians but flatly rejects 'their Sophistic Subtilties' to accept the 'plain Doctrin' of Trinitarian scripture" (103–4). I am convinced, however, that Hunter misreads.

78. See my "De Doctrina Christiana and the Question of Authorship," *Milton Studies* 41, edited by Albert C. Labriola (Pittsburgh: University of Pittsburgh Press, 1990), 172–230.

79. Compare the corresponding chapters in the *Racovian Catechism* (sec. 1, chaps. 1–3) devoted to the authenticity and authority of Scripture. Although the *Racovian Catechism* acknowledges the possibility that certain aspects of Scripture have been corrupted in transmission, none of these corruptions is sufficient to compromise the full meaning of the text (*RC,* 5).

80. Compare the *Racovian Catechism:* "Although some difficulties do certainly occur in them; nevertheless, those things which are necessary to salvation, as well as many others, are so plainly declared in different passages, that every one may understand them" (*RC,* 17). In *De Doctrina Christiana,* the discussion of "the right method of interpreting the Scriptures" (including knowledge of languages, consideration of intent, ability to distinguish between literal and figurative meaning, attention to context, and willingness to compare one text with another) is iterated in a corresponding passage in the *Racovian Catechism* (18).

81. This runs contrary to the Socinian belief in the absolute power of reason. Without right reason, "we could neither perceive with certainty the authority of the sacred writings, understand their contents,

discriminate one thing from another, nor apply them to any practical purpose" (*RC*, 15).

82. As has been noted before, the emphasis upon number is a significant characteristic of Milton's *Artis Logicae*, particularly in the association it advances between number and essence: "Things which differ in number also differ in essence . . .: *Here let the Theologians take notice [Evigilent hic Theologi]*" (YP 8:233; CM 11:58–59). The passage has been variously interpreted. See Hunter, *Visitation Unimplor'd*, 115–16.

83. In his note to this passage in the Yale *Prose*, Kelley cites the *Racovian Catechism* for an analogous view (YP 6:213 n. 32).

84. See Kelley's editorial note to this passage in YP 6:419–20 n. 18. Kelley cites the ancient Jewish-Christian sect of Ebionism as a source as well. William B. Hunter approaches Milton's views on the Incarnation from the perspective of Nestorianism. See Hunter, "Milton on the Incarnation," in *Bright Essence: Studies in Milton's Theology*, ed. William B. Hunter et al. (Salt Lake City: University of Utah Press, 1971), 131–48.

85. Another departure concerns the all-important matter of "satisfaction." Whereas the Socinians categorically dismissed the idea of Christ's satisfaction in the atonement for sins in the Crucifixion, the author of *De Doctrina Christiana* endorses the doctrine of satisfaction without qualification. "Satisfaction means that Christ as Theanthropos fully satisfied divine justice by fulfilling the law and paying the just price on behalf of all men [*pro omnibus*]." The argument for the efficacy of "satisfaction" in *De Doctrina Christiana* appears to be taking into account the precise argument against the efficacy of "satisfaction" among the Socinians, who argue that the words "Christ died for us" (1 John 3:16) means not "*pro quo*" (for whom) but "*propter quem*" (for [or on account of] whom). See the discussion in *De Doctrina Christiana* (YP 6:443–46; CM 15:314–15, 322–25). Milton endorses the doctrine of satisfaction throughout his poetry. See *Upon the Circumcision* (20–21); *Paradise Lost* 3.209–12, 294–97; 12.415–35.

86. Introduction to John T. Shawcross, ed., *Milton: The Critical Heritage* (London: Routledge, 1970), 25.

87. In *The Early Lives of Milton*, ed. Helen Darbishire (1932; reprint, New York: Barnes and Noble, 1965), 188–92. See John T. Shawcross's entry on John Toland in *A Milton Encyclopedia*, 8:69–70. For the genesis of the idea of a "*System of Divinity*" among Milton's early biographers, see Hunter, *Visitation Unimplor'd*, 19–33.

88. In *A Milton Encyclopedia*, 8:69–70. "Toland's first book *Christianity Not Mysterious*, finished while he was still a student at Oxford, was published in 1696 and plunged him into religious controversy, which raged the rest of his life. He espoused deism and

Socinianism against the orthodox view, and brought his beliefs into his 'Life of Milton.' " In response to Toland's "Life," Reverend Offspring Blackall published *Remarks on the Life of Mr. Milton* (London, 1699). Responding to Blackall, Toland, in turn, defended himself in *Amyntor; or, A Defense of Milton's Life* (London, 1699). Other tracts followed (*A Milton Encyclopedia*, 8:69).

89. See *Christianity Not Mysterious; or, A Treatise Shewing, That there is nothing in the Gospel Contrary to Reason, Nor Above it: And that no Christian Doctrine can be properly call'd A MYSTERY* (London, 1696). Interestingly, this tract ventures statements that appear to be *critical* of Arianism and Socinianism: Neither the Arians nor the Socinians "can make their Notions of a *dignifi'd and Creature-God capable of Divine Worship,* appear more reasonable than the Extravagancies of other Sects touching the Article of the *Trinity*" (25). In response to Toland's tract, Thomas Beverly published *Christianity, the great mystery in answer to a late treatise: Christianity not mysterious, that is, not above, not contrary to reason* (London, 1696), as well as other tracts such as Jean Gailhard's *The blasphemous Socinian heresie disproved and confuted* (London, 1697). Among the Socinian works attributed to John Toland is *Socinianism truly Stated; Being An Example of fair Dealing in all Theological Controversys . . . Recommended by a Pantheist to an Orthodox Friend* (London, 1705). Providing an excellent overview of Socinian doctrine, this tract is supposed to represent the first instance of the use of the word "pantheist." In this regard, see Toland, *Pantheisticon* (New York: Garland, 1976).

90. John Dennis, "The Grounds of Criticism in Poetry" (1704), *The Critical Works of John Dennis,* 2 vols., ed. Edward Niles Hooker (Baltimore: The Johns Hopkins University Press, 1939), 1:344–45.

91. Jonathan Richardson, *Explanatory Notes and Remarks on Milton's "Paradise Lost." By J. Richardson, Father and Son. With the Life of the Author, and a Discourse on the Poem. By J. R. Sen.* (1734), in *Milton 1732–1801: The Critical Heritage,* ed. John T. Shawcross (London: Routledge, 1972), 84.

92. See the selections from the *Gentleman's Magazine* (1738) in *Milton 1732–1801,* 93–98.

93. See Theophilus Lindsey, *The Apology of Theophilus Lindsey, M.A., on the Resigning the Vicarage of Catterick, Yorkshire* (Dublin, 1774).

94. References are to the entry on Theophilus Lindsey in *The Dictionary of National Biography,* 29 vols., ed. Sir Leslie Stephen and Sir Sidney Lee (London: Oxford University Press, 1917), 11:1196–97.

95. Theophilus Lindsey, *A Sequel to the Apology on Resigning the Vicarage of Catterick, Yorkshire* (London, 1776), 404–9. For further discussion of Lindsey's views of Milton, see Wallace, *Antitrinitarian*

Biography, 1:331–33. See Thomas Newton's edition of *Paradise Lost*, 2 vols. (London, 1749). According to Shawcross, Newton "produced the most reprinted life of Milton and the texts generally employed for editions of Milton's poems during the last half of the eighteenth century" (*Milton 1732–1801*, 153). McLachlan notes that in later years Samuel Taylor Coleridge also found Socinianism in *Paradise Regained*. According to Coleridge, Milton had "represented Satan as a sceptical Socinian . . . as knowing the prophetic and Messianic character of Christ, but sceptical as to any higher claim." On the other hand, John Keats, whose brother George was a Unitarian, "failed to discern the heretical tendencies" in Milton (*The Religious Opinions of Milton, Locke, and Newton*, 18–19). For the Romantic contexts of Milton's works, see *The Romantics on Milton: Formal Essays and Critical Asides*, ed. Joseph Wittreich (Case Western Reserve University Press, 1970).

96. Lindsey, *An Historical View*, xxi–xxii. Lindsey also produced *Two Dissertations: I. On the Preface to St. John's Gospel. II. On Praying to Jesus Christ* (London, 1778). In section 1 of *On Praying to Jesus Christ*, Lindsey invokes *Paradise Lost* 2.561: "And found no end, in wandring mazes lost" (66).

97. Charles R. Sumner, "Preliminary Observations," *A Treatise of Christian Doctrine, Compiled from the Holy Scriptures Alone*, trans. Charles R. Sumner (Cambridge: Cambridge University Press, 1825), xxxiii–xxxv. Shortly after its discovery in 1823, the treatise was known as *De Dei Cultu;* see William B. Hunter, "*De Doctrina Christiana: Nunc Quo Vadis?*" *MQ* 34 (October 2000): 98.

98. Francis E. Mineka, "The Critical Reception of Milton's *De Doctrina Christiana*," *University of Texas Studies in English* 22 (1943): 115–47. See also Maurice Kelley, "The Recovery, Printing, and Reception of Milton's *Christian Doctrine, HLQ* 31 (1967): 35–41.

99. *Evangelical*, n.s. 3 (1825): 507, cited in Mineka, "Critical Reception," 119.

100. *Evangelical*, n.s. 4 (1826): 51, cited in Mineka, "Critical Reception," 121.

101. *Congregational Magazine* 8 (1825): 588, cited in Mineka, "Critical Reception," 127.

102. *Gentleman's Magazine* 95 (1825): 344–45, cited in Mineka, "Critical Reception," 141. In response to the publication of *De Doctrina Christiana* and the review of it in the periodical literature, Samuel Taylor Coleridge, *The Notebooks*, 4 vols., ed. Kathleen Coburn and Merton Christiansen, Bollingen Series L (Princeton: Princeton University Press, 1990) expressed astonishment at the views of God and the godhead reflected in the theological treatise. Alluding to the treatise in the context of earlier discussions of the Socinian movement, Coleridge maintains (May–November 1825)

that *De Doctrina Christiana* prompts one to "exclude all Philosophy! Extinguish all Ideas! Hold in contempt all Church Tradition," and "in short, depose at once Reason & the Church from the Chair of Interpretation." As applied to "Absolute Being," Milton's words (for Coleridge) are "nonsense." The very idea of what such thoughts of godhead may lead to is a "shriek of a Delirium!" According to Coleridge, Arians and, by implication, Socinians will "reap the harvest" of such an endeavor. The Deists, the Behmenists, and the Swedenborgians, among others, fall into the same camp (vol. 4, items 4797, 5213, 5262). I am grateful to my colleague Mark Canuel for alerting me to this material.

103. In his *Critical Heritage* volumes, Shawcross calls attention to Henry John Todd, Milton's important nineteenth century editor, whose revision of his fourth variorum edition in 1842 "registers shock and disbelief and acceptance and discomfort. Todd did not want to accept Arian influence on *Paradise Lost,* and yet he could not deny its tenets in *De Doctrina Christiana.* The poem and its author had fallen irretrievably in his judgment" (see Shawcross, introductions to *Milton: The Critical Heritage,* 25; and *Milton 1732–1801: The Critical Heritage,* 26). Of corresponding interest is the figure of Thomas Burgess, Bishop of Salisbury, of whom Hunter provides interesting accounts in *Visitation Unimplor'd,* 4–7, and passim. As discussed in my "De Doctrina Christiana and the Question of Authorship," Burgess, who disputed the notion of the Miltonic authorship of *De Doctrina Christiana,* produced *Milton Not the Author of the Lately Discovered Arian Work "De Doctrina Christiana," Three Discourses, Delivered at the Anniversary Meetings of the Royal Society of Literature, in the Years 1826, 1827, and 1828, to which is Added Milton Contrasted with Milton and with the Scriptures* (London: Thomas Brettell, 1829). Of particular interest is the section entitled "Milton Contrasted with Milton and with the Scriptures," which constructs two personas, that of the orthodox Trinitarian Milton of *Paradise Lost* and that of the heterodox Antitrinitarian (that is, Arian *and* Socinian or Unitarian) Milton of *De Doctrina Christiana.* For Burgess, one is entirely incompatible with the other. Alluding to Samuel Johnson's observation in his *Life of Milton* (1779) that "Milton appears to have had full conviction of the truth of Christianity, and to have been untainted with any heretical peculiarity of opinion," Burgess remains steadfast in his adherence to the orthodox Milton (165–66). Even Burgess, however, is prompted to acknowledge the distinctly "*human* existence" of Jesus in *Paradise Regained,* an idea, Burgess suggests, apparently at odds with "the eternal Divinity of the Son of God" in *Paradise Lost.* For a brief moment, the persona of a Socinian Milton arises in Burgess's criticism, but the idea is entertained, only to be dismissed (171–72).

For additional commentary, see James Ogden, "Bishop Burgess and John Milton," in *Bibliographical and Contextual Studies*, nos. 29 and 30 (Lampeter, Wales: University of Wales, 1997), 79–98.

104. Mineka, "Critical Reception," 130–33.

105. *Monthly Repository* 20 (1825): 692, cited in ibid., 131.

106. References are to the entry on William Ellery Channing in *American National Biography*, 24 vols., gen. ed. John A. Garraty and Mark C. Carnes (New York: Oxford University Press, 1999), 4:680–81. The estimate of Channing as "the single most important figure in the history of American Unitarianism" is from David Robinson, *The Unitarians and the Universalists* (Westport, Conn.: Greenwood Press, 1985), 229.

107. *American National Biography*, 4:681.

108. References to the *Remarks on the Character and Writings of John Milton* are to the third edition (Boston: Benjamin Perkins, 1828). The work was originally issued in the *Christian Examiner* (1826). For an extended study of Channing's treatment of Milton's *De Doctrina Christiana*, among his other works, see Kevin P. van Anglen, *The New England Milton: Literary Reception and Cultural Authority in the Early Republic* (University Park, Pa.: The Pennsylvania State University Press, 1993), 81–108. According to van Aglen, Channing's *Remarks* is "the most important treatment of Milton by any Unitarian" (82). During Channing's lifetime, his essay came under attack on the Trinitarian front by the Reverend Frederick Beasley of New Jersey in a pamphlet that questioned the theological arguments of *De Doctrina Christiana* and emphasized those aspects of *Paradise Lost* that bore an anti-Unitarian imprint (105). Van Anglen also explores what he calls "The Unitarian Milton," that is, the reception of Milton among the New England Unitarian community (40–79). Important to the Unitarian reception of Milton's works, including *De Doctrina Christiana*, is Robin Grey, *The Complicity of Imagination: The American Renaissance, Contests of Authority, and Seventeenth-Century English Culture* (Cambridge: Cambridge University Press, 1997), esp. 38–45. See also Keith W. F. Stavely, *Puritan Legacies: "Paradise Lost" and the New England Tradition, 1630–1890* (Ithaca, N.Y.: Cornell University Press, 1987).

109. Channing, *Remarks*, 66–68, 70–71.

110. Ibid., 75–79. Along with Milton's "Antitrinitarianism," Channing is determined to see in *De Doctrina Christiana* a lack of conviction in the author's treatment of the doctrine of satisfaction: "With respect to Christ's mediation, he [Milton] supposes, that Christ saves us by bearing our punishment, and in this way satisfying God's justice. His views indeed are not expressed with much precision, and seem to have been formed without much investigation" (94).

111. It is interesting that by the time Ralph Waldo Emerson

produced his lecture "John Milton" (1835), *The Early Lectures of Ralph Waldo Emerson*, 3 vols., ed. Stephen E. Wicher et al. (Cambridge: Harvard University Press, 1959–72), Emerson was able to dismiss the discovery of *De Doctrina Christiana* in 1823 as an event of only passing interest: "But the new-found book having, in itself, less attraction than any other work of Milton, the curiosity of the public has quickly subsided, and left the poet to the enjoyment of his permanent fame" (145). For a discussion of the influence of Channing's review on Emerson's essay, see van Anglen, *New England Milton*, 109–37.

Notes to Chapter 8

1. See John P. Rumrich, "Milton's Arianism: Why It Matters," in *Milton and Heresy*, edited by Stephen B. Dobransky and John P. Rumrich (Cambridge: Cambridge University Press, 1998), 76. For Richardson, see *Explanatory Notes and Remarks, on Milton's "Paradise Lost"* (London, 1734), in *Milton 1732–1801: The Critical Heritage*, edited by John T. Shawcross (London: Routledge, 1972), 84. In his "Preliminary Observations" to the 1825 edition, Charles Sumner, *A Treatise on Christian Doctrine, Compiled from the Holy Scriptures Alone* (Cambridge: Cambridge University Press, 1825), asserts that "this summary [of the treatise] will be sufficient to show that the opinions of Milton were in reality nearly Arian" (xxxiv).

2. See William B. Hunter, *Visitation Unimplor'd: Milton and the Authorship of "De Doctrina Christiana"* (Pittsburgh: Duquesne University Press, 1998).

3. See my "*De Doctrina Christiana* and the Question of Authorship," *Milton Studies* 41, edited by Albert C. Labriola (Pittsburgh: University of Pittsburgh Press, 1990), 172–230, regarding the issue of authorship. The scholarship on Milton's views of godhead is vast, particularly in the context of the Trinitarian/ Antitrinitarian debates. Crucial to the debates (and arguing against the notion of an "Arian Milton") is William B. Hunter, C. A. Patrides, and J. H. Adamson, *Bright Essence: Studies in Milton's Theology* (Salt Lake City: University of Utah Press, 1971), as well as Hunter's other studies, including "Divine Filiation," in *Visitation Unimplor'd*, 99–119. Of corresponding importance is John T. Shawcross's *Rethinking Milton Studies: Time Present and Time Past* (Newark: University of Delaware Press, 2005), 103–68. Among others, these studies adopt the so-called Subordinationist position. Firmly in the opposing camp is Michael Bauman, *Milton's Arianism* (Frankfurt am Main: Peter Lang, 1987), which defends the Arian position adopted by Maurice Kelley, *This Great Argument: A Study of Milton's "De Doctrina Christiana" as*

a Gloss on *"Paradise Lost"* (Princeton, N.J.: Princeton University Press, 1941). Early in the debate but still of interest is Louis Aubrey Wood, *The Form and Origin of Milton's Antitrinitarian Conception* (London, Ontario: Advertiser Printing Co., 1911), as well as Ruth M. Kivette, "Milton on the Trinity" (Ph.D. diss., Columbia University, 1960), and Ira Clark, "The Son of God in the Works of John Milton," (Ph.D. diss., Northwestern University, 1960.

4. See the "Ordinance for the punishing of Blasphemies and Heresies, with the several penalties therein expressed" (May 2, 1648) and the "Act against several Atheistical, Blasphemous and Execrable Opinions, derogatory to the honor of God, and destructive to humane Society" (August 9, 1650), in *Acts and Ordinances of the Interregnum, 1642–1660*, 2 vols., ed. C. H. Firth and R. S. Rait (London: Wyman and Sons, 1911), 1:1133–36, 2:409–12, respectively.

5. Socrates Scholasticus, *The Ecclesiastical History* (1.38), in *A Select Library of Nicene and Post-Nicene Fathers of the Christian Church, Second Series*, ed. Philip Schaff and Henry Wace (Edinburgh: T. & T. Clark, 1989), 2:34–35 (hereafter cited as *A Select Library*).

6. Ephraim Pagitt, *Heresiography; or, A description of the Hereticks and Sectaries of these latter times*, 3rd ed. (London, 1646), 134–35. For a discussion of Pagitt's polemic against Milton (in this case as a "divorcer"), see, among other accounts, William Riley Parker, *Milton's Contemporary Reputation* (Columbus, Ohio: Ohio State University Press, 1940), 74–75. The standard account of the so-called heresiarchs of the Antitrinitarian stamp (including Legate and Wightman) is Robert Wallace, *Antitrinitarian Biography; or, Sketches of the Lives and Writings of Distinguished Antitrinitarians*, 3 vols. (London: E.T. Whitfield, 1850).

7. Rowan Williams, *Arius: Heresy and Tradition* (London: Darton, Longman and Todd, 1987), 1. Maurice Wiles adopts this "archetypal perspective" in his *Archetypal Heresy: Arianism through the Centuries* (Oxford: Clarendon Press, 1996). Additional works of interest include Thomas A. Kopecek, *A History of Neo-Arianism*, 2 vols. (Cambridge, Mass.: The Philadelphia Patristic Foundation, 1979); and Johannes Quasten, *Patrology* (Westminster, Md.: The Newman Press, 1960).

8. Williams, *Arius*, 1.

9. Ibid., 82, 234.

10. Cited in Wiles, *Archetypal Heresy*, 4.

11. Williams, *Arius*, 95. Even the available "Arian" texts (distinct from those embedded in the writings of Arius's enemies) are ascriptions. These include (1) the confession of faith presented to Alexander of Alexandria, (2) Arius's letter to Eusebius of Nicomedia, and (3) the confession submitted by Arius and Euzoius to the emperor in 327, or possibly 335 (Williams, 95). See Athanasius, *Athanasius Werke, hrsg. Im auftrage der Kirchenvater-kommission der Preussischen*

akademie der wissenschaften, 3 vols., ed. Hans-Georg Opitz (Berlin: W. de Gruyter, 1934).

12. Williams, *Arius,* 98–103. Extracts from both versions are offered in Williams's account.

13. Ibid., 105.

14. According to Roy J. Deferrari's translation of Eusebius Pamphilus, Bishop of Caesarea's *Ecclesiastical History,* books 1–5 (Washington, D.C.: Catholic University of America Press, 1953), "Arius was himself not the real author of the heresy that bore his name, but rather his instructor Lucian, from whom he learned its essentials. . . . They who in the early days of the heresy were known as staunch Arians had all been disciples of Lucian, and were carrying on their master's principles" (7).

15. J. N. D. Kelly, *Early Christian Doctrines,* 2nd ed. (New York: Harper & Row, 1960), 226–27. For a correspondingly informative account of Arian doctrine, see Adolph Harnack, *History of Dogma,* 4 vols., trans. Neil Buchanan (New York: Dover, n.d.), 4:15–19. In the patristic literature, accounts of the so-called Arian beliefs are plentiful (and varied). For translations of the original documents, see Athanasius, *Select Works and Letters,* in *A Select Library,* vol. 4. This volume includes works that are germane to the Arian debate, such as the "Deposition of Arius," "Defence against the Arians," "De Decretis," "Four Discourses against the Arians," and "De Synodis."

16. Kelly, *Early Christian Doctrines,* 227–29. See also Kelly, *Early Christian Creeds* (New York: David McKay, 1960), 233. Despite the idea that the Son is mutable, there is apparently for Arius (or the doctrines attributed to him) a sense in which the Son is "unalterable and unchangeable," a feature that seems to be in opposition to what the heresiarch is purported to have said in other contexts. Wiles, *Archetypal Heresy,* attempts to reconcile the conflict (16–17).

17. *Creeds of the Church: A Reader in Christian Doctrine from the Bible to the Present,* 3rd ed., ed. John H. Leith (Atlanta: John Knox Press, 1982), 30–31. (I have silently altered the translations in spots to accord more closely with the original: *poieten* as "maker," rather than "creator," and *poiethenta* as "made," rather than "created.") In the Constantinopolitan Creed (associated since the Council of Chalcedon, 451, with the Council of Constantinople, 381), the Holy Spirit is accorded greater attention. For distinctions among the creeds, see Gerald Bray, *Creeds, Councils and Christ* (Downers Grove, Ill.: Inter-Varsity Press, 1984). In their use of "begotten" (as opposed to "made"), the orthodox drew a distinction between *gennetos* ("begotten") and *genetos* ("contingent") (Kelly, *Early Christian Creeds,* 234).

18. For an account of the transitions, see the excellent discussions by C. A. Patrides, "Milton on the Trinity: The Use of Antecedents," and William B. Hunter, "Further Definitions: Milton's Theological

Vocabulary," in *Bright Essence*, 3–13, and 15–25, respectively. See also Kelly, *Early Christian Creeds*, 216, 243.

19. Kelly, *Early Christian Creeds*, 216, 243. The later followers of the heresy ascribed to Arius proposed (as a substitute for *homoousios*) the term *homoiousios* ("of a similar *ousia*"), which in itself resulted in a struggle. See Jaroslav Pelikan, *The Emergence of the Catholic Tradition (100–600)*, 5 vols. (Chicago: University of Chicago Press, 1971), 1:209.

20. The quotation from Martin Luther is drawn from *Rationis Latomianae Confutatio*, as cited in Hugh MaCallum, *Milton and the Sons of God: The Divine Image in Milton's Epic Poetry* (Toronto: University of Toronto Press, 1986), 25.

21. Deferrari, translation of Eusebius, 11. See also G. L. Prestige, *God in Patristic Thought* (London: S.P.C.K., 1952), 210.

22. Wiles, *Archetypal Heresy*, 89.

23. For additional accounts of the philosophical basis of Arian thought, see G. C. Stead, "The Platonism of Arius," *Journal of Theological Studies*, n.s. 15 (1964): 16–31, and Rowan Williams, "The Logic of Arianism," *Journal of Theological Studies*, n.s. 34 (1983): 31–55.

24. See, in particular, Wiles's chapter, "The Rise and Fall of British Arianism," *Archetypal Heresy*, 62–93.

25. Wiles, *Archetypal Heresy*, 62–63.

26. Such a stance would certainly be consistent with a host of Reformation theologians, including Luther and Calvin, not to mention Ames and Wolleb, all of whom greatly influenced Milton's theology and who subscribed to beliefs contrary to those attributed to Arius and the Arian heresy.

27. Milton's judgment is indeed harsh. The early church accounts of Eusebius of Caesarea, Socrates Scholasticus, Sozomenus, and Theodoret do not (to my knowledge) implicate Constantine in this way. Constantine purportedly did receive Arius back into the fold, against the wishes of Athanasius, who was banished for his resistance; but, according to Socrates Scholasticus, among others, that is because Constantine was taken in by Arius's duplicity. For this account, see *The Ecclesiastical History* (1.38) of Socrates. In his entry "Of Curiosity" in the Commonplace Book, Milton adopts a very positive attitude toward Constantine, whom Milton considers wise in his handling of the Arian controversy (YP 1:380). See also Milton's discussion in *The History of Britain* (YP 5:113–27).

28. For other declarations of Milton's Trinitarian stance in the antiprelatical tracts, see *Of Prelatical Episcopacy* (YP 1:645).

29. The Apostle's Creed (which professes belief in God the Father, Jesus Christ the Son, and the Holy Spirit) is the statement of faith adopted not only by Roman Catholics but by Anglican and many

Protestant churches as well. Although the Creed was traditionally looked upon as a document composed by the 12 apostles, it is the product of the early church. It reached its final form in the late sixth or early seventh century. In his *Apology for Smectymnuus*, Milton counters the argument "that if wee must forsake all that is Rome's, we must bid adieu to our Creed." He declares, "I had thought that our Creed had been of the Apostles; for so it beares title." But if it must be abandoned in order to do away with the Catholic Church, "let her take it." For, he says, "we can want no Creed, so long as we want not the Scriptures" (YP 1:943). The Bible itself is the ultimate "creed."

30. Milton associates such "traditions and additions" with popery throughout his career as a polemicist.

31. Responding to the statement that begetting is a literal act, Kelley reminds us that three paragraphs earlier the author "holds that the [scriptural] texts containing 'today' . . . do not concern the literal generation of the Son." Kelley asks, "Is Milton contradicting himself or indicating that by their own proof texts the orthodox cannot establish the eternal generation of the Son?" (YP 6:210 n. 24).

32. The translation in the Yale *Prose* is "whatever that means," and in the Columbia Milton "in whatever sense that expression is to be understood."

33. "The Son also teaches that the attributes of divinity belong to the Father alone, and that even he is excluded from them" (attributa etiam divina solius esse Patris docet Filius, excluso etiam seipso) (YP 6:227; CM 14:227).

34. In this instance, I use the Columbia Milton translation because it is more accurate, but for *renuntiemus* I substitute "renounce," which I believe is closer to the spirit of the original than either the "discard" of the Columbia Milton or the "disregard" of the Yale *Prose.*

35. See, for example, Kelley's puzzlement over what he feels is the inconsistent handling in *De Doctrina* 1.5 of the distinction between "essence" and "hypostasis": "With this paragraph, Milton's argument becomes puzzling, for though professing not to do so, he seems to be employing *hypostasis* here [in 1.5] in a sense different from that used in chapter ii" (YP 6:224 n. 56).

36. For elaboration on this point, see Harnack, *History of Dogma,* 16–17; and Kelly, *Early Christian Doctrines,* 229.

37. Kelley is in agreement with Kivette's observation that Milton is "the father of his own theology" ("Milton on the Trinity," 106–16).

INDEX

accommodation, theory of, 131, 137–41, 143, 149–50, 155–57
Acts, 58, 70
actuality, and potentiality, 99–100
Alsted, Johann Heinrich, 28
amanuenses, 18–20, 44–45
Ames, William, 22–25, 28–32, 47, 48, 52–53, 142–43, 172, 176
amor Dei. See love, God's
Anabaptists, 238
Ancient of Days, 116–17
Andrewes, Lancelot, 292n58
Animadversions (Milton), 270
Anselm, 54–56
Anthropomorphites, 141, 301n26
anthropopatheia, 129. *See also* passibility of God's
Antitrinitarianism, 217–18, 222, 224, 231, 255–56, 258–59, 262. *See also* Arianism
Apology for Smectymnuus (Milton), 176–77, 327n75, 338n29
apophatic theology, 73, 77, 122, 291n49, 292n51
The Apostolical and True Opinion concerning the Holy Trinity (Biddle), 225
Aquinas, Thomas, 56–57
Areopagitica (Milton), 214, 233, 237

Arianism, 261–78; concept of, 263–65, 335n11, 336n14; *De Doctrina Christiana* and, 255, 272–77; doctrines commonly ascribed to, 265–67; Milton and, 269–78; Milton's comments on, 238–40, 269–71; in Milton's poetry, 278; opposition to, 262–69; *Paradise Lost* and, 251, 252, 254, 278; Socinianism conflated with, 224–26, 238, 320n15, 323n42
Aristotle, 25, 53, 56, 99
Arius, 262–65, 276, 336n14
Arminians, 238
Art of Logic (Artis Logicae) (Milton), 25, 48–49
Athanasius, 229, 231, 263–64
atheism. *See* belief/disbelief in God
Augustine, 73, 135–38

baptism, 221
Bauthumely, Jacob, 6
Beardslee, John, 34
belief/disbelief in God: in Ames and Wolleb, 52–53; Anselm on, 55; Calvin on, 59; in *De Doctrina Christiana*, 63–69; in early church, 53

339